Economic Behaviour in Adversity

Economic Behaviour in Adversity

Jack Hirshleifer

THE UNIVERSITY OF CHICAGO PRESS

Jack Hirshleifer is Professor of Economics at the University of
California, Los Angeles.

The University of Chicago Press, Chicago 60637

Wheatsheaf Books, Ltd., Brighton

Library of Congress Cataloging in Publication Data

Hirshleifer, Jack.
   Economic behaviour in adversity / Jack Hirshleifer

      p. cm.
   Includes index
   1. Natural disasters — economic aspects. 2. War — economic
   aspects.
I. Title.
HC79.D45H57 1987   330.9—DC19   87-19846

ISBN 0-226-34282-4

Contents

List of Tables

List of Figures

Introduction

I am grateful to the publishers for taking the initiative in making some of my previous published and unpublished essays available in this volume. The general subject of the essays is economic behaviour in disaster and conflict — a momentous topic that as yet has been only barely explored by economists.

To say that conflict, disaster and destruction have overarching significance for human life is not news. We think most immediately about the threat of nuclear war. But even 'conventional' weapons can have truly horrendous consequences, especially when amplified by war-caused disruption of economic life. Nor can war, which after all may only be the consequence of *resisting* aggression, be assigned the full blame. It was only after organized resistance ceased in Indo-China that the recent Cambodian holocaust could take place. And while modern times have brought man-made disasters to the fore, natural catastrophes like earthquakes and plagues remain serious threats. I cannot claim that the essays collected here provide ready solutions. But learning something of the causes and operative mechanisms of disaster and conflict may help to ward off or at least to alleviate some of the worst consequences.

There is a second, less obvious, warrant for studying human behaviour in adversity. Methodologically, engineers know that gaining knowledge about the sources and limits of strengths in materials and structures requires experiments that test to destruction. Deliberately carrying out tests upon human subjects to the point of ruin or collapse would be monstrous. But natural and man-made disasters provide us with all too many instances of such destructive trials. These events have generated a wealth of scarcely exploited data that are relevant not only for comprehending human responses to abnormal stress, but even for understanding the normal functioning of individuals and social structures.

The essays collected in this volume are grouped under two main

1

headings. The first part is titled *Disaster and Recovery*. In this part of the book I have taken the opportunity to reproduce some early historical studies of disasters that have not heretofore appeared in print, together with a number of analytical papers that follow up certain implications of the disaster experience. The second part of the book is headed *Cooperation and Conflict*. The essays contained here are, for the most part, somewhat more abstract. They represent attempts to model the emergence of cooperation and conflict under a variety of assumptions, each such model being designed to correspond to a particular challenge posed to humans and to human societies. It was Charles Darwin's view that not only the bodily forms but the behavioural characteristics and even the social mechanisms of species are strategies of competition for survival in the 'economy of Nature'. In the Darwinian spirit, the papers in this section represent an ultimately biological (or more specifically, *bioeconomic*) approach to the human problem of cooperation and conflict.

All the essays in the volume appear essentially in their original form except that a number of the citations have been updated, and some evident typographical and stylistic slips corrected. I would like to thank my research assistant Laurel Clark Hyde for assistance in gathering and evaluating potential materials for the volume. In addition, I am grateful to the Earhart Foundation, to the Research Center for Managerial Economics and Public Policy (UCLA) and to the Ford Foundation which helped support portions of this research.

Part I
Disaster and Recovery

1 Disaster and Recovery: An Historical Survey*

*   *   *

Background of this Chapter

This survey of the causes, characteristics and consequences of important historical disasters was undertaken for The RAND Corporation under a US Air Force contract. In view of the well-known role of RAND as think-tank for US military agencies, outsiders might reasonably infer that the study constituted part of a purposefully organized military research programme. Some might deplore such research, taking it as evidence that the US was planning to initiate that great potential disaster of the present age — nuclear war. Others might feel reassured that appropriate agencies of the American government were thinking seriously about a threat that, regardless of our wishes and actions, might yet occur. But actually there was no such organized research programme to be deplored or commended. At least in this period, research at RAND was conducted under exceptional conditions of intellectual freedom. It was not only the case that the analytical techniques employed and the conclusions arrived at by individual researchers like myself remained free of any censorship (except in cases where military classification was involved). What was even more remarkable, the research topics themselves were very largely those proposed by RAND's staff, rather than commissioned by the sponsor. The topics and the quality of research were indeed subject to review by a professional hierarchy within RAND, but this process was quite decentralized and permissive.

---

* Originally distributed as The RAND Corporation Memorandum RM-3079-PR (April 1963). Views or conclusions contained in this memorandum should not be interpreted as representing the official opinion or policy of the United States Air Force. Reproduced by permission of The RAND Corporation.

As regards the paper reproduced here, it was my own conviction about the importance of the topic that led me, a very junior staff member at RAND, to propose the research. There was no interference of any kind, on the part of the RAND hierarchy or the Air Force, with the conduct of the analysis or the dissemination of the results. (The opposite side of the coin, perhaps, is that the research may have had no practical value for decision-makers.)

Substantively, the historical review here suggests an extraordinary resiliency of human populations and social structures. It is of course impossible to prove that social breakdown will never occur in the aftermath of disaster, especially when we contemplate the unprecedented catastrophe of nuclear war. But the lurid picture of post-disaster regression to savagery, that staple of fiction and of popular thought, can draw no support from the historical record.

*   *   *

INTRODUCTION

This historical survey of the economic causes, characteristics and consequences of certain important historical disasters was initially projected to help provide intellectual tools and insights for the comprehension and analysis of the great potential disaster of the present age — nuclear war. In this paper, however, the topical motive remains somewhat in the background, and only limited and tentative conclusions or inferences will be drawn about the prospects for national survival and recuperation from atomic holocaust. In any case, a survey of historical disasters can stand alone as a topic of the greatest interest and significance in its own right; the behaviour of economies under extreme stress may teach us something about even the normal functioning of economic relationships.

The word 'disaster' is used to refer to any substantial impoverishment due to an unusual source of stress that takes place within an economic system. The term 'economic collapse' denotes a disastrous situation in which the stresses are so great, or the internal corrective mechanisms so defective or damaged, as to lead to progressive economic deterioration. Symptoms of economic collapse, in addition to general drops in statistical indexes of production and consumption, are such phenomena as fall in population, emigration from cities, and cessation of internal trade. Unless the process can be reversed, the consequence is a breakdown in the complex system of production through division of labour, which is the source of the enormous productivity of modern economies. One central theme of this investigation is: Under what conditions do external or internal stresses lead beyond disaster to

economic collapse? A secondary theme is: Granted some remission of
the original source of stress (for example, termination of a destructive
war), what are the conditions promoting or hindering recovery?

Historical disasters may be divided into two categories according to
geographical extent: localized and generalized. A *localized* disaster is
usually due to some specific event: tornado, explosion, air raid, and
so on. Though geographically limited, it may be very violent or intense,
as when the town of St Pierre on the island of Martinique, with all its
30,000 inhabitants, was wiped out in minutes by the 1902 eruption of
Mt Pelée. Localized disasters are typically sudden in their onset.
Historical *generalized* disasters covering entire societies have been
caused by complex social phenomena such as war, famine, revolution
or pestilence. In the past, these have all taken extended periods of
time to develop their full effects. Thermonuclear war would be unique
in its combination of suddenness of destruction and generalized scale
of effect. For this historical review, it was felt desirable to look at both
the violent but limited-scale calamities, and the slower developing but
generalized catastrophes, since each type of experience may have a
great deal to contribute to our understanding of the economic impact
of, and responses to, nuclear attack.

In fact, there has been an intensive investigation of the disaster
phenomenon in the postwar period, though limited almost entirely to
specific World War II bombing experiences and to postwar localized
events. For localized disasters, we can probably now say that the crucial
socio-psychological phenomena are well understood, including the
immediate and delayed reactions of the victim population, the established leadership, host populations in case of evacuation, and so on.
For this reason, only a brief summary of the general findings about
localized disasters has been incorporated here.

For generalized disasters, in contrast, data are typically unavailable,
incomplete or unreliable; statistical series are usually interrupted at the
height of the crisis, and are always subject to considerable changes in
coverage, content and accuracy. In addition, the development of a
disaster over extended areas and times, the reactions of varied and
divided populations, and the difficulties of determining the nature and
success of complex policies, all pose overwhelming problems for analysis.
Accordingly, relatively extensive discussions have been provided of
four separate historical generalized disasters to help fill the larger gap
in our knowledge. The four historical experiences reviewed in detail
are: (1) the period of Russian war communism, 1918–21, (2) the
American Confederacy, 1861–65, (3) Japan during and after World
War II, and (4) Germany during and after World War II.

This survey is based entirely upon secondary sources, as interest here
is not in the historical events for their own sake but in the questions

of economic behaviour and policy on which the events cast some light. For this reason, and because of the weaknesses of the factual record, in each section the major sources upon which the analyses and conclusions are based will be indicated, thus making clear that reliance upon the understanding and interpretations of specialists in each of the experiences surveyed is as great as or greater than reliance upon 'objective' facts or data.

One crucial issue will reappear in almost every historical instance of disaster and recovery surveyed: Was the cause of collapse, or of failure to recover adequately from disaster, *technological* or *organizational*? If the cause is *technological*, the production possibilities available to the economy have been so impaired by the stresses imposed as to make recovery (or even, in some cases, maintenance of current levels) difficult or impossible even with perfect organization of the surviving resources. Clearly, where the economic stress takes the form of increasing physical destruction of the resource base, by bombing (as in the case of Japan), or by progressive enemy occupation of the nation's land area (as in the case of the Confederacy), eventually a point will be reached where the economy will break down; the productivity of even the surviving resources will be radically reduced because of functional dependence upon inputs from resources no longer available. In such cases there may be organizational difficulties in addition — policy mistakes, unwise resource allocations, and so on — but the technological explanation would suffice to explain the final result.

If we are to have even a potential recovery, there must be some cessation of the stress responsible for the disaster. Nevertheless, it does not follow that a rapid rebound from a depressed economy towards more normal historical levels of production and income is technologically possible. Even without a visible source of continuing stress, the lingering damage to key economic resources or systems may make it impossible to maintain the surviving resources and population. Bottlenecks or vicious circles may be so pervasive that economic conditions must get worse before a stable level is reached from which growth can be resumed. Or, as a less extreme situation, the economy may not necessarily go downhill, but still not improve without a long interlude of seeming stagnation. However, a thorough exploration of post-disaster technological production possibilities was not attempted in this study. In the historical instances surveyed, whenever failure to recover was observed, organizational difficulties (inflationary monetary and credit policies, interference with the price mechanism, unwise public expenditures, and the like) have seemed to provide an adequate explanation. In some cases, rather direct visible technological consider-ations seem to have been of supplementary significance. (On the other hand, if we were to consider the more massive levels of destruction in thermonuclear war, and especially the possibilities for the disruption of key ecological or physical systems, lasting *technological* impairment of recovery potentialities might be serious indeed.) For the cases observed here, the contention that technological limitations were the main source of difficulty should be kept in mind as an alternative hypothesis that cannot be dismissed without a more rigorous investigation than could be provided.[1]

LOCALIZED DISASTERS: A SUMMARY[2]

Even a narrowly limited disaster is, of course, 'total' for those who do not survive it, and sufficiently catastrophic for anyone suffering severe personal and material damage. Accordingly, small disasters have a great deal to teach us about the social and psychological consequences of quite large ones. In general, for any disaster it is useful to consider three zones of effect: the total destruction zone, the partially damaged zone, and the economically linked but physically undamaged support zone. Property and human damage are not perfectly correlated, of course; in Hiroshima, there were human survivors even in the 'total destruction' zone for property. Still, the distinctions remain generally useful. Among the best documented of the more severe localized disasters are the San Francisco earthquake and fire of 1906 (500 dead), the Halifax explosion of 1917 (2000 dead), and the World War II bombings of Hamburg (40,000 dead), Hiroshima (80,000 dead) and Nagasaki (40,000 dead).

Most studies of localized disasters have emphasized the psychological determinants of the behaviour of the population in the impact area, of its leaders, of supporting groups in neighbouring areas, and so on. These determinants are not our present concern. However, the typical psychological pattern of reaction to disaster is so well established that it is worth reviewing as a reliable input into analyses of the economic impact of disaster.

In general, it has been found that the 'disaster syndrome' displayed by a population suddenly struck by disaster does not include the wild, asocial behaviour described by the more lurid popular writers on such themes. Panic does not ordinarily occur.[3] Survivors first reorient and extricate themselves, and then their families. Some, even when seriously injured themselves, assist others. If there is reason to fear another hazard (explosion, spreading fire, renewed bombing, etc.), there may be hasty flight. All this is rational behaviour. Others seem to become temporarily stunned or apathetic, in which condition they will respond to direction but are incapable of independently useful action. In the immediate post-impact period, a strong feeling of community identification is generated, promoting cooperative and unselfish efforts toward repair and relief activity. Gradually, however, this stimulus wears off, after some days or weeks, and concern over unfairness of relief distribution and the like typically leads to considerable recrimination as a more normal society is restored.

A very marked psychological pattern, the 'counter-disaster syndrome', typically takes place in the support area outside the impact zone of the disaster. The crisis calls forth an outburst of generous assistance, both personal and material, from this zone. Volunteer rescuers converge on the disaster area; food and medicines are freely contributed; refugees are welcomed in reception areas. For many smaller disasters, the material support has been so great as to exceed emergency needs. Some time later, however, a reaction may set in, leading to bad relations between victim and support populations and accusations of ingratitude.

The effect of disaster upon community leadership and essential workers is interesting and important. The conventional leaders may be wiped out by the disaster; but even if not, their effectiveness is at first limited by shock, communications breakdown, and loss of facilities and personnel. Furthermore, within these limitations, leaders and essential workers may function poorly for lack of plans and training in how to deal with emergencies. One crucial problem is conflict between personal and public roles; leaders must worry about their own family needs as well as community needs. Many leaders and essential personnel, it appears, abandon their posts in order to see to their own families' safety. Frequently, it is found, transmitted messages will not suffice, and only the assurance afforded by face-to-face confrontation with other members of the family will permit the worker to return to his task. Personnel who respond most effectively to the emergency are typically those with normal quasi-disaster functions, the army, the police, fire-fighters, and so on. The abdication of conventional leadership often leads to the rise of emergent leaders, who are frequently those with less emotional involvement, or with some specialized knowledge or talent. There may also be entrance of leaders from the support area.

Looking at matters now from the economic point of view, the urgent needs in the impact period are rescue, escape, fire-fighting, medical aid, and so on; in general, protection from physical hazards. At first, most useful endeavours to these ends are necessarily unspecialized and uncoordinated. The shattering of customary patterns and the breakdown of communications limit assistance to those in the immediate neighbourhood. However, some specialized organizations may spring rapidly into action: fire departments, hospitals, civil defence, utility repair services, for example. If these groups are well trained and prepared, they may perform prodigies; if not, they may not function at all.

After the physical hazard abates, the relief phase begins. The prime needs are shelter (in inclement weather), food and water, and clothing. In localized disasters, at least in the recent history of the western world, relief pours in so quickly and copiously as to preclude any substantial degree of what might be called 'secondary mortality' from exposure and starvation, though of course there will still be much suffering. Planning and training for the required social services in the relief period are of the greatest value.

Finally, there is the recuperation phase in which measures are put under way to restore the economic viability of the damaged area. Here the most crucial needs seem to be utilities — communications, power, water, sewage, and gas — to permit industry to function once more and to make the area habitable. Also vital are housing and restoration of transportation. Even in great historical disasters, it has proved technologically and organizationally possible to restore the functioning of the impact area, and the surviving population have generally been strongly motivated to return and rebuild rather than emigrate.[4]

In Iklé's analysis of recovery from bomb destruction, he makes use of the concepts of 'consumer-resource ratio' and 'elasticity'.[5] Disasters destroy resources, but also tend to reduce the demands upon some classes of resources because of mortalities, impoverishment and decline in economic activity. The demands for a few critical services may not contract, however, and in fact may expand manifold in the face of the destruction of capacity. These critical resources usually include medical facilities and repair or construction services.

'Elasticity' refers to the expansibility of services performed by the surviving resources. For example, remaining housing can be crowded beyond its normal capacity.[6] Similarly, medical facilities can be spread by reducing care for the sick to a Spartan level; transport facilities by crowding; and repair facilities by improvised minor restoration (cardboard replacing broken glass windows, for example), by ignoring merely ornamental damage, and so on. The higher the pre-disaster standards, the more elasticity in meeting minimal post-disaster needs.

The availability of certain services that depend upon complex functioning systems cannot always be analysed in this simple quantitative fashion. For example, electric power generators may survive very well, but if the electrical distribution system is thoroughly smashed it may be impossible to provide electrical service. This is peculiarly important because power is a vital input into almost every other critical service. This suggests one other helpful category, which we may call 'substitutability'. At least in good weather, huts or tents may be satisfactory minimal substitutes for housing; lorries may possibly substitute for buses and trains; couriers for telephone services, and so forth. There is, however, no practicable substitute for power in most uses, which underlines the importance of this service. Emergency generators are, to the extent available, a valuable substitute for network power.

It is sometimes suggested that a community hit by disaster tends to rebound, and may in the long run actually be better off. Prince's pioneer study of Halifax, for example, indicates that the explosion changed social mores in that city from a conservative mould inhibiting economic expansion to a more progressive and commercial attitude. The recoveries of San Francisco, Halifax, Hiroshima and Nagasaki have also been widely hailed as remarkable. In the case of Hamburg, the long statistical series available suggests that the wartime incidents represent only a temporary break in the city's overall pattern of development.[7] It seems safe to conclude that there is a very powerful tendency to rebound to normal trends, but whether the rebound actually tends to carry beyond what would have been the normal level must remain in doubt.

Following is a brief review of what is known about the economic impact of two of the greatest localized disasters of history: the fire raids on Hamburg and the atomic attack on Hiroshima. Hamburg was a city of around 1.7 million before the war, but pre-attack evacuation (mostly of non-essential personnel) had reduced the population at risk to some 1.5 million.[8] A series of raids over a period of ten days in July and August of 1943 destroyed about half of the buildings in the city. The attack was mainly incendiary, and perfect weather conditions, combined with the exceptional density of combustible materials in Hamburg, overwhelmed well-prepared and heroic civil defence measures (though fire-fighters did succeed in saving whole neighbourhoods at the fringes of the mass fires). People proved tougher, generally speaking, than property; the 40,000 fatalities[9] were around 3 per cent of the population at risk. Most of the casualties were suffered in the night of 24–25 July, when a firestorm (a ring of mass fire) was touched off, destroying almost everything within its periphery.

In the aftermath of the raids, Hamburg found itself with approximately as many injured survivors as fatalities. Over two-thirds of hospital beds were destroyed. During the course of the attacks about half of the population had fled the city. Reception areas had been prepared with food stocks and large-scale cooking equipment, and relief services for casualties and refugees were efficiently handled. A considerable effort was put into salvage of consumer goods; and cash grants were made to permit refugees to purchase replacements. Mortuary services also required extraordinary efforts. During this relief phase, support was provided by the Hamburg suburban areas, with supplementation from all over Germany.

Over a period of months, around 300,000 of the refugees were rehoused in the city, while some 500,000 were permanently evacuated. Rehousing required compulsory billeting; makeshift shelters proved unsatisfactory and new emergency construction too costly. A 'dead zone' of the city was closed off. In the rest of the city, extraordinary effort had to be put into repairs of all kinds. During this recuperation phase, water supply was a difficult problem, even though emergency wells had been dug before the attack. Tank trucks were used to distribute water in areas where the system failed. Disruption of water supply made flush toilets inoperative in some areas, and privies were used. Electricity and gas were adequate within a few days after the last attack. Within four days the telegraph was functioning normally, and the mails within twelve days. Heavy loss of street and elevated cars kept the transit system from full recovery, and the reshuffling of housing in relation to places of work tended to increase transport crowding further. The railroad yards were heavily damaged, but through traffic was resumed in a few days. During the recuperation phase, substitute administrative centres which had been prepared in the suburbs proved very valuable. On the seventh day the central bank was reopened, and business began to function normally. Hamburg was not a dead city. The Strategic Bombing Survey reported that within five months it had recovered up to 80 per cent of its former productivity.[10]

The 1940 census population of Hiroshima[11] was 345,000, but some wartime evacuation had cut the population at risk to perhaps 300,000.[12] Hiroshima had escaped previous bombing, and perhaps for this reason the civil defence system was not very efficient. A substantial programme of demolition for firebreaks, however, had made considerable progress by the date of the atomic attack, 6 August 1945. Immediate deaths were caused mainly by mechanical injuries from collapse of structures, by direct heat and gamma radiation, and by fire. Deaths at Hiroshima are estimated at 80,000, including fatalities from radiation sickness (mostly in the ensuing few weeks). It is worth noting that there were survivors in shelters and strong buildings practically at ground zero. As at Hamburg, there was a firestorm in the central area. This led to complete destruction of the zone affected, but tended to limit expansion of the fire. (In Nagasaki there was no firestorm, but a moving conflagration, and the fire carried into a less built-up area.) As at Hamburg, people proved tougher than structures. Almost 70 per cent of the buildings in Hiroshima were destroyed, compared with around 30 per cent of population.[13]

Again as at Hamburg, injured survivors about equalled fatalities; both were on a much higher proportionate scale than at Hamburg, however. Medical facilities were severely damaged, and the surviving capacity overwhelmed. A flight of population took place immediately after the disaster, a rational move in view of the terrible fire threat, the destruction of the economic mechanisms of the city, and fear of possible second attack. People began returning within 24 hours, and by November 1945, the city population was back to 140,000. Although information on this topic is not entirely clear, it appears that the lack of efficient civil defence prevented the rescue of many trapped individuals who perished from fire. The fire-fighting and police services do not appear to have functioned effectively on the day of the disaster. Surviving hospital and medical services performed to the limits of the supplies and personnel available. Military support and organized rescue and relief activity began to take effect on the next day, 7 August.

In the recuperation phase, it is worth noting that the air-burst bomb generally left underground utility networks intact. The gas-producing plant and water pumping station survived, but destruction of gasholders prevented service and lack of electricity stopped the water supply. Sewers were undamaged, but sewer pumping stations were inoperative. On 7 August power was generally restored to surviving areas, and through railway service commenced on 8 August. Telephone service started on 15 August. Hiroshima was also not a dead city. The US Strategic Bombing Survey reported that plants responsible for three-quarters of the city's industrial production could have resumed normal operations within 30 days (the newer and larger plants in Hiroshima were on the outskirts of the city, and both physical premises and personnel generally survived).[14] By mid-1949 the population had grown to over 300,000 once more, and 70 per cent of the destroyed buildings had been reconstructed.[15]

For localized disasters, the overall experience in the crisis and in recovery afterwards is broadly favourable. Organizational difficulties do not seem to have been crucial, once the impact phase of the disaster was past. Technologically, several of the elements of the productive mechanism take on critical importance (for example, power and water supply), but in the scale of disaster surveyed the recovery potentials were present to provide sufficient base for a rebound in the direction of normal levels. The repeatedly demonstrated willingness of populations to put out extraordinary efforts with an exceptional degree of unselfishness in the crisis period is a crucial element in making recovery possible.

WAR COMMUNISM IN RUSSIA, 1917–1921[16]

Great disasters destroy established social relationships as well as physical structures. This is increasingly the case as the scale of disaster expands from a localized calamity, in which the physical and social environment surrounding the impact area may be scarcely affected, to a truly society-wide phenomenon. From the wreckage of the established way of things the community emerges in a somewhat plastic state. The pieces of the social structure must be put together again, but can be reassembled in a number of different ways. In the aftermath of thermonuclear war, for example, it is questionable whether a surviving community would re-establish an economic system based upon private ownership and monetary exchange. We might see, instead, one form or another of what has been called 'disaster socialism'. The term has no unique accepted referent, but presumably goes beyond the governmental regulation and intervention in the economy experienced in the US in World Wars I and II, some distance towards the complete substitution of centralized direction over resources in place of the institutions of private property and voluntary exchange. It may go so far as to include total labour conscription in which free choice of occupation, or in effect, private property in one's own person is abolished. Since such an ordinarily 'unthinkable' policy may become a real possibility in the plastic post-disaster state, it is of interest to examine 'war communism' in Russia, the most extreme effort in modern times to do away with the system of private property and voluntary exchange. The war communism policy arose, of course, out of a uniquely disastrous situation, but the attempts of the Bolsheviks to cope with the consequences of external stresses and of their own disruptive policies may convey much relevant information about disasters in general.

The Tsarist regime in Russia was overthrown in favour of the Provisional Government in March 1917, and the Provisional Government in turn was overthrown by the Bolsheviks in November 1917. The following four years probably represent the historical ultimate in national social disorganization. Apart from the complete overturn of established political, economic and social relationships in Russia, there also took place beginning in 1918 a complex civil war. Reactionary forces, democratic and non-Bolshevik socialist factions, independent peasant movements, and minority national separatists struggled with and against each other and the Bolsheviks. The German role was also important before the defeat of the Central Powers. Germany looked benignly upon the Bolsheviks in Russia proper because of their anti-war position, but at the same time it attempted with some success to incorporate the Ukraine and other areas within its own sphere of rule. Allied interventionists supported the White forces in northern Russia, Siberia and elsewhere, and in addition the Bolsheviks warred with newly independent Poland, Had all these forces combined their efforts against the Bolsheviks, it seems impossible that the communist regime could have survived, but such coordination was never achieved; even so, the success of the Bolsheviks in escaping one threat after another seems to have required miracles of improvisation. By the end of 1920 these various campaigns had come to an end, but dissidence within the Soviet forces flared into the Kronstadt revolt of March 1921, which led directly to the adoption of the New Economic Policy (NEP) in the interests of regaining the popular support lost by the policy of war communism.[17]

Turning to economic affairs, the almost complete confiscation or nullification of property rights that occurred in revolutionary Russia was not a deliberately planned undertaking of the Bolsheviks. Rather, recognizing their limited capacity for economic administration and sensing the need to feel their way in the transition period, the communist leaders planned originally only to seize and control 'the commanding heights' of industry. The pace of confiscation was largely determined by 'the elemental forces' of the Revolution. Throughout Russia, peasants were seizing estates, workers were taking over factories, and managers and capitalists were abandoning their properties. Total central control was believed necessary to combat the syndicalist tendencies of such developments, since the usurpers of seized properties frequently began to operate them to their own parochial advantage. In addition, extensions of central state control were thought to be required to overcome the resistance or sabotage of disaffected managers of nationalized or remaining private and cooperative enterprises.

In industry, the final situation was an all-encompassing (in theory) state monopoly. Agricultural products above those necessary for farm subsistence were requisitioned from the peasants by government collectors. Even though the help of the poorer peasants was enlisted, so that the effect was in large part to expropriate those who were better off, considerable resistance was encountered in the countryside. The produce so garnered was rationed to the urban population.[18] Industrial products were also distributed by administrative arrangements to both urban and rural consumers. At first payment was required for the products distributed, in low, fixed prices. But as the inflation progressed these became meaningless, and finally free distribution to consumers was undertaken in the interests of attaining a 'natural' (moneyless) economy. In pursuit of this utopian goal, money accounts and profitability calculations were abandoned in operations of and transactions among state enterprises. As for labour, 'By the end of this period, labor was conscripted, militarized, and attached to the place of work'.[19] The entire economy ran, in principle, under orders like an army; the process of voluntary exchange was rejected and prohibited.

However, black market trade in the form of informal barter, as well as more professional illegal activities by specialized 'bagmen', was very important throughout this period. According to Carr, well over half of the foodstuffs consumed by town-dwellers came through extra-legal channels, and a degree of toleration of the trade became a necessity.[20] Indeed, the existence of this illegal trade was of importance to the Bolsheviks in a variety of ways, one of which was that trade required a medium of exchange and thus created a demand for the money produced by the Bolshevik printing press. The Soviets possessed the plates for Tsarist and Kerensky currency as well as Bolshevik, and permitted all of them to circulate legally. In fact, they concentrated on expanding the older currencies (which were preferred by the public) and thus succeeded in diverting a considerable part of the community's wealth to the service of the government.[21]

One question of topical concern is whether the experience with war communism lends any support to proponents of a policy of disaster socialism for other possible disaster situations, specifically, in a post-thermonuclear war environment. The policy of war communism did contribute to the specifically Bolshevik goal of irretrievably smashing the old social order, but as a method for conducting economic affairs it did not seem to work. It is somewhat difficult to validate this conclusion statistically since, aside from the defects of the statistical record, the disruptive effects of the civil war upon the economy are confounded with the effects specifically caused by the war communism policy. However, the negative conclusion on the workability of war communism is supported by observers on all sides of the political spectrum, and of course corresponds with the action of the Bolsheviks themselves in abandoning the policy for the NEP.[22] Furthermore, it seems to be the case that economic conditions were rapidly deteriorating towards complete collapse in the spring of 1921, after the definitive Bolshevik victory had ended the civil war.[23]

A number of points related to the statistical tables call for comment. Table 1.1 shows the catastrophic decline of industrial production to 20 per cent of the pre-war level by 1920,[24] markedly worse for large-scale than small-scale enterprises. Since administration of the large-scale plants was certainly more centralized, this is a rather suggestive result. It is related to the following somewhat puzzling question: How did the economy succeed in supporting the Bolshevik civil war effort in 1918–20, if it approached complete collapse in the period after Bolshevik victory?

Table 1.1   Output Indexes for Russian Industry, 1913–1920*

Year	Large-scale	Small-scale	Total
1913	100.0	100.0	100.0
1916	116.1	88.2	109.4
1917	74.8	78.4	75.7
1918	33.8	73.5	43.4
1919	14.9	49.0	23.1
1920	12.8	44.1	20.4

* These indexes were calculated by State Planning Commission (Gosplan), as quoted in Baykov, p. 8.

To some extent, the answer may be that the Bolsheviks in effect used up in the earlier years that portion of the nation's capital wealth formerly in the hands of nobles, bourgeoisie, wealthier peasants and foreign investors;[25] only towards the end did the impoverishment bear primarily upon the Bolsheviks' own class support. Another and possibly more important explanation is that illegal private or cooperative-syndicalist enterprise continued to function in large sectors of industry, and this, together with illegal 'bagman' trade of products (which grew to huge proportions in 1920),[26] served to maintain a minimally tolerable economy during the civil war. While theoretically all industry was operating under total state administration, a census of 1920 reported the existence of some 37,000 state industrial enterprises, of which only 7000 were on the books of the central control agency and thus subject to even nominal control.[27] The view that the maintenance of the economy depended to a large extent upon the non-controlled enterprises is supported, of course, by the lesser output decline for smaller enterprises revealed in Table 1.1. This view is also consistent with the economic collapse after the conclusion of the civil war. At this point, the Bolsheviks were able to turn to the liquidation of illegal industry and trade, and to centralize what had in the confusion escaped control, thus (on this interpretation) destroying or paralysing the only effectively functioning portion of the economy. In addition, many small capitalists who had stayed on in the hopes of Soviet defeat decamped and abandoned their enterprises. Consequently, the paradox of economic collapse only after political and military victory.

Table 1.2 suggests the magnitude of the agricultural problem. It seems to be universally agreed that the policy of compulsory requisition of produce above farm subsistence levels (in effect, a 100 per cent tax

Table 1.2   Output and Stock Measures for Russian Agriculture, 1909–1921

Year	Sown area (million desyatin)	Gross yield of crops (million poods)	Number of horses (millions)	Number of cattle (millions)	Number of sheep and goats (millions)
1909–13	83.1	3,850			
1916	79.0	3,482	31.5	49.9	80.9
1917	79.4	3,350			
1920	62.9	2,082	25.4	39.1	49.8
1921	58.3	1,689	23.3	36.8	48.4

Quoted from official sources by Baykov, p. 23. The data do not refer to the whole territory of the USSR, but to the territory on which the census of 1920 was carried out (using the same territory for all years).

Table 1.3   Russian State Budget and Note Issue, 1917–1921 (milliard roubles)

Year	Revenue	Expenditure	Deficit	Note issue
1917	5.0	27.6	22.6	16.4
1918	15.6	46.7	31.1	33.5
1919	49.0	215.4	166.4	164.2
1920	159.6	1215.2	1055.6	943.6
1921	4139.9	26,076.8	21,936.9	16,375.3

Source: Baykov, p. 36.

upon marginal production of the peasant) led directly to reductions in sown area and declines in output.[28] The key provision signalling the inauguration of the New Economic Policy was the March 1921 abolition of compulsory requisitions in favour of a proportional tax (in kind, at first) upon peasant production.[29] Permitting the peasants to retain a fraction of their produce above subsistence levels led, by an obvious step, to the legalizing of markets in which the surplus could be exchanged for desired goods.

Tables 1.3 and 1.4 provide data upon the state budget, the note issue, and price levels. As commonly occurs in disaster situations, the vast bulk of government operations in 1917–22 were financed by the printing press. When such a practice has continued long enough to create a crisis of confidence, historical experience indicates that the price level tends to rise faster than the volume of money.[30] The

Table 1.4   Real Value of the Total Volume of Paper Money, Russia,
1914–1922

Year (figures for July or August)	Index of notes in circulation (July 1, 1914 = 1)[a]	Index of prices (1913 = 1)[a]	Real value of volume of money (millions of roubles)[b]
1914	1.0		3015
1918	26.8	88.5	493
1919	62.0	656	154
1920	313.9	8140	63
1921	1439.6	80,700	29
1922	196,288.4[c]	5,795,000[c]	55

Notes:
[a] Official figures, quoted in Arnold, p. 91.
[b] Calculated by dividing the volume of paper money by the official All-Union Price Index, in Arnold, p. 93.
[c] Arnold, p. 129.

consequent decline in the real value of the money stock represents another dimension of impoverishment of the community.[31] In addition, from the government's point of view, the process may be proceeding so fast that the real revenue obtained from new currency issues no longer justifies the cost of printing and distributing the notes. This apparently was the situation in early 1921.[32] In the USSR, of course, the threat of repudiation implicit in the ideological drive towards a moneyless economy further reduced the incentive to hold currency. And the spread of barter, facilitated by payment of wages in kind, contracted the range of uses of money. When markets were legalized under the NEP and money-wage payments were gradually restored, the use of and need for money vastly increased, thus permitting the Bolsheviks to proceed further in the direction of hyperinflation in 1922. In that year they expanded the note issue well over 100-fold, but the increased demand for currency held down the price increase; the real value of the total money volume substantially increased. The printing press operation was thus a highly profitable one in 1922, thanks to the NEP, and the Soviets were enabled to continue the hyperinflation through 1924. Nevertheless, definite economic recovery did take place from 1921 to 1924 under the NEP. By 1924, industrial production in particular returned to almost half the level of 1913 (see Table 1.5), while the money supply was rising to some 500,000,000 times the 1914 level, and the price index to 60,000,000,000 on the base 1913 = 1.

Table 1.5   Output, Money, and Prices Under the NEP, USSR, 1920–1924

Year	Index of notes in circulation (July 1, 1914 = 1)[a]	Index of prices (1913 = 1)[a]	Index of industrial production (1913 = 100)[b]	Index of agricultural production (1913 = 100)[b]
1920	314	8140	20[d]	65
1921	1440	80,700	13	55
1922	196,288	5,695,000	24	69
1923	5,546,713	117,569,000	35	76
1924	496,702,887[c]	61,920,000,000[c]	49	69

Notes:
[a] Arnold, pp. 91, 129, 186–7. Figures are for July (unless otherwise specified).
[b] From a study by Jean Dessirier, quoted in Phillip Cagan, 'The Monetary Dynamics of Hyperinflation', in Milton Friedman (ed.), *Studies in the Quantity Theory of Money*, p. 117.
[c] March, 1924.
[d] From Table 1.1 above.

A somewhat better grasp of the magnitude of the economic disaster Russia suffered in the period of war communism may be obtained from demographic statistics. (Though here, in particular, it must be remembered that not all the loss can be attributed to the policy of war communism, since the military operations of the civil war were also significant.) Reasonable estimates are that in the period 1917–22 the population of the territory that became the Soviet Union fell by about 16 million, not counting war deaths and emigration.[33] City reports generally show, comparing 1920 with 1914, marked increases in death rates per 1000 and decreases in birth rates.[34] However, perhaps the most significant demographic statistics, from the economic point of view, are those showing depopulation of cities in this period. When people abandon the cities it is usually a sign of a serious breakdown in the division of labour such that physical closeness to sources of food becomes an important requisite for survival. Sorokin reports estimates that 8 million people left the towns for the villages between 1918 and 1920;[35] Baykov describes the exodus as reducing the town population by 33.4 per cent between 1917 and 1920; in the greatest and most advanced cities, Moscow and Petrograd, the decline was 58.2 per cent.[36]

It may be convenient to summarize here the main features of war communism for possible comparison with hypothetical policies of disaster socialism:

1. Practically all property rights of upper classes (aristocracy, bourgeoisie, wealthier peasants and also foreign investors), and the bulk of private properties in 'means of production' outside of agriculture were confiscated.
2. In agriculture, the confiscated properties were divided among the peasants, and operated individually for the most part. 'Surplus' production over subsistence levels was requisitioned.
3. Labour was conscripted and subjected to quasi-military discipline; wages were paid largely in kind.
4. All industry was, in theory, centrally directed and administered. Private production and trade were illegal.
5. Government operations were financed by printing money, to the extent that resources were not acquired by direct compulsion.
6. Low, fixed prices were promulgated for the procurement of supplies and materials and the distribution of finished goods on a rationed basis to consumers. As the inflation made these close to meaningless, free distribution was undertaken.
7. There was an attempt to abandon money settlements and money accounts in the operations of and transactions among state enterprises.

The NEP, in contrast, was characterized by the following policies:

1. A proportional tax upon farm production was substituted for compulsory requisitions.
2. Private trading was legalized for both agricultural and industrial products, and in fact trade was soon dominated by private businessmen, often called 'Nepmen'.[37]
3. Cooperative productive enterprises, and even those privately owned, were permitted to some extent. In general, however, state enterprises were not denationalized.
4. Total centralized planning of operations of state enterprises was abandoned, and separate enterprises were permitted to contract for acquisition of supplies and disposal of products. In addition, money accountability was restored, and enterprises were expected to show a credit balance.
5. Compulsory labour service and wage payment in kind were abolished.
6. The government continued to employ the printing press as a major source of state revenue.

The policies of the NEP, as indicated in Table 1.5, were associated, despite hyperinflation, with a considerable economic recovery in the years 1922–24. This recovery, however, still left the Soviet economy far below the levels of production attained in pre-Revolution years.

Russian war communism was, clearly, an organizational crisis, recognized as such at the time and by almost all students of the era since. There were certainly elements present for substantial technological difficulty: human losses in combat and by emigration, destruction of property and loss of production in World War I and the civil war, and cessation of foreign trade. However, the worsening of conditions after the Bolshevik victory and, especially, the dramatic though partial recovery following institution of the NEP, constitute almost a crucial experiment between the organizational and technological explanations. This experience is perfectly consistent with the hypothesis that it was the policy of war communism as an organizing technique that was fatally defective. Under the alternative hypothesis, it would have to be argued that some increasingly severe technological constraint was suddenly mitigated in 1922, and the reversal of economic policy was merely coincidental. The major possibility here would seem to be the civil war itself: a lagged effect might be called upon to explain the observation that the economic disaster waxed as the fighting waned. But the scale of physical destruction following the end of the civil war was insufficient to explain the drastically low production levels reported in Table 1.5. The failure to surpass, by 1924, the level of 50 per cent of the industrial output of 1913 is again consistent with the explanation that the state-dominated economy, even with the enlarged role assigned to the private sector by the NEP, was not organizing resources properly.

THE AMERICAN CONFEDERACY, 1861–1865[38]

In Kahn's great study of nuclear warfare, it is suggested that a modern economic system may be thought of as integrating an 'A Country' and a 'B Country'. The A Country consists of the cities, which might be destroyed by bombing, and the B Country consists of the hinterland, too dispersed to be vulnerable in the aggregate.[39] Kahn goes on to argue that the B Country can survive without the A Country (the hinterland without the cities) and, in fact, contains the resources and skills necessary to rebuild the destroyed centres,[40] by a process presumably analogous to that in which cities first arose in the course of economic development. The Confederacy, after the interdiction of trade with the northern states, was in a position somewhat like the hypothetical 'B Country' in Kahn's analysis. After secession, populations of the loyal and seceded areas were around 22 million and 9 million respectively (about 3,500,000 of the latter total were slaves).

But of the united nation's ten largest cities, only one (New Orleans, captured by Union forces in April 1862) was in the Confederacy, as were only ten of the 102 cities of 10,000 population or more. The seceded states accounted for less than one-tenth of the total value of manufactured products.[41] The South, furthermore, suffered from an additional disadvantage in that even as a hinterland its economic structure in isolation was extremely unbalanced; the agriculture of the Confederacy was highly specialized in the production of cotton and, secondarily, tobacco. It was, therefore, dependent in peacetime upon trade with the outside world not only for manufactured goods, but even for food. Thus, we see that the self-sufficiency, even on a low level, of a 'B Country' should not be casually assumed.

Somewhat counterbalancing the disparity of resources was that the military goal of the South could be more modest than that of the North. To crush the rebellion the Union forces had to conquer; to keep it alive, it was sufficient for the Southern forces to achieve a military stalemate or draw. And, in fact, it was freely predicted by foreign observers that the military conquest of a nation of the geographical extent and with the human and material resources of the Confederacy was quite impossible. The ability of the thirteen colonies to maintain their independence of Great Britain in the American Revolution was given as an example.

In many ways, of course, the South put up an impressive war effort. Estimates vary on the forces enrolled, but at the height of the war they probably comprised between 500,000 and 600,000 men; about 50 per cent of the male white population between the ages of 15 and 50.[42] The effectiveness of the Southern armies needs no elaboration here. Aside from the vast military enrolment, pressures on the economy included the scarcity of food, clothing and war materials; blockade of foreign trade and interdiction of normal peacetime trade with the North; gradual paralysis and breakdown of manufacturing and transport systems for want of vital parts and replacements; occupation and raiding of key areas by Federal forces; and the administrative problems of a new nation, compounded by strong states' rights sentiment in the recently seceded states. Despite all these, the economy somehow supported the armies for four years of hard fighting before the collapse. Even then, it may be somewhat debatable as to what extent the Southern collapse was economic and what purely military. However, it is generally agreed that, by the end of the war, the Southern economy had collapsed, and that the proximate cause was breakdown of transportation.

Before going into the origin of the Southern economic collapse, it is vital to appreciate the fact that it took place under the conditions of increasing strain and pressure described above. So far as the disaster represented by the separation from the industrialized North was concerned, the South made an excellent adjustment. The main economic problems that the Confederacy faced (in addition to providing the war goods, manpower and resources and supplies required for military purposes) were to shift its redundant capacity for producing cotton and tobacco towards other agricultural products, especially food and wool; to set up manufactures for consumer goods and for producing replacements for capital goods of all kinds; and in so far as possible to trade surplus cotton and tobacco externally for the vitally needed manufactured goods. A good beginning was made on a number of these problems.

Cotton production, 4.5 million bales in 1860 and only slightly less in 1861, was cut back sharply in the 1862 crop. Little direct control was employed; the main factors behind the reduction were the unmarketability of cotton and strong moral suasion.[43] The 1863 crop fell below 1 million bales, and output was halved again in the following years. Tobacco production was also reduced, the consequence of both weakness of markets and direct pressure on producers. As for manufacturing, the Confederate authorities energetically and success-fully made provision for the supply of such vital war goods as cannons, small arms, powder, tents, and so on. The provision of shoes and clothing for the armed forces was less successfully managed, but perhaps minimally adequate.[44] On the consumer level, private enterprise and individual ingenuity partially succeeded in producing substitutes for the manufactured goods previously imported or whose local manufacture was previously dependent upon imported supplies or materials. Perhaps the most successful development was homespun cloth.[45]

Unfortunately, there appear to be no general production statistics for manufacturing under the Confederacy to assist in gauging the magnitude of industrial development. However, we can note that the Southern cities grew rapidly in population, despite the lack of resources for new housing construction. Richmond, Charleston, Wilmington, Atlanta, all became desperately crowded.[46] This crowding was in large part caused by rising industrial and administrative employment. (Especially in the later years, another important factor was the influx of refugees from Northern-occupied or threatened areas.) One of the most remarkable new industrial developments was the huge munitions complex at Selma, Alabama. In sum, it appears that here was a 'B Country' building an 'A Country' — a hinterland, largely deprived of customary urban services, providing for them by building new cities, or rather, by enlarging existing ones. That this development could take place, even though only partially, during a period of steady diminution and attrition of the aggregate resources of the South, lends considerable support to Kahn's thesis.

Nevertheless, despite partial success along this line, the Confederate economy ultimately collapsed. The fundamental cause was the increasing pressure of the war, that took two main forms: first, the steady drain upon resources of all kinds as they were channelled into direct fighting needs and away from economically productive employments and, even more important, the attrition of the country's physical base by Union occupation and interdiction. The fighting between the capitals of Washington and Richmond was largely inconclusive for four years, but the Union forces were, during all this time, making continual inroads upon the Confederacy's western and coastal fronts. In 1861 Missouri was largely cleared of Confederate forces and Kentucky and West Virginia held for the Union; also, several ports were captured or closed to the Confederates, including Port Royal, S.C. In April 1862 came the disastrous loss of New Orleans to Federal amphibious forces. Also in 1862 western Tennessee was captured, including Memphis, leaving only a narrow stretch of the Mississippi open to the South. The ports of Savannah and Jacksonville were also closed. In 1863 Union conquest of the entire Mississippi cut the Confederacy in two, and the Federals also partially blocked the land connection of Texas with Mexico. In 1864 came Sherman's march through Georgia, cutting the Confederacy through once again, with the consequent loss of the cities of Atlanta and Savannah.

The progressive loss of territory and resources made the task of creating an economy able to bear the crushing war burden quite impossible. Nevertheless, it will be worth our while to trace the main features of the economic collapse in some detail. We have seen that direct war needs for munitions were generally met, and the food and clothing situation was at least barely tolerable. Where the Confederate authorities failed (but unavoidably, in the circumstances) was in maintenance of the supporting economy underlying the war goods industries. Establishments that could have been used to manufacture replacements for vital machinery in all sectors of industry were wholly converted to direct war production. All civilian industry, even the most essential, was seriously hampered by the preferential manpower and supply arrangements for war goods production. Conscription of skilled labour was an important problem everywhere. The railroads of the South were in generally poor condition even before the war began, consisting of a collection of small roads with limited interconnections and varying gauges. A few vital links and interconnections were constructed to meet war needs, but no railroad iron was rolled during the war, so new construction required taking up secondary lines. The railroads suffered from loss of skilled labour, war destruction and accelerated wearing out of facilities, and general lack of replacements, materials and supplies. Meanwhile, coastal and river commerce was substantially stopped by Federal control of the waterways, and horses and wagons were largely impressed for the Confederate army. Break-down of transportation was the proximate cause of the economic collapse. Towards the end of the war, resources and stocks of goods lay everywhere useless and subject to looting and deterioration, while the armies and factories were unable to secure vital materials.

We shall now turn to a consideration of several policies of the Confederate government which, then and now, have been assigned large roles in the defeat of the Confederacy by some commentators and defended by others. These policies include inflationary finance, the foreign trade policy, and the practices of impressment and price controls. The position adopted here, as can be appreciated by review of the foregoing, is that the Southern economy was crushed by *force majeure*; even ideal policies could not have redressed the imbalance of resources, given the intense commitment of the North to the struggle. It is still of interest to examine possible Confederate mistakes. Lack of consideration for the problems of the vital supporting economy underlying the war goods industries has already been alluded to. (Assistance could perhaps have been provided by increased exemption of skilled labour from conscription, more provision of unskilled slave labour, import of needed materials through the blockade, and so on, though it is doubtful whether any great improvement was really possible.)

The policy of the Confederate government on trade does seem to have been somewhat perverse. Export of the huge cotton surpluses in 1861 and 1862 would have been possible, but was discouraged by the government. In the last peace season, 1860–61 (the 1860 crop), the South is reported to have exported around 2 million bales, and perhaps an equal amount was shipped North before the war began. But in 1861–62, despite loss of the Northern market, only 13,000 bales are reported as exported of a 4 million bale crop.[47] This, despite the fact that the blockade was scarcely effective in the early years of the war.[48] The reason was the 'Cotton is King' fallacy; by withholding cotton the South hoped to coerce Northern and foreign (especially British) industrialists into supporting the Confederacy. In each of the years 1863 and 1864, with blockade and blockade-running in full swing, amounts on the order of 130,000 bales are reported to have reached England.[49] Exports in these later years received the advantage of a European cotton price as much as five times higher than normal; however, the optimal policy for the Confederacy would have been to export while it had the opportunity, possibly holding cotton stocks abroad as a speculation. Not until early 1864 did the Confederate government organize blockade-running systematically. And as is well known, a large fraction of the goods imported were luxury items.[50]

An even more striking error was the policy of the Confederate government that banned trade through the lines with the North, partly on moralistic grounds, partly again to withhold 'King Cotton'. This was illogical for several reasons, one of which was that much of the cotton run through the blockade to Cuba or Bermuda was trans-shipped to the North anyway. But more important, a strict ban on trade through the lines was, for the Union, a logical complement to the sea blockade, a component of the 'anaconda' policy of strangling the Southern economy, dependent as it was upon trade with the outside world. In contrast, it was in the interest of the South to break this overland ban almost as much as it was to evade the sea blockade. It is true that the cotton and tobacco that could have been sent north would, to some degree, have helped the Northern war economy; but the Confederacy, its economy collapsing because of inability to dispose of its surpluses for needed imports of all kinds, was in a position where it had to grasp every opportunity. Actually, a substantial (though unrecorded) amount of illegal trade did pass through the lines; despite the attempts of officials on both sides to stop the practice, the temptations to corruption and the real needs of the Southern economy at times proved to be an overwhelming combination.[51] Curiously, even today historians commonly take a moralistic attitude on this question, and fail to appreciate the fundamental asymmetry in position that made maintenance of the land blockade a wise policy for the Union, but an unwise one for the Confederacy. If anything, it appears that the Union government was more tolerant of 'trade with the enemy' than was the Confederate, so that according to this analysis the policies of both sides were somewhat defective; but, of course, the North could more afford to commit mistakes than the South.

Confederate inflationary finance through multiplication of the note issue is often cited by historians as a crucial error of policy, and a major cause of economic collapse. We have seen, however, that even a hyperinflation was not inconsistent with economic recovery in Russia under the New Economic Policy, and of course the American Revolutionary War was successfully prosecuted despite an analogous depreciation of the Continental currency. Inflation is undoubtedly a disturbing factor: if the price level rises faster than the money supply, a real impoverishment occurs because of decreased real liquidity, and if prices rise so fast that no one will hold money, trading must be reduced to a barter basis. This latter effect is an especially fearful loss

to an advanced economy; and there was, in fact, considerable resort
to barter in the last years of the Confederacy. Still, the inflationary
policy was probably more a consequence than a cause of collapse.

The government's problem, of course, was to acquire resources for
the support of the war. Only small amounts were secured from foreign
loans and partially external sources such as import and export duties
and profits from state trading. More important, but non-recurrent, was
acquisition of property of the Federal government and of Union citizens
upon the outbreak of war, supplemented by some war booty later on.[52]
The major sources were necessarily internal: in addition to the
printing press these included loans, donations, taxes and impressments.
Impressments (that is, compulsory sales) were requisitions of goods,
originally only for the direct needs of the armed forces. Since the sale
price was commonly the officially controlled price or some other 'just
price' when the market value was much higher, impressment was often
practically confiscation. Furthermore, a huge amount of impressed
goods was never paid for, and the 'sellers' were left with uncollectable
Certificates of Indebtedness. The military were also able to contract
for factory-produced goods (blankets, shoes, and so on) on favourable
terms by threat of conscription of the labour force and by control over
raw materials and transportation.

Systematic year-by-year budgets for the Confederate Treasury do
not seem to have been compiled. However, the overall totals of
revenues from various sources may be put together from Todd's study
(see Table 1.6), though these totals are in the fluctuating medium of
Confederate dollars. Roughly speaking, the Confederate government's
wartime $3 billion of income was distributed as follows: taxes, 7 per
cent; seizures, 17 per cent; loans, 24 per cent; and note issue, 52 per
cent.[53] This indicates the source of the inflationary problem.

The successive financial programmes of the government were measures of increasing desperation, and only a few comments will be made
on them here: (1) The proportion collected by taxes was low for a
number of reasons: uncooperativeness of Congress in passing legislation,
resistance of state authorities, underestimates of prospective expenditures, popular failure to appreciate the anti-inflationary potential of
tax collections as opposed to financing through loans or, especially,
through printed money;[54] and sheer physical difficulty of collections
under a new and improvised administration in confused wartime
conditions.[55] (2) The bond issues were moderately successful at first,
but as the depreciation of the currency accelerated, bonds tended to
become unsalable since the real yield to holders was negative.[56] (3)
The problem of physical production of the currency notes was an
immense one in an economy largely without engravers, suitable papers

Table 1.6   Income Sources of the Confederate Government

Source	Amount (millions of $C)	Per cent of total
Taxes[a]		
Import and export duties	3.5	0.1
Tax in kind (estimate)	62.0	2.1
Ordinary taxes	142.0	4.8
Subtotal, taxes	207.5	6.9
Seizures and Donations[b]		
Federal funds	0.7	0.0
Sequestration of alien property[c]	7.5	0.3
Specie reserve of New Orleans banks[d]	4.2	0.1
Donations (estimate)	2.0	0.1
Impressments, certified by unpaid Certificates of Indebtedness (estimate)[e]	500.0	16.7
Subtotal, seizures and donations	514.4	17.2
Loans[f]		
Foreign (Erlanger loan)	15.0[g]	0.5
Domestic	697.0	23.3
Subtotal, Loans	712.0	23.8
Treasury Notes[h]	1554.1	52.0
Grand Total[i]	2988.0	100.0

Notes:
[a] Todd, p. 156.
[b] Ibid., p. 174.
[c] No estimate available for property taken over from Federal government, other than Federal funds.
[d] Confiscated upon Federal occupation of New Orleans.
[e] Not the total of impressments, but only those not paid in Treasury notes or other money.
[f] Todd, pp. 83–4.
[g] Amount realized (in foreign exchange figuring $5 = £1 sterling) was $7.7 million (ibid., p. 184). Schwab, after deducting certain costs, estimates the proceeds at $6.25 million (p. 42).
[h] Todd, p. 120.
[i] Certain minor sources, such as profits from government enterprises (including blockade-runners), appear to be omitted, in addition to the value of confiscated Federal properties already mentioned.

and inks, and so on. The quality of the notes was unsatisfactory and they were easy to counterfeit. The shortage of currency was such that the government resorted to honouring counterfeits.[57] State, municipal and private notes ('shinplasters'), as well as Federal greenbacks,[58] circulated freely.[59] There was also a good deal of barter.[60] (4) The real cause of the seeming money scarcity, as of the money famine of the Russian inflation and of other inflationary incidents, was the fact that the price level was rising faster than the money supply thus reducing the real command over goods and services represented by the money stock. In inflations generally, the price level tends to rise beyond the money supply once inflationary expectations become established in the public mind. In the Confederate case (see Table 1.7), this pattern was reinforced by the growing fear of total loss of exchange value of Confederate treasury notes as a result of ultimate Federal victory. (5) One of the expedients employed to arrest the rise in the money supply and commodity price level was a currency reform. The reform provided that all currency not converted into bonds before 1 April 1864 had to be exchanged for new notes at the rate of 3 : 2. While a temporary dip in the price level was thus achieved, the basic inflationary processes continued unabated, and prices soon resumed their upward march.

We may now turn to a consideration of the much-debated Confederate policies of price control and impressment. Throughout history, kings and governments in need have debased the coinage and multiplied the note issue. Typically, the contemporary publics have blamed the consequent inflation of prices upon the greed of speculators, merchants, blood-suckers, and the like. Legislation to hold prices down by fiat is thus an almost universal concomitant of monetary inflation. In the Confederacy, maximum prices were first fixed, apparently, to regulate the compensation for impressed goods. The scope of impressment steadily widened; at first only direct military needs of the national government were so met, but eventually impressment was employed for all purposes of all government units in the Confederacy. In addition, there was heavy pressure upon private transactions to comply with the published price lists.

The consequence of these policies was a partial breakdown in the commerce between city and countryside. A farmer, bringing his produce to city markets, had to risk impressment or other unremunerative sale of his produce. Often, impressment of horse and wagon was an even more serious threat. As a result, provisions were scarce and expensive in all the cities, yet often plentiful in the countryside.[61] The next step, therefore, was the dispatch of impressment officers into the countryside. This measure caused great bitterness and political disaffection; the impressment system collapsed in 1865, and the government was forced

Table 1.7   Money and Prices in the Confederacy

Date[a]	Index of stock of money (Jan. 1861 = 1)[b]	Index of commodity prices (Jan. 1861 = 1)[c]	Index of real value of money stock[d]
1861:			
January	1.0	1.0	1.00
April	1.3	1.0	1.29
June	1.3	1.1	1.17
October	1.8	1.4	1.34
1862:			
January	2.5	1.9	1.33
April	3.0	2.8	1.07
June	3.4	3.3	1.02
October	5.0	5.2	0.95
1863:			
January	6.9	7.6	0.90
April	6.7	11.7	0.57
June	9.6	13.0	0.74
October	11.3	18.6	0.61
1864:			
January	11.6	27.8	0.42
April		44.7	
June		42.0	
October		40.0	
1865:			
January		58.2	
April	20[e]	92.1	0.22

Notes:
[a] Figures through January 1864 from E. M. Lerner, 'Money, Prices, and Wages in the Confederacy', p. 29.
[b] Treasury notes plus bank notes and deposits. Not adjusted to eliminate interbank deposits, but excludes supplementary currencies circulating.
[c] From April 1864 on, the general price index of the eastern section of the Confederacy is used (ibid., p. 24).
[d] Index of Stock of Money divided by Index of Commodity Prices.
[e] Crude estimate of author, summing $1,550 millions in Confederate notes, $250 millions for bank notes and deposits, and adding around $200 million for supplementary currencies.

to pay market prices with its last specie hoards.[62] During the time it was effective, the threat of impressment led to concealment of goods and production for subsistence rather than for marketable surplus; both were catastrophic in the economic situation of the Confederacy. It is unclear, however, whether one characteristic phenomenon of economic collapse — flight of population from the cities back to the countryside — was actually observed in the Confederacy. (The unsettled state of the countryside, with Northern troops, Southern deserters, hungry refugees, and freed or escaped slaves roaming about, tended to deter flight from the cities.)

The following few comments are added about phenomena observed in the Southern Confederacy that may be of wide relevance for disaster situations:

1. There was a good deal of state and local discord, often bordering upon disloyalty, in the Confederacy. Quite apart from pro-Union sentiment in some areas, there were innumerable instances of uncooperative actions, particularly on the state level. Such vital war measures as conscription[63] and tax collections[64] were obstructed by some Governors. North Carolina retained the products of its textile industry for its own troops and civil population exclusively.[65] In Georgia, the Governor prevented effective coordination of the militia with the Confederate forces opposing Sherman.[66]

2. Class antagonisms also grew more intense. The main conflict was between the slave-holding aristocracy (which group supplied the great bulk of the Confederate leaders) and the less affluent whites. The conviction gradually spread among the latter that they were fighting someone else's battle.[67] The bitter feeling against *nouveaux riches* — blockade-runners, merchants and speculators — should also be mentioned.

3. The policy of the Union government toward Confederate financial arrangements seriously increased the difficulties of the South. From the first, there was no question of Confederate currency or debts of the Confederate government (including its bonds) ever being honoured in any way by the Federal government. In consequence, the usefulness of Confederate currency as a store of value was seriously impaired from the beginning, and became increasingly poor as the prospect of Federal triumph neared. As had already been noted, Federal greenbacks successfully competed with Confederate notes and played a substantial role as both circulating medium and store of value behind the Confederate lines.[68]

Only a very limited discussion of the postwar recovery of the former Confederate states can be provided here.[69] In the postwar years the South was heavily burdened by the human and material losses of the war; social disorganization caused by problems of adapting to the changed status of the former slaves; and what amounted to a continuing indemnity in the form of taxes collected for service of Union war bonds and war pensions (Confederate bonds were, of course, voided, and no Federal pensions were paid for Confederate war service).

The Southern economy appears to have recovered faster in the manufacturing than in the agricultural sector. Table 1.8 provides a selection of significant statistics. In general, the physical data for agriculture show recovery by 1880 to about the levels of 1860. The farm value data actually show 1880 as still well below 1860, but this seems to be largely a reflection of cyclically low farm prices in the years just before 1880. The gross farm income data in Table 1.9, on the other hand, show a rather rapid recovery that contrasts with the depressed farm value series. The two series are not logically inconsistent, in that a sharp increase of farm costs of production (especially, of course, the need to hire free labour) could explain high gross income but low farm values. The difference in price levels should also be borne in mind. The consumer price index was 167 in 1866 (1860 = 100), and declined to 142 in 1870 and 110 in 1880.[70] Thus, the comparative steadiness of the postwar gross farm income data really represents gradually rising physical production combined with gradually falling prices. In manufacturing, although the value of products, considered in real terms, did not rise as fast as the number of labourers employed, the recovery was nevertheless superior to that in agriculture; production was approaching the real prewar level by 1870. Transportation, especially rail, also recovered rapidly.[71]

The dominating reason for the differential recovery pattern was the need to reorganize both techniques and social relations in agriculture, which was formerly conducted predominantly by slaves. Manufacturing, on the other hand, had a predominantly white labour force. As compared with this organizational factor, all other possible explanations seem to be insignificant. However, on the technological side it should be mentioned that there were severe losses in livestock in the war; this form of agricultural capital is, for biological reasons, peculiarly difficult to expand rapidly in the absence of substantial imports of stock.

JAPAN'S ECONOMY: DEFEAT AND RECONSTRUCTION[72]

Japan's problem in World War II was in some ways very similar to, in other ways interestingly different from, that of the Confederacy in the Civil War. Like the Confederacy Japan was, economically, hopelessly inferior to her enemy. Her grand strategy required quick military victories and then a stubborn defence to induce the enemy to agree to a negotiated peace on acceptable terms. Japan's economy, again as in the case of the Confederacy, was highly unbalanced and critically dependent upon external trade; for Japan, however, it was imports of

Table 1.8 Postwar Southern Recovery — Agriculture Versus Industry, 1860–1880

Year	Agricultural statistics						Industrial statistics			
	Milch cows		Farm acreage		Farm value		Labourers		Value of products	
	Thousand	Index	Million	Index	Million $	Index	Thousand	Index	Million $	Index
1860	2706	100.0	200	100.0	1,851	100.0	111	100.0	155.5	100.0
1870	1852	68.4	157	78.2	977	52.8	144	130.3	199.0	127.9
1880	2818	104.1	197	98.3	1,235	66.7	172	155.0	240.5	154.6

Source: E. M. Lerner, 'Southern Output and Agricultural Income, 1860–80', in Ralph Andreano (ed.), *The Economic Impact of the American Civil War*, pp. 92–3.

Table 1.9 Postwar Southern Recovery of Agricultural Production, with Special Reference to Cotton

Year	Gross farm income, cotton		Gross farm income, 11 crops[a]		Year	Cotton output	
	Million $	Index	Million $	Index		Million pounds	Index
1859	278	100.0	576	100.0	1859	2373	100.0
1866	337	121.2	490	85.1	Annual average, 1866–70	1213	51.1
1867	245	88.1	500	86.8			
1868	236	84.9	543	94.4			
1869	311	111.9	527	91.6			
1870	339	121.9	602	104.7			
1875	280	100.7	588	102.2	Annual average 1876–80	2395	100.9
1880	351	126.3	608	105.7			

Note:
[a] The eleven crops are cotton, tobacco, sweet potatoes, wheat, potatoes, corn, oats, hay, rye, sugar cane and rice.

Source: E. M. Lerner, 'Southern Output and Agricultural Income, 1860–80', in Ralph Andreano (ed.), The Economic Impact of the American Civil War, pp. 90–103.

raw materials rather than of manufactures and capital goods that were vital. Japan's crucial scarcities, in rough order of urgency, were of petroleum, iron ore and bauxite. For each of these only a very small fraction of needs could be met from home sources. Next most serious were coal and foodstuffs, both produced predominantly at home but with considerable import supplementation.

To meet military requirements for these scarce commodities Japan counted upon heavy initial stocks, continued imports from areas already under her domination (chiefly Korea, North China and Manchuria, and Formosa), and captures of stocks and of producing capacity in the Philippines, East Indies, China and Southeast Asia. This programme was completely successful at first. But the Japanese soon found the American blockade (primarily by submarine, secondarily by air) unexpectedly effective in cutting off supplies from and shipments to the newly captured and even the old subject areas. As the net tightened inexorably in the later years of the war, almost all of the merchant marine was sunk[73] and Japan's military machine and war industry became strangled by interlocking shortages. The Allied recapture of such areas as Burma and the Philippines contributed only to a minor extent in worsening the situation, since the sea blockade had already largely cut off those regions. Finally, the great air attacks were effective in causing unprecedented civilian death and misery, with consequent impact upon morale. Economically speaking, however, the air attacks were somewhat redundant in that the industrial capacity destroyed was already largely idle for lack of materials.[74]

In view of these insurmountable technological difficulties — poverty of resources at home, interdiction of vital imports, and the ever increasing weight of bombing attack — no economic policy available to Japan could have prevented the collapse. To illustrate the source of the difficulty, Table 1.10 shows the constriction of supplies of three crucial materials: iron ore, crude petroleum and coal — commodities that represent different degrees of import dependence. In all three cases, imports dropped off catastrophically in 1944, and were practically nil in 1945. One point worth noting is the enormous inventory level in petroleum carried by Japan before war began, equal to around two years' normal consumption. This was a deliberate policy of the Japanese military leaders in preparing for war; it contributed enormously to the effectiveness of the Japanese war machine. Nevertheless, the fuel stringency eventually became so severe as to hinder even the most urgent military measures, such as tactical movements of major naval vessels.[75]

By using up accumulated stocks of materials and goods in process, production of finished goods was maintained at a high level for some

Table 1.10 *Japan's Wartime Supplies of Three Crucial Materials*

Fiscal year[a]	Iron ore[b]			Crude petroleum[c]				Coal[d]		
	Iron content of domestic production	Iron content of imports	Total iron content	Domestic production	Imports	Total new supply	Inventories[e]	Domestic production	Imports	Total production plus net imports
1940	564	3095	3659	2063	22,050	24,113	49,581	57,309	10,123	65,941
1941	745	3021	3766	1941	3130	5071	48,893	55,602	9585	63,448
1942	1179	2911	4090	1690	8146	9836	38,229	54,178	8748	61,330
1943	1459	2147	3606	1814	9484	11,662	25,327	55,538	6029	60,467
1944	1911	925	2836	1585	1641	3226	13,816	49,335	3135	51,756
1945-I[f]	1376	268	1844	1624	0	1624	4946	43,508	752	44,012
—II[g]	na	na	na	1612	0	1612	3029	20,952	0	20,952

Notes:

na = not available.

[a] The Japanese fiscal year begins in April of the same calendar year. Thus, the first quarter of fiscal 1940 consists of April, May and June of calendar 1940.

[b] Thousands of metric tons in home islands. Cohen, *War and Reconstruction*, p. 116.

[c] Thousands of barrels, Japanese Inner Zone. Ibid., p. 134.

[d] Thousands of metric tons, Japan proper. Ibid., p. 160.

[e] Crude plus refined petroleum, at beginning of period.

[f] First quarter, annual rate (except petroleum inventories).

[g] Second quarter, annual rate (except petroleum inventories).

Table 1.11   Expansion and Decline of Japanese War Production
(1941 = 100)

Category	December 1941	September 1944	July 1945
Aircraft	126	502	221
Army ordnance	116	224	127
Navy ordnance	113	581	250
Naval ships	100	233	110
Merchant ships	103	461	92
Motor vehicles	134	35	9
Total	115	339	139

Source: Cohen, *War and Reconstruction*, p. 196.

Table 1.12   Rice in Wartime Japan (thousands of metric tons)

Year	Domestic production[a]	Imports[b]	Total new supply	Stocks[c]
1941	8245	2517	10,762	1178
1942	9999	2581	12,580	392
1943	9422	1183	10,605	435
1944	8784	874	9658	384
1945	6445	268	6713	133[d]

Notes:
[a] Cohen, *War and Reconstruction*, p. 368.
[b] Ibid., p. 369.
[c] Ibid., p. 367. Figures are for 31 October of each year.
[d] An additional 245,000 tons of rice was set aside as an emergency reserve from military stocks in November 1944. Of these, 130,000 tons were destroyed in air raids by the end of the war.

little time after the downturn in imports (the overall peak of war production occurred in September 1944). After that date, output in all categories dropped sharply, as indicated in Table 1.11. A particularly significant commodity is rice, figures for which are shown in Table 1.12. Even these figures understate the seriousness of the situation, for the supplemental foods were in relatively poorer supply than was rice. In the last months of the war, the government in desperation cut back imports of all other materials in favour of foodstuffs.[76] Nevertheless, there would have been starvation in Japan had the war continued through another winter.[77]

As in the case of the American Confederacy, we can conclude that the economy of Japan was crushed by *force majeure*. Again, it will be of some interest to examine the policies pursued in the course of the collapse. But we shall pass over these rather quickly, in order to concentrate upon the period of recovery from collapse under the postwar Occupation.

It is worth noting, first of all, that Japan's war economy was administered in much the same way as were the war economies of Germany, Great Britain and the United States, in orthodox twentieth-century style, so to speak. The government secured resources primarily by market or contract purchases from the private sector, financed by creation of credit through the banking system or by direct multiplication of currency. (The purchases were not always on a voluntary basis, however. Farmers in Japan, for example, were required to deliver pre-assigned quotas to the government collectors at the low legal prices — a practice suggesting the requisitions of war communism or impressment under the Confederacy.) The accumulation of financial claims in the private sector, coinciding with a real diversion of resources to government war activities, led to strong upward pressure on prices. An attempt was made to contain this pressure by a universal price freeze, leading in turn to other difficulties.

First, the prices frozen at low levels relative to the supply/demand balance could no longer serve the function of allocating resources effectively. There were shortages everywhere. On the consumer level this led to rationing in order to assure a more even distribution of food, clothing, and so on. On the producer level, control agencies were established on an industry basis to organize production, arrange for provision of raw materials and labour, and for distribution of output. Alongside the legal method of administered distribution of resources under controlled prices flourished black markets, with illegal exchange of commodities for money at uncontrolled prices.[78] Barter and 'trekking' to the countryside to barter for food were important activities. As many as 900,000 persons are reported as trekking from Tokyo on a single Sunday.[79] (Trekking is not only an extremely inefficient mode of food distribution, but perhaps even more harmful as a cause of factory absenteeism.)

The next difficulty caused by the price freeze was the reduction in incentives to produce. As necessary inputs became scarce at legal prices, the real costs of production rose. Farmers, in particular, tended to withhold supplies from the market, and may be presumed to have redirected their production patterns away from the market and toward farm self-sufficiency. This tendency was countered by a number of government policies. First, the government granted increases in the official price list fairly frequently.[80] Second, the black market was tolerated to a degree: in the case of food, the government concentrated attention upon the controlled distribution of the rice ration, so that other foods were distributed primarily through illegal channels.[81] Third, the government resorted to a system of compulsory quota deliveries for farmers, while industrial production was at least theoretically under such control from the beginning. Here the policy was rather ingenious, in that while the compulsory quota delivery had to be made at a low price, deliveries beyond the quota levels received the benefit of a premium incentive price. Finally, and most important, the government made use of the expedient of general production subsidies in an attempt to maintain high prices for producers and low prices for consumers. (Such subsidies were also employed, not quite to the same extent, by Germany, Britain and the United States in World War II.) A subsidy of sufficient magnitude for a particular commodity can, of course, provide the same incentive to produce as a similarly high uncontrolled price. On the other hand, the low price paid by buyers tends to discourage economizing on use of the subsidized commodity (for consumers who can actually obtain a supply). The differential between producer and consumer prices in Japan could only be financed by the government through further creation of credit, thus intensifying the very sources of the inflation whose effects the government was attempting to ameliorate or disguise.

Table 1.13 contains some salient data relating to the financing of the Japanese war effort. We can observe that between year-end 1941 and year-end 1945 the note issue was multiplied around ninefold. The total money supply (currency plus demand deposits) rose about fourfold, from around 44 to 175 billion yen in this period. (The ratios of increase would be somewhat lower if calculated to the termination of hostilities instead of year-end 1945.[82]) The real price level approximately trebled during this period; apparently, the type of inflationary expectations associated with flight from money and consequent acceleration of prices beyond the money supply had not definitely set in during the Japanese wartime period. However, as we shall see, the willingness of the Japanese public to absorb further increases in money supply was limited.

The following are some remarks on various organizational aspects of the Japanese war economy:

1. In wartime Japan, the army and navy successfully resisted civilian regulation of war production under their auspices. In competition with the civil administration and with one another, the army and navy failed to turn over materials under their control, issued

Table 1.13 *Wartime Financial Data for Japan (billions of yen)*

Fiscal year[a]	Government revenue[b]	Government expenditure[b]	Deficit[b]	National debt[c] (end of fiscal year)[d]	Note issue	Bank deposits (except Bank of Japan)[g]	Index, 1941 = 100	
							Retail prices, official[h]	Retail prices, real[i]
1940				31.1	4.8	31.2	99	86
1941	5.8	19.2	13.4	41.8	6.0	37.8	100	100
1942	9.8	24.7	14.9	57.0	7.1	46.6	101	130
1943	13.4	32.1	18.7	85.1	10.3	56.3	113	153
1944	18.5	77.6	59.1	150.8	17.7	77.9	139	191
1945	27.2	103.8	76.6	177.7[e]	55.4	119.8	169	na

Notes:

na = not available.

[a] The Japanese fiscal year begins in April of the same calendar year (see footnote to Table 1.10).

[b] Cohen, *War and Reconstruction*, p. 88.

[c] Ibid., p. 89.

[d] The figure for the national debt at the end of the fiscal year refers to 31 March of the following calendar year. Thus, the 1940 figure refers to 31 March 1941.

[e] This figure is as of 30 September 1945.

[f] Figures for 31 December of calendar year. S. Shiomi, *Japan's Finance and Taxation, 1940–1956* (New York: Columbia University Press, 1957), p. 4.

[g] Ibid.

[h] Cabinet Bureau of Statistics consumer price index for wage earners in Tokyo, cited in Cohen, *War and Reconstruction*, p. 356.

[i] Morita index calculated to include black market transactions (ibid.).

overriding priorities to their suppliers, and sometimes even refused to report important data on production and imports.

2. The Japanese did not undertake a dispersal programme for industry until much too late, in 1945. The effect was catastrophic, as the attempt to disperse under conditions of heavy air attack and a collapsing economy only compounded the disaster. The few firms that had dispersed earlier on their own initiative made the transition successfully.[83]
3. The Japanese had a war damage indemnity programme that apparently worked successfully to the end of the war.[84]
4. Although taxes covered only about 20 per cent of government expenses, a compulsory national savings association was organized that helped hold down civilian consumption. Savings were deposited in financial institutions which in turn were enabled to lend money to war industry or to government. Almost all bond sales were to the banks rather than the public.

During the postwar recuperation of Japan, in contrast with postwar Allied policy toward Germany, the Occupation authorities did not attempt to dismantle the entire Japanese political and civil structure. Instead, Japanese forms and institutions were used for Occupation purposes, subject to purging of unwholesome individuals and forces. A Japanese administration, therefore, was more or less responsible for economic recovery throughout the period, although it was subject to the overriding directives and less formal pressures of SCAP (Supreme Commander, Allied Powers), the Occupation authority. Of course, the objectives of the two administrations were rather different. The goal of SCAP was, at first, to reform Japanese social and economic arrangements in the belief that this would prevent Japan from menacing other nations in the future. In time, the goal gradually shifted to that of incorporating a reformed democratic Japan into the worldwide system of alliances against Soviet expansion. Consequently, while the Japanese administration was presumably concerned with economic recovery from the beginning, the Occupation at first was scarcely interested in that objective.[85] The prior interest of SCAP was, rather, in reparations to other nations, victims of Japanese imperialism, subject only to maintaining Japanese per capita income at an austere minimum level (fixed at that of 1930–34).[86] SCAP soon grew concerned about recovery, however, when it became apparent that American financial aid would be necessary to maintain minimal living standards and that an economy in distress provided a poor background for social and political reforms.

At the beginning of the Occupation Japan was economically prostrate.

Practically all industrial production statistics plunged rapidly towards zero in 1945. The 1944 rice crop had been about 10 per cent below normal, but the 1945 harvest, not yet in at the date of the surrender, proved to be disastrous, 30 per cent or more below normal. In addition, the supplemental foods (grain, vegetables, fish) were in very low supply,[87]and imports had practically stopped. Furthermore, around one-third of the nation's urban housing had been destroyed;[88] stocks of crucial materials (coal, oil and iron ore) were exhausted; the merchant marine had been sunk; all overseas investments and colonies were lost; and the list of difficulties, aggravated by population increase through natural growth and voluntary or forced repatriation of Japanese nationals from abroad, could be extended indefinitely.

The situation was not entirely without bright spots. Almost immediately upon surrender, the economy was relieved of the burden of supporting a huge military machine. In 1943 and 1944, war expenditures had amounted to around 40 per cent of the gross national product.[89] In all sectors of the economy, withdrawal of resources from war and war-supporting industry made potentially available the means for a vast increase in civilian production. To cite one example, during the war fertilizer production had been cut back to promote the manufacture of explosives; starting with the 1946 crop, increased availability of fertilizer could be expected to augment domestic farming yields. Increased labour supply from demobilization of the armed forces and release of workers from war factories could also be expected to contribute substantially to agricultural production. Elimination of military demands on industry should have made it possible for the latter to make available once again supplies of vital farm tools, processing equipment, and so on. Another potential bright spot to a country subject for years to increasing, and finally total, blockade was the reopening of international trade. In a postwar world desperate for goods, Japan's talent for cheap mass production could reasonably have been expected to yield substantial income with little delay.

Despite these favourable factors, Japan's recovery was slow and halting in the early postwar years until 1950, the year we shall take as the end of the recuperation period. The Dodge reforms of 1949 finally pointed the way out of the economic morass, while the Korean war beginning in mid-1950 launched Japan into her first postwar boom. The Korean fighting tapered off in 1951 and finally ended in 1953, the Occupation having terminated in 1952, but the Japanese recovery continued, becoming a phenomenal (if irregular) economic expansion persisting unabated to the present date. Such a course of events would have seemed unbelievable in the distressed early postwar years, when only massive American aid prevented starvation in Japan.

Table 1.14 presents a number of statistical indicators of the unsatisfactory state of the economy in the early postwar years. For the reasons already cited, the last eight months of the war in 1945 was a period of catastrophic economic decline, while the confusion attendant upon the inauguration of the Occupation can easily account for failure to show improvement in the remainder of 1945. But 1946 was, generally, still worse than 1945 despite cessation of bombing and blockade and release of resources from war activities.

The index of agricultural production on the 1934–36 base did rise from 60 in 1945 to 77 in 1946, but the index of industrial production fell from 60 to 31. From that low point a slow upswing began. Even by 1950, however, the index of industrial production was only 84 on the 1934–36 base, and there had been a 20 per cent increase in population in the interim. But by 1956, industrial production attained an index of 219, substantially over the wartime peak on an aggregate basis, and just about equalling the peak on a per capita basis after a 25 per cent population increase.

From a purely statistical point of view, it might be questioned whether we are really justified in regarding the progress to 1950 as unsatisfactory, while calling the post-1950 results a splendid performance. From the Industrial Production Index in Table 1.14, it might seem that there is a fairly continuous curve of economic expansion from the low point of 31 in the year 1946 to 84 in 1950 and 219 in 1956. Contrasting the results of the two periods is, however, well justified, for the following reasons. It is a far easier feat for an economy to recover to levels of production already achieved in the past than to attain new high ground; to a large degree, the former involves only putting existing capacity into production, but the latter requires heavy additional investment. This is especially the case when it is remembered that 100 on the index refers to the long-past depression period of 1934–36; even if we leave out of consideration the high wartime levels, industrial production indexes over 140 had been attained in Japan as far back as the year 1938. The results up to and including 1950 incorporate substantial amounts of US aid (see Table 1.15); however, by 1950 this had begun to taper off, and from 1952 on aid was not a factor.[90]

The questions now to be explored are: what were the forces or frictions holding back the progress of the Japanese economy in the early postwar years; what shares of the blame can be assigned to the various adverse factors; and how did the forces of growth eventually gain ascendancy? Certain explanations of a technological nature could be put forward as hypotheses to explain the lagging postwar recovery. For example, it might be maintained that the war so impaired Japan's

Table 1.14 Japanese Economic Indicators — Early Postwar Years

Year	Index of industrial production[a]	Index of agricultural production[b]	Index of public utilities[c]	Real net national income (billion yen)[d]	Index of population[f]	Index of per capita production[f]
1944	179	na	154	15.4	105.5	170
1945	60	60	88	na	104.0	58
1946	31	77	109	8.2[e]	105.6	29
1947	37	75	124	8.7[e]	112.8	33
1948	55	86	138	10.2[e]	115.9	47
1949	71	93	155	11.8[e]	118.1	60
1950	84	99	168	13.9[e]	120.2	70
1956	219	122	295	22.1	130.4	168

Notes:
na = not available.
[a] 1934–36 = 100. Cohen, *Postwar Economy*, p. 47.
[b] 1933–35 = 100. Allen, p. 192.
[c] 1934–36 = 100. Cohen, *Postwar Economy*, p. 15.
[d] In 1934–36 prices. Ibid., pp. 12–13. Average national income for 1934–36 was 14.4 billion yen.
[e] Fiscal year.
[f] 1934–36 = 100. Ibid., p. 47.

capital stock in quality and quantity as to reduce, in a way difficult to remedy, her ability to produce. Another hypothesis would emphasize not the aggregate capital stock but specific disproportions and bottle-necks created by selective bombing and other war-related causes. A rigorous test of these hypotheses would take more time than could be allowed here, and only some impressionistic comments will be provided. It does not appear that the overall resources available to the Japanese economy were reduced much as a result of the war, especially when the enlargement of human resources is offset against the limited decline in material capital stock. The argument involving disproportions is harder to dismiss; it might be argued, for example, that the increase in labour resources could not be used until after a slow process of industrial reconversion, filling of inventory pipelines, and the like. The author's impression is that this sort of consideration played a role in the immediate post-surrender period, but disproportions and bottle-necks should have disappeared rapidly in the absence of policy errors in the allocation of the society's available resources.

The possible adverse factors to be considered in some detail are: (1) restrictive and punitive policies of SCAP; (2) social and political disorganization, possibly caused in part by SCAP reforms of Japanese government and society; and (3) the financial-monetary policy of repressed inflation. All three factors are organizational in nature (though from the point of view of Japanese decision-makers, the policies of SCAP were a kind of natural constraint not unlike a technological limitation).

In contrast with the pastoralization programme adopted for Germany, limitations placed on production or consumption levels as deliberate Occupation policy in Japan were relatively innocuous (the austere level of 1930–34 referred to earlier was supposed to be a *minimum*, with no maximum specified for Japanese per capita income). However, the programme of extensive reparations laid down in the Pauley Report early in the period was, in fact, a pastoralization programme for Japan. The report proposed removal of the bulk of Japan's steel capacity, three-quarters of shipbuilding, over three-quarters of machine-tool inventory, and all of aluminium and magnesium capacity (in addition, of course, to all war goods facilities). Production limitations were also recommended.[91] While this programme was fierce enough (one consequence of its adoption would have been a sharp reduction in the population that could have been maintained on an economically viable basis in the Japanese islands), it was not actually put into effect. Nevertheless, there are indications that SCAP production-level limi-tations interfered with at least some branches of production,[92] and uncertainty about just what would be taken as reparations was definitely deleterious. SCAP gradually scaled down, and finally abandoned, the reparations programme in 1947 and 1948, together with other elements of the 'Reform-Punishment' philosophy. The main reason, at least in the case of reparations, was the obvious distress of the Japanese economy. The actual removals for reparations during the recovery period appear ultimately to have amounted to very little.[93] (In the years since 1950 Japan has voluntarily signed combined commercial and reparations agreements by which she has contracted to pay out huge sums to the various nations injured by Japanese imperialism in World War II. Apparently, the motive was largely to promote trade.)[94] Another burden on Japan is the debt owed to the United States for the costs of occupation and rehabilitation, in the amount of some $2 billion.[95] However, this was not a drain upon the Japanese economy during the recovery period considered.

A rather stronger case for the harmful effect of Occupation restrictions can be made in the crucial field of foreign trade. In this special field SCAP did not play a merely supervisory role; rather, SCAP directly controlled and monopolized all of Japan's external trade. Not until August 1947 were private foreign traders admitted to Japan, and not until August 1948 could Japanese exporters make direct contracts with foreign buyers.[96]

What the motives for such stringent controls may have been will be discussed shortly, but the results are all too clear (Table 1.15). Japan's foreign trade throughout the recovery period remained extremely low, and over half of imports through 1950 were financed by U.S. aid.[97]

It seems certain that the prohibition of private trading was an important adverse element in Japan's postwar foreign trade situation, but it was by no means the only source of difficulty. There is no clear evidence that SCAP had a deliberate policy to hold down trade. It appears instead that the restrictions on trade (like so much of economic policy during this period) constituted an erroneous set of measures from the point of view of recovery, but were not motivated to hold back recovery.[98] It has been suggested that a hold-down policy on trade existed, either to weaken Japan strategically or perhaps to gain some commercial advantages for nations that feared her export competition,[99] but the evidence does not support this interpretation. Furthermore, a number of other factors contributed to the poor progress of Japan's trade recovery. Among these were the decline in demand for silk, loss of the merchant marine, and legal changes in customer countries discriminating against or removing special privileges in favour of Japanese imports. However, probably more important than all of these was the general depression of production, largely due to the domestic policy of repressed inflation to be discussed below. It is shown

Table 1.15 International Trade, Postwar Japan

Period	Index of volume of exports (1934–6 = 100)[a]	Index of volume of imports (1934–6 = 100)[a]	Export-import balance (million $)[b]	U.S. aid[b] (million $)	Special procurement (million $)[b]
Sept. 1945– Dec. 1946	na	na	−202	193	c
1947	na	na	−352	404	c
1948	8	18	−425	461	c
1949	16	28	−395	535	c
1950	30	33	−154	361	149
1956	73	103	−729	0	595

Notes:
na = not available.
[a] Allen, p. 197.
[b] Cohen, *Postwar Economy*, p. 110. The export-import balance figures exclude 'invisibles', but apparently Japan had also a deficit on invisibles during the period under consideration (Allen, p. 165).
[c] 'Special Procurement' did not begin until 1950.

in Table 1.15 that even by 1956 Japan's exports were well below the 1934–36 base period. Evidently, certain shifts in international trade patterns had led Japan to reduce her proportionate reliance upon foreign trade as a source of real income. One such change is visible in the 'Special Procurement' column of the table. This item represents, primarily, services to American military forces based in Japan. Special procurement provided Japan with an important source of foreign exchange that is accounted as an 'invisible' rather than an export in the trade statistics. The general conclusion in this section is, then, that no very large share of the responsibility for the poor Japanese recovery to 1950 can be assigned to a deliberate Occupation policy of holding down the Japanese economy.

We turn now to the question of the possible effects upon the economy of social and political disorganization during the Occupation period. There was, of course, an organizational crisis between the surrender date and the time SCAP effectively asserted control. After 15 August 1945, it has been alleged,[100] Japanese disbursing officers improperly paid out huge amounts of government funds — some 40 billion yen in the six weeks after surrender.[101] Government stocks were also appropriated by individuals and channelled into the black market. Impressed Korean and Chinese labourers left their jobs, creating difficulties in the coal mines. This crisis was terminated by the end of September, when SCAP's actions made it clear that the Occupation would maintain the legal system of Japan, would not expropriate property rights (with some exceptions), and would work to reform rather than destroy Japanese customs and establishments (particularly, the Emperor institution).

These conservative policies of SCAP contributed to the minimal restoration of confidence necessary to get the productive mechanism going again. Nevertheless, among the major goals of the Occupation were certain legal and social reforms that SCAP felt impelled to achieve, even if to some degree at the expense of Japanese recovery. The purge of militarists and of wealthy beneficiaries of Japan's expansionist policies (especially the elite clique of great financial and industrial families known as the *Zaibatsu*) was rigorously pursued, even though it stripped government and industry of a large fraction of their leading personnel. Deprivation of property and exclusion from public offices and important business positions were based primarily upon membership in certain social groupings (for example, career officers of the armed services, major officials of all large private corporations, relations of *Zaibatsu* families); proof of individual complicity in war guilt was not required.

Among the other economic reforms were anti-monopoly and deconcentration legislation, and abolition of industry 'control associations'. These associations, which served in part as cartels, were also the agencies that determined the allocations of supplies and distribution of products for the various industries — a necessary function since, under the policy of repressed inflation, the price mechanism was not working to guide the allocation of resources. Since the repressed-inflation policy was continued, the control associations had to be succeeded by newly organized 'public corporations'.[102] This led to charges that *Zaibatsu* monopolies were being replaced by state monopolies.[103] The final effect of the anti-monopoly legislation may well have been highly favourable to the Japanese economy, and Occupation anti-trust policy can perhaps be awarded some of the credit for Japan's competitive vigour in the 1950s. However, during the recovery period the problem of reorganizing much of Japanese industry caused a great deal of confusion and uncertainty, and very probably detracted from production.

Measures adopted in 1946 for a capital levy and for abolition of war damage indemnities combined reformist and fiscal motives. The capital levy brought in revenue of over 40 billion yen, while the indemnity abolition cancelled government obligations of some 90 billion yen.[104] (For the fiscal significance of these totals, see Table 1.16). The measures were considered to be important from the reform point of view, because the highly progressive nature of the capital levy achieved a substantial levelling of the wealth structure.[105] Furthermore, the bulk of the war damage indemnities would have been paid to corporations and wealthy individuals. The cancellation of war damage indemnities was particularly disruptive in its effects, as a huge number of corporations thereby became insolvent. Little attention seems to have been paid to the problem of equity in regard to those individuals who were the unfortunate victims of Allied bombing, and whose legal claims for compensation from their fellow citizens were thereby cancelled.[106]

Another measure strongly pushed by SCAP was land reform. This was supposedly directed against great feudal landowners, a group believed to be an important element of Japan's military ruling class. Unfortunately, SCAP apparently was unaware of the fact that feudal landowners did not hold any substantial fraction of Japan's arable land,[107] so that the effect was to extinguish a rural middle class by expropriation of even tiny holdings.[108] Over 65 per cent of Japan's cultivated land was taken by the government, with only negligible compensation, under this programme. The agricultural disruption must have been considerable, although the agricultural sector nevertheless performed better than the industrial sector up to 1950. The final effect was to eliminate the great bulk of farm tenancies in Japan in favour of owner-operated farming, typically on a very small scale.[109]

Table 1.16 Monetary and Financial Statistics, Postwar Japan

Year	Budget deficit, fiscal year (billions of yen)[a]	National debt (billions of yen)[b]	Note issue (billions of yen)[c]	Total money supply (billions of yen)[d]	Wholesale price index (1934–6 = 1)[e]
1941	13.4	31	6	na	na
1945	76.6	151	55	140 (Dec.)	3.5
1946	65	178	93[h]	309[h] (Mar.)	na
1947	103	na	219	390 (Mar.)	na
1948	166	446[g]	355	646 (Mar.)	na
1949	62[f]	531[g]	355	787[i]	209
1950	+125 (surplus)	316[g]	422	na	247
1956	na	na	785	na	358

Notes:

na = not available.

[a] Cohen, *War and Reconstruction*, pp. 450–1; *Postwar Economy*, pp. 84, 87. Fiscal year begins in April of same calendar year.

[b] 31 March of calendar year (end of previous fiscal year). See Table 1.13 and Cohen, *Postwar Economy*, pp. 84, 87.

[c] Cohen, *War and Reconstruction*, p. 448; *Postwar Economy*, pp. 84, 91. S. Shiomi, p. 4. Figures for end of calendar years.

[d] Note issue plus adjusted demand deposits. Compiled from various sources.

[e] Cohen, *Postwar Economy*, p.92 (figures for March).

[f] Ibid., p. 87. This figure is reported for 1948, apparently in error.

[g] Mid-year figures.

[h] After currency reform.

[i] Beginning of year.

Another set of Occupation reforms achieved the abolition of the various labour control measures effective in Japan, introduced 'fair labour standards' and protection of employment security, provided a system of unemployment insurance and, most important, promoted the growth of trade unionism. Unions grew rapidly in numbers and in militancy under radical leadership. Seizure of plants by the unions became a serious problem in 1946. In 1947 SCAP intervened to stop a general strike and in 1948 had to prohibit strikes of government employees. Collective bargaining remained vigorous throughout the Occupation period, however.

Some comment on communist activities during the Occupation is also called for.[110] The political atmosphere in 1945 and 1946 was, of course, very different from that today; it seems hard to credit that SCAP did not merely legalize the Communist Party but for some time looked benignly upon communist activity as a counterweight to the reactionary forces the Occupation sought to crush. The Communist Party in Japan in 1945 and 1946 posed as a moderate and non-violent organization, a true friend of Occupation principles, and it had on that basis considerable influence in some SCAP circles. With the purge of reactionaries and militarists from all branches of Japanese public life, vacancies in positions of leadership and influence in universities, trade unions, newspapers and radio, and so forth, were created, and these were often filled by Communists. However, the hardening of the cold war led to increasing incompatibility between the communist line and Occupation policy, and the resort of the communists to direct action (sabotage and violence) on the political and labour fronts finally elicited strong SCAP action. As a result, a 'Red purge' in 1949 and 1950 followed the 'reactionary purge' of 1945 and 1946. In the early postwar years, however, the internal communist threat may have been (though not so recognized by SCAP) an important source of social instability from the point of view of Japanese investors.

To summarize this section on social and political disorganization, economic progress in an economy in which private enterprise plays an important role requires assurance that property rights will be protected. No one will be motivated to save or invest or perform on contracts unless he has reasonable confidence that he will not be deprived of his right to the yield of such activities. The various reform measures reviewed here were considered by SCAP to be justified as essential elements of a plan to change the social structure of Japan so as to prevent a militarist revival. Some adverse effect upon production was probably anticipated, as a cost of making the necessary changes. Just how great the adverse effects may have been is rather difficult to say; it seems reasonable to consider them of significant magnitude, in such a period of thorough-going political and economic turmoil. One could hardly deny that confidence in social stability and in property rights was at a low ebb in Japan during the Occupation period up to 1950. However, the worst from this point of view came relatively early, in 1946. After that time, the legal and political background for private economic activity substantially improved. Since the overall performance of the economy remained highly unsatisfactory, it seems likely that other factors must be given the major weight.

We have seen that the Japanese war economy was financed by the technique of repressed inflation, leading by the end of the war to something like a five-fold increase in note issue, $3\frac{1}{2}$-fold increase in overall money supply, and also around a three-fold increase in the real price level (that is, the price level calculated to include black market transactions). The Occupation administration continued the same type of financial-monetary policy in the postwar period (or, rather, permitted the postwar Japanese governments to pursue this policy). As Table 1.16 suggests, Japan's lack of success with repressed inflation was more evident in the postwar period, undoubtedly because of growing unwillingness of the public to hold a depreciating currency. Although it is difficult to find mutually consistent data for the wartime and postwar periods, it appears to be roughly the case that the price level rose around 50-fold in the postwar period up to 1950 as compared with only a trebling in the wartime period. Furthermore, postwar results are in spite of the currency conversion of March 1946, which reduced the currency from 62 billion to 15 billion and free bank deposits from 128 to 13 billion.[111] Allowing for this revaluation, a better estimate would be a 200-fold price rise in the postwar era.

The engine of inflation in the postwar period was the heavy government deficit, financed by currency expansion and central bank credit. A second factor was lavish credit extended in the form of loans to industry by a government agency, the Reconstruction Finance Bank (and its predecessors).[112] Since these loans were at low interest rates in a period of rocketing prices, the fortunate borrowers were relieved of the necessity of repaying more than a fraction of real value; hence, 'reconstruction loans' proved to be very popular.[113] They were financed by advances from the Bank of Japan, and thus led directly to increases in the money supply. The government's deficit was achieved despite certain extraordinary deflationary factors, such as the termination of military expenditures, the cancellation of war damage indemnities, and the capital levy. The currency reform had no lasting effect because the sources of the inflation continued unabated. Subsidies to industry to hold down consumer end-product prices were a major expenditure.[114]

Only around 20 per cent of budget expenditures were covered by taxation.[115]

Unlike inflations due to overriding causes such as war destruction or support of a tremendous military effort, this postwar Japanese inflation seems to have been almost entirely the result of deliberate but erroneous policy.[116] The inflation was quite suddenly terminated in 1949–50 when the recommendations of the Dodge mission were put into effect. Subsidies were sharply reduced and the budget so heavily overbalanced that 25 per cent of the accumulated internal debt was retired. The Reconstruction Finance Bank's operations were severely curtailed. At the same time stock exchanges were reopened, and the government corporations responsible for supply allocations were eliminated. Export trade was freed from the complex and inefficient system of multiple exchange rates, and the new rate was fixed at the realistic level of 360 yen to the dollar. The note issue fell slightly, and the consumer price index fell around 15 per cent from its 1945 peak by mid-1950.[117] (As it happened, the Korean War beginning in June 1950 led to a renewed inflationary development in Japan. However, this latter inflation was relatively mild and was an accompaniment of a Japanese boom rather than of economic stagnation.)

During the earlier postwar inflationary period, SCAP and the Japanese authorities were continually trying to 'hold the line' against price increases by the familiar devices of price controls, rationing, and subsidies. Although legal ceilings were frequently raised, they were continually lagging behind costs, and an extensive black market accounted for a very large fraction of sales.[118] The government continued to acquire commodities by the wartime technique of compulsory deliveries at low, fixed prices but, fortunately, did allow premium prices to farmers, in particular, for above-quota production. Even so, substantial diversions to the black market occurred. To the extent that relief was not granted through one legal device or another — a raised ceiling, a premium for over-quota delivery, a production subsidy, or a reconstruction loan — the only alternatives were the black market or barter. All of these 'solutions' detract substantially from economic efficiency, and any attempt to close the loopholes and rigorously enforce price controls is liable to break down the division of labour and paralyse trade entirely. The familiar disaster phenomenon of trekking to the countryside to barter for food also took place in postwar Japan, and the fact that agricultural output recovered faster than industrial suggests that at least a relative shift of population from the cities took place. The partial breakdown in the division of labour, and the diversion of production and exchange into devious and inefficient channels to evade the price control and allocation mechanisms, both due ultimately to the repressed-inflation policy, seem to have been the major causes of the unsatisfactory recovery up to 1950.

Why was such a catastrophic economic policy not reversed earlier? One reason was simple ignorance; the policy of repressed inflation was more or less standard procedure everywhere during and after World War II. The examples of some of the European countries that succeeded in mastering their postwar inflations by the use of orthodox fiscal and monetary policies were not immediately appreciated elsewhere. The turning point, perhaps, was the German 'miracle' of mid-1948, to be discussed in the next section. Here the analogy to the Japanese situation was so close that it could not have been missed by either SCAP or the Japanese authorities. We may remark, however, that there were some groups who were definite beneficiaries of the repressed-inflation policies. Prosperity among the farmers was proverbial, because of elimination of the real value of their debts, together with ability to dispose of produce via barter or black market. Black market operators were also an obvious category of beneficiaries. Perhaps most significant for Japanese policy was a group well hidden from public opprobrium: beneficiaries of reconstruction loans from the government financial institutions, recipients of production subsidies, and those so placed with the materials-control agencies as to receive favourable allocations of scarce supplies through low price legal channels. In the aggregate, these undoubtedly comprised an important interest group with a stake in the repressed-inflation system.

GERMANY'S RECOVERY FROM COLLAPSE, 1945–1948[119]

Germany's war effort was financed by the technique of repressed inflation, as were the war efforts of Japan, Britain and the United States. The main features were easy credit and deficit financing on the fiscal level, priorities and allocation systems for controlling the distribution of resources to industry, and rationing and price controls on the consumer level. The priorities and allocation system developed slowly; as in Japan, the military resisted systematic central control.[120] The consumer control system is generally considered to have worked well; black markets were minor during the war.[121]

The aspect of the German war economy most commented upon by postwar observers was the failure of the Germans to mount an all-out effort on the industrial front until much too late in the war.[122] Surprisingly (in view of the early German military victories), Hitler did

Table 1.17 German Industrial and Munitions Production, World War II

Year	Industrial production and construction (1939 = 100)[a]	Munitions production (1939 = 100)
1939	100	100[b]
1940	106	145[b]
1941	117	146[b]
1942	118	193[b]
1943	132	302[c]
1944	133	376
1945	na	197[d]

Notes:
na = not available.
a USSBS, *German War Economy*, p. 27.
b Klein, p. 97.
c Munitions figures for 1943 and later from USSBS, *German War Economy*, p. 275.
Linked to Klein's series by multiplying by ratio 193/142.
d March — last figure available.

not have a quantitatively enormous war machine at the beginning of the war; furthermore, on the basis of successes on the Russian front, demobilization of war industries was actually begun in 1941, and considered again in 1942. The employment of women was discouraged throughout the war as contrary to National Socialist 'ideals'. Only at the end of 1942 did the magnitude of the industrial output required for Nazi survival, not to mention victory, become appreciated. After that point, a substantial expansion of industrial output, and of munitions production in particular, was achieved (see Table 1.17). In the face of an increasing scale of air attack and adverse shifts of the fighting fronts this was an impressive performance, but it was fatally limited by the failure to expand basic capacity earlier, when the opportunity existed.

It is rather difficult to divide the responsibility for the German economic breakdown between the two major sources of stress: air attack and loss of territory. Bombing became important in 1943; the attacks upon oil and transportation were particularly damaging. Allied military conquests first cut off regions supplying raw materials and some manufactured products to German industry, and of course eventually overran the German national territory itself. It is evident, though, that the collapse was entirely ascribable to these technological pressures and not to any endogenous breakdown of the social mechanism.

In the wake of their victorious armies the Allies found a collapsed German economy. On a national basis the postal, telephone and telegraph services had stopped in 1945, and in many areas even the vital utilities (power, gas and water) were not in service. Transportation had generally stopped, and with it practically all industrial production.[123] The whole system of division of labour seemed to be completely broken. The economic paralysis was greater than that in Japan, for a number of reasons. First of all, in Japan there was no battlefield damage in the home islands, and no scorched-earth policy like that carried out by the Nazis under Hitler's 'Nero plan'.[124] Though impressed Korean and Chinese labourers did pose some difficulty in Japan, the effect was minor compared to the problems created in Germany by some 4½ million liberated displaced persons and 2 million prisoners of war,[125] plus Germans fleeing from the Russian zone or expelled from Eastern Europe. Perhaps most crucial of all, government had collapsed almost everywhere. Nazi officials deserted their posts with the retreating German armies, and the Allies repudiated the entire government apparatus (including ordinary civil servants) as hopelessly Nazi-dominated.

In Allied planning before final victory, no preparations had been made for restoration of a collapsed German economy. Rather, attention had been directed almost exclusively to the problem of keeping postwar Germany disarmed, economically weak, and free of Nazi resurgence. In fact, under the famous directive JCS/1067 to the American Commander, general assistance to the economy was forbidden. However, the directive provided a loophole. To the minimum extent necessary to avoid starvation, disease and unrest, the Commander was directed to facilitate the restoration of transportation and utilities, repair and construction of minimum shelter for the civilian population, and the production of coal and other civilian goods.[126] In practice, assistance during the emergency period had to be provided on a substantial scale to get the wheels of the economic mechanism moving again so as to prevent mass starvation. Aid was crucial in restoring communications and transportation, but perhaps even more important was the lead taken by the Occupation forces in preserving civil order and restoring the functioning of government. As in Japan, property rights (in the Western zones) were generally respected, except, of course, for confiscation of properties of National Socialist institutions and of leading Nazis, and restitution of looted properties of Allied citizens and persecutees. Banks were permitted to reopen on an individual, local basis in the American zone; confidence had been restored to such an extent that by early 1946 deposits exceeded withdrawals.[127]

When the extreme crisis of this interregnum period was overcome with the aid of the military conquerors, the German economy in the

Table 1.18   Production in Postwar Germany

Year	Food production (1935–39 = 100)[a]	Industrial production (1938 = 100)[b]	Population (1938 = 100)[c]	Industrial production per capita (1938 = 100)
1946	67	29	111.0	26
1947	58	33	112.9	29
1948	79	52[d]	115.9	45
1949	93	74	118.3	63
1953	118	132	123.4	107
1958	na	199[e]	131.0	152

Notes:
na = not available.
[a] Mendershausen, *Two Postwar Recoveries*, p. 8. Data in source are shown for crop years (c.g. 1946–47), believed to correspond approximately to calendar years shown.
[b] Ibid., p. 6. Bizonal area to 1948.
[c] *Statistisches Jahrbuch für die Bundesrepublik Deutschland*, 1961, p. 36.
[d] First half of 1948 (prior to currency reform), 45; second half, 59.
[e] 1958 figure from United Nations, *Patterns of Industrial Growth 1938–1958*, p. 247, linked to 1953 index in table.

Western zones faced longer-run problems. Housing was particularly bad; the effects of war destruction were aggravated by the inflow of millions of refugees and expellees. As late as 1950, one-quarter of all West German families had no regular home; they were either sharing quarters or living under emergency shelter conditions.[128] However, once the rubble was cleared away industrial war damage proved to be much less than originally believed. It was estimated at about 20 per cent of prewar capacity.[129] Food was an even more urgent problem than housing because the Western zones were cut off from former food-supplying areas in eastern Germany. Until 1948, in fact, economic planning in Germany was dominated by the hand-to-mouth problem of finding sufficient food to prevent starvation. Another overriding shortage was of coal because of the loss of the Silesian and Saarland supplies. As in Japan, there were potentially offsetting factors on the positive side: again, the most important were the elimination of any need to support a huge war effort (though Occupation costs had to be met), and the reopening of world trade.

Despite these favourable factors recovery was painfully slow until the currency reform 'miracle' of June 1948. Table 1.18 presents some suggestive data. Perhaps a better impression of the distressed state of the economy is the tabulation of General Clay's remarks on the food ration during this period (Table 1.19). Throughout this period the

Table 1.19   Food Rationing in Postwar Germany (General Clay's comments)

Date	Remark
July 1945	US Zone ration set at 950 to 1150 calories. Only 950 distributed.
August 1945	Official ration set at 1550 calories. Not met.
Winter 1945/46	1550 calorie ration met for a few months.
February 1946	Downward trend resumed.
May–June 1946	Low point, 1180 calories.
End of June 1946	Increase to 1225 calories.
October 1946	1550 calorie ration met.
January 1947	Fusion of British and US zones prevents maintenance of 1550 calorie ration.
April 1947	Authorized allowance dropped to 1040 calories.
June 1947	Ration started upward again.
April 1948	1550 calorie allowance met.
July 1948	Ration set at recommended 1990 calorie level.

Source: Clay, pp. 263–70.

ration goal, set on a fairly spartan level to correspond with general policy on the German standard of living, remained at 1990 calories per day. It was estimated that perhaps 200 calories, on the average, were obtained by German consumers from black market or other unaccounted sources,[130] but in the absence of clearer evidence of mass starvation, it seems that greater amounts must have been so obtained.[131] Until the excellent 1948 harvest, it should be mentioned, such distribution as was attained depended upon external aid — the commitment of SHAEF's 600,000 ton grain reserve in 1945/46, and some millions of tons of later relief imports.

A number of competing hypotheses can be put forward as to the sources of the lagging German economy before the mid-1948 currency reform which initiated the postwar boom. There are possible technological explanations in terms of wartime aggregate destruction of capital, or, alternatively, selective and disproportionate destruction leading to bottlenecks. The importance of these hypotheses warrants fuller and more detailed explanation than there is space for here. The impressionistic comment, made earlier with reference to Japan, can be repeated: the overall level of destruction does not seem to have been sufficient to lead to the observed economic stagnation in the German case either, and selective bottlenecks should have yielded to an appropriate application of resources after only a relatively short delay.[132] On the organizational side, three categories of forces paralleling those considered in Japan will be distinguished: restrictive or punitive policies of the Occupying powers; social and political disorganization, possibly caused partly by reformist or other Occupation policies; and the monetary-fiscal policy of repressed inflation. One factor appears in Germany that did not appear in Japan — the zonal division. From the point of view of the West Germans, restrictive Occupation policies (and the zonal division) were effectively technological constraints outside of their ability to modify. From the point of view of the Occupation authorities, however, at least some of these constraints were capable of modification as a policy matter.

The first factor to be considered is the deliberate Allied policy of holding down the German economy. The initial US intention was to 'pastoralize' Germany, under the policy most strongly advocated by Treasury Secretary Morgenthau.[133] British assent to this policy was, apparently, obtained at the second Quebec conference in September 1944.[134] The Morgenthau plan set the tone of JCS/1067, the directive to the American Commander, though the Potsdam protocol of August 1945 (agreed upon by the Occupying powers, excluding France) was somewhat more moderate.[135] In general, the British were in favour of a moderate policy on level-of-industry and economic restrictions, while the French were perhaps more extreme than the Americans. Under the Potsdam formula, all capital equipment in Germany in excess of the amount judged necessary to maintain a standard of living not greater than the average level of other European nations (excluding Great Britain and Russia) was to be dismantled and made available for reparations.[136] The Potsdam Agreement fixed 55 per cent as the maximum level for permitted German production in relation to 1938 output, exclusive of war production in 1938. Steel was to be limited to about 30 per cent of pre-war, machine tools 10 per cent, chemicals 40 per cent, textiles 75 per cent, and so forth, while a number of industries were prohibited completely, including aircraft, ball-bearings, shipbuilding, munitions and synthetic oil.[137] In late 1945 four-power agreement was obtained on all-German steel production: an output of 5.8 million tons and capacity of $7\frac{1}{2}$ million tons,[138] compared with prewar capacity of some 22 million tons.[139]

Whatever one thinks of the wisdom of this 'Carthaginian peace' policy, it does not appear that the slowness of the recovery can be attributed to it in any great degree. The observed economic performance was, in general, far below the intended economic limitations throughout the period. Furthermore, the limitations themselves were successively relaxed, usually well before they constituted any brake upon production. In the case of steel, for example, in 1947 after the abandonment of four-power negotiations, bizonal limitations were fixed at 10,700,000 tons of production and capacity of 13,000,000 tons.[140]

Punitive measures other than level-of-industry controls included dismantling for reparations, confiscation of the German merchant marine and of all external assets including patents, and the retention of German prisoners of war as forced labourers. The programme of dismantling, initially envisaged on an enormous scale to correspond with the level-of-industry restrictions, was successively cut back. Although there was some impact upon production, the pace of dismantling was so slow and the levels of actual production before the currency reform so low, that adverse effects were not suffered until after the 1948 reforms (when the vigorously expanding economy began to utilize all the capacity available). One estimate places the cost of the programme to Germany at around 2 billion Deutsche marks,[141] perhaps $400 million. The confiscation of external assets for the purpose of reparations may have amounted to around 1 billion dollars,[142] to which should be added the value of some 1.4 million tons of shipping seized.[143] The number of German prisoners of war retained as forced labour amounted to perhaps 1 million in the West (primarily in France and England), and 3 million in the East.[144] The Western countries did not free all their prisoners until the end of 1948; perhaps half of those taken by Russia never returned. Quite aside from the humane aspects of the question, the loss of this labour force was undoubtedly serious to the German economy. The postwar German population had an extremely unbalanced distribution with respect to the proportion fit for work even without this further distortion. However, given the unsatisfactory functioning of the economy, it is questionable how large a fraction of the prisoners could have been successfully integrated into productive employments during the pre-reform period.

Another drain upon the German economy that bears mentioning is Occupation costs. In the early years of the Occupation this category accounted for around 40 per cent of all budgeted government expenditure, representing perhaps 15 per cent of the low gross national product of those years.[145] After the reform, the annual levy was set at 7.2 billion Deutsche marks, still a very substantial sum.[146]

In the aggregate, these various penalties did amount to a very substantial burden upon the German economy. However, they were counteracted by two positive factors: first, the relaxation of the most severe constraints (especially level-of-industry controls and dismantling) before they became very limiting, and second, Allied aid to the German economy. The motives for the gradual easing of Allied policy are, of course, generally familiar. Politically, the continual worsening of relations with the Soviet Union led eventually to the formation of the NATO alliance with German participation. Discussions on the creation of a German army did not begin until 1951, though attitudes were shifting long before. However, in the 1945–48 period it appears that the economic motive predominated in the policy shift. It was gradually brought home, first to the Occupation authorities on the spot and with some delay to top policy-makers in Washington and other capitals, that Germany could not be pastoralized without mass starvation or assignment to a permanent dole. Germany simply could not feed itself as an agricultural nation; it could only live by producing and exporting manufactured products in a complex division of labour with the rest of the world. Also, it was slowly realized that the German economic morass was holding back recovery in the rest of the world. Not only did the drain on American and British taxpayers limit the assistance these nations could provide to other countries, but Europe as a whole was hindered by the lack of German nonpastoral products such as coal, steel, chemicals and machinery, as well as products of German consumer industries. The formal recognition of the need for German recovery as part of a revived European economy came in late 1947 with the announcement that Germany would participate in the Marshall Plan.

Returning to the question of the role of deliberate Allied policy in holding down recovery, the negative effects of that policy must be weighed against the positive contributions of Allied assistance under the 'avert disease and unrest' formula. The role of the Occupying forces in restoring communications, transportation and utilities during the immediate post-surrender crisis period has already been mentioned. This role involved not only direction and organization, but also material aid; for example, 25,000 US railway carriages were brought into Germany.[147] After the passage of the crisis, Occupation economic policy was dominated by the overriding problem of food, and most assistance was provided in this form. Marshall Plan aid in support of the general economy did not arrive, however, until after the currency reform.[148] The relief programmes designed to 'avert disease and unrest' totalled some $2.5 billions, though not all of this arrived in the pre-reform period; assistance under the European Recovery Programme and its successors, all coming after the reform, amounted to around $2 billion more.[149] The magnitude of these contributions weighs heavily against the negative effects of other Occupation policies.

As in the case of Japan, the Occupation control of foreign trade was especially rigorous. All foreign trade was monopolized by the Occupation authorities, and Germans were not permitted even personal commercial contacts with foreigners. During the early period, perhaps two-thirds of imports were aid-financed (see Table 1.20). In view of the levels later attained, one can certainly say that in the pre-reform period foreign trade was paralysed.[150] There is no reason to believe that the Occupation authorities were deliberately trying to strangle

Table 1.20   Postwar Balance of Payments, West Germany (millions of dollars)

Year[a]	Exports	Imports	Services (net)	Current account balance	Foreign aid
1945	na	na	na	na	64[c]
1946	160[b]	na	na	na	468[c]
1947	320[d]	825	10	−495	611
1948	645	1585	45	−895	1059
1949	1136	2247	93	−1018	861
1950	1985	2543	−49	−607	491
1954	5271	4278	−160	+833	69

Notes:
na = not available.
[a] Figures for 1947 and 1948 from A. K. Cairncross, 'The Economic Recovery of Western Germany', *Lloyds Bank Review* (October 1951), p. 28. Later data from Wallich, p. 238.
[b] Zink, p. 256. American and British zones only.
[c] Wallich, p. 66. Figures refer to aid-financed imports, and exclude direct aid by military units.
[d] This appears in conflict with the figure of $225 million (American and British zones only) in Clay, p. 173.

German trade for competitive or strategic reasons. Rather, the main deterrent to exports was the same system of multiple exchange rates linked with price controls that largely eliminated incentives to export in Japan. As General Clay explains, 'Military Government could not let German products be sold below world market prices without arousing justified resentment.'[151] Accordingly, products that were cheap in Germany, such as china, were sold for foreign currencies at high 'world market prices', but remittance was then made to the German producer at a steeply unfavourable exchange rate to correspond with the low internal ceiling price. Commodities whose internal prices were high were, correspondingly, awarded a favourable exchange rate. Imports were valued only at their internal ceiling prices, so that a manufacturer receiving an import allocation 'got very high value for his mark'.[152]

Despite the best of intentions on the part of Occupation authorities, this system failed. It seems evident that the system neatly cancelled out the incentives for German producers to sell abroad, especially for logical export commodities that could be produced cheaply in Germany. Producers receiving only the internal ceiling price in any case, preferred to sell on the domestic market where various 'grey market' tricks provided some possibility of return in excess of the unrealistic legal ceilings. And, at the same time, the control system subsidized imports. But the policy was a mistake rather than a diabolical plot; it was a natural concomitant of internal price ceilings, since with a single rate producers of commodities with low internal prices would be under strong incentives to ship all their output abroad.[153] It may be mentioned that a large fraction of German exports in this period was in the form of coal, badly needed to support revival of industry in Germany itself. The coal exports were compulsory rather than commercial in nature, and the price received was only about half of the world market price.[154]

Social and political disorganization represents a possible alternative explanation of unsatisfactory economic performance. It is plain that there was in fact an organizational crisis in Germany during the transition period after Nazi collapse. However, after the assumption of power by the Occupation authorities, law and order were firmly established, and property rights were not endangered (in the Western zones) except under the legal procedures set under way for restitution, denazification, and so on. Perhaps because of the all too obvious lesson provided by East Germany, Communism won little support in the Western zones and did not constitute a considerable threat after the interregnum period. In these circumstances, while the zonal divisions were important economically because of the hindrance to trade, the lack of a central German government does not seem to have created anything like a crisis of confidence.

The denazification and decartelization policies of the Occupation authorities have been accused of disorganizing the productive powers of the economy. Denazification was a major programme in the American zone: over 930,000 individuals were tried, 500,000 were fined, and some 122,000 were restricted in employment. Also, some 74,000 individuals were interned for up to three years, and of these around 39,000 were sentenced in addition to prison or special labour.[155] The most serious economic effect lay in the employment restrictions handed down either by Occupation edict or by denazification proceedings; for some time almost all important industrial executives were assumed to share the Nazi guilt, and could work only as common labourers. The German economy was undoubtedly deprived of the services of some efficient executives under these provisions, but it seems difficult to believe that the overall effect was very great. It might be added that denazification was much less stringent in the other zones, and the US zone did not contain the major industrial centres of Germany.

The programme for decartelization and deconcentration of industry was designed to prevent concentrations of economic power believed to be partially responsible for German aggression. Again, this was a policy

embraced more enthusiastically in the American than in the other
zones. Cartels in Germany were, in fact, completely ineffective in the
period considered here, and it would therefore be difficult to argue
that dissolution of such market-sharing organizations interfered with
production. The deconcentration policy, on the other hand, involved
the break-up of productive organizations. Such dissolution did promote
competition, but the attendant confusion may have had an adverse
economic effect. At one point, General Clay prevented the dissolution
of a German firm that was a principal supplier of locomotives, in the
belief that the urgency of transport needs made it inadvisable to subject
this firm to reorganization proceedings.[156] Here again it should be
remembered that the more extreme American policies on deconcentration did not apply in the British zone, which contained the bulk of
the great German industry.

Certainly more important than either the punitive or the reformist
policies[157] described above were the economic consequences of the
division of Germany into four Occupation zones superimposed upon
the loss of eastern territories to Poland and Russia and of the Saar to
France. From the time of surrender on, trade of the Western zones
with East Germany and with Eastern Europe in general was practically
stopped.

Furthermore, the economic merger of even the Western zones was
slow and halting. At first, indeed, trade was controlled at the county
level and often stopped there, though intra-zonal trade was freed before
very long. But in May 1946 General Clay reported that all four zones
had tight boundaries closed to commodities, persons and ideas.[158]
Economic merger of the British and American zones was agreed upon
in July 1946 and became effective soon thereafter. It was particularly
vital because the British zone had the Ruhr's heavy industry, while
the American zone had finished-products assembly and some food
production. The French zone, however, remained separate until the
currency reform of July 1948. Although it is difficult to adduce evidence
showing quantitatively how significant the zonal divisions and the loss
of trade with Eastern Europe were in hampering German recovery,
the effect must have been very substantial. In addition to the transitional
problems faced by firms in finding new suppliers and customers, trading
channels, and the like, there was a permanent loss due to the inferior
economic solutions arrived at after the disruption of previously existing
trading relations.

As a cause of the desperate lag in production during the pre-reform
period, however, even the zonal division and the break-off of trade
with Eastern Europe must yield first place to the policy of repressed
inflation. As a result of the monetary and fiscal policies pursued by

the National Socialist regime, when peace came the economy was saturated with liquid funds in the hands of the public (currency hoards, Reich debt, bank accounts, and so on). Reich tax collections covered only 26 per cent of expenditures between 1939 and 1945.[159] From 1935 to 1945, the public debt rose from 15 billion to 400 billion Reichsmarks (not counting potential war damage claims, perhaps equal in amount), while the money supply (currency plus bank deposits) rose from RM35 to more than RM200 billion.[160] At the same time, the productive capabilities of the economy had been substantially reduced by war damage to human and material resources, by loss of territory, and general exhaustion. Furthermore, ordinary German consumers had been deprived of a normal flow of consumer goods for many years,[161] and there were overriding urgent needs on the part of millions of people who had been bombed out or who were refugees or expellees from the East.

The disproportion between the supply of goods and the intensity of desires — desires backed by enormous liquid funds — dictated a new equilibrium level of money prices (in the absence of price controls) substantially higher than that prevailing under the Nazi regime. Alternatively, the current price level could have been maintained at an equilibrium by provisions for cancelling or sterilizing the bulk of the liquid funds in the hands of the public (as was finally done in the currency reform). Instead, an attempt was made to operate the economy as a 'disequilibrium system'. It should be mentioned, however, that the American authorities appreciated the urgent need for a currency reform quite early, and a plan to that effect was proposed in the Dodge–Colm–Goldsmith report in 1946.[162] However, the need for Four-Power agreement foiled all such plans until the Western powers finally went ahead without Russia in 1948.

The decision to maintain and enforce the National Socialist system of ceiling prices was made on a four-power basis shortly after the surrender, and in fact this decision reaffirmed earlier actions of the zone Commanders. In the postwar situation, the controlled prices were hopelessly unrealistic; relative prices were drastically out of line with supplies and demands, but even these distortions were swamped by the disproportion between the general price level and the overall amount of liquid funds. As a result, over most of the economy, production for legal sale could take place only at a financial loss. In addition, the prices initially established were very difficult to modify because all four occupying powers had to consent to any change.[163] A system of price ceilings may be workable in a situation where the public regards current shortages as a temporary phenomenon; the near prospect of a return to normality makes people willing to accumulate liquid hoards in the belief that they will be able to spend their money, without too great a price penalty, in the not too distant future. This was substantially the situation for the *wartime* repressed inflations of Germany, Britain and the United States. And, in the victorious countries, public confidence (mistaken though it was) in the restoration of normal price levels persisted for some years afterward. But no one in postwar Germany could believe in the return of normality, so this vital stabilizing element was lacking. Furthermore, in most historical situations ceilings have been adjusted to keep the margin between legal and realistic prices within bounds, a necessary accommodation if the controls are to be workable at all. But in postwar Germany the ceilings were initially based upon a Hitler price freeze dating as far back as 1936[164] (liquid funds having risen more than ten-fold in the interim) and then were maintained with exceptional rigidity.[165]

It is very instructive to compare the Japanese and German post-war inflations. In Japan there were also price controls. But there, in the hope of stimulating industrial recovery, the financial authorities pursued an extreme cheap-money policy which continued to multiply money and credit. Fiscal and monetary policy in Occupied Germany was, in contrast, very conservative; balanced budgets were the order of the day,[166] and the banking system was not in a position to create very much credit. In Japan there was a dynamic or 'run-away' inflation, based upon ever-increasing expansion of money and credit, and a consequent flight from money on the part of the public. The Japanese price ceilings were flexible and adjusted fairly rapidly; even so, they fell behind the actual course of developments. As a result, a large fraction of transactions took place on the black market, which could not be rigidly suppressed. But in Germany the inflation was static. Current fiscal and monetary policy did not augment the inflationary pressure, which was entirely due to an initial overhang of excess liquidity. The price ceilings were rather tightly maintained, and the black market did not play a very major role, representing perhaps 10 per cent of transactions.[167] In Germany, however, the term 'black market' was given a very narrow definition: outright trading of goods for cash at illegal prices, a practice professionally engaged in by a specialized class of disreputable individuals.[168] In contrast, *everybody* engaged in a form of transaction known as 'bilateral exchange' or 'compensation trade', apparently without moral taint. This trade took place at legal prices in money, except that no one could acquire goods or services for money alone, but, rather, only upon exchange of some compensation in real goods and services. The compensation system was apparently even more important on the wholesale and manufacturing levels than at retail; estimates are that from one-third to one-half of all transactions took this form.[169] Even the Occupation authorities engaged in it, as the noon meal provided all German employees of the Occupation administration (at legal prices, of course) was often the chief attraction of such employment. In addition, incentives in kind were found necessary to increase production in certain vital fields, particularly coal mining.[170]

What was taking place in both Japan and Germany was the elimination of money as a medium of exchange. In Japan barter trading did not develop so far, because the more realistic price ceilings and the wider scope of the black market still left a useful role for money (though at the cost of a substantial hidden tax paid by individuals in the form of depreciation of money value during any period in which they held money without spending it). In Germany, barter trading in the form of compensation trade was dominant, the money aspect of the transaction being a *pro forma* demonstration to preserve legality and morality. Transactions by barter are, of course, extremely inefficient. They require a matching of the commodity needs of buyer and seller that is very difficult to achieve under complex production arrangements.

Since the German difficulty was due to the static overhang of excess purchasing power, rather than to continual creation of additional liquidity, it was amenable to a once-and-for-all cure. Once the currency reform scaled down the liquid funds, the enforcement of price controls could be abandoned,[171] and trade and then production leaped ahead. In Japan, by contrast, the early monetary reform of 1946 cured nothing, since the government continued the policy of inflationary deficits and lavish creation of credit. The cure here was monetary and fiscal conservatism, imposed in 1949 by the Dodge reforms.

Certain characteristic symptoms of a breakdown of the monetary trade mechanism were evident in Germany, as in others of the disaster cases reviewed here:

Trekking to the countryside to barter or forage for food was very prevalent. After the currency reform when trekking stopped, short-haul railroad passenger traffic dropped immediately to less than 40 per cent of its pre-reform volume.[172]

Quotas were imposed upon farmers for compulsory delivery of products at legal prices. (The policy of impressment under the Confederacy was somewhat similar, though less systematized.) In Germany, however, the sensible Japanese system of a price premium for over-quota deliveries was not adopted; authorities refused to countenance the weakening of the legal ceilings that such 'market-splitting' would represent.

Subsidies to hold down end-product prices had been an important element in the cumulative build-up of inflationary pressures in Japan.

Such subsidies had been fairly substantial under the Nazi regime, but were soon abandoned by the Occupation, probably because the balanced-budget policy left no funds available for that purpose. Subsidies, of course, would have been pointless in aiding consumers, as the money prices of commodities were already a negligible consideration. To make the subsidies significant in the calculations of producers would have required embarking upon the Japanese course of dynamic inflation.[173]

The currency reform, need for which had been appreciated long before (by the American authorities, at any rate), was postponed until June 1948 in the hopes of obtaining Soviet acquiescence. To go ahead without Soviet agreement meant adopting a separate money for West Germany, abandoning the common currency that represented one of the few remaining symbols of German unity. The stumbling block in the negotiations was the Soviet insistence upon control of a separate set of plates; the Russians rejected the proposal of a single set of plates under four-power control.[174] The Americans were adamant against a separate Russian set of plates, after their painful experience with the military marks.[175] After urgent last-minute negotiations, the French agreed to accept the currency reform and to merge their zone at this time.

The currency reform represented radical surgery. It was based upon a 10 : 1 conversion of old Reichsmarks for new Deutsche marks. This was the scale used for revaluing private bonds, mortgages, annuities, and so on; public debt of the Reich was cancelled, except for the possibility of claims under future projected legislation for equalization of war burdens. The actual conversion rate for currency and demand and savings deposits was more severe — 100 : 6½ — while the reform had a levelling feature in that substantial 'initial allotments' on a per capita basis[176] were made even in the absence of Reichsmarks presented for conversion. Table 1.21 presents some summary data on the money supply as of April 1949 showing the effects of the currency conversion. It will be noted that in the aggregate the 'initial allotments' exceeded the balances resulting from Reichsmark conversion. The amounts shown with 'credit creation' as source are all post-reform, so that the reform created some DM12.6 billion. The amount of the true pre-reform money supply is unknown; some 122.4 billion Reichsmarks were presented for conversion, but it is believed that there was considerable slippage as holders of large balances had to satisfy the authorities as to their source and legitimacy.

A number of other measures complementing the monetary reform were adopted concurrently or soon thereafter. Personal income and business taxes were reduced from their very high levels. A uniform

Table 1.21 Volume of Money in West Germany, 30 April 1949 (millions of Deutsche marks)

1. *By source*		
a. Initial allotments		6690
To individuals	2780	
To businesses	470	
To German governments (including		
state-owned railroad and postal systems)	2670	
To military governments	770	
b. Reichsmark conversion		5910
c. Credit creation		6560
Total		19,160
2. *By type*		
a. DM notes in circulation		6330
b. Bank deposits		12,830
Total		19,160

Source: Walter W. Heller, 'Tax and Monetary Reform in Occupied Germany', *National Tax Journal*, vol. 2 (1949), p. 216.

link between the DM and the dollar, initially set at $0.30, replaced the system of multiple exchange rates or conversion factors. All-comprehensive price, rationing and allocation controls were withdrawn. Not all controls were immediately abolished; the Occupation authorities offered some resistance on this score. But enforcement was so relaxed that the black and legal markets gradually merged into a unified free market. The wage stop was also abolished soon after the reform.[177]

The effects of the monetary reform and companion measures were attested to with remarkable unanimity, though there was some disagreement as to the more fundamental causes of the dramatic recovery of trade and production. General Clay declares, 'The effect on the German economy was electric although it was given too much credit for the recovery which followed.'[178] On the other hand, Wallich says: 'Observers, left-wing as well as right-wing, agree that it transformed the German scene from one day to the next. On June 21, 1948, goods reappeared in the stores, money resumed its normal function, black and gray markets reverted to a minor role, foraging trips to the country ceased, labour productivity increased, and output took off on its great upward surge.'[179] Heller, writing in September 1949, says of the reform: 'It has unquestionably proved an economic success. It quickly re-established money as the preferred medium of exchange and monetary incentives as the prime mover of economic activity. Coupled with Marshall Plan imports, a good harvest, tax reform, and the removal of many direct controls, it touched off an expansion ...'[180] Economists were generally able to perceive what seemed to be the main lesson: Germany had been 'a country without a currency';[181] now, 'It was as if money and markets had been invented afresh as reliable media of the division of labour.'[182]

Disagreements still persist on a number of major economic features of the period, however. General Clay's contention seems to be that the pre-reform Occupation period did not represent economic stagnation, but rather a generally satisfactory picture of steady recovery under adverse conditions. The statistical indicators (see Table 1.18) support the view that in the pre-reform period some recovery did take place. But almost all observers agree that in view of the failure to return to anywhere near pre-war levels the rate cannot be called satisfactory.[183] Mendershausen (while describing with enthusiasm the consequences of the 1948 currency reform) suggests that had the reform and the associated decontrol measures been imposed earlier the results would have been no more satisfactory than were the results of the repressed-inflation policy actually pursued, in view of 'the protracted disorganization of government, social life, and foreign supplies.'[184] However, the analysis here indicates that social and political disorganization was not too significant as an independent factor after the crisis of 1945, while the *economic* disorganization caused by the lack of an effective monetary mechanism persisted until the reform.

Gottlieb, who served as an economist on the staff of the American military government in this period, represents still another point of view. He argues that failure to adopt an early currency reform was a major error, but for a reason quite different from the one adduced here. Gottlieb does not regard the techniques of rationing, controls, and centralized assignment of resources — the only available means of resource allocation under repressed inflation — even as necessary evils. In his view they are, at least in principle, positively desirable tools, superior to the market mechanism as means of organizing production and achieving social objectives under conditions of impoverishment and dislocation like those in post-war Germany.[185] The unfortunate results achieved, actually employing just these tools in post-war Germany, he ascribes to policy mistakes and to general inefficiency on the part of German agencies and governments and Allied Occupation authorities.[186] The failure to adopt a monetary reform earlier was such a policy mistake in his view since the swollen money supply undermined the wage and price controls and encouraged black markets.[187] There is, however, concurrence of opinion that, whatever the potential excellence of repressed-inflation controls may be for good, they can also be used to bad effect, and indeed were, in Germany.

CONCLUSION: COMMON THEMES IN DISASTER

This survey has been an exploratory investigation into the natural history of disaster, rather than a scientific testing of clearly formulated hypotheses about the causes, characteristics or consequences of disasters. The primary results of the investigation are, therefore, clarification of concepts, gathering of evidence and materials for further study, and certain inferences of a more or less conjectural nature about the laws that govern disaster phenomena. These inferences may be divided between those that seem to be fairly reliable empirical generalizations of the evidence surveyed, and more speculative ideas that must remain at the level of surmise because of a scarcity of evidential base. In what follows, an attempt will be made to indicate the degree of reliability of the conclusions, or at least to label clearly those that must be considered mere surmise.

The term *disaster* has been used here to refer to a substantial, sharp reduction in material resources available to a community. Economic *collapse*, in contrast, refers not to mere impoverishment but to a failure in the mode of functioning of the economic system, in essence, a breakdown in the division of labour. The causes of the impoverishment or breakdown may be divided into exogenous versus endogenous with respect to the economic mechanism, though there is some difficulty in classifying in this way such causes as social revolutions.

Bombing is clearly an exogenous source of stress. Conventional bombing in World War II was not heavy enough to bring about economic collapse by the generalized effects of sheer material destruction. However, in wartime Germany, attacks on transportation, oil and power in combination with loss of territory from combat operations did lead to collapse. Apparently, essential connecting links in the economic system were broken, so that production fell even more than did the resources available. In the Confederacy, a similar effect resulted from loss of territory in combination with blockade of an economy highly dependent upon external trade. It appears that blockade took first place and bombing second place in order of importance as causes of the collapse of the Japanese war economy in 1945. Other exogenous sources of stress, less important in modern than in earlier times, are famine from crop failure or other natural catastrophes (for example, the Irish potato blight), and disease (for example, the Black Death).

The endogenous causes of disaster or collapse are more subtle, in as much as no obvious destruction of resources may be visible. Those observed here were dissolution of or threats to the institution of property, and disruption of the mechanism of monetary exchange. In the case of Russian war communism there was almost total destruction of property rights, involving an attempt to replace a system of production based upon voluntary exchange with a system of total bureaucratic administration of the economy. Recovery under the NEP required reinstitution of markets and of a considerable degree of private ownership. (The modern Soviet system retains the essential element of voluntary exchange represented by free choice of occupation in return for monetary reward, that is, private ownership of one's own labour power.) The threat of communism, also, may be as potent a force as the actuality: Who will sow if he believes that he will not be permitted to reap? Such fears may have been a significant element in the lagging post-war recoveries.

Difficulties with the monetary mechanism observed here were all connected with inflation, or with the attempt to repress inflation or cope with its consequences through the device of price ceilings. In an unrepressed inflation, the inflationary tax on holding money (the rate of increase of prices) may become so great as to lead to the abandonment of the monetary medium. In a repressed inflation, the same effect may come about if exchange becomes impossible at legal ceiling prices, and if the safety valve of the black market is rigorously suppressed. In either case, the consequence is resort to barter. The general substitution of barter for money exchange interferes so drastically with the division of labour as to be a fairly reliable indicator of a collapsed economy. It should be mentioned that monetary disorders at the opposite end of the spectrum — of a deflationary rather than an inflationary nature — are intimately connected with the crises and panics frequently encountered in financial history. Indeed, in terms of magnitude of effect (aside from direct human casualties), an event like the great Depression of 1929–33 may rank with some of the greatest disasters of history.

Perhaps the most striking outcome of this survey is the remarkable similarity in the general sequence of events characterizing large-scale generalized disasters. The term 'disaster syndrome' is already reserved for the typical social-psychological pattern of response to sharp *localized* disasters; we shall therefore use the term 'generalized disaster phenomenon' to refer to this characteristic course of events.

The generalized disaster phenomenon seems to hinge on the food/money exchange relationship between countryside and city. The initiating event is, let us say, an exogenous stress such as blockade on bombing that leads to a substantial reduction in the material resources of the community. As a result, consumer commodities become scarce — the more so if the government is subject to some continuing source of pressure such as external war or revolution. Especially in such a case, the government will be driven to finance its urgent needs through the printing press. Scarcity of goods and excessive quantities of money combine to raise prices, especially food prices in the cities. The impoverishment may be so great as to dictate a new long-run locational equilibrium entailing a movement of population back to the land from the cities, but the government resists this tendency: it may be vital to maintain war production, or perhaps the political base of the government may be in the cities. At any rate, the next step of the government (if not already taken) is to introduce price ceilings and urban food rationing. The result is that farmers tend to stop bringing food to the cities at the low prices legally ruling, worsening the situation more than ever. Unofficial mechanisms of food distribution develop: black markets, barter, trekking. These all involve some loss of urban productive capacity, and are perhaps unacceptable to the government on other grounds. Consequently, the carrot and the stick are put to work on the farmers: compulsory quotas for food deliveries are imposed, and some type of subsidy is offered to overcome the negative effect of the low maximum prices. The subsidies, however, can only be financed by inflationary means, thus adding fuel to the inflationary fire roaring by this time. If the breakdown is severe enough, the government may use military force to collect food supplies from the farmers, a process yielding a temporary return at a severe cost in terms of production for the next harvests, not to mention adverse political effects. The generalized disaster phenomenon may culminate in a number of ways. First, economic collapse may occur. Alternatively, there may be a cessation of the external source of stress before economic collapse takes place (or afterward). With such a remission, recovery generally becomes possible; the policies associated with the disaster phenomenon may survive, however, to become a drag on the recovering economy. The economy may achieve a new equilibrium at a lower level of economic organization, or the monetary mechanism and markets may be restored to functioning by the abandonment of inflationary policies or of price ceilings. Foreign relief may provide a vital leeway in easing the transition to a viable economic system.

Each one of the particular historical experiences surveyed displays some variations from this archetypal pattern, of course. In Russian war communism the restoration of markets and the freeing of food prices under the NEP led to a considerable recovery *despite* the continuance and intensification of inflationary financial policies on the part of the government. The Confederacy did not formally institute price controls and rationing, though food was taken from the countryside by forced impressment at 'fair' prices. Post-war Germany did not pursue inflationary fiscal and monetary policies; instead the difficulty was caused by the previous inflation of liquid assets under the National Socialist regime. Other departures from the general pattern may be

Table 1.22   Urban Fraction of the Total Population, Germany and Japan

West Germany		Japan	
Date	% Urban	Date	% Urban
May 1939	70.5	October 1940	37.9
October 1946	68.6	February 1944	41.1
September 1950	71.1	November 1945	27.8
		April 1946	30.4
		August 1948	34.6
		October 1950	37.5
		October 1955	56.3

Source: United Nations, *Demographic Yearbook (1960)* (New York: 1961), pp. 383, 387.

cited, but the overall uniformity of the generalized disaster phenomenon in such very different political and economic situations remains the dominating feature. It is entirely probable that the generalized disaster phenomenon is being reproduced in such economically catastrophic situations as China, and possibly Cuba, today. And the aftermath of a future war is likely to provide still more instances, at least if we consider possible wars with enough human and material survival to allow an advanced society.

It follows from this analysis that the urban/rural composition of the population should provide an indicator of the development of the disaster and recovery processes. Table 1.22 shows the data available for Germany and Japan. For Russia, systematic data are not available, but we have seen estimates that between 1917 and 1920 the aggregate population of towns fell by around one-third, and of the two great cities of Moscow and Petrograd by over one-half. The Confederacy may provide an exception, however. There the breakdown of law and order in the countryside seems to have led to a movement of refugees from the more remote rural areas into the cities. One possible explanation is that the local rural environs of the Southern towns largely sufficed to feed the urban population, since Southern agriculture was devoted mostly to non-food crops where it was not on a merely subsistence basis.

It will be noted that the particular course represented by the generalized disaster phenomenon involves both technological and organizational elements. Bombing or blockade may be sufficient to bring on economic collapse, whatever the policies pursued, but the steps taken by the government in an attempt to cope with this stress are almost certain to bring on the second phase of the disaster — a breakdown in the functioning of markets and of monetary exchange. To the extent that the distress is due to these secondary causes, it is eminently curable by a reversal of the policies responsible, as evidenced by the success of the NEP in Russia, of the German currency reform, and of the Dodge fiscal reforms in Japan. Why did the reversal not occur earlier in these instances? For the Bolsheviks, of course, smashing the previous social order and economic system had important positive values to be weighed against whatever loss of production ensued. The Japanese inflation seems less explicable, though simple error certainly contributed. The financial gains to the beneficiaries of government credits almost certainly created an influential class with a vested interest in continued inflation. In Germany, the benefits of a currency reform were widely (but *not* universally) appreciated in advance; the delay was caused by fruitless diplomatic negotiations with the Soviets.

One of the major objectives of repressed-inflation policies, and the source of much of their political appeal, is epitomized by the slogan, 'fair shares'. Especially in a disaster situation, it may seem intolerable that anyone live much better than his fellows, even if the equality imposed is an equality of misery. Unfortunately, the pursuit of short-run equality will almost certainly be at the expense of economic productivity, and even possibly at the expense of long-run equality. But in a crisis situation where the average level of the population may not be far from the margin of starvation, it has proved politically difficult to break away from what could be claimed to be policies of 'fair shares' or at least 'equality of misery'. Alternative policies involving restoration of the market mechanism do create possibilities of enrichment for the few (for example, by removal of price ceilings on scarce commodities) in the course of general economic improvement.

All this goes some distance toward explaining why repressed-inflation policies were maintained for so long in Germany and Japan. One other consideration that should be brought out is the view of some government economic decision makers that the repressed-inflation system, possibly after some reforms and improvements, can be made to yield results that are fundamentally superior to those of the market system. Such views may explain the seemingly permanent attachment of several important Latin American countries to repressed-inflation policies in the face of accumulated adverse experience.

To sum up on this point, it may be regarded as a well-established generalization that, whatever the technological impact of an initial disaster upon the productive potentialities of an economy, there is likely to be a characteristic organizational response to the crisis in the form of adoption of monetary-fiscal policies of repressed inflation. At the extremity of the crisis, when the stress is at its utmost effectiveness, it would be hard to say if such a policy really worsens matters. However, in the initial response to the threat the effective use of the society's resources is likely to be impaired by a repressed-inflation policy; and, almost certainly, recovery after cessation of the external pressure will be impaired. (It must not be forgotten, however, that the damage inflicted by the source of stress will have a lasting component. Even ideal policies cannot produce instantaneous recovery, and perhaps not complete recovery at any time.)

Generalized disasters are a relatively infrequent historical event, so that there seems to be rather little learning from one instance to the next.[188] However, after World War II a number of countries were thrust simultaneously into rather similar circumstances, so that learning could more easily take place. The success of 'orthodox' (anti-inflationary) fiscal and monetary policies in Belgium provided an early clue, while the Einaudi reforms of 1947 in Italy terminated the inflation in that country. Both of these instances almost certainly influenced German sentiment against continuance of the repressed-inflation policy, while the role of Joseph M. Dodge in both Germany and Japan indicates that there was some learning from the former to the latter situation.

We now turn from the relatively well-established generalizations to the more conjectural inferences from the experiences reviewed. Since they are clearly speculations, they must remain as bare hypotheses for future study.

The first such conjecture is that, by and large, population appears to have been tougher than property under physical blows like bombing or combat damage. This conclusion would obviously not apply to radiological or bacteriological warfare, however.

The second conjecture is that the speed and success of recovery in the observed historical instances have been due in large part to the proportionately smaller destruction of population than of material resources. That the proportionate survival of population may be the critical factor is suggested also by the fact that completely depopulated cities have often failed to regain their former size and prosperity,[189] in comparison with cities largely destroyed physically, but where substantial fractions of population survived (for example, Hiroshima). And again, this conjecture is reinforced by such historical instances as the economic decline of Ireland following the large emigration of population because of the potato blight.

While economists have written astonishingly little on the subject of disaster, this view linking the possibility of recovery to the degree of depopulation was expressed over a century ago by John Stuart Mill.[190] Mill presents a somewhat defective argument for this position, contending that the destruction of capital that takes place in disaster is very little more than the normal process of using up of the capital stock that would require its replacement by the community in any case.[191] Such an analysis treats capital wealth as if it were only a stock of consumables, a diminution of which is automatically corrected by the 'involuntary privation' that necessarily results. What is omitted here is that capital contributes enormously to productivity, so that the production necessary to replace the capital stock is itself hampered and impaired by the scarcity of tools, machines, usable buildings, and inventories of all kinds. Even if capital wealth did consist entirely of a stock of consumables, it is clear that lack of food, for example, would in general have an adverse effect upon production. A sounder argument for the conjecture could be based upon the propositions that: (1) the fraction of the community's real wealth represented by visible material capital is small relative to the fraction represented by the accumulated knowledge and talents of the population, and (2) there are enormous reserves of energy and effort in the population not drawn upon in ordinary times, but which can be utilized under special circumstances such as those prevailing in the aftermath of disaster.

A third, somewhat related, conjecture is that economic recovery seems possible over an extremely wide range of damage. Certainly, there is no question that a rather prompt recovery was technologically possible in any of the instances here reviewed, granted a cessation of the external stress. Mill also remarks:

... what has so often excited wonder, the great rapidity with which countries recover from a state of devastation; the disappearance, in a short time, of all traces of the mischiefs done by earthquakes, floods, hurricanes, and the ravages of war. An enemy lays waste a country by fire and sword, and destroys or carries away nearly all the moveable wealth existing in it: all the inhabitants are ruined, and yet in a few years after, everything is much as it was before.[192]

The A Country, B Country hypothesis of Herman Kahn (see above) is also lent some conjectural support by our data. Generally speaking, it has proved relatively easy to rebuild great cities after destruction if the hinterland has remained largely intact. On the other hand, the cities cannot maintain themselves without the hinterland, since adverse developments in the countryside interfering with food supplies lead to rapid depopulation of the cities (Russia under war communism).

As an additional generalization, it is worth noting that the catastrophes reviewed here seem not to have led directly to as much danger of popular revolt from the rule of the established authorities as might have been anticipated. The chief exception is farmer resistance to enforced crop collections, which led to armed conflict in Russia and even to some extent in the Confederacy. In the circumstances, these seem to have been put down with surprising ease by the authorities.

Finally, it may be mentioned that the subject of disaster and recovery could be regarded as a kind of special case of the general problem of economic development. There might, therefore, be reason to suspect that the causes of lagging recovery from acute disaster may often also be the causes responsible for chronically lagging normal growth in certain national economies, for example, in Latin America.

NOTES

1. A theoretical study of such technological limitations, as applied to the hypothetical problem of recuperation from nuclear war, will be found in Sidney G. Winter, Jr, *Economic Viability After Thermonuclear War: The Limits of Feasible Production*, The RAND Corporation, RM-3436-PR (September 1963).
2. Major sources employed were F. C. Iklé, *The Social Impact of Bomb Destruction* (Norman, Oklahoma: University of Oklahoma Press, 1958); S. H. Prince, *Catastrophe and Social Change* (New York: Columbia University Press, 1920); *Human Organization* (Special issue: 'Human Adaptation to Disaster', N. J. Demerath and A. F. C. Wallace (eds.), vol. 16 (Summer 1957)). In the *Human Organization* issue is an 'Annotated Bibliography on Disaster Research', by Jeanette Rayner. The Iklé volume also contains a bibliography. An extremely valuable source, containing abstracts and summaries of many separate contributions to the literature, is R. D. Popper and W. A. Lybrand, *An Inventory of Selected Source Materials Relevant to Integration of Physical and Social Effects of Air Attack*, Human Science Research, Inc., October 1960.
3. By 'panic' is meant extreme and irrational, disfunctional or self-defeating physical action. It is rational and therefore not panicky to make all possible haste in fleeing a raging fire. But panic has been observed where, for example, those attempting to flee have jammed a narrow exit so that none could escape. Only rarely do disasters produce this panic-generating condition.
4. St Pierre has never recovered more than a minor fraction of its previous population, but there the entire original population perished. The same holds true for a number of cities in ancient history destroyed by conquest or natural calamity. During World War II, the St Georg district of Hamburg was abandoned after the fire raids of 1943, as it was judged too costly to restore under war conditions.
5. Iklé, pp. 7–8.
6. In Hamburg after the fire raids, only 51 per cent of the pre-war dwellings survived, but those sheltered 64 per cent of pre-war population. Ibid., p. 40.

7. Ibid., p. 220.
8. This discussion is based upon data and analysis in Iklé.
9. Fatality estimates for Hamburg vary widely, and figures up to 100,000 are found in various accounts. The 40,000 figure is based upon the detailed report of the Hamburg Police President, and is accepted by Iklé, p. 24.
10. United States Strategic Bombing Survey, *Over-all Report (European War)*, 30 September 1945, p. 72.
11. Supplementary sources used here were Report of the British Mission to Japan, 'The Effects of the Atomic Bombs at Hiroshima and Nagasaki' (1946), and US Strategic Bombing Survey, 'The Effects of Atomic Bombs on Hiroshima and Nagasaki' (1946).
12. The US Strategic Bombing Survey estimates the population at risk as 245,000, while the British Mission indicates a figure closer to 320,000. The Research Department of the Hiroshima Municipal Office is reported to have estimated the population in the city as 407,000, in *Hiroshima* (Hiroshima Publishing Company, 1949).
13. These proportions are the estimates used by the US Strategic Bombing Survey report. The Hiroshima Municipal Office calculations show an even greater disparity, reporting 22 per cent of population killed and missing but some 89 per cent of buildings as destroyed or needing reconstruction (*Hiroshima*)
14. USSBS, 'The Effects of Atomic Bombs at Hiroshima and Nagasaki', p. 8.
15. *Hiroshima*.
16. The main sources employed in this section were M. Dobb, *Soviet Economic Development Since 1917* (New York: International Publishers, 1948), Chs. 4–7; A. Baykov, *The Development of the Soviet Economic System* (Cambridge, England: University Press, 1947), Chs. 1–9; A. Z. Arnold, *Banks, Credit and Money in Soviet Russia* (New York: Columbia University Press, 1937), Chs. 4–8; and E. H. Carr, *The Bolshevik Revolution, 1917–1923*, vol. 2 (London: Macmillan, 1952), Chs. 17–19.
17. Dobb, p. 120.
18. Differential rations were employed so as to provide more food to the manual workers and other preferred Bolshevik categories than to remaining sectors of the population. Members of the former bourgeoisie ranked lowest, generally receiving only around one-third the ration of the preferred groups (Carr, p. 232).
19. Baykov, p. 42. A full discussion of the question of the 'militarization' of labour will be found in Carr, pp. 208–27.
20. Ibid., pp. 241–2.
21. It has actually been reported that older currencies exchanged, at times, at a 50-fold premium over Bolshevik (Arnold, p. 82).
22. Lenin later described war communism as 'a mistake', and 'in complete contradiction to all we wrote concerning the transition from capitalism to socialism' (quoted in Dobb, p. 123). The following more extended quotation from Lenin may also be of interest:

We are living in such conditions of impoverishment and ruin, of overstrain and exhaustion of the principal productive forces of the peasants and the workers, that for a time everything must be subordinated to this fundamental consideration — at all costs to increase the quantity of goods ... On the economic front, in our attempt to pass over to Communism, we had suffered, by the spring of 1921, a more serious defeat than any previously inflicted on us by Kolchak,

Denikin or Pilsudsky. Compulsory requisition in the villages and the direct Communist approach to the problems of reconstruction in towns — this was the policy which interfered with the growth of the productive capacity of the country and proved to be the main cause of a profound economic and political crisis which confronted us in the spring of 1921. (Quoted in Baykov, p. 48)

23. Baykov, p. 47. See also Lenin quotation in note 22 above.
24. Even more extreme estimates appear in some of the sources. Dobb quotes statistics showing 1920 industrial production as only 14.5 per cent of the pre-war level (p. 100). Carr cites 1920 production indexes as 12.9 per cent of 1913 (in pre-war rouble values) for fully manufactured products, and 13.6 per cent for semi-finished goods (p. 195). Detailed statistical production data for a wide range of commodities and industries are tabulated in G. Warren Nutter, *Growth of Industrial Production in the Soviet Union* (Princeton, N.J.: Princeton University Press, 1962), Table B-2, pp. 420–59.
25. 'The main material resources on which the country lived during this period were provided not by fresh production but by existing stocks of raw materials, unfinished and finished goods inherited from the pre-revolution period, by compulsory requisitioning of agricultural products and by confiscation from the "bourgeoisie".' (Baykov, p. 47)
26. Dobb, p. 107.
27. Baykov, p. 7n. Carr adds that only some 4500 were regarded as 'effectively nationalized' (p. 175).
28. Carr, following a common Bolshevik opinion of the period, places some blame upon the shift to small-scale production (as large estates were converted into individual peasant holdings) as a major cause of the decline in agricultural output and of the trend to subsistence farming (Carr, pp. 168–9). In view of the remarkable output performance of the small permitted private holdings in contrast to the collective farms in the modern Soviet economy, it seems dubious to assign more than a minor negative role to the technological consideration of smallness of scale, in comparison with the effect of the policy of compulsory requisitions. It is an almost universal observation that farmers will work much harder, and produce much more, on their own proprietary holdings than they will as employees on large private or government estates, or on collective farms.
29. The 1921 crop, however, was hit by a disastrous drought. Foreign relief played an important role in the 1921–22 famine.
30. See Phillip Cagan, 'The Monetary Dynamics of Hyperinflation', in Milton Friedman (ed.), *Studies in the Quantity Theory of Money* (Chicago: University of Chicago Press, 1956).
31. This decline explains the paradoxical complaints often heard about 'shortages' of money in such extreme inflationary situations; in fact, the increasing money stocks do represent lesser real command over goods. Needless to say, such a money shortage will not be cured by printing still more currency. See Arnold, p. 96, for comments on the 'currency famine' in Russia.
32. Ibid., p. 94.
33. Pitirim A. Sorokin, *The Sociology of Revolution* (Philadelphia: Lippincott, 1925), p. 197. Lorimer estimates the 'population deficit' between 1914 and 1926 at around 28 million, excess civilian deaths accounting for some 14 million of this total (the other categories were military deaths, emigration

and birth deficit). Frank Lorimer, *The Population of the Soviet Union* (Geneva: League of Nations, 1946), p. 41.
34. Sorokin, pp. 202–3.
35. Ibid., p. 244n.
36. Baykov, p. 41.
37. Baykov reports private trade as accounting for over 90 per cent of product distribution in 1922 and 1923 (p. 55). Dobb provides somewhat lower estimates, three quarters of retail turnover and one fifth of wholesale trade being described as in private hands in 1923 (p. 143). The Nepmen also served as middlemen in trading even among state enterprises.
38. Major sources used were E. M. Lerner, 'The Monetary and Fiscal Programs of the Confederate Government, 1861–65', *Journal of Political Economy*, LXII (December 1954), and 'Money, Prices and Wages in the Confederacy, 1861–65', ibid., LXIII (February 1955); Clement Eaton, *A History of the Southern Confederacy* (New York: Macmillan, 1954), especially Chs. 7 and 12; Richard C. Todd, *Confederate Finance* (Athens, Georgia: University of Georgia Press, 1954); John C. Schwab, *The Confederate States of America, 1861–65: A Financial and Industrial History of the South During the Civil War* (New York: Scribner's, 1901); E. Merton Coulter, *The Confederate States of America 1861–1865* (Baton Rouge: Louisiana State University Press, 1950); and Ralph Andreano (ed.), *The Economic Impact of the American Civil War* (Cambridge, Mass.: Schenkman Publishing Co., 1962).
39. Herman Kahn, *On Thermonuclear War* (Princeton, N.J.: Princeton University Press, 1960), pp. 74–95.
40. Ibid., p. 78.
41. The South produced only about 3 per cent of the iron ore, and 6 per cent of the rolled iron. It contained around 10 per cent of cotton milling capacity, and 3 per cent of woollen milling. See Albert D. Kirwan (ed.), *The Confederacy* (New York: Meridian Books, 1959), p. 63.
42. About 900,000 served at one time or another as Confederate soldiers. Eaton, p. 89.
43. The fall in cotton prices imposed hardships on cotton planters, who demanded assistance from the government. Various sophistical arguments were put forward as to how the economy would benefit from government purchase of the cotton crop at normal peacetime prices. Secretary of the Treasury Memminger was generally successful in resisting these pressures; the proposed purchase, of course, as well as straining government finances, would have deterred the desired shift from cotton production. See Lerner, 'Monetary and Fiscal Programs', pp. 514–15.
44. On these points, see especially Eaton, Ch. 7, and Schwab, Ch. 12.
45. M. E. Massey, *Ersatz in the Confederacy* (Columbia: University of South Carolina Press, 1952), Ch. 5.
46. Ibid., Ch. 6.
47. Schwab, p. 238.
48. Eaton, p. 147.
49. Schwab, p. 238. Eaton reports 1,250,000 bales as carried from the Confederacy by blockade-runners during the whole war. Eaton's figures do not seem consistent with Schwab's, even when allowance is made for exports lost or delivered elsewhere than to England. Illegal trade with the North may account for the difference.

50. 'When Captain Hobart Pasha of the *Venus* asked a Southern woman in England what was most needed in the Confederacy, she unhesitatingly replied, "Corsets"' (Eaton, p. 144).
51. Schwab has an extensive discussion of this trade (pp. 258–66).
52. See Table 1.6. The $700,000 or so in currency and specie funds of the United States seized in 1861 was minor compared with the aggregate of Federal property obtained. The naval shipyard at Norfolk and the Harper's Ferry arsenal are worth special mention.
53. Lerner estimates the proportions of money received by the Confederacy to October 1864 as follows: taxes, 5 per cent; miscellaneous, 5 per cent; bonds, 30 per cent; printing press, 60 per cent ('Monetary and Fiscal Programs', p. 507). These estimates broadly parallel Todd's when it is recalled that Lerner omits the huge amount of impressments unpaid and evidenced only by Certificates of Indebtedness.
54. Secretary of the Treasury Memminger appears to have had a remarkable grasp of these relationships, but Congressional and state opposition was insuperable. Nevertheless, Memminger has been commonly regarded by historians as incompetent. He is strongly defended in Lerner, 'Monetary and Fiscal Programs'.
55. The tax in kind proved particularly difficult and wasteful.
56. Memminger repeatedly proposed a compulsory loan, but it was not adopted (Lerner, 'Monetary and Fiscal Programs', p. 516).
57. Ibid., p. 520.
58. The use of Federal greenbacks as medium of exchange or store of value represented a real loss to the South. If they had not served as currency (that is, if Confederate issues had monopolized the monetary function) the greenbacks in Southern hands could have secured more resources for the Confederacy by purchases abroad or through the lines.
59. Schwab, Ch. 8.
60. Ibid., p. 164.
61. Schwab, p. 180. Physical difficulty of transportation was also an important explanation for this disparity.
62. Todd, p. 169.
63. Schwab, pp. 200–1; Eaton, p. 264.
64. Lerner, 'Monetary and Fiscal Programs', p. 509.
65. Eaton, p. 251.
66. Ibid., p. 264.
67. Ibid., pp. 271–3; Schwab, p. 224.
68. It is worth remarking here that Union policy toward enemy finances in the Civil War was much more intelligent than the corresponding Allied policy in World War II. In the occupation of enemy territories during World War II, it was Allied practice to introduce new currency at par with the old, the latter continuing to play a major role as the circulating medium. Since enemy governments (for example, Mussolini's 'Fascist Republic') held the plates for old currency, they were able to produce claims upon the resources behind the Allied lines simply by printing more notes. See W. D. Grampp, 'The Italian Lira', *Journal of Political Economy*, LIV (August 1946), p. 322. (The old currency, being valid on both sides of the fighting lines, had superior acceptability for this reason as well as having the advantage of familiarity.) Repudiation of the enemy currency would have impaired its utility and thus would have diminished the real revenue

obtainable by the enemy through his printing press.
69. The main source used for this section is Eugene M. Lerner, 'Southern Output and Agricultural Income, 1860–80', in Andreano (ed.), *Economic Impact of the American Civil War*. A secondary source is James L. Sellers, 'The Economic Incidence of the Civil War in the South', ibid.
70. Andreano, p. 181.
71. Lerner, in ibid., p. 97.
72. Major sources used in this section were Jerome B. Cohen, *Japan's Economy in War and Reconstruction* (Minneapolis: University of Minnesota Press, 1949), and *Japan's Postwar Economy* (Bloomington, Indiana: Indiana University Press, 1958); G. C. Allen, *Japan's Economic Recovery* (London: Oxford University Press, 1958); and United States Strategic Bombing Survey, *The Effects of Strategic Bombing on Japan's War Economy* (December 1946).
73. There were 5296 thousands of gross tons of shipping operable on 7 December 1941. In addition, 3293 thousands of gross tons of new shipping was built during the war, and 822 thousands captured or salvaged — a total of 9411 thousands of gross tons. Of this total, 8617 thousands or 91.6 per cent were sunk during the war (Cohen, *War and Reconstruction*, p. 267).
74. Ibid., p. 107. However, the Strategic Bombing Survey pointed out that the economic effectiveness of air attack was limited by the mission assigned to it. To facilitate a ground force invasion of Japan anticipated for the near future, the bombing plan dictated attacks on such targets as oil refineries, aircraft plants, etc. Had the mission of the air attack been to contribute optimally to the economic collapse of Japan, an attack on land transport systems (especially rail) would have intensified the effects of the sea blockade (USSBS, *Japan's War Economy*, p. 3).
75. Cohen, *War and Reconstruction*, p. 144.
76. Ibid., p. 107.
77. Ibid., p. 386.
78. It has been estimated that 80 per cent of all perishables were sold on the black market towards the end of the war (Cohen, *War and Reconstruction*, p. 378).
79. Ibid.
80. Ibid., p. 359.
81. Ibid., p. 374.
82. The note issue as of 15 August 1945, when the war ended, has been reported at 30 billion yen (Cohen, *Japan's Postwar Economy*, p. 84), representing only a five-fold multiplication of the figure for 31 December 1941. Unfortunately, we have only the year-end figure for bank deposits, but it is believed that in the case of deposits there is not a large disparity between the figures for the two dates. These considerations lead to the conclusion that total money supply was multiplied around 3½-fold in the wartime period proper. (It should be noted that certain contradictions appear in the statistics quoted for this unsettled period.)
83. Cohen, *War and Reconstruction*, p. 82.
84. United States Strategic Bombing Survey, *Final Report Covering Air-Raid Protection and Allied Subjects in Japan* (February 1947), p. 14.
85. The Basic Initial Post-Surrender Directive to SCAP, forwarded on 8 November 1945, specified: 'You will not assume any responsibility for

the economic rehabilitation of Japan or the strengthening of the Japanese economy.' Edwin M. Martin, *The Allied Occupation of Japan* (Stanford, California: Stanford University Press, 1948), p. 135.

86. This level was specified in a directive of 23 January 1947, at a time when the performance of the economy fell far short of that standard (Cohen, *War and Reconstruction*, p. 419).

87. Ibid., p. 368. There is some reason to believe, however, that the food crops may have been substantially understated because of diversion of production from legal channels into the black market.

88. USSBS, *Japan's War Economy*, p. 41.

89. Ibid., p. 84.

90. A very convincing indicator of the difference between the two periods is the contrast between Cohen's two volumes on the Japanese economy. *War and Reconstruction* (1949) is more than gloomy in its conclusions as to the prospects for Japanese recovery (pp. 501–4), while nothing could be more ebullient than the discussion of 'Japan's Amazing Recovery' (pp. 11–26) in *Postwar Economy* (1958).

91. Cohen, *War and Reconstruction*, p. 420.

92. Allen, p. 94.

93. Cohen, *War and Reconstruction*, pp. 421–6.

94. The scale of the agreements signifies the recent strength of Japan's economy. The agreement with Indonesia in 1957, for example, provided for payments of reparations in the amount of $225 million over a period of years, cancellation of Indonesian trade debt to Japan in the amount of $175 million, and Japanese loans and investments in Indonesia in the amount of $400 million (Cohen, *Postwar Economy*, p. 165).

95. Ibid.

96. Ibid., p. 500.

97. Aid amounted to over $2 billion between 1945 and 1951 when it terminated (Allen, p. 165).

98. Of course, simple inefficiency played a role, too. Cohen remarks that while Japan had been largely strangled by blockade in the last months of the war, peace brought with it absolute cessation of foreign supplies for a considerable period while SCAP worked out the regulations and procedures to permit trade to be conducted at all (Cohen, *War and Reconstruction*, p. 418).

99. In a Foreword to Cohen's *War and Reconstruction*, Sir George Sansom states that policy was originally to limit Japan's foreign trade, on a mixture of grounds: 'partly political, partly strategic and partly competitive' (p. ix). However, the text does not bear out this contention, nor does it seem to be confirmed elsewhere.

100. Cohen, *War and Reconstruction*, pp. 417–8.

101. Cohen, *Postwar Economy*, p. 84.

102. Cohen, *War and Reconstruction*, p. 431.

103. Ibid., p. 426. See also Allen, *Economic Recovery*, p. 139.

104. Cohen, *War and Reconstruction*, p. 429.

105. The capital levy rates rose to 90 per cent of the wealth in excess of 15 million yen (the yen at this time was fixed at 50 to the dollar). However, the progress of the inflation was so rapid that the real effect of the capital levy was considerably less than intended.

106. However, a Non-war Sufferers' Special Tax was enacted in 1947 to redress the balance somewhat. See Henry Shavell, 'Taxation Reform in Occupied Japan', *National Tax Journal*, I (1948), p. 139.
107. Allen, *Economic Recovery*, p. 52.
108. Absentee landlords were dispossessed completely; other landlords were permitted to retain only 1 *chobu* (2.5 acres) on the main islands. Owner-farmers could retain 3 *chobu* (ibid., p. 57).
109. In order to prevent a recurrence of landlordism, it was specified that the land so acquired could not be resold for thirty years except with official permission. Such a provision, tying the farmer to the land, is certainly reminiscent of the feudalism the programme was designed to attack. It also interferes with efficiency by making it difficult for the farmer to obtain credit, since land cannot be pledged as security.
110. This discussion is based upon Harry E. Wildes, *Typhoon in Tokyo* (New York: Macmillan, 1954), pp. 269–316.
111. Cohen, *War and Reconstruction*, p. 455.
112. Ibid., p. 449.
113. Debentures of the RFB, which began operations in January of 1947, rose to 131 billion yen by March 1949 (Cohen, *Postwar Economy*, p. 85).
114. In the 1949–50 fiscal year, they accounted for 202 billion of a total expenditure of 704 billion yen (Cohen, *Postwar Economy*, p. 86). Occupation costs were also a large budget item — it is not clear whether or not these costs were fully balanced by corresponding US credits, though we know that Japan accumulated a $2 billion debt because of Occupation costs.
115. Cohen, *War and Reconstruction*, p. 451.
116. The following statement by Ishibashi, one of the early Finance Ministers, exemplifies the reasoning employed: 'The advance of commodity prices is caused more by the decrease of commodities than by the expansion of currency. Therefore, relief must be sought more in the increase of goods than in curtailing the amount of currency, and for that reason an expansion policy becomes more necessary than retrenchment'. From 'Danger of Retrenchment Policy', *Zaisei*, Tokyo (December 1945), as quoted in Cohen, *War and Reconstruction*, p. 450.
117. Cohen, *Postwar Economy*, p. 88.
118. About one-third to one-half of the 1946 national income was believed to have been transacted on the black market (Shavell, p. 129).
119. The main sources employed were Harold Zink, *The United States in Germany 1944–1955* (Toronto, Canada: Van Nostrand, 1957); Lucius D. Clay, *Decision in Germany* (Garden City, New Jersey: Doubleday, 1950); H. C. Wallich, *Mainsprings of the German Revival* (New Haven: Yale University Press, 1955); Horst Mendershausen, *Two Postwar Recoveries of the German Economy* (Amsterdam: North-Holland Publishing Co., 1955), and 'Prices, Money and the Distribution of Goods in Post-war Germany', *American Economic Review*, XXXIX, 646–72; B. H. Klein, *Germany's Economic Preparations for War* (Cambridge, Mass.: Harvard University Press, 1959); United States Strategic Bombing Survey, *The Effects of Strategic Bombing on the German War Economy* (1945); and Manuel Gottlieb, *The German Peace Settlement and the Berlin Crisis* (New York: Paine-Whitman Publishers, 1960).

120. Klein, pp. 156–7.
121. Wallich, p. 64. Of course, this is not a fully satisfactory criterion of a successful control system. Ruthless suppression of black markets may well be associated with paralysis of legal trade as well.
122. Klein, pp. 173–205.
123. The rate of industrial production in the American zone from May through December 1945 was estimated at 5 per cent of normal. Zink, p. 254.
124. Eugene Davidson, *The Death and Life of Germany* (New York: Knopf, 1959), p. 51.
125. Ibid., p. 53. A substantial fraction of these could not or would not return to their country of origin. One of the most cruel features of the period was the forced repatriation of Russian and East European nationals.
126. See text of JCS/1067 in Carl J. Friedrich and Associates, *American Experiences in Military Government in World War II* (New York: Rinehart, 1948), pp. 385–95.
127. Clay p. 203. General Clay remarks that this indicated a degree of 'public confidence perhaps not warranted by the facts'. Most of these deposits were wiped out in the currency reform of 1948.
128. Wallich, pp. 171–2.
129. Zink, p. 253.
130. Clay, p. 266.
131. An interesting technique, used to estimate the degree of general malnutrition, was the employment of teams to stop Germans in the street for random weighings.
132. One example will have to suffice on this point. General Clay makes repeated reference to the interdependent coal and food problems: it was difficult to keep men working and productive in the coal mines when they lacked food, while lack of coal hindered transportation and industrial activities essential for maintaining food output. However, it is doubtful that the vicious circle was technological in origin. In postwar Germany there were many essentially unemployed labourers who could have been attracted to the coal mines by a higher real wage. It was the effective abandonment of the money-wage mechanism, with rationing of all important consumer goods, that made it impossible to offer a higher real wage to recruit coal miners (and the low fixed product price for coal largely eliminated any incentive toward unusual efforts on the part of the coal firms).
133. Dale Clark, 'Conflicts over Planning at Staff Headquarters', in Friedrich, pp. 220–31.
134. Clay, p. 11.
135. Ibid., pp. 41–2.
136. Clay, pp. 108–9.
137. Zink, p. 258.
138. Clay, p. 108.
139. Klein, p. 115.
140. Clay, p. 322.
141. Wallich, p. 370. The total number of plants in the Western zones finally removed was around 700, compared with original plans to dismantle some 1500.
142. Ibid., p. 359.
143. Gustav Stolper, *German Realities* (New York: Reynal and Hitchcock, 1948), p. 85.

144. Davidson, pp. 166 ff.
145. Mabel Newcomer, 'War and Postwar Developments in the German Tax System', *National Tax Journal*, vol. 1 (March 1948), pp. 1–2. Gottlieb estimates the drain at about 10 per cent of overall industrial output in the bizonal area, and at over 25 per cent of social product for the Soviet and French zones (Gottlieb, p. 69).
146. Wallich, p. 361. Wallich points out, however, that the Occupation levy may be regarded as a rather cheap substitute for German defence expenditure.
147. Clay, p. 188.
148. Ibid., p. 216.
149. Wallich, pp. 355–7. See also Zink, p. 263.
150. 'Foreign trade had practically ceased and come to be replaced largely by the intake of foreign relief and the outgo of foreign levies.' Mendershausen, 'Prices, Money, and Goods', p. 646.
151. Clay, p. 197.
152. Ibid., p. 198.
153. In some circumstances multiple exchange rates may represent an efficient way for a country to reap extra advantages from international trade. The difficulty here lay in the link between the exchange rate system and the internal price ceilings.
154. Wallich, p. 362. A similar situation existed with respect to timber exports (Gottlieb, p. 68).
155. Clay, pp. 260–1.
156. Ibid., p. 330.
157. A land reform programme was also carried out in the American zone. Its effects were minor, in as much as the agriculture of the zone, to begin with, was practically free of large-scale farming.
158. Clay, p. 73.
159. Newcomer, pp. 3–4.
160. Howard P. Jones, 'Currency, Banking, Domestic and Foreign Debt', in Edward H. Litchfield and Associates, *Governing Postwar Germany* (Ithaca, New York: Cornell University Press, 1953), p. 419.
161. Though, it must be recalled, Germans were generally quite well fed at least until 1945, in contrast with the wartime experience of the European populations under German domination.
162. OMGUS (Office of Military Government, US) Special Report: 'A Plan for the Liquidation of War Finance and the Financial Rehabilitation of Germany' (20 May 1946). See Clay, pp. 209–10. Aside from the scaling-down of currency, the report proposed a progressive capital levy for equitably redistributing wealth so as to equalize war burdens. Reich debt was to be repudiated. See Gottlieb, pp. 112–15.
163. There were characteristic divergences between the different national policies. The Russians favoured rigid price ceilings as a device to make private production unprofitable; they set up Soviet corporations in their zone, and exempted these from the price regulations. The Americans approached the problem with a dogged 'hold-the-line' spirit. The British, appreciating the economic advantages of price increases but also concerned for the political effects of any relaxation, had a vacillating policy. See Mendershausen, 'Prices, Money, and Goods', p. 648.
164. Klein, p. 154.

165. Prices were not absolutely rigid, though the movement was very small. A wartime cost-of-living index calculated at legal prices showed 1943 as 110 per cent of 1936 (ibid.), while a post-war index showed May 1948 as 131 per cent of 1938 (Mendershausen, 'Prices, Money, and Goods', p. 649).
166. Newcomer, p. 8; Jones, p. 424.
167. Mendershausen, 'Prices, Money, and Goods', p. 652.
168. Ibid., p. 653.
169. Ibid., p. 655.
170. Clay, p. 195.
171. Alternatively, the abandonment of price controls in the absence of currency reform would have led to a rapid shift to a higher price level, but not to a progressive inflation, given continued budgetary conservatism. It appears, from the rather hostile description in Gottlieb's book, that British financial advisers favoured this solution. Gottlieb, pp. 107 ff.
172. Clay, p. 191.
173. For a contrary contemporary view, see F. A. Burchardt and K. Martin, 'Western Germany and Reconstruction', *Bulletin of the Oxford Institute of Statistics*, vol. 9 (December 1947), pp. 405–16.
174. Clay, pp. 208–9.
175. When Allied fighting forces entered Germany, they were supplied with military marks for use in making local purchases; troops were permitted, also, to draw part of their pay in military marks for personal use. The Allied military mark circulated freely in the German economy at par with the Reichsmark. The Western Allies were all supplied with marks from one accountable source, but upon Soviet demand, a duplicate set of plates with inks and paper was provided to the Russian authorities. The Soviets proceeded to print large quantities of marks and refused any accounting or settlement. Since Allied military marks were convertible into US dollars by American personnel (the Soviets did not permit conversion into roubles), the marks came by various means into the hands of US personnel. General Clay indicates (p. 63) that $300 million of such notes were converted; on this interpretation, the Soviets had in effect printed up this quantity of US dollars for their own purposes. Gottlieb casts doubt on Clay's assertion, however. He argues that the actual amount converted is inconsistently reported in various documents and that there were other possible sources of 'excess' marks, mainly unrecorded issues by Western Allied military or occupation authorities (Gottlieb, pp. 117–21). Gottlieb considers the Russian source to have been at least a contributing factor, however, and in any case the Americans were unwilling to take a similar risk again.
176. Initial allotments were made on a per capita basis to individuals, and on the basis of a variety of formulas to businesses and government units.
177. For a general discussion of these points, see Mendershausen, 'Prices, Money, and Goods', pp. 659–69.
178. Clay, p. 214.
179. Wallich, p. 71. See also Jones, p. 425.
180. Heller, p. 215.
181. Stolper, p. 95.
182. Mendershausen, 'Prices, Money, and Goods', p. 646.
183. Mendershausen reports that for other (presumably more or less compar-

able) countries (but excluding Japan) industrial production indexes were generally better than 75 per cent of pre-war *by 1947*. ('Prices, Money, and Goods', p. 647.) Table 1.18 indicates that the German index was only 45 on a 1938 base for the first half of *1948* (pre-reform).

184. Ibid.
185. Gottlieb, pp. 7–8.
186. Gottlieb indicates that waste and misdirection were worst or at any rate most harmful precisely in those industries subject to the most thoroughgoing controls — the coal–steel complex. Ibid., p. 78. This curiously parallels the experience under Russian War communism reported earlier.
187. Rather inconsistently perhaps, Gottlieb argues at one point that reform was desirable in enlarging the role of markets and of decentralized decision making (pp. 98 ff.) — a view more in consonance with that expressed here.
188. As an illustration of the difficulty of the learning process, consider the following. Burckhardt, writing in 1852, reports that in the disaster year 302 the annals record that 'the Emperors at that time commanded that there should be cheapness'. Their edict declared: 'Unprincipled greed appears wherever our armies, following the commands of the public weal, march, not only in villages and cities but also upon all highways, with the result that prices of foodstuffs mount not only fourfold and eightfold, but transcend all measure.... Our law shall fix a measure and a limit to this greed.' Burckhardt goes on to comment: 'The inevitable consequences ensued. Goods were hidden, despite the prohibition they grew dearer than ever, and countless sellers were made liable to the death penalty, until the law was rescinded.' Jacob Burckhardt, *The Age of Constantine the Great* (Garden City: Doubleday, 1956), pp. 51–2. Despite the accumulation of at least 1600 years of historical knowledge of the behaviour of economies under disaster conditions with inflated money supplies, Allied military government attempted to impose price controls upon the disrupted Italian economy during the course of World War II, with equivalent lack of success. See William D. Grampp, 'The Italian Lira, 1938–45', *Journal of Political Economy*, vol. 54 (August 1946), pp. 309–33. In the event of thermonuclear attack on the United States, the National Plan for Civil Defense and Defense Mobilization calls for institution of a universal price freeze to 'stabilize' the post-attack economy.
189. Aside from St Pierre in modern times, there are ancient examples such as Melos and Babylon. An interesting case is Carthage, which revived as a Roman city only after a century of desolation.
190. 'The possibility of a rapid repair of their disasters, mainly depends on whether the country has been depopulated. If its effective population have not been extirpated at the time, and are not starved afterwards; then, with the same skill and knowledge which they had before, with their land and its permanent improvements undestroyed, and the more durable buildings probably unimpaired, or only partially damaged, they have nearly all the requisites for their former amount of production.' *Principles of Political Economy* (New York: J. A. Hill & Co., 1904), Book I, Ch. 5.
191. 'There is nothing at all wonderful in the matter. What the enemy have destroyed, would have been destroyed in a little time by the inhabitants

themselves: the wealth which they so rapidly reproduce, would have
needed to be reproduced and would have been reproduced in any case,
and probably in as short a time. Nothing is changed, except that during
the reproduction they have not now the advantage of consuming what
had been produced previously.' Ibid.
192. Ibid.

BIBLIOGRAPHY

Allen, G. C., *Japan's Economic Recovery* (London: Oxford University Press,
     1958).
Andreano, Ralph (ed.), *The Economic Impact of the American Civil War*
     (Cambridge, Mass.: Schenkman Publishing Co., 1962).
Arnold, A. Z., *Banks, Credit, and Money in Soviet Russia* (New York:
     Columbia University Press, 1937).
Baykov, A., *The Development of the Soviet Economic System* (Cambridge,
     Mass.: Harvard University Press, 1937).
British Mission to Japan, Report of, *The Effects of the Atomic Bombs at
     Hiroshima and Nagasaki* (1946).
Burchardt, F. A. and Martin, K., 'Western Germany and Reconstruction',
     Bulletin of the Oxford Institute of Statistics, vol. 9 (December 1947),
     pp. 405–16.
Burckhardt, Jacob, *The Age of Constantine the Great*, trans. Moses Hadas
     (Garden City, N.J.: Doubleday, 1956).
Cagan, Phillip, 'The Monetary Dynamics of Hyperinflation', in Milton Friedman
     (ed.), *Studies in the Quantity Theory of Money* (Chicago: University of
     Chicago Press, 1956).
Cairncross, A. K., 'The Economic Recovery of Western Germany', *Lloyds
     Bank Review* (October 1951).
Carr, E. H., *The Bolshevik Revolution, 1917–1923*, vol. 2 (London: Macmillan,
     1952).
Clay, Lucius D., *Decision in Germany* (Garden City, N.J.: Doubleday, 1950).
Cohen, Jerome B., *Japan's Economy in War and Reconstruction* (Minneapolis:
     University of Minnesota Press, 1949).
—— , *Japan's Postwar Economy* (Bloomington, Ind.: Indiana University Press,
     1958).
Coulter, E. Merton, *The Confederate States of America, 1861–1865* (Baton
     Rouge, La.: Louisiana State University Press, 1950).
Davidson, Eugene, *The Death and Life of Germany* (New York: Knopf, 1959).
Demerath, N. J. and Wallace, A. F. C. (eds.), 'Human Adaptation to Disaster',
     Human Organization, vol. 16 (Summer 1957).
Dobb, M., *Soviet Economic Development Since 1917* (New York: International
     Publishers, 1948).
Eaton, Clement, *A History of the Southern Confederacy* (New York: Macmillan,
     1954).
Friedrich, Carl J. and Associates, *American Experiences in Military Government
     in World War II* (New York: Rinehart, 1948).
Gottlieb, Manuel, *The German Peace Settlement and the Berlin Crisis* (New
     York: Paine-Whitman Publishers, 1960).

Grampp, W. D. 'The Italian Lira, 1938–45', *Journal of Political Economy*, vol. 54 (August 1946).

Grosser, Alfred, *The Colossus Again*, trans. Richard Rees (New York: Frederick A. Praeger, 1955).

Heller, Walter W., 'Tax and Monetary Reform in Occupied Germany', *National Tax Journal*, vol. 2 (1949).

Hiroshima Publishing Company, *Hiroshima* (1949).

Iklé, F. C., *The Social Impact of Bomb Destruction* (Norman, Okla: University of Oklahoma Press, 1958).

Jones, Howard P., 'Currency, Banking, Domestic and Foreign Debt', in Edward H. Litchfield and Associates, *Governing Postwar Germany* (Ithaca, N.Y.: Cornell University Press, 1953).

Kahn, Herman, *On Thermonuclear War* (Princeton, N.J.: Princeton University Press, 1960).

Kirwan, Albert D. (ed.), *The Confederacy* (New York: Meridian Books, 1959).

Klein, Burton H., *Germany's Economic Preparations for War* (Cambridge, Mass.: Harvard University Press, 1959).

Lerner, Eugene M., 'The Monetary and Fiscal Programs of the Confederate Government, 1861–65', *Journal of Political Economy*, vol. 62 (December 1954).

——, 'Money, Prices and Wages in the Confederacy, 1861–65', *Journal of Political Economy*, vol. 63 (February 1955).

Lorimer, Frank, *The Population of the Soviet Union* (Geneva: League of Nations, 1946).

Martin, Edwin M., *The Allied Occupation of Japan* (Stanford, Calif.: Stanford University Press, 1948).

Massey, M. E., *Ersatz in the Confederacy* (Columbia, S.C.: University of South Carolina Press, 1952).

Mendershausen, Horst, 'Prices, Money and the Distribution of Goods in Postwar Germany', *American Economic Review*, vol. 39 (June 1949).

——, *Two Postwar Recoveries of the German Economy* (Amsterdam: North-Holland Publishing Co., 1955).

Mill, John Stuart, *Principles of Political Economy* (2 vols.) (New York: J. A. Hill & Co., 1904).

Newcomer, Mabel, 'War and Postwar Developments in the German Tax System', *National Tax Journal*, vol. 1 (March 1948).

Nutter, G. Warren, *Growth of Industrial Production in the Soviet Union* (Princeton, N.J.: Princeton University Press, 1962).

OMGUS (Office of Military Government, U.S.) Special Report: 'A Plan for the Liquidation of War Finance and the Financial Rehabilitation of Germany' (20 May 1946).

Popper, R. D. and Lybrand, W. A., *An Inventory of Selected Source Materials Relevant to Integration of Physical and Social Effects of Air Attack*, Human Sciences Research, Inc. (October 1960).

Prince, S. H., *Catastrophe and Social Change* (New York: Columbia University Press, 1920).

Rayner, Jeannette, 'Annotated Bibliography on Disaster Research', *Human Organization*, vol. 16 (Summer 1957).

Schwab, John C., *The Confederate States of America, 1861–65: A Financial and Industrial History of the South During the Civil War* (New York: Scribner's, 1901).

Shavell, Henry, 'Taxation Reform in Occupied Japan', *National Tax Journal*, vol. 1 (1948).
Shiomi, Saburo, *Japan's Finance and Taxation, 1940–1956*, trans. S. Hasegawa (New York: Columbia University Press, 1957).
Sorokin, Pitirim A., *The Sociology of Revolution* (Philadelphia: Lippincott, 1925).
Statisches Jahrbuch für die Bundesrepublik Deutschland, 1961.
Stolper, Gustav, *German Realities* (New York: Reynal and Hitchcock, 1948).
Todd, Richard C., *Confederate Finance* (Athens, Ga.: University of Georgia Press, 1954).
United Nations, *Patterns of Industrial Growth 1938–1958* (New York: United Nations, 1960).
United Nations, *Demographic Yearbook (1960)* (New York: 1961).
United States Strategic Bombing Survey, *The Effects of Atomic Bombs at Hiroshima and Nagasaki* (1946).
——, *The Effects of Strategic Bombing on the German War Economy*, Overall Economic Effects Division (31 October 1945).
——, *The Effects of Strategic Bombing on Japan's War Economy*, Overall Economic Effects Division (December 1946).
——, *Final Report Covering Air-Raid Protection and Allied Subjects in Japan*, Civil Defense Division (February 1947).
——, *Over-all Report (European War)* (30 September 1945).
Wallich, Henry, C., *Mainsprings of the German Revival* (New Haven: Yale University Press, 1955).
Wildes, Harry E., *Typhoon in Tokyo* (New York: Macmillan, 1954).
Winter, Sidney G., Jr, *Economic Viability After Thermonuclear War: The Limits of Feasible Production*, The RAND Corporation, RM-3436-PR (September 1963).
Zink, Harold, *The United States in Germany, 1944–1955* (Toronto, Canada: Van Nostrand, 1957).

2   Disaster and Recovery: The Black Death in Western Europe*

*   *   *

Background of this Chapter

This RAND study is an extension of the previous paper's historical
analysis of the disaster-recovery process. Though sponsored by the US
Atomic Energy Commission rather than the Air Force, like the previous
paper it was produced under conditions of complete intellectual
freedom.

*   *   *

INTRODUCTION**

A previous RAND study examined a number of great disasters of
modern times[1] in order to explore such questions as: (1) How rapid
and successful were the recoveries from disaster? (2) Which government
policies promoted, and which hindered, recovery? (3) To what extent
was the loss due to disaster (or the failure to recover from disaster) an
unavoidable consequence of the narrowed technological possibilities
and resources of the post-disaster society, and to what extent was it
the consequence of organizational failures and mistakes in the utilization
of surviving resources? The major conclusion arrived at was that, in
the instances examined, rather prompt recovery (say, within four or
five years) to pre-disaster levels of well-being was technologically
possible and did, in fact, take place, with some 'slippage' due mostly
to avoidable mistakes in monetary policies.

* Originally distributed as The RAND Corporation Memorandum RM-4700–TAB
(February 1966). Views or conclusions contained in this Memorandum should not be
interpreted as representing the official opinion or policy of the Atomic Energy
Commission. Reproduced by permission of The RAND Corporation.
** In the body and footnotes to this paper, citations will be given in abbreviated form.
Full descriptions of sources may be found in the Bibliography.

Table 2.1   Chronology[a]

1310–22	Wars of Edward II, King of England, with Scottish and Irish barons.
1324	Fighting with French in Aquitaine.
1327	Revolt in England. Abdication and murder of Edward II, King of England; accession of Edward III.
1328–36	English intervene in Scottish dynastic conflict.
1328	Accession of Philip VI, King of France.
1328	French suppress peasant insurrection in Flanders.
1336	*Beginning of Hundred Years' War.*
1337	English support revolt in Flanders.
1341	Fighting in Brittany begins between English and French candidates for dukedom.
1346	English victory over Scots at Neville's Cross; and over French at Crécy.
1348–50	*Black Death.*
1350	Death of Philip VI, King of France; accession of John II.
1356	English victory at Poitiers; John II of France captured.
1357–59	Near-anarchy in France. *Jacquerie* suppressed. Dynastic intrigues of Charles the Bad, King of Navarre. Du Guesclin's tactics exhaust English.
1360	Truce of Brétigny.
1360–61	*Recurrence of plague.*
1364	Death of John II, King of France; accession of Charles V.
1367–69	Fighting in Spain ends in victory of French-backed contender, Don Henry.
1369	*Recurrence of plague.*
1369–75	Resumption of Hundred Years' War; French successes.

This, like other related RAND studies,[2] was intended to cast some light on the aftermath of the great potential disaster of our age — thermonuclear war. No disaster of modern times, however, really compares to a large-scale nuclear war, in geographic scope, suddenness of impact and intensity of effect. There are, of course, a number of historical instances of violent destruction of particular cities (for example, Hiroshima in World War II). There are also some examples of substantial population declines over wider areas (for example, Ireland after the potato famine), but these latter instances have been more in the nature of slow decay than sudden destruction. The Black Death of 1348–50 was much closer to a hypothetical nuclear war in its geographical extent, abruptness of onset, and scale of casualties. Of course, in other important respects its impact was unlike that of nuclear war; in particular, there was no physical destruction of material property. (Thus, the Black Death is a closer analogy to *bacteriological* than to nuclear war.) And, in addition, the fourteenth century is so distant in time from the current period as to preclude the drawing of easy parallels. Nevertheless, we may hope that the study of even such a remote historical experience will help provide some depth of understand-

1374	*Recurrence of plague.*
1375	Truce of Bruges; English retain only Calais and small portion of Gascony.
1376	'Good Parliament' in England; independence of Commons.
1377	Death of Edward III, King of England; accession of Richard II.
1380	Death of Charles V, King of France; accession of Charles VI.
1381	Peasants' Revolt in England.
1382	French crush English-backed insurrection in Flanders.
1399	Revolt in England. Deposition of Richard II, accession of Henry IV.
1402–6	English defeat Scots.
1400–16	Revolt of Welsh suppressed.
1413	Cabochian riots in Paris.
1413	Death of Henry IV, King of England; accession of Henry VI. Resumption of war with France.
1415	English victory at Agincourt.
1418	English occupy Paris.
1420	Burgundians ally themselves with English.
1422	Death of Henry V, King of England; accession of Henry VI. Death of Charles VI, King of France; accession of Charles VII.
1429	French victory at Orleans; Joan of Arc.
1429–53	French gradually reconquer national territory.
1450	Jack Cade's Rebellion.
1453	*End of Hundred Years' War*; English retain only Calais.

Note:
[a] Based mainly on Previte-Orton, *Cambridge History*, Ch. 29, 33.

ing as to the human potentialities for recovery from great catastrophes. A point heightening interest in this historical episode is that it has been cited, by at least one author, in the course of a pessimistic evaluation of the prospect for recovery from the potential disaster of atomic war.[3]

Another difficulty in the evaluation of social consequences specific to the Black Death is the fact that the period in which it fell was one of great turbulence in Western Europe. The effects of the pestilence are not easily separable from those of the destructive Hundred Years' War; in addition, the Western European nations and especially England and France suffered also from internal dynastic conflicts, class warfare and regional separatism. Table 2.1 provides a chronology of the major events of the period surrounding the Black Death.

Finally, the reader must be warned that any attempt to evaluate the overall lessons to be drawn from complex phenomena such as disaster-recovery experiences must, necessarily, be in large part subjective and impressionistic. In the case at hand the force of this caveat is strengthened by the paucity and defects of the data available, together with all the other problems of comprehending individual and social behaviour in a social and historical context very different from our own.

THE BLACK DEATH

Throughout the historic period, plague has been endemic in certain permanent centres of infection. Three great outbreaks of the disease are recorded.[4] The first is the so-called plague of Justinian, which raged over the known world in the latter half of the sixth century. After this waned, human plague was for centuries almost unknown to Western Europe until the great pandemic of 1348–50. (Some maintain that there was a precursor plague around 1316.[5] Thereafter, repeated onslaughts recurred on a gradually diminishing scale; the last London plague was in 1665, and in Western Europe the last great outburst was at Marseilles in 1720. The third outbreak began around 1890 in China; in the West its effects have been held in check by modern sanitary knowledge.

Plague is primarily a disease of rodents, carried to man by the flea. Some historians have blamed the plague of 1348–50 upon the arrival of the rat in Europe, but others disagree.[6] The gradual decline of the disease over the following centuries has been attributed to the replacement of the black rat (*Rattus rattus*) by the brown rat (*Rattus norvegicus*). The latter, a better fighter, has driven out the former except on shipboard and in the vicinity of ports. From the human point of view, the brown rat is a less unpleasant neighbour, as it prefers to live out-of-doors — and even more important, its fleas have more aversion to biting human beings than do those of the black rat.[7]

Plague in human beings takes two main forms: bubonic and pneumonic (a third form, the septicemic, is sometimes reported). *Bubonic* plague is characterized by swellings (buboes), especially in the groin and armpits. This is the less fatal form, with a typical mortality rate of perhaps 50 per cent. It is not infectious from man to man but requires the intervention of the flea. The *pneumonic* form is seated in the lungs; it is extremely infectious and nearly always fatal. In the bubonic form an outbreak of the disease dies down in the winter, but in the pneumonic form it will rage more violently than ever in the cold season. Pneumonic plague is less common, but when it occurs the mortalities may be enormous; the Black Death itself was a combined attack of both forms of plague.

There have been some fluctuations of opinion over the years about the scale of mortality attendant upon the original plague of 1348–50, and the later visitations during the next quarter-century. The reports of contemporary chroniclers abound with tales of total or near-total depopulation, often still repeated in non-technical writings. Generally speaking, however, historians today place a more moderate estimate on the scale of casualties. Without necessarily dismissing all the early reports as fabulous, it is evident that there is a tendency for occasional

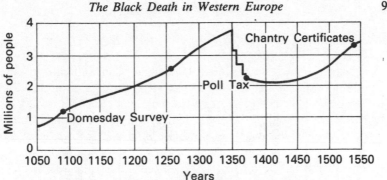

Figure 2.1 Trends of gross population in England

chronicles to record, even if they do not exaggerate, the extreme and unusual as opposed to the typical. Modern historians, in contrast, are in a position to base opinions on patchy but nevertheless rather extensive surviving manorial, legal and church documents.[8] The impression one gains from such records is that the Black Death proper carried off between a quarter and a third of the population of Western Europe, while the later attacks — the *Pestis Secunda* of 1360–61 and the plagues of 1369 and 1374[9] — may each have swept away around 5 per cent of the populations remaining.[10]

Russell's detailed study for England,[11] seemingly the only attempt to weigh the demographic evidence scientifically, comes to a somewhat different conclusion (see Table 2.2). Russell's data tend to discount the scale of the original Black Death somewhat (in comparison with the general opinion of scholars), and to magnify the later blows. The demographic factors, not previously appreciated, explaining the differences are: (1) making a proper allowance for age distribution of the initial populations and of the survivors, rather than simply averaging the documented mortality rates; and (2) deducting normal mortality. This latter is especially significant, since the Black Death extended over a period of 2 to 3 years. As Russell estimates the normal annual mortality at 3 per cent, this factor reduces the observed mortality rate of 23.6 per cent over the Black Death period to around 16.6 per cent, which may be interpreted as the proportionate 'excess mortality' associated with the disaster. Table 2.2 indicates that the 1369 visitation produced an excess mortality of 10.0 per cent in one year, a *per annum* rate greater than that of 1348–50. Cumulatively, the later attacks outweighed the Black Death itself. (See also Figure 2.1, reproduced from Russell's book.)

With respect to overall population trends, Postan (one of the leading students of this era) argues on the basis of price and occupancy data that population decline began some 30 years *before* the Black Death.[12]

Disaster and Recovery

Table 2.2 *Mortality and Population in England*[a]

	Mortality Rate in Period (per cent)	Normal Mortality in Period (per cent)	Excess Mortality in Period (per cent)	Population Remaining	Population Index (1348 = 1)
1348				3,757,500	1.0
Plague periods					
1348–50	23.6	7	16.6	3,127,500	0.836
1360–61	18.7	6	12.7	2,745,000	0.730
1369	13.0	3	10.0	2,452,500	0.657
1374	11.6	3	8.6	2,250,000	0.600

Notes:
[a] Data are reproduced as shown in the cited source. There seem to be minor discrepancies in the calculations. Also, the technique of deducting the 'normal' 3 per cent mortality is strictly correct only if the population would have been stationary under that mortality rate. (I am indebted to Russell T. Nichols for this point.)

Source: Russell, *British Medieval Population*, p. 263.

(The question of whether the plague *initiated* the population decrease of the following century takes on considerable importance in interpreting the evidence as to the post-disaster recovery or lack of recovery.) Russell admits some retardation in the rate of growth before 1348, but nevertheless his chart (Figure 2.1) shows a rising population curve to that date.[13]

The discussion of the Black Death and its aftermath as a disaster-recovery experience will be divided into two main headings. The first will take up the real or alleged *immediate and relatively early* consequences, distinguishing between social and political effects on the one hand and economic on the other. The timespan considered is up to perhaps a decade in length; during this period the line of causation, as to what are properly effects of the plague as such and what are coincidental consequences of other acting forces, is fairly clear. The next section will take up a much longer period, up to perhaps a century, in which *long-term* effects of the Black Death have been asserted to play a significant role. In dealing with this latter topic, the key problem will be to isolate the effects of the initial plague disaster from those of other events leaving their mark upon the same period.

AFTERMATH — THE EARLY PERIOD

There are curious divergences in the contemporary reporting of social and political events during and immediately after the Black Death. Some writers describe extremes of socially disruptive behaviour (flagellant cults, massacres of Jews,[14] flight of upper classes), whereas the reports of other chroniclers emphasize the continuity of established forms and institutions.[15] That there was some flight from the cities seems certain, and yet it is clear that government did not collapse. (One reason, perhaps, is that the disease did not strike a whole nation at once; in Britain it began in the southeast in the fall of 1348, waxed greatly while spreading north and west during 1349, and by 1350 was mostly limited to Scotland.) The following remarks on the enrolment of wills in London's Husting Court are suggestive of the course of the disease. They also signify the continuation of this bureaucratic function through all but a few months:

Those who died of the plague leaving wills were, of course, but a small fraction of the whole mortality; but the wills during some eight months of 1349 are ten or fifteen times more numerous than in any other year before or after, excepting perhaps the year of *pestis secunda*, 1361. Starting from 3 in November 1348 (none in December), the probates rise to 18 in January, 1349, 42 in February, 41 in March, none in April (owing to paralysis of business, doubtless), but 121 in May, 31 in June, 51 in July, none in August and September, 18 in October, 27 in November, and then an ordinary average.[16]

A similar continuity of agricultural records is shown by Miss Levett, who accordingly denies the earlier view that anarchy reigned in the countryside.[17]

The English Parliament was prorogued on account of the plague several times during 1349; it did not meet again until 1351. However, a considerable number of ordinances and decrees on economic matters were issued by the King's Council in 1349 and 1350. The Hundred Years' War was in a period of truce, but in the last days of 1349 Edward III led troops in combat before Calais. During 1350 a great feast was held at Windsor to celebrate the institution of the Order of the Garter. Also during this year, extensive military and naval preparations were organized, and a Spanish fleet was defeated in a great engagement. Froissart reports great celebrations in France upon the accession of John II (1350); the Order of the Star was instituted about this time. The French *parlement*, which ordinarily convened only when the King needed funds, did not meet until 1355. In that year, it issued large grants for the conduct of the war. Also in 1355 began the campaign of the Black Prince that ended in the great English victory at Poitiers (1356). It is evident from this recital that paralysis of government in England and France, if it occurred at all, was limited to the period when the plague was actually raging.

Turning to the economic impact of the disaster, traditional doctrine tells us that the equilibrium rate of wages must have risen consequent upon the new scarcity of labour. And a rapid rise in wages certainly did occur. The following is illustrative (data refer to England):

Threshing will be taken as being the most significant type of labour ... Up to the time of the Great Plague, threshing was paid at steady, and on the whole low, rates. But directly afterward the wages were doubled. The increase due to the plague is 32 per cent for the threshing of wheat, 38 per cent for barley, 111 per cent for oats in the eastern counties. In the middle counties the percentages of rise are 40, 69, 111; in the south, 33, 38, 75; in the west, 26, 41, 44; in the north, 32, 43, and 100.[18]

One of the most interesting developments was the Statute of Labourers in England (1351), a parliamentary enactment that had been anticipated by an ordinance of the King's Council in 1349.[19] The Statute fixed wages at the pre-disaster level, forbade idleness, and required reasonable prices for necessities. It would appear that serious efforts were made for some years to enforce these regulations.[20] The French Statute of Labourers[21] had a similar origin, but seems to have been largely a dead letter. That per capita income of the lower classes (the vast majority, of course) tended to rise is evidenced by innumerable reports of individuals of lower status stepping up to fill vacant places, of remissions and recontracts of feudal dues, as well as by complaints against unwontedly lavish living by 'wasters' and *nouveaux riches*.[22] Correspondingly, however, the scarcity of labour led to falling rents.[23] As a result, high-status individuals tended to suffer diminution of income.

In the aftermath, economic as well as political recovery from the crisis took place promptly. Agriculture was of course the overwhelmingly dominant industry; vacant manorial places were rapidly filled by a general upgrading of holdings, with abandonment of some marginal lands no longer worthy of cultivation by the thinned labour force. Direct evidence on trade and industry is largely lacking, but the ability of the English and French kings to call for and obtain renewed support for military campaigns (see above) seems to deny the possibility of any but short-lived paralysis in the non-agricultural sectors. It appears that competition was lively between country and town for scarce labour, newly 'mobilized' by the widened opportunities everywhere.[24]

AFTERMATH — LONG-TERM

Several authors have asserted that the short-term recovery from the Black Death, described above, was but temporary or illusory and that a long-lasting depression set in shortly thereafter.[25] Others, without necessarily tying the onset of the recession to the event of the Black Death, have maintained that the century following 1350 was generally depressed.[26] There are two great questions about this 'economic depression of the Renaissance': First, did it really occur? And second, if so, was the Black Death its cause?

There has been a lively controversy among economic historians as to whether the century following the Black Death was in actuality a period of economic recession. In view of the reduced population, that *aggregate* production was on the whole lower in 1350–1450 than in 1250–1350 is obvious but hardly relevant; the question at issue is whether there was a depression in the sense of impoverishment — whether per capita production fell. Historians writing on this topic have, regrettably often, been unable to keep these two questions apart and may thus have debated at cross-purposes.[27] The following points, however, can be regarded as established in comparing the century after 1350 with the century before. (1) A great *increase* in real wages and the standard of living of the labouring classes, both rural and urban,

Table 2.3 Daily Wages of Agricultural Labour on the Estates of the Bishops of Winchester

Years	Index of wages in silver pence	Index of wages in grains of silver	Index of wages in wheat
1300–19	100	100	100
1320–39	124	125	140
1340–59	133	117	148
1360–79	169	142	154
1380–99	188	153	235
1400–19	189	143	210
1420–39	189	130	200
1440–59	189	125	236

Note: Postan, 'Some Economic Evidence', p. 226. The index in grains of silver has been calculated from other data in the source.

took place;[28] (2) A very considerable *decline* in rents, and therefore in the incomes of the propertied classes, also occurred.[29] In short, the long-term effects paralleled the short-term ones with respect to the relative position of the two great social classes.

The first of these points and, by implication, the second are illustrated by the English data in Table 2.3 showing wage indexes in nominal monetary units, in grains of silver, and in wheat. Postan remarks, in a footnote, that the figures probably understate true wages in the period during which the Statute of Labourers was effective (presumably, the first decade or two after 1350) as the Bishop tended to make a show of conformity while actually evading the law.

The fall in the price of wheat relative to wages, that provides quantitative support for the innumerable reports of declining land rents, is also displayed by the data in Table 2.4. Note that the wheat price indexes also reach a peak in the 1301–50 period, falling steadily thereafter until 1500.

Among the points that may be regarded as still in doubt are the *overall* behaviour of per capita income when rising wages and falling rents are considered together. There is another interesting question, the relative prosperity of towns versus countryside, on which the historical authorities seem hopelessly divided. Langer argues that a depression in agriculture took place first, leading to a massive movement of rural population to the towns.[30] Postan denies that any net movement took place; also, he indicates that urban and rural wages rose in about the same proportion.[31] Creighton emphasizes disparities from one town

Table 2.4 Wheat Prices and Real Wages

Years	Index of wheat prices, France (1721–45 = 100)	Index of wheat prices, England (1721–45 = 100)	Index of real wages, England[a] (1721–45 = 100)
1201–50	41.9	35.8	—
1251–1300	51.5	47.8	110.0
1301–50	75.9	53.1	115.7
1351–1400	65.4	43.9	145.7
1401–50	61.7	36.1	182.9
1451–1500	31.8	27.7	170.0
1501–50	57.8	30.0	182.9[b]

Notes:
[a] Threshing labour, piecework.
[b] This figure is perhaps a typographical error. Other sources agree that real wages were significantly *lower* for this period.
Source: Slicher van Bath, pp. 326–7.

to the next.[32] Robbins draws a contrast between an urbanization trend in England, and urban depopulation due to war and brigandage in France.[33] Herlihy reports a greater decline of the rural than the urban population of Pistoia in Italy.[34]

In the hundred years 1350–1450, on *a priori* grounds there would have been considerable reason to anticipate a rather definite increase in per capita income overall. First, the short-term aftermath of the disaster in all probability led to a jump in real per capita wealth — recovery from the crisis was associated with a general upgrading of holdings. Since population did not increase rapidly thereafter (see Figure 2.1), the continuing long-term trend of improvement in technology, plus the possibilities for reallocating resources in line with the changed availabilities of land and labour, could operate without encountering increased numbers of mouths to feed. Leaving aside the question of whether an overall reduction in per capita income may have taken place, it would appear that failure to achieve a marked *increase* in this period may have been a significant development lending some support to pessimistic views of the ability of societies to recover from massive disasters.

A number of hypotheses have been put forward to explain what seems to be a lagging pace of economic development in Western Europe during the hundred years after 1350. Hypotheses involving forces other than the Black Death will here be considered first, after which an attempt will be made to place the role of the Black Death in its proper perspective.

Apart from the plague, war is the most obvious factor damaging the Western European economies during this period. England was heavily burdened by wars with Scotland, Spain and the Hanseatic League, and rebellions in Ireland and Wales in addition to the conflict in France; furthermore, the final outcomes were mainly adverse for her. But France was even more severely affected by the repeated ravages of the armies of England and her separatist allies, not to mention recurrent class conflicts and periods of near-anarchy. The evidence that most strongly suggests the impact of war is the comparative fate of urbanization in England and France during this period. For England the records of city growth in the century after 1350 are very uneven; some towns, and especially Norwich (previously the second city in the kingdom), declined sharply,[35] while others, including Bristol and Coventry, definitely grew. London is reported as 'no less populous'.[36] By way of contrast, the French territory involved in the Hundred Years' War was largely depopulated, and Paris itself seemed almost deserted in the fifteenth century.[37] One author contrasts the war-caused destruction in France with an asserted rapid growth of urbanization and industrialization in England.[38]

A second economic drag upon the recovering society has been emphasized by several authors: the *continuing* drain represented by the onslaughts of plague following the Black Death itself.[39] The great pandemics of 1361, 1369 and 1374 have already been mentioned; and recurrences of considerable magnitude continued, on a gradually declining scale, for centuries. The impact of this upon levels of per capita well-being (limiting the discussion to the purely material elements of loss) would be due primarily to the wholly or partially wasted investments in child-rearing, and in education and training.[40] It is true that the impact of early mortalities is less in an agricultural society than it would be in an industrial community, because of the lesser degree of training involved as well as the earlier start of productive contributions on the part of the child. Even so, the loss must have been very considerable. A further point worth noting is that recurrences of plague disproportionately attacked the young, presumably because older individuals tended to possess some degree of natural or acquired immunity.

A third independent cause of decline has been suggested: that there may have been an adverse climatic change in Western Europe beginning in the fourteenth century.[41] There is indeed some evidence that a cooler, wetter phase set in about this time in the North Atlantic area. The climate of Greenland and Iceland definitely deteriorated. As for

England, cultivation of vineyards for wine was still at its height in the thirteenth century, but had disappeared by 1400.[42] (As an incidental point of interest, it is possible that the onset of plague in the fourteenth century and its decline in later centuries were ecologically connected with such changes in climatic conditions.) It might be argued, however, that the same climatic change ought to have been beneficial for countries like Italy and Spain, and there is no clear evidence for this. Furthermore, some sources maintain that climate in the prosperous 1150–1300 era was worse than the climate in the following centuries.[43] But perhaps the chief argument against the climate theory is that the period from 1300 on was characterized by falling wheat prices (see Table 2.4), suggesting good harvests rather than bad.[44]

Finally, there is still another view holding that a level of overpopulation had been attained by 1300, not permanently maintainable with the available resources and technology:

As long as the colonization movement went forward and new land was taken up, the crops from virgin lands encouraged men to establish new families and settlements. But, after a time the marginal character of marginal lands was bound to assert itself and the honeymoon of high yields was succeeded by long periods of reckoning, when the poorer lands, no longer new, punished the men who tilled them with failing crops and with murrain of sheep and cattle. In these conditions a fortuitous combination of adverse events, such as the succession of bad seasons in the second decade of the fourteenth century, was sufficient to reverse the entire trend of agricultural production and to send the population figures tumbling down.[45]

Thus, Postan and a number of other authors contend that population decline and/or economic 'depression' began well before the Black Death.[46] At least in the Malthusian form put forward by Postan and Slicher van Bath, however, the argument is vulnerable to the same criticism these very authors levy against the climatic theory. Overpopulation relative to the long-term capacity of the soil should have led to a period of failing harvests and low real wages until the population fell to a maintainable level. But, from Tables 2.3 and 2.4, it is evident that the period 1350–1400, during which the bulk of the decline in population took place (see Figure 2.1), was a period of relatively low wheat prices (good harvests) and high real wages.

Integrating some portions of the different theories outlined above, the following is put forward as an hypothesis consistent with the main body of evidence as to economic phenomena in the period under consideration. The initiating, autonomous cause of a break in economic trends was the onset of plague — a source of ecological pressure upon the human population beginning with the Black Death of 1348–50 (or beginning some 30 years earlier, according to some authors). The sudden population decline due to the arrival of the plague, with material property left essentially unaffected, raised overall per capita wealth in the short-term while drastically shifting relative returns and incomes in favour of the labouring and against the property-owning classes. In terms of price statistics, the short-term effects included a rise in wages and fall in wheat prices.[47] Under normal circumstances, Malthusian forces would then be expected to operate to increase population once again — if so, the longer-term aftermath would have been associated with rising population, falling real wages, and a recovery in wheat prices. But in this special situation the corrective forces were inhibited by the *continuing* plague now endemic, and recurrently breaking out in great attacks. Not only did the plague directly wipe out substantial fractions of what would have been a recovering population, but it reduced incentives to bear children and raise families. Consequently, population continued to fall throughout the fourteenth century, leading to further declines in wheat prices and increases in wages. Secondary effects included shifts to less labour-intensive crops; tillage often gave way to pasture.[48] Furthermore, it is plausible to argue that whereas agriculture benefited by being able to abandon marginal lands, industry (being subject to increasing returns with respect to population size) suffered a loss of relative position.[49] Eventually, with the attenuation of the pressure of plague, the Malthusian forces began to assert their dominance; thus, in the latter part of the fifteenth century real wages decline once again.

The explanation offered above ascribes primary responsibility for the lag in aggregate recovery to *plague recurrences*. The alternative explanation of *war* need not be entirely rejected, especially in relation to stricken France. A high rate of real daily or hourly wages could have been in effect whenever conditions were peaceful enough to permit work — but, with armies and marauders often about, the opportunity to engage in productive work may have been severely limited, quite apart from actual destruction. Thus, war tends to engender high wage rates but lower labour income (and per capita production). The third explanation mentioned, *over-population* entailing a natural self-corrective reaction, does not appear to be defensible.[50]

The explanations considered above were all in the nature of alternatives to an hypothesis that specifically relates the long-term depression to the *shock* engendered by the Black Death as a unique event — comparable in some ways to the possible shock of a nuclear war.[51] Langer's analysis outlines the supposed mechanism in economic terms: The great contraction of population, by reducing aggregate demand, led to a semi-permanent state of depression — only relieved when population growth began once more.

For a short time the towns and cities experienced a flush of apparent prosperity. Many survivors of the epidemic had suddenly inherited substantial amounts of property and money ... The rural areas, on the other hand, virtually collapsed. With fewer people to feed in the towns and cities, the farmers lost a large part of the market for their crops. Grain prices fell precipitately ... the rural population fled to the cities en masse.... And of course in the long run the depression of agriculture engulfed the cities in depression as well.[52]

Langer clearly has in mind depression in the sense of *impoverishment* (decline in per capita income) and he is evidently referring to impoverishment of the mass of the population. But although the course of *overall* per capita income may be in doubt, it is substantially certain, as we have seen, that per capita income for the mass of the population *rose* considerably (except possibly in war-torn France).[53] It is true that 'farmers' (lords?) lost a large part of their markets, but surviving farm tenants were able to extend and up-grade their holdings, and farm labourers were able to command higher wages. Labour in *both* city and countryside was scarce relative to the demand; far from there being flight *en masse* to the cities, it remains in doubt whether there was any substantial net shift of population at all. Leaving aside what seems (to the present author) to be very dubious reasoning about the economic mechanism of the supposed downward spiral, Langer's picture of events is not consistent with the evidence reviewed earlier.

The same author has also emphasized the psychological consequences of the Black Death: the interest in death and the macabre, the intensification of religious feeling, and the tendency toward licentious yet guilt-ridden behaviour.[54] The view that there were such effects appears to have considerable justification.[55] An argument might conceivably be offered that this psychological transformation was associated with the economic depression, perhaps by leading to a withdrawal from worldly economic activities to otherworldly religious ones. But the evidence of the chronology in Table 2.1 suggests that, when we leave the economic sphere and turn to government and politics, the period was characterized by normal and even hyper-normal levels of energetic worldly activity. Nor was all this activity of a destructive nature. In England, for example, the same period saw significant developments in the direction of national unification and parliamentary independence.[56]

Turning to long-term socio-political effects, one question is the bearing of the Black Death upon the decline of the feudal system in Western Europe. Since the manorial system was decaying in any case, the plague catastrophe was more of an auxiliary force than an underlying cause of the great social change. The feudal system was, of course, status-oriented and tradition-bound. Although there seems to be great disagreement about the progress of commutation of personal services by the time of the Black Death,[57] there nevertheless was enormous rigidity in the established terms of economic relationships. The system was ill-adapted to cope with the pressures for changes in these terms dictated by the new scarcity of labour relative to land. Hence the complaints about flight of labour, vagrancy and the like, and legislative attempts (for example, in the Statutes of Labourers) to reverse by fiat the concessions granted perforce by individual lords. On this hypothesis, outbursts like the Peasants' Revolt in England (1381) were caused basically by attempts to insist upon and enforce feudal dues and rights or status relationships no longer economically maintainable in the changed circumstances.[58] (The immediate cause of the Peasants' Revolt was the imposition of a severe poll tax, highly oppressive to the lower classes.) The pressure of labour scarcity contributed to the decay of the vestiges of serfdom, and a shift toward a contractual form of employment relationship.[59]

CONCLUSIONS

1. The Black Death of 1348–50 swept away perhaps one-quarter of the population of Western Europe, though the 'excess mortality' was somewhat lower. Among all recorded catastrophes, it is the one most comparable in suddenness, geographical scope, and scale of casualties to a hypothetical thermonuclear war. On the other hand, in contrast with war, there was no direct destruction of material property.
2. Although there are literary reports of organizational breakdowns in cities during the period when the plague was at its height, it is evident — from records of governmental proceedings, and the fact of large-scale military and naval activity — that the mechanisms of government did not collapse. It should, of course, be appreciated that 'government' in the fourteenth century was a simpler and more limited activity than government today. (And, indeed, it might be conjectured that the socio-political structure of the fourteenth century had evolved so as to be particularly resilient to disaster.)[60]
3. The short-term economic aftermath of the Black Death was very much in line with what economic theory would predict: a rapid rise in wages and per capita incomes of the labouring classes, and downward pressure on rents and the incomes of the propertied classes. The attempt to stem these pressures by government fiat (Statutes of

Labourers) had only limited success. Economic recovery from this initial blow was rapid.

4. The century following the Black Death is usually considered by historians to be a period of depression, and some authors have attributed the depression to the Black Death. Review of the evidence indicates that it remains questionable whether the period saw an actual decline in per capita well-being in comparison with the level prevailing before the Black Death. And the century was a prosperous one for the labouring classes, the mass of the population. But economic improvement was less than might have been expected, especially as population was relatively stable. The stagnation of this century appears to have been mainly due to the continuing recurrences of plague, secondarily to the effects of war (the latter applying especially for France).

5. The Black Death accelerated the decline of feudalism and the shift to modern contractual economic relationships. Although this development was proceeding in any case, the suddenly changed relative scarcities of labour and land dictated a 'new deal' that the tradition-bound feudal system was unable to provide.

6. Direct inferences can hardly be drawn from this fourteenth-century catastrophe as to possible consequences of thermonuclear war. But we can state the negative conclusion that this historical record provides no support for contentions that social collapse or an economic downward spiral are necessary or likely consequences of massive disasters.

NOTES

1. Hirshleifer, RM-3079-PR. Among the large-scale disaster-recovery experiences investigated were the Southern Confederacy during and after the American Civil War, Russia under war communism (1918–21) and Germany and Japan during and after World War II.
2. Winter, RM-3436-PR; Clark and Bear, P-2093; Clark, RM-1809; Hirshleifer, P-674.
3. Stonier, *Nuclear Disaster*, Ch. 13, especially pp. 159–61, 166–7.
4. Saltmarsh, pp. 30–2.
5. Slicher van Bath, p. 88.
6. Langer, 'The Black Death', p. 114.
7. Saltmarsh, pp. 32–4.
8. The reference here is to mortalities in England and France. It cannot be definitely determined whether the plague produced relatively greater casualties in other European countries. As an example of the sort of disagreement that may arise, a modern art historian concludes (on the basis of chroniclers' reports) that 'during the summer months of 1348 more than half the inhabitants of Florence and Siena died of the bubonic plague'

(Meiss, p. 65). Such a conclusion about a particular city or cities is not beyond the bounds of credibility, but is more likely exaggerated.

9. Some sources date this recurrence in 1375.
10. Saltmarsh, pp. 34–8; Bean, p. 424; Langer, 'The Black Death', p. 114.
11. Russell, *British Medieval Population*.
12. Postan, 'Some Economic Evidence', p. 245.
13. Russell, pp. 259–60, 280.
14. Massacres took place primarily in Germany. The Jews had previously been expelled from England and, for the most part, from France.
15. Boccaccio's *Decameron* opens with a famous description suggesting a breakdown of organized society in Florence. Froissart, in his *Chronicles*, also comments on the flagellants and the persecution of the Jews, but his reports on government and Church activities suggest that established institutions continued to function. Froissart indicates that the Jews were despoiled at the instance of the lords, and were protected in papal territories. As indicated in a footnote earlier, it is possible that Florence suffered unusually high mortality. On the other hand, mortality was certainly high in London (Creighton, p. 128) where no breakdown occurred.
16. Creighton, pp. 117–18.
17. Levett, pp. 72, 142–3.
18. Robbins, p. 463. Note the seeming inconsistency between the generalization about the 'doubling' of wages and the particular percentages shown; the generalization may refer only to 'panic' rates in the immediate aftermath. See also Seebohm, p. 269; Creighton, p. 185; Mullett, p. 23; Robbins, p. 470.
19. Ordinances in the same year forbade migration to Scotland, and taking money out of the kingdom. See Mullett, p. 23.
20. Robbins, p. 476.
21. Ibid., pp. 474–5.
22. Creighton, p. 187; Robbins, p. 450. In England, a Statute of Dress of 1363 forbade the lower classes to imitate upper-class attire. (But even in 1336, it is reported, a law forbade many courses at meals.).
23. Robbins, pp. 461–2.
24. Creighton, p. 197; Robbins, pp. 468–73.
25. Saltmarsh, pp. 25–6; Langer, 'The Black Death', p. 118.
26. For example, Postan ('Some Economic Evidence', p. 245) and Slicher van Bath (pp. 89, 132) suggest that the depression was a natural reaction to excessive agricultural expansion in the previous centuries (see below).
27. For example, Lopez and Miskimin, among the leading proponents of the 'depression' hypothesis, show only that aggregate production fell and state their inability to draw conclusions as to per capita income (p. 410). Cipolla, an 'anti-depression' scholar, does not deny the fall in aggregate production but argues that per capita income rose (pp. 523–4).
28. Cipolla, pp. 523–4; Postan, 'Some Economic Evidence', pp. 225–9; Beveridge, pp. 164–5; Slicher van Bath, pp. 137–40. War-ravaged France may have been an exception to the general European picture, however (ibid., p. 139).
29. Postan, 'Some Economic Evidence', p. 237, 'The Fifteenth Century', pp. 161–2; Robbins, pp. 461–2.
30. Langer, 'The Black Death', p. 118.
31. Postan, 'Some Economic Evidence', pp. 231–4.

32. Creighton, pp. 195–7.
33. Robbins, pp. 471–3.
34. Herlihy, p. 231.
35. Creighton, pp. 193–4. But on Norwich compare Mullett, p. 26.
36. Creighton, p. 195.
37. Robbins, p. 454n.
38. Ibid., pp. 478–9. The plague in France is described as 'almost incidental', 'an aggravation of an already desperate situation', whereas in England the disorder attendant upon the pandemic provided an opportunity for the villein to desert the manor for the growing towns.
39. Saltmarsh, passim. In a critique of Saltmarsh's thesis, Bean has argued that the fall in England's population probably terminated by about 1400, around which date the rise in agricultural wages stopped (see Table 2.3 above) and in urban wages slowed down (Bean, pp. 435–6). This is an assertion about the date at which the Malthusian forces — tending to bring about an increase in births in response to the high level of wages — began to overcome the direct and indirect effects of the plague.
40. A discussion of such losses in a different historical context appears in Hansen, 'The Cost of Children's Mortality'.
41. Utterstrom, 'Climatic Fluctuations'.
42. Ibid., p. 10.
43. Slicher van Bath, p. 161.
44. Ibid.
45. Postan, 'Rapport', p. 235.
46. Postan, 'Some Economic Evidence', pp. 245–6; Lopez and Miskimin, p. 412; Slicher van Bath, p. 89. Florence suffered a profound economic crisis beginning about 1340; the King of England, because of reverses in the Hundred Years' War, defaulted upon enormous loans contracted from the great Florentine banks (see Meiss, pp. 61–2, Burckhardt, p. 50).
47. Wheat production is the resultant of property inputs (land, primarily) and labour inputs. With labour suddenly more scarce, but land as available as before, wheat production would tend to decline but *in lesser proportion* than the decline in labour input. Hence, there would be relatively good harvests in a per capita sense, and low wheat prices.
48. Slicher van Bath, p. 142.
49. As indicated above, however, the data are inconclusive as to the relative contraction of the rural and urban populations.
50. Still other, less cogent, explanations of the recession or lagging recovery have been offered, including an autonomous slowdown in technological advance, and reduced supplies of gold and silver.
51. Stonier's discussion (pp. 160, 165) suggests this hypothesis, though it is not explicitly stated therein.
52. Langer, 'The Black Death', pp. 118, 121.
53. Perroy, writing specifically of France, presents data casting considerable doubt upon earlier conclusions that real wages tended to rise in that country after 1350. He also remarks, however, that in this period we must *not* conclude that the wage-earners led a miserable life (p. 235).
54. Ibid., p. 121. See also Meiss, passim.
55. Not entirely dissimilar phenomena occurred in the *pre*-Black Death period, however. The flagellant cult began earlier, for example as did expulsions and massacres of Jews. The Children's Crusade of 1212, and the 'dancing

114 Disaster and Recovery

manias' beginning in the thirteenth century might also be cited.
56. *Cambridge History*, pp. 895–6.
57. For a view of this question as it concerns England, see Miss Power's study. Evidently, in England commutation had progressed considerably though unevenly before 1350.
58. It is suggestive that the burden of villein services was heavy in a number of the countries where the revolt was most violent. Power, p. 115.
59. Seebohm, p. 277; Creighton, p. 192, Robbins, pp. 468–9.
60. This point was suggested to the author by Michael Arnsten.

BIBLIOGRAPHY

Bean, J. M. W., 'Plague, Population, and Economic Decline in England in the Later Middle Ages', *The Economic History Review*, 2nd ser., vol. 15 (April 1963).

Beveridge, W. H., 'The Yield and Price of Corn in the Middle Ages', *The Economic Journal* (Economic History Series No. 2), May 1927, pp. 155–67.

Boccaccio, *Decameron*.

Burckhardt, Jacob, *The Civilization of the Renaissance in Italy* (Phaidon Press, Oxford, 1945).

Cipolla, Carlo M., 'Economic Depression of the Renaissance?', *The Economic History Review*, 2nd ser., vol. 16 (April 1964).

Clark, Paul G., *Vulnerability and Recuperation of a Regional Economy: A Study of the Impact of a Hypothetical Nuclear Attack on New England*, The RAND Corporation, RM-1809 (October 1956).

Clark, Paul G. and D. V. T. Bear, 'The Importance of Individual Industries for Defense Planning', The RAND Corporation, P-2093 (September 1960).

Creighton, Charles, *A History of Epidemics in Britain*, vol. 1 (Cambridge, 1891).

Froissart, Sir John, *Chronicles of England, France, and Spain*, trans. Thomas Johnes.

Hansen, W. Lee, 'A Note on the Cost of Children's Mortality', *Journal of Political Economy*, vol. 65 (June 1957).

Herlihy, D., 'Population, Plague and Social Change in Rural Pistoia, 1201–1430', *The Economic History Review*, 2nd ser., vol. 18 (1965).

Hirshleifer, Jack, 'Some Thoughts on the Social Structure After a Bombing Disaster', The RAND Corporation, P-674 (August 1955).

——, *Disaster and Recovery: A Historical Survey*, The RAND Corporation, RM-3079-PR (April 1963).

Langer, William L., 'The Next Assignment', *The American Historical Review*, vol. 63 (January 1958).

——, 'The Black Death', *Scientific American* (February 1964).

Levett, A. Elizabeth and Ballard, A., *The Black Death*, Oxford Studies in Social and Legal History, vol. 5, Paul Vinogradoff (ed.) (Oxford, 1916).

Lopez, R. S. and Miskimin, H. A., 'The Economic Depression of the Renaissance', *The Economic History Review*, 2nd ser., vol. 14 (1961–62).

Meiss, Millard, *Painting in Florence and Siena after the Black Death* (Harper Torchbooks: Harper & Row, New York, 1964).

Mullett, Charles F., *The Bubonic Plague and England* (University of Kentucky Press, 1956).

Perroy, E., 'Wage Labour in France in the Later Middle Ages', *The Economic History Review*, 2nd ser., vol. 8 (1955).

Postan, M., 'Revisions in Economic History: IX — The Fifteenth Century', *Economic History Review*, 2nd ser., vol. 2 (1949–50), pp. 160–7.

——, 'Some Economic Evidence of Declining Population in the Later Middle Ages', *The Economic History Review*, 2nd ser., vol. 2 (1950).

——, 'Moyen Age: Rapport' in *Rapports du IXe Congrès International des Sciences Historiques*, I, pp. 225–41.

Power, E. E., 'Historical Revisions: VII — The Effects of the Black Death on Rural Organization in England', *History*, new series, vol. 3 (1918), pp. 110–16.

Previte-Orton, C. W., *The Shorter Cambridge Medieval History* (Cambridge University Press, Cambridge, 1953), v. 2.

Robbins, Helen, 'A Comparison of the Effects of the Black Death on the Economic Organization of France and England', *Journal of Political Economy*, vol. 36 (August 1928).

Russell, Josiah Cox, *British Medieval Population* (University of New Mexico Press, Albuquerque, 1948).

Saltmarsh, John, 'Plague and Economic Decline in England in the Later Middle Ages', *Cambridge Historical Journal*, vol. 7 (1941).

Seebohm, F., 'The Black Death, and Its Place in English History', *Fortnightly Review*, vol. 2 (1865) (in two parts).

Slicher van Bath, B. H., *The Agrarian History of Western Europe, A.D. 500–1850* (Edward Arnold; London, 1963), Olive Ordish, trans.

Stonier, Tom, *Nuclear Disaster* (Meridian Books: World Publishing Co.; Cleveland, 1963).

Utterstrom, Gustaf, 'Climatic Fluctuations and Population Problems in Early Modern History', *The Scandinavian Economic History Review*, vol. 3 (1955).

3 War Damage Insurance*

*   *   *

Background of this Chapter

This article, also produced under the sponsorship of The RAND Corporation, represents research performed and published earlier than the first two papers in this volume. But in terms of logical arrangement it seems better to place this policy-oriented analysis after the historical studies that help provide factual background.

The threat of nuclear war is explicitly addressed here. The paper argues in favour of an insurance programme that would, over a long period, help promote passive adaptations (like industrial dispersal and protective construction) to the bombing threat. It must be remembered that at the time of writing the fission weapon was still quite new, and the drastically more powerful fusion weapon just coming into view. For the present 'age of nuclear plenty', the discussion may seem hopelessly dated. According to the now dominant view in the West, it is useless to attempt even to moderate the consequences of nuclear destruction.

There are two responses I would make. First, that the logical issues as to compensation versus insurance remain much the same when it comes to disasters like floods and earthquakes that are, on this cosmic scale, somewhat less fearsome than nuclear war. And second, that it is wrong to assume that even nuclear war's destruction must necessarily be beyond any hope of alleviation. Is it good news or bad news to insist that there may be 'small' as well as all-out nuclear wars? And even for major nuclear wars, destruction *may* be kept short of total —

* Originally published in the *Review of Economics and Statistics*, 35: 144–53 (May 1953). Reproduced by permission of the President and Fellows of Harvard College.

as a result of arms limitations, of the development of active defences, or of the mutually rational adoption of damage-limiting targeting tactics on the part of the belligerents.

*   *   *

If the United States becomes engaged in a new major war, we must expect that enemy aircraft will attack our cities and industry with nuclear weapons of mass destruction. That we cannot wholly prevent such attacks from being launched or intercept them before enormous damage may have been inflicted upon us is a matter of common knowledge. In these circumstances, *passive defence* — actions designed to minimize the consequences of bombing on the assumption that the enemy will have at least partial success in getting his planes and bombs through to the targets — becomes a vitally needed supplement to our active defence weapons.

People tend to think of atomic bombs as absolute weapons, pulverizing whole cities at one blow, overwhelming all possible defences. While the effects of such weapons are in fact enormous, it does not follow that we are helpless in devising protective measures. For example, much of the destruction in the past has been due not to the atomic blast itself but to the general conflagration which followed; fire-resistant construction and strengthening of city fire departments may yield great returns by reducing this latter risk. In addition, shielding can be of great utility in protecting vital machinery, and the reduction of flying glass hazards equally vital for the protection of personnel.

Despite these considerations, as of this moment practically nothing has been done in the way of passive defence. There are several sound arguments which may partially explain this neglect. First of all, there is the question of alternative uses of the money and resources which might be expended on passive defence — perhaps it would be better to spend that money on bombers or on tanks. Secondly, even if it is generally agreed that something should be spent on passive defence, we can come to no concrete decision until we have some idea how far to go in this direction. Finally, the proponents of passive defence have possibly harmed their case by laying excessive emphasis upon relocation, especially dispersal, which is only one of several methods of reducing vulnerability, and by no means always the best.

It is the contention of this paper that at least a partial way out of the present impasse concerning passive defence would be to offer *war damage insurance* to protect property-owners from the chance distribution of losses due to enemy action. It will be shown that an appropriate method of insuring property against war damage can be expected, over a period of years, to encourage purely *private* actions which will, aside from any governmental measures, tend to reduce the physical and economic vulnerability of our cities and industry to enemy bombing. This crucially important effect seems never to have been noted in any of the public discussions of war damage insurance.[1] The desired effect can be achieved by providing the war damage insurance according to a schedule of differential rates — allowing relatively cheap insurance to property located in safe areas, possessing bomb-resistant structure, and built of non-inflammable materials; and only relatively expensive insurance to property located in dangerous areas, not of sound construction, and susceptible to fire. The subject of this paper is of particular urgency because, as will be shown, alternatives now under consideration would have a positively harmful effect on vulnerability.

The overall objective of such an insurance programme is to induce socially desirable private behaviour through the mechanism of the price system. Under this proposal, private calculations of profit and loss in terms of differential insurance costs will minimize the role of administrative fiat in encouraging the vitally needed reduction of vulnerability to bombing. Lest hopes be raised too high, it should be pointed out immediately that a number of qualifications make this proposal no short-cut to national safety. (1) The desired objective will not be attained in the short run; a definite improvement may be attained in perhaps ten years, but hardly in one or two. (2) It follows from (1) that, at least for urgently needed improvements, administrative fiat cannot be entirely dispensed with. (3) The argument along welfare lines which is used in this paper is only correct to a rough approximation, since the insurance premiums to be charged will be far from perfect estimates of risk. (4) In addition, there are administrative problems which must not be minimized, as well as serious political objections on the part of interested groups.[2] These difficulties will be discussed in detail below. While they undoubtedly weaken the case for the proposal made here, it will also be shown that no available alternative — including doing nothing — is free from objections which, in the author's opinion, are even more damaging.

THE BACKGROUND

The term 'war risk insurance' is frequently used to refer to several different types of insurance coverage: (1) insurance of ships and cargoes in war zones, (2) life insurance where enemy action in war is the cause of death, (3) re-insurance of carriers of workmen's compensation insurance where injury or death due to enemy action is suffered while on the job, and (4) insurance against property losses due to enemy action. In this paper, we shall be discussing only item (4), property insurance — hence the term 'war damage insurance', rather than the broader 'war risk insurance'.

The subject is limited in this way in order to keep the paper within reasonable bounds, and there is no intention to minimize the importance of other types of war risk insurance. Insurance against death or injury due to enemy action in war is a particularly important and pressing problem, especially since an insurance programme can be designed to encourage measures tending to reduce human casualties as well as property damage. Such a programme could be combined and administered jointly with the programme of war damage insurance proposed here. This type of insurance raises, however, various special difficulties which it was thought best to leave aside at this time.

Both the United States and Great Britain had war damage insurance programmes in effect in World War II. In each case the programme did not become effective until after war had begun, and so did not have time to bring about a more favourable passive defence situation.[3] Besides these two, a number of other nations had war damage insurance or indemnity programmes. An indemnity programme is one of government compensation for war damage without any prepayment insurance feature. France and Germany both had plans of the indemnity type.[4]

The steadily worsening international situation, especially after the opening of hostilities in Korea, led to a demand in the United States for a new programme of war damage insurance. A number of bills to reinstitute the World War II programme were introduced in both the 81st and 82nd Congresses, though none has yet become law.[5] From our point of view, their most important characteristics were: (1) As in the World War II programme, the financing of the proposed War Damage Corporation was restricted to $100 million of capital stock to be subscribed by the RFC and an advance of not more than $1 billion from the same agency; and (2) The Corporation was directed to establish uniform rates for each type of property according to an estimate of risk. The House report on H.R. 0802 in the 81st Congress interpreted 'uniform rates' to mean uniform with respect to geographical location. These Bills cannot be considered satisfactory since, as will be shown: (1) financial resources limited to $1 billion would be quite inadequate, and (2) the restriction to geographically uniform rates would weaken the favourable effect on vulnerability which an insurance programme could bring about.

During 1951, the Budget Bureau, on behalf of the executive agencies, opposed all war damage insurance legislation. The Bureau proposed that, instead of a war damage insurance measure, Congress pass an act authorizing the President simply to grant compensation up to the amount of $22 billion to indemnify those suffering losses from enemy action.[6] The proposal of the Bureau has the considerable advantage of administrative convenience, since little need be done until the bombs fall. It will be shown, however, that simple compensation programmes of this type tend actually to discourage private actions which would reduce vulnerability, thereby *increasing* the overall national risk. In the author's opinion, if the harmful effect on vulnerability of the Bureau's proposal can be shown, this should be considered a fatal objection to the proposal. In its criticisms of war damage insurance, the Budget Bureau totally missed the favourable effect on vulnerability of insurance and the harmful effect of their own proposal. It is remarkable that, so far as we have been able to discover, even the *proponents* of insurance failed to note this effect in the *Hearings*.

VULNERABILITY AND DIFFERENTIAL RATES

In order to influence vulnerability in a favourable sense, it is proposed here that as far as possible war damage insurance rates be based on the risks involved in insuring different types of property. For example, certain locations will be safer than others; certain types of construction will be more resistant to blast and others less; and some materials will be less likely than others to burn and to ignite other structures and materials. In all these cases, it would be desirable to insure the safer property at a relatively low rate, and the poor risk at a high rate. This obviously makes sense from an insurance point of view, though a Federal War Damage Corporation would not have to be bound by ordinary commercial insurance practice.

Rates and incentives
What is more important is that such a schedule of differential rates will, through the price system, tend to encourage voluntary private actions in the direction of reducing vulnerability to bombing. For every possible step in this direction, an appropriately reduced insurance premium would (ideally) be offered. Clearly, rational self-interest would lead to the adoption of all measures such that the private cost of change is less than the private gain in terms of reduced premiums. When these conditions apply, we may say that, at least as a first approximation, the social cost of change (diversion of resources) is less than the social cost (the risk of destruction) of maintaining the status quo. While movement in the opposite direction (the abandonment of protective measures where the cost of maintaining them is greater than the gain in terms of insurance premiums) is also theoretically possible

and will undoubtedly occur to some extent, it is not believed that this will be very important in practice — always assuming that the premiums are correctly adjusted. Underlying this opinion is the belief — based on empirical observation — that our economy has not as yet taken sufficiently into account the new bombing risks. The insurance programme should, therefore, lead on balance to a net reduction of vulnerability. As a matter of fact, wherever the costs of maintaining protective measures are greater than fair insurance differentials received, there is a *prima facie* case in favour of abandoning those measures on the ground that the social cost exceeds the social gain.

It may then be asked: Would not the absence of insurance lead to exactly the same result? The answer to this question is yes — in principle — but only under the assumption that the government's policy will be *not to offer compensation for war damage*. In the author's opinion, in the absence of an insurance programme, it will be politically impossible for the government not to compensate for damage.[7] Simple compensation without insurance tends to discourage private efforts designed to reduce vulnerability, since those making the expenditures involved do not gain relative to those who leave their property in a highly vulnerable condition. In fact, simple compensation will encourage the abandonment of any protective measures of non-zero cost as already exist. In terms of the effect on vulnerability, therefore, war damage insurance will be superior to simple compensation. Whether or not it would be superior to no insurance combined with a policy of *not* compensating is a much more doubtful question. Since the combination of no insurance with no compensation is considered close to impossible politically, the question is more of theoretical than practical importance.

The two main feasible methods for spreading the burden of loss are, then, a simple programme of government compensation or a scheme of war damage insurance.[8] It should be noted that partial compensation, being a compromise between simple compensation and no compensation at all, would have consequences for vulnerability intermediate between the harmful effect of the former and the favourable effect of the latter. The improvement with respect to vulnerability, however, is purchased at the expense of the inequity of forcing unlucky individual property-owners to bear the uncompensated fraction of losses due to enemy action.

Participation: Voluntary or compulsory?
Should the insurance coverage be completely voluntary? A compulsory insurance programme would solve many difficult problems. In particular, there need be no worry about adverse selection of risks (the tendency of poor risks to take out insurance and of good risks to self-

insure), because no one has the option of remaining outside the insurance programme. In addition, under a compulsory programme it would be possible to make better estimates and projections of the inflowing revenue and better guesses of the probable liability. Perhaps most important of all, universal coverage (not achievable under a voluntary plan) would entirely eliminate the problem of demands for compensation sure to arise after bombing on behalf of those who have failed to take out insurance.

The chief argument against compulsion, of course, is that the latter is always undesirable in principle and might prove unacceptable to the American people in this case. It is possible that some compromise may be adopted, applying the compulsory principle to certain classes of risks and leaving others in the voluntary category. In the remainder of this paper it will be assumed (unless otherwise specified) that a purely voluntary programme is in effect. Even in this case, it will be argued, the insurance programme will have a beneficial effect.

Structure of rates

According to the arguments developed above, rates should be based on the risks involved in order to achieve the desired effect on vulnerability. The overall levels of rates should reflect the overall degree of risk, and relative rates should reflect relative riskiness of different properties. In this section, we shall emphasize relative rates as between properties of differing degrees of risk. The absolute level of rates will be discussed in connection with the financing problem.

What type of actions do we wish to encourage? These fall roughly into three general categories concerning location, construction and other protective measures. With respect to location, we frequently hear demands for the utmost in the way of dispersal of cities and industry. Even aside from the costs involved, it is by no means clear that dispersal is always wise from the point of view of defence. For example, if a certain limited area could be made invulnerable, it might well be best to concentrate our vital facilities within that area. In general, the advantages in the way of concentrating the defence must be weighed against the increase in attractiveness of the target resulting from concentration. In practice, we would probably like to spread vital facilities far enough apart so that only one at a time would fall within the lethal area of a single bomb — but it would be quite doubtful whether we should want to encourage a general migration to the Great American Desert. Popular belief seems to be that dispersal necessarily means relocation in some remote part of the country, whereas mere spreading out of industrial concentrations into the neighbouring countryside may be more desirable from the defence point of view.[9]

As far as construction is concerned, it is quite clear that we would wish to encourage the building of new structures and the improvement of existing ones so as to increase the number which will survive the blast and fire dangers associated with atomic bombing. In the book, *The Effects of Atomic Weapons*, prepared under the direction of the Los Alamos Scientific Laboratory, design suggestions for new buildings and for improving existing buildings are made.[10]

In addition to location and construction, we would wish to encourage certain protective measures, both individual and community-wide, which could greatly ameliorate the vulnerability situation. The improvement of municipal fire-fighting organizations (with special attention to the protection from the bomb explosion of the organization itself and of the water supply) and the construction of adequate firebreaks are examples of such measures.

To reflect the degree of risk and to influence behaviour appropriately, the rate structure should take all these factors into account.[11] It appears that, for large properties at least, the presently existing schedules of fire insurance rates can be used as a starting point. This is possible because fire is one of the chief agents of destruction. It is also convenient, as it is likely that the detailed administration of the plan will have to be handled largely through private fire insurance companies (as in the World War II programme). In addition, some account would have to be taken of the blast risk as well as of the fire risk. Secondly, and far more importantly, the differential *bombing* risk (depending upon enemy strategy) would have to be superimposed upon the pure fire risk dependent on chance factors.

Setting the insurance rates will involve judgement and, therefore, the differential rates will not have the ideal effects on incentives which could be claimed for the true rates. Nevertheless, we believe that this is a case where judgement would have to go very far astray to produce really perverse effects on incentives, which is all we need be afraid of. We shall not get optimality, but we can expect improvement.[12]

The practical effect

The question might well be asked: Will the effect of the proposed programme be substantial enough to produce a noticeable reduction in the nation's vulnerability to bombing? It must be remembered, first of all, that the proposal made here aims at a long-run effect — it will not make the United States invulnerable tomorrow. Even granting this, it might be thought that insurance differentials will be only a very small element in the whole complex of factors which influence a firm's decision to locate, for example, in one city or another. Similarly, a typical person will not be inclined to change his place of residence merely because he can get cheaper war damage insurance on his household goods in a different locality.

Arguments of this sort fail to take into account the fact that changes in economic circumstances always influence only persons and firms on the margin. It is not an effective argument to say that a typical firm will not be influenced to move solely by insurance differentials. The *typical* firm may not be induced to move, but there will be some firms, perhaps atypical, who were close to the margin of moving anyway. The extra inducement of the insurance will, for such firms on the margin, be sufficient to swing the balance toward change. In fact, if any firm is not induced by profit-and-loss calculations to move, there is a *prima facie* case in favour of the proposition that it *should not move*, since the economic advantages of its present site remain dominant even considering the bombing risk. Furthermore, as we have pointed out, relocation is not the only way, and probably not the most effective way from the national point of view, of reducing vulnerability to bombing; effective and less costly methods of protection will also be encouraged by the insurance differentials.

It will be cheaper, in general, to incorporate vulnerability-reducing features in new construction than to add them to already existing buildings. This is especially clear for drastic changes like relocation, which may require abandonment of such plant, fixtures and machinery as cannot conveniently be moved. Therefore, it is to be expected that the most powerful influence of the differential insurance rates may be upon the location and construction of new facilities for expansion or for replacement of worn-out or obsolete equipment or plant. In 1951, gross private domestic investment amounted to \$59.1 billion.[13] In addition, there was a substantial amount of investment under the auspices of federal, state, and local governments. It is evident that an enormous amount of new investment will, over a number of years, be subject to the influence of the differential insurance rates.

The costs of change

The various risk-reducing measures to be encouraged by the proposed insurance programme all involve certain social costs. These costs are of two types: the direct cost of making the change (e.g. abandoning a still useful plant in a vulnerable area), and the continuing cost either in terms of direct outlay (as in maintaining fire-protection equipment) or loss of economic efficiency (e.g. producing at a safer but economically inferior location). The question before us now is the consideration which should be given to such costs as an argument against attempting to influence vulnerability through an insurance programme. This objection is, in a sense, opposite to the above argument that the programme may not have *enough* effect. Assuming that the insurance rates can be made to reflect the risks, it is maintained that this argument should be given no weight whatsoever.

The reason for this assertion, which may seem extreme, is simply that the existence of the threat of atomic bombing has changed the peacetime situation with respect to the economic efficiency of, say, one location as against another. In all economic calculations from now on, the threat of bombing is a factor which should be given weight. The insurance programme does not influence vulnerability by *creating* a new set of incentives; rather, it *reflects*, by inserting the new data into the price system via an insurance mechanism, the situation already created by the threat of bombing. The costs of change represent the normal adaptation of the economy to a changed situation and, presumably, would not be undertaken unless they were less than the costs of maintaining the status quo in the face of the changed situation.

The problem of equity

There is a possible objection on equity grounds to a war damage insurance programme embodying a schedule of differential rates based on the risk of loss through bombing. After all, it might be argued, is it fair to charge, for example, safer rural properties lower insurance rates than more dangerous urban ones? Aren't the armed forces supposed to protect the entire country, and don't city-dwellers pay their share of taxes?

The counter-argument here is the same as the answer to the objection about the costs of change: differential insurance rates proportioned to risks do not *create* any inequity which may exist, they merely *reflect* it. The 'inequity' here is that vested interests are disturbed by the new threat of bombing; they are so disturbed in the absence of any insurance at all. Whether or not there is insurance, a man with vulnerable property is in a poorer position than a man with safe property, although property values may not yet have changed to take this fully into account. We could, of course, attempt to restore the previous status of vested interests by providing insurance either free or without rate differentials according to risk. Aside from the harmful effect on vulnerability which such a programme would entail, it could not wholly succeed in restoring the status quo. To the extent that transactions exchanging properties have already taken place at values reflecting the new pattern of risks (reports have been made in the press that the threat of bombing has been a factor in the rise of prices of farm land relative to city properties), the gains and losses occasioned by the changed pattern of risk have already been realized, and the attempt to restore the status quo will result in windfall losses and gains to new owners.

Furthermore, as long as the insurance plan remains voluntary, it is hard to see what valid objection can be brought on equity grounds. The government is not *imposing* a new set of property values; it is rather offering a simple business proposition: does or does not the property-owner want insurance at rates reflecting risks? Assuming that the rates are correctly set — and that is not in question here — is there any justification for a man with a poorly built house demanding as cheap insurance as a man with a well-constructed house? If the rates failed to discriminate against the poorer risks, the owners of safer properties might well have equally valid grounds for complaint. So long as the programme is voluntary, either has the option of not taking out insurance.

THE FINANCING PROBLEM AND AVERAGE PREMIUM

An attempt will be made to give the roughest sort of guess as to the probable liability of a war damage insurance programme. The term 'probable liability' is used as opposed to 'potential liability'; the latter is the entire value of policies issued, while the former is an estimate of the damage likely to be suffered in actuality by policy-holders. In order to have an average rate-level reflecting the degree of risk, the probable liability must be corrected by a factor representing the probability of war, and then divided by the total of policies outstanding. The result of this calculation is the average annual premium.

Since we only want orders of magnitude, we shall simply guess here at figures of $800 billion in March 1952 dollars of potential coverage,[14] a 10 per cent damage level,[15] and a 10 per cent risk of war occurring in a given year.[16] Then to get an approximately correct effect on incentives, rates should be set capable of accumulating one-tenth of a fully paid-up fund in the given year. (We wish to set the rates *as if* we were accumulating such a fund; whether or not to establish a reserve fund is a separate problem.) One further modification is that, for reasons to be explained later, at a 10 per cent damage level it will only be desirable to compensate at the rate of 90 per cent for losses.

This calculation would require $7.2 billion to be paid in during the given year. (No adjustment for interest is made.) Since the figure for total wealth insured is $800 billion, this implies an annual premium of 0.9 per cent of value on the average. The rate could conceivably go up to almost 10 per cent for property whose complete destruction was certain in the event of war and, on the other hand, would be essentially zero for exceptionally safe property. It will be noted that the fiscal problems involved in handling such collections will be of the first magnitude.

These problems are in one respect mitigated but in others made worse by the probability that the plan will be, as discussed here, voluntary rather than compulsory. The fact that no one needs to sign up will mean that the potential liability, the probable liability, and the required premium income will all be less by an unknown but probably large factor. This will reduce the magnitude of the financial problem, but will leave the average rate required as high as before. In fact, the element of adverse selection will tend to raise the average rate required.

The chief problem connected with a voluntary insurance programme, however, is the fact that people will be tempted to speculate on the probability of war. That is to say, they may not take out insurance until the international situation becomes very threatening — especially since the premium rates will necessarily be rather high. In theory, the check on this should be variation of rates over time to take account of the changing risks. Another check, and one that might well be very effective, would be the granting of policies which do not become effective except after a waiting period of perhaps a year or six months. Such a provision would make speculation on the probability of war very dangerous, since one would have to guess about the situation six or twelve months from now, and not about the very immediate future. These and other devices should enable the War Damage Corporation to hold down speculation on the probability of war (adverse selection in respect to time) to a tolerable level.

The loss figures shown above assume complete coverage. Let us say that only 50 per cent of potential coverage is written. This may come about because some property-owners fail to take out policies or because some or all policies may be written with a coinsurance feature (where the insured continues to bear part of the risk, only a fraction being covered by the insurance policy). If the rate remains about the same,[17] annual premium income will be about $3.6 billion, reflecting potential liability of $400 billion and probable liability of about $36 billion.

The proposed War Damage Corporation Acts of 1950 and 1951 would have given the Corporation resources of $1.1 billion. These figures show that, unless our estimates are wildly in error, the scope of the programme was completely misconceived. In fact, a single bomb in certain highly valuable and concentrated areas might create valid damage claims in excess of a billion dollars.

The Budget Bureau's simple compensation proposal referred to earlier called for authority to expend up to $22 billion for compensation purposes. This figure corresponds to our $80 billion of probable damage to the entire economy, if we can assume that the Budget Bureau figure represents an estimate of overall national loss. Without an extensive study, it cannot be decided whether our guess or the Budget Bureau's estimate (if it is such) is likely to be closer to the truth.[18] Accepting the Budget Bureau's figure for probable damage while retaining our other assumptions would reduce the annual premium income with full coverage and the average rate of premium required by a factor of about four — that is, to about $2 billion and 0.2 per cent of value, respectively. This lower premium rate would certainly make the insurance more palatable, though less powerful in reducing vulnerability. The lesser effectiveness of lower rates is not necessarily an argument against them, for the optimal effectiveness depends on the unknown true degree of risk.

At this point the reader may quite justifiably be worried. We have made blind guesses at the overall probable loss and the probability of war, but will anything better than a blind guess ever be possible? If not, we might set rates so as to push people into less vulnerable situations ten times too fast relative to the true risks, or else not one-tenth fast enough![19] This objection is undoubtedly a serious one and it further weakens — to the vanishing point, some will think — the force of the welfare arguments used initially.

Nevertheless, we must always view the problem in terms of the alternatives, and especially the leading alternative — simple compensation. If we do not move fast enough, we are at least going in the right direction, while simple compensation would be pushing us in the wrong direction. We might indeed move too fast, but in view of all the administrative and political pressures in favour of the status quo, the danger of moving very much too fast seems quite slight.

It should perhaps be noted that any attempt to reduce vulnerability, whether or not through an insurance programme, would face the same difficulty of deciding how quickly the change should take place. In fact, some estimate of the probability of war and of the overall risk of loss is implicit in all decisions relevant to national defence. The necessity of setting an overall level of risk for war damage insurance would only force this estimate to be made explicitly.

Reserves and compensation
We cannot here enter into a discussion of proper reserve and compensation policy, but it will be useful to make clear what the fundamental objective of this policy should be. Without extended argument, we shall assert that the objective — which we shall call the Equitable Principle — should be to restore the *relative* position of those

who lose property by the bombing so that they are no worse off than the nation as a whole. Since the bombing will reduce the real national wealth, the restoration of the *absolute* position of those who lose property would mean an actual gain for them relative to the rest of the community. It follows from the Equitable Principle that the proportion of actual loss compensated should be 1 minus the overall proportionate loss of national wealth; if, for example, 10 per cent of the national wealth is destroyed in the bombing, the real value of the compensation should be at the rate of 90 per cent of the real value of the loss. This calculation assumes that money and other claims to wealth are not destroyed, or else that such assets are separately insured under a parallel programme, as they were in World War II.

An ordinary insurance company must have a reserve fund in order to maintain solvency in periods when cash outgo may exceed cash income. For war damage insurance, in the period before war comes there will be only income and no outgo; should war occur, however, outgo is likely to exceed income by far. If, therefore, the War Damage Corporation is to operate on sound insurance principles, it might seem absolutely necessary that the Corporation build up a reserve fund to meet its future liabilities. However, there is a fundamental difference between liabilities of private individuals or corporations and liabilities of the government, and so it does not necessarily follow that the War Damage Corporation — an instrument of the federal government — must or even should follow sound business practice appropriate for a private insurance company. By its taxing power and its ability to create money, the government is in a position to call into existence assets to meet its own liabilities. With respect to war damage insurance, this means that after the bombing the government can create purchasing power in favour of those who have lost property in the bombing or can tax the rest of the population so as to achieve the Equitable Principle of restoring the relative position of the former — without accumulating any reserve at all.

Whether it would be wise to conduct the insurance programme without a reserve can only be determined by an exploration of the likely consequences of the several different possible policies, which cannot be done within the limits of this paper. We may merely mention that, in the absence of a reserve, the appropriate procedure to redistribute the remaining national wealth would involve a capital levy. In all probability, a very considerable inflation would be unavoidable. To the extent that a reserve exists, of course, assets will be available for meeting compensation claims without calling on the general credit of the government.

THE PROPOSED PROGRAMME AND ALTERNATIVES

There are a number of possible actions the government might take which are not alternative to the insurance programme and so are not precluded by it. These actions include making some specified reduction of vulnerability a condition for the granting of government contracts, certificates of necessity for accelerated tax amortization, or priorities and allocations under the defence production programme. Such direct measures will be appropriate where special circumstances (e.g. new construction of a facility in a highly critical industry) make reliance upon the milder generalized pressure of the insurance programme insufficient. The Committee Staff of the Congressional Joint Committee on the Economic Report has proposed the use of such devices.[20] Unfortunately, the report proposed them only in connection with dispersal, which is only one of the aspects of the vulnerability problem. Because of the dangers involved in arbitrary *ad hoc* decisions varying from case to case, direct intervention should probably be limited to special situations concerning critical industries.

Even after all qualifications are made, this review indicates, in the opinion of the author, that a great opportunity to influence vulnerability in a favourable direction will be lost if we fail to provide a suitable type of insurance for war damage. In the absence of such a programme, political realities will probably require compensation for damage. The expectation of compensation will encourage a socially harmful type of behaviour with respect to vulnerability.

On the other hand, even if we do offer an insurance programme, the effect on vulnerability may not be favourable unless rates are proportioned to risk. Such differentiation of rates was done only in the most perfunctory fashion in the World War II programme. At that time, the fault was not important because (1) the risk was not very great, and (2) the effect on vulnerability can be only a long-term one, and the insurance programme was not put into effect until after war had begun. Nevertheless, the element of adverse selection, which always appears when rates are not properly proportioned to risk, was very conspicuous in the World War II programme.[21] For a prospective future war, neither of the factors mitigating the failure to differentiate will apply. The risk of damage due to enemy action is liable to be great, while on the other hand war may not come for a number of years or may not come at all. Therefore, we have both a great need for insurance and an opportunity to introduce it early enough to have a large effect on vulnerability. This effect will not be achieved unless considerable care is exercised in establishing rates according to risk, and this will not be done unless the connection between the insurance and the vulnerability problem is recognized by the federal government. Such has not been the case up to the present time.

Finally, it should be recognized that the financing problem will be of an entirely greater order of magnitude than it was in World War II. This problem merits the close attention of those responsible for fiscal policy and for the overall behaviour of the economy. The results may be positively dangerous if the programme is narrowly conceived as only a special form of insurance, and left solely in the hands of a small agency with purely insurance responsibilities.

ACKNOWLEDGEMENTS

The author would like to express his appreciation to A. P. Lerner, H. J. Barnett, P. A. Samuelson, and C. J. Hitch for criticisms received in discussions of this problem dating back to early 1951.

NOTES

1. Except for a letter to the *New York Times*, 29 July 1951, signed by Professors E. S. Mason, P. A. Samuelson, J. Tobin and C. Kaysen, which argues in the same direction as this paper.
2. Regional objections to dispersal of war plants have been a stumbling-block for passive defence proposals in the past. As a matter of fact, dispersal (in view of its enormous cost) seems less promising in many (perhaps all) instances than less radical alternatives like shielding machinery. While war damage insurance would offer a cheaper rate to safer areas, it would also give credit to these alternative measures. It is hoped, therefore, that regional objections will be less intense than to dictated dispersal programmes.
3. The American programme is described in *Encyclopedia Americana*, 1950 edn., XXVIII, 677. For the UK programme, see *The Economist*, CIL (15 December 1945), 883; and *Monthly Labor Review*, LIII (August 1941), 371–3.
4. Comparative data and analysis of the war damage insurance or indemnity programmes of various countries are available in two studies by the United States Chamber of Commerce. They are entitled: 'War Damage Indemnity' (September 1950), and 'Analysis of War Damage Indemnity Laws' (October 1950).
5. War Damage Corporation Act 1951, Hearings Before a Subcommittee of the Committee on Banking and Currency, US Senate, 82nd Congress, 1st session (US Government Printing Office, 1952).
6. *Hearings*, pp. 171 ff., 211 ff.
7. In the Budget Bureau proposal already mentioned, simple compensation was put forward as an alternative to insurance. The inequity of the

fortuitous distribution of losses is so generally recognized that the only practical question seems to be whether to spread risks through an insurance programme or without such a programme.

8. Differential insurance rates are not the only method for achieving the desired effect. An appropriately differentiated special 'passive defence tax' might be levied, or there could be differentiated compensation schemes in which the proportion of loss to be redeemed for various types of risks might be announced to property-owners in advance, to encourage them to reduce vulnerability. These proposals, unlike simple compensation, would all work in the right direction. They have been rejected on grounds of administrative or political impracticality.

9. See National Security Resources Board Document No. 66, 'National Security Factors in Industrial Location', 22 July 1948.

10. Los Alamos Scientific Laboratory, *The Effects of Atomic Weapons* (September 1950), pp. 376–86.

11. They should not be revised, however, to take into account the pattern of active defences. The theoretical justification for this position (there are practical justifications as well) is that the active defence which must be provided for highly vulnerable areas confers an unearned benefit on a special group at a cost to the entire nation. If we lower insurance premiums because of the active defence provided, we lessen the incentive to undertake those vulnerability-reducing measures which would tend to remove the need for active defences in the area concerned.

12. Space limitations prevent an adequate discussion of this problem, but in support of the above view it should be noted that a considerable body of experience has been accumulated by this date (in actual warfare or experimentation) on such risk elements as the blast and heat effects of atomic and conventional explosives, strength of structures, inflammability of materials, etc. Nor would the element of judgement involved here be unique, since private insurance rates for fire, theft and other contingencies also are ordinarily based on informed judgement.

13. *Survey of Current Business* (March 1952), p. S-1.

14. This figure assumes full participation of eligible property in the plan. It was arrived at by using $502.4 billion as the value of reproducible tangible assets in the United States in 1946 (in R. W. Goldsmith, 'A Perpetual Inventory of National Wealth', *Studies in Income and Wealth*, vol. XIV, published by the National Bureau of Economic Research, p. 18), other types of property being considered uninsurable. A March 1952 figure was arrived at by the rough device of assuming that this element of national wealth was in the same proportion to current gross national product at that date as it was in 1946. The exact figure derived by this procedure was $807.7 billion.

15. Such a figure seems too high for the current situation, but as atomic stockpiles of potential enemies mount it becomes more reasonable.

16. While guessing at this figure for each year is particularly dubious, such a procedure is implicit in our recurrent budgetary decisions on national defence; for example, deciding to what extent we should invest in increasing productive capacity for the future as an alternative to building up military stocks today involves much the same estimate of probabilities.

17. The element of adverse selection will tend to increase it, while co-insurance tends to decrease the rate required.

18. It will be remembered that our figure was based on 10 per cent damage, an estimate which was considered high for the immediate future but possibly low for the more distant period.
19. There is a further complication in that the true risks are not constant but depend on enemy strategy, which may well be affected by our decisions on passive defence.
20. 82nd Congress, First Session, Joint Committee Print, 'The Need for Industrial Dispersal'.
21. A tabulation of the policies issued shows a highly disproportionate amount of policy coverage in the coastal states (the most vulnerable regions) as opposed to, say, the Midwestern states. See *Encyclopedia Americana* (1950 ed.), XXVIII, 677.

4   Disaster Behavior: Altruism or Alliance?

*   *   *

Background of this Chapter

This paper, originally an internal document prepared in 1967 for The RAND Corporation, has been kindly released for publication in this volume. While supposedly not publicly available up to now, as it happened the paper did receive some informal circulation which led to its being discussed in the open literature.

After the Alaskan earthquake of 1964, a humanly gratifying but seemingly 'irrational' development was the degree of mutual aid and cooperativeness displayed by both victim and support populations. Such a syndrome is in fact an historically normal societal response to disaster, at least in the immediate aftermath, as has been summarized in detail in my first essay in this volume. The specific question at issue was whether, from the viewpoint of economic theory, catastrophic events are best regarded as changing people's underlying *attitudes* ('tastes', in the economist's inadequate jargon) or else their *opportunities*. The contention here is that the latter is the more parsimonious and accurate basis on which to explain the observations.

*   *   *

Anomalies play a crucial role in the development of a science. When a well-verified and widely supported theory is found to be in direct opposition to an observed fact, we need not throw the theory overboard; every theoretical structure, at all times, has had some such skeletons in the closet. The challenge is there, however. Attempts to explain the anomaly, whether by a 'normal' further articulation of the received theory or by a more or less radical revision of it, have been responsible for much of our intellectual progress.[1] The analysis of even seemingly trivial anomalies (e.g. very minor divergences from the predicted orbit of Mercury) has led in the past to important scientific advances.

I

Kunreuther and Dacy[2] have recorded just such an anomaly for economic theory: market behaviour after the Alaskan earthquake of 1964. In circumstances where prices might have been expected to rise sharply, they were unchanged or actually fell (see Table 4.1), remaining at abnormal levels for a period of weeks or months. This pattern held even for commodities in exceptionally urgent demand, e.g. milk and canned juices in a period when public water supplies were out of commission. Nor was this a matter of informal rationing by the merchant, at a disequilibrium price; rather, the evidence suggests that the customers rationed themselves, taking no more than some minimal or 'equitable' quantity from the shelves. Investigating further, Dacy and Kunreuther found similar phenomena in other disasters: refugees from floods or tornadoes, for example, have received shelter in private homes, sometimes for periods of months, at little or no charge (e.g. the Dutch floods of 1953).

In explanation of this phenomenon, Kunreuther and Dacy theorize that disaster induces a flourishing of 'community feeling'. Consider a vital commodity, whose demand curve would be expected to remain essentially unchanged post-disaster while the supply is sharply reduced. In the absence of community feeling, the equilibrium price must rise;[3] this is contradicted by the evidence. In the presence of community feeling, the demand curve shifts to the left because of self-rationing. Conceivably also, suppliers may be willing to provide their services on unselfishly generous terms,[4] shifting the supply curve back to the right. On this hypothesis, a price increase is not a necessary consequence. The anomalous movement of (some) prices, their failure to rise, provides support for the contention that community feeling — an element omitted from conventional economic theory — must at times be taken into consideration.

Going beyond the conventional limits of economics, we can note that the Kunreuther–Dacy observation is consistent with a remarkable generalization that has been arrived at by students of social behaviour during and after disasters. Before seeing the evidence, it might have been very plausible to conjecture that the weakening of the normal control mechanisms of society would allow anti-social elements to violate laws and customs, and that even normally law-abiding individuals would attach much higher priority than before to the selfish necessities of personal survival and well-being as against serving community needs or interests. Nevertheless, reports on recent disasters have emphasized that the opposite tends to occur. Disaster seems to mobilize certain reserves for constructive communal action that are not apparent in

Table 4.1 Pre- and Post-Earthquake Retail Food Prices in Anchorage for Selected Items,[a] 23 March–15 June 1964

Food Item	Unit	Price, $[b]							
		23 March[c]	30 March[a]	6 April[d]	20 April	4 May	18 May	1 June	15 June
Normal market-basket goods:									
Bread, Mrs Wright's white std. lge. loaf	22½oz.	0.47	0.47	0.47	0.47	0.47	0.47	0.47	0.47
Milk, fresh, Lucerne	quart	0.45	0.43	0.43	0.43	0.43	0.43	0.43	0.43
Eggs, large, Grade AA, Cream of the Crop	doz	0.77	0.77	0.75	0.75	0.75	0.75	0.75	0.74
Coffee, Edwards	lb	0.83	0.83	0.83	0.83	0.83	0.87	0.87	0.87
High-demand goods:									
Canned beef stew	24 oz	0.65	0.65	0.65	0.65	0.65	0.69	0.69	0.69
Pream	7 oz	0.65	0.65	0.65	0.65	0.65	0.65	0.65	0.65
Grapefruit juice, Townhouse	46 oz can	0.63	0.63	0.63	0.63	0.69	0.69	0.69	0.69
Cigarettes	Carton — all brands & sizes	2.79	2.79	2.79	2.79	2.79	2.79	2.79	2.79

Source: Kunreuther and Dacy, op. cit.
Notes:
a Source: Safeway Stores.
b Underscored numbers indicate price changes.
c Monday preceding quake.
d Monday following quake.

normal times. The most impressive evidence is the way in which the populations of England, Germany and Japan stood up to bombing attacks in World War II with little loss of productivity, or even weakening of the will to continue resistance.[5] Similar results have been observed for other disasters, from the Halifax explosion of 1917[6] to the New York power blackout of November 1965[7]. Indeed, some social theorists regard shared communal disaster as a unifying experience without equal.[8] It must be pointed out that opinion is not quite unanimous on this question.[9] Some writers have maintained that disaster releases a variety of extreme behaviours, both selfish and altruistic, that are not normally observed.[10] A number of disaster experiences of earlier and modern times do not reveal quite so happy a picture; incidents of looting during the Chicago blizzard of February 1967 might be mentioned as a recent example counterbalancing the evidence of the New York blackout. Nevertheless, the generalization about 'good behaviour' seems to be the dominant note, if only as a corrective to *a priori* expectations of 'bad behaviour'.

In what follows, I shall attempt to provide an interpretation consistent with the observed patterns of mutual cooperativeness under *some, but not all*, disaster circumstances.

II

The Kunreuther–Dacy explanation that disaster leads to an increase in community feeling does not carry us very far. If the explanation means that disaster brings about a shift in the utility function, the phenomenon lies in the realm of psychology — so there is little for the economist to discuss. It may be remarked, however, that the instances noted above of post-disaster bad behaviour remain to be explained.

De Alessi[11] has argued that we need not call upon a shift of the utility function, since the Alaskan evidence is consistent simply with a movement *on* a given utility map, in consequence of the changed availability of goods. Assume that (almost) every person normally spends some fraction of his income for altruistic ends, thus evidencing (assuming rationality) a positive taste for charity. We might think of the utility curves as drawn on coordinates *My real income* and *Other fellows' real income*, with a normally negative slope reflecting the fact that the partial effect of either 'commodity' upon the function is positive. If my indifference curves have the normal convex curvature, and if both commodities are superior goods, an impoverishment of others *relative to* myself would raise the relative marginal utility to me of others' consumption. Assuming that I can still transfer at par a dollar's worth of my consumption for a dollar's worth of his, I will indeed be inclined to make some additional transfers. Thus we have an explanation of why relatively better-off individuals in disaster tend to help their less fortunate neighbours.

This argument is appealing, as it does explain the universally observed fact that relief (in financial, physical and emotional form) tends to flow into a damaged area from the untouched outside. The opposite side of the coin, the implication that those relatively worse-off tend to be less altruistic than before, is also plausible, but there seems to be no evidence relating degree of altruistic activities inversely to the degree of relative deprivation. Also, this view provides no explanation as to why *general* impoverishment is met with general good behaviour, nor as to why exceptional cases occur in which bad behaviour is observed.

III

In the alternative explanation I would now like to offer, taste for altruism will be assumed away. I do not deny that many people do have a positive taste for altruism, and that the effects of relative deprivation upon their behaviour would then be essentially as outlined above. However, I would deny the premise that substantially *everyone's* utility map has a positive partial derivative with respect to 'other fellows' income'. Indeed, depending upon the individual and varying from culture to culture and with relative wealth levels, there will be many cases of a *negative* taste for altruism — at least on the margin. If keeping up with the Joneses is a problem, I will not view Mr Jones' salary raises with unalloyed joy.[12] If there are *conflicting* tastes for altruism, the effect upon behaviour of a general impoverishment will be even less clear.

If altruism will not serve as our social cement, we shall need an alternative. In my formulation, this alternative is rational selfish calculation of the advantage of maintaining that *alliance* we call society. That the continuation of a highly organized society is of enormous importance, to essentially everyone within it, will command general assent. Even criminals, or rational criminals at any rate, want a prosperous society. The problem, however, is to explain why alliance-supportive activities (community feeling in the Kunreuther–Dacy formulation; altruism for De Alessi; good behaviour in the historical record) are *particularly* prevalent under conditions of disaster.

The explanation lies in the economics of alliance.[13] The key point is that alliance-supportive activities are an example of the class of collective goods, the main benefits of which are not realized as private gains but are diffused throughout the entire community. Despite the enormous value to the typical individual of maintaining the social alliance in a healthy and prosperous state, the perceived *marginal* effects of his own alliance-preserving actions will normally be very small. Thus the criminal can engage in disruptive activities *because* he is confident that the community will survive anyway, assuring him of a pleasant environment in which to spend his ill-gotten gains.

On this view, individuals have mutually bound themselves, in a social contract, to certain *duties* (both positive and negative injunctions of an alliance-supportive nature) in consequence of which they can anticipate the benefits of having an organized society. The contract is in some part self-enforcing; the conversion of duties into customary behaviour is one of the prime purposes and achievements of early education (constituting, presumably, an important justification for social subsidy of private education). But even the best of us are rarely enthusiastic about paying taxes, and the policeman plays a still necessary role in all known societies — evidence that a degree of compulsion remains necessary to induce good behaviour in normal times.

However, those few who can perceive a direct connection between their actions and the health and survival of the alliance will on this theory behave quite differently. We are not surprised, therefore, to hear of the gruelling hours and intense pace of work at high levels in the national administration in Washington. An even clearer example for our purposes is the soldier, who is willing to place his life in danger to defend his community (or communities).[14]

Returning to the main argument, the contention here has been that alliance-supportive activities are of the nature of a collective good, and thus normally under-supplied on the basis of individuals' private decisions — except in so far as duties under the social contract are enforced by custom and policemen.[15] What happens to change this in cases of disaster? Suddenly the state of the society's health, or even its continued existence, may be thrown into question. The marginal effectiveness of individual actions upon the outcome is then multiplied by a large factor. Consider a military example: Soldiers are manning a rampart, and all will be in grave peril if any gives way. Or a non-military example: when the river is in flood, an entire community drops its normal tasks and stands by the dykes — for it is not absurd to imagine that even one man may make the difference. In the Alaskan case, each man could reason that even a single individual's selfish behaviour could trigger an explosion of hoarding from which all would lose. In such circumstances, and regardless of whether the taste for altruism is positive or negative, we would expect to see a high level of alliance-supportive activities.

This interpretation leads readily to an explanation of circumstances in which bad behaviour will be observed. Bad behaviour will be more likely the more plausible the argument: 'Since at least one deviant individual is liable to start a hoarding spiral anyway, I might as well get an early start myself.' In military terms again, once the conviction grows that defeat is probable, *sauve qui peut* is the only rational policy. On this theory, the 'goodness' of behaviour to be expected will be a characteristic function of the intensity of the threat. If it is sufficiently small, there is no reason for anyone to be any more alliance-supportive in his behaviour than before. As the threat grows to a certain critical level, where the balance hangs by a hair, alliance-supportive behaviour is maximized. Once the balance seems to be swinging the other way, alliance-supportive behaviour drops off. Indeed, because of the positive feedback element of any individual's defection upon the calculations of all others, breakdown is liable to be very swift once the process starts. Again, military examples abound.

Of course, the degree of alliance-supportive behaviour is not a function *only* of the size of the threat. Social customs and culture will affect each individual's perception of others' behaviour, with the same positive feedback noted above. The less duty-bound the individual considers others to be, the less reasonable his standing to his own post. Presumably, the more deeply divided internally the society is, the less each individual will value maintenance of a community containing the incompatible group. And the larger group in question, the less the confidence that each individual can have in the behaviour of others.

IV

The conclusion arrived at, then, is that the perceived advantage to the individual of society-supportive as opposed to narrowly selfish activities explains why 'good behaviour' is sometimes, but not always, observed in connection with disaster. Alliance theory leads to an expectation of a definite optimum stress from the point of view of eliciting alliance-supportive behaviour — if stress intensifies beyond that point, rapid collapse of the alliance is to be anticipated.

NOTES

1. See T. S. Kuhn, *The Structure of Scientific Revolutions* (Chicago: University of Chicago Press, 1962).

2. H. Kunreuther and D. Dacy, 'The Peculiar Economics of Disaster'. Later published in D. Dacy and H. Kunreuther, *The Economics of Natural Disasters: Implications for Federal Policy* (New York, 1969).
3. It is true that, other things equal, the 'income effect' would tend to reduce demand and thus prices, as a result of community impoverishment. But the actual overall wealth decline in Alaska was not great (especially considering the prospect of federal relief), whereas the supply of some vital commodities was sharply reduced by destruction of stocks and interruption of transport.
4. Truck freight rates to Alaska were reduced after the disaster. To underline the anomalous element for conventional theory, the truck rates were lowered only for those commodities that could *not* be conveniently shipped by boat — the competitive mode of transport.
5. See especially Fred C. Iklé, *The Social Impact of Bomb Destruction* (University of Oklahoma Press, 1958).
6. S. H. Prince, *Catastrophe and Social Change* (Columbia University Press, 1920).
7. A. M. Rosenthal and Arthur Gelb, *The Night the Lights Went Out* (Signet, 1965).
8. C. E. Fritz, 'Disaster', in R. K. Merton and R. A. Nisbet, *Contemporary Social Problems* (Harcourt, 1961).
9. Robert N. Wilson, 'Disaster and Mental Health', in G. W. Baker and D. W. Chapman, *Man and Society in Disaster* (Basic Books, 1962).
10. P. A. Sorokin, *Man and Society in Calamity* (Dutton, 1942).
11. Louis De Alessi, 'The Utility of Disaster', later published in *Kyklos*, vol. 21 (1968).
12. I would be inclined to hypothesize that for many (most?) people the marginal utility of 'other fellows' income' remains positive only up to some level safely below their own income. Indeed, few obey the old injunction addressed to the poor 'to take delight in the prosperity of elevated persons'.
13. See Mancur Olson, Jr and Richard Zeckhauser, *An Economic Theory of Alliances*, RM-4297-ISA, The RAND Corporation, October 1966. Also published in *Review of Economics and Statistics*, vol. 48, August 1966.
14. Of course, 'the' community is an over-simplification, because men actually live in an overlapping set of communities ranging from the family through the nation and even perhaps to the human species as a whole. The soldier's willingness to sacrifice himself is not only a function of his identification with the national society, but with the narrower military communities from squad to army.
15. As a matter of political philosophy, we can note that the charge made against free societies, that they encourage people to be 'more selfish' than people would like to be, may have a degree of merit. For while the social contract can bind us to unselfish conduct, the enforcement costs are liable to increase disproportionately with the rigorousness of the duties imposed. Given heavy enforcement costs, the optimum social contract will then tend to be biased in the direction of minimizing those duties.

Part II
Cooperation and Conflict

5 From Weakest-link to Best-shot: The Voluntary Provision of Public Goods*

* * *

Background of this Chapter

While there is a considerable time-gap, this study is a later development of themes suggested in the preceding essay. The observed powerful tendency to provide mutual aid in times of disaster, and the concept of such cooperation as a voluntary contribution to a public good — the survival of society as an alliance — led me gradually to believe that the standard economic theory of public goods was inadequate. In the generalized version proposed here, there is a spectrum of cases. At one extreme, as in the post-disaster syndrome, much more of the public good will be provided than allowed for in standard theory (the Weakest-link case). At the other extreme, even less will be voluntarily offered than standard theory predicts (the Best-shot case).

An addendum to the paper corrects a technical error in the original.

* * *

ABSTRACT

It has traditionally been assumed that the socially available amount X of a public good is the simple sum of the separate amounts x_i produced by the $i = 1, \ldots, I$ members of the community. But there are many other possibilities of practical importance. Among them are: (i) Weakest-link rule, where the socially available amount is the *minimum* of the quantities individually provided, and (ii) Best-shot rule, where the socially available amount is the *maximum* of the individual quantities. The former tends to

* Originally published in *Public Choice* 41: 371–86 (1983); Correction in ibid., 46: 221–3 (1985). Reproduced by permission of Martinus Nijhoff Publishers.

arise in linear situations, where each individual has a veto on the total to be provided (e.g. if each is responsible for one link of a chain); the latter tends to arise when there is a single prize of overwhelming importance for the community, with any individual's effort having a chance of securing the prize.

In comparison with the standard summation formula of ordinary public good theory, it is shown that under-provision of the public good is moderated in situations where the Weakest-link function is applicable, but aggravated when the Best-shot function is applicable. In time of disaster, where the survival of the community may depend upon each person's doing his duty, the conditions for applicability of the Weakest-link rule are approximated. This circumstance explains the historical observation that disaster conditions tend to elicit an extraordinary amount of unselfish behaviour.

Anarchia is a perfectly circular island, and each citizen owns a wedge-shaped slice (not all equal) from the centre to the sea. Like the Netherlands, Anarchia is protected by dykes from occasional storms that threaten to flood the land. But since Anarchia has no government, everyone makes his own decision as to how high a dyke to build. While the height of each citizen's dyke is perfectly visible to all, the customs of Anarchia forbid enforcement of any threat, inducement or contract whereby some parties might influence the choices of others. In times of flood the sea will penetrate the sector belonging to whichever citizen has constructed the lowest dyke, but the topography of Anarchia is such that no matter where the sea enters, damage will be suffered equally over the whole island. The economists of Anarchia have long realized that flood protection for their island is a public good. Many centralized schemes for motivating individuals to build dykes of the socially optimal height have been discussed, but Anarchia's citizens find any such social planning intolerable. It so came about, however, that the United Nations generously paid for an analysis of the situation by the well-known international consulting firm of economists, Arthur 'Dam' Little & Co. To everyone's surprise, the conclusion was that Anarchia's citizens have voluntarily invested in dykes (and therefore have provided themselves with the public good of flood protection) to almost all (98.17 per cent, to be exact) of the socially efficient amount.

ALTERNATIVE SOCIAL COMPOSITION FUNCTIONS

Public goods, by definition, have a peculiar feature on the demand side: the amount produced, however determined, is equally available for concurrent consumption by all members of the community. Our standard models have assumed, however, that there is nothing at all special on the supply side, in the social technology for the *production* of public goods.

More specifically, it has always been assumed that the socially available amount X of a public good is nothing but the simple sum of the separate amounts x_i produced by the $_i = 1, \ldots, I$ members of the community. But many other possibilities come to mind. I shall speak of these alternative possibilities as *social composition functions*, i.e. as different possible ways of amalgamating individual productions into social availabilities of a public good.

I shall concentrate on three especially simple cases:

Social Composition Functions

(1) $X = \sum_i x_i$ Summation

(2) $X = \min_i(x_i)$ Weakest-link

(3) $X = \max_i(x_i)$ Best-shot

Imagine a team markmanship contest. Suppose that the pay-off in the form of glory goes as a public good to all the members of the winning team, collectively. Now, it is perfectly easy to imagine that the relevant social composition function, the formula for calculating a team's score, might be (among many other possibilities) any one of the three rules above: the team declared the winner might be the one with the best total score, or the highest minimum score (the best of the individual marksmen's worst shots), or the highest maximum score (the best single shot).

While in this illustration the alternative social composition functions represent contrived formulas for judging a social pastime, other examples can be instanced that correspond to 'natural' environmental payoff structures. The Anarchia fable is an instance of the Weakest-link function. More generally, the Weakest-link measure approximates a wide variety of 'linear' situations where each member of a social group successively has a kind of veto power over the extent of collective achievement; for example, if each member is responsible for one link of a chain. As for the Best-shot function, imagine a number of anti-missile batteries ringing a city, firing at a single incoming nuclear-armed ICBM, where destruction for all will be the consequence if the enemy device gets through the defensive ring. Then, for all practical purposes, the only relevant question is whether the single best defensive shot is good enough to destroy the incoming bogey. Or a logically similar situation: the supporters of two claimants to the throne might engage in battle, with all the combatants on each side instructed to aim exclusively to kill the rival pretender.

As a different kind of example, consider the 'natural economy' of families. In modern evolutionary-genetic theory, the behaviour of animals is ultimately determined by the need to maximize reproductive survival. For a diploid organism, survival of an offspring represents a public good for its two parents. Since parents share equally in the genetic heritage of their offspring, any genetic payoff to the father due to enhanced offspring survival is equally an achievement for the mother, and vice versa. If father and mother forage separately for food, nutritional success for offspring might essentially depend only upon the total of the calories they bring back to the nest (Summation). Or, perhaps mother and father forage for distinct nutritional elements needed in fixed proportions by the offspring (Weakest-link). Or, more fancifully, the distinct elements may be equally useful but incompatible, rather like pickles and ice cream, so that the offspring will feed only on the larger of the two loads brought home by the two parents (Best-shot).

Of course, all kinds of intermediate cases and combinations can be imagined. Social composition functions observed in practice may well involve strands of all three rules mentioned above, as well as of others not yet identified. Not the best shot or the highest total but the location of the top decile, or the total of the best three shots, or the average of the best and worst shots, or the variance or skewness (and so on in indefinite variety) might be the relevant scoring formula. And there may be trade-offs: an excellent best-shot might partially compensate for a mediocre total, etc. When we think of the variety of collective enterprises — families and nations and armies and firms — and the vast range of their associated activities, we can realize how descriptively incomplete has been our standard assumption that all social composition functions take the form of simple summation.

EFFICIENT AND EQUILIBRIUM SOLUTIONS — SUMMATION VERSUS WEAKEST-LINK

In this section, I shall examine Nash–Cournot equilibrium outcomes versus efficiency conditions for provision of public goods, comparing the standard textbook Summation situation with the Weakest-link composition function of our Anarchia fable.

In making the comparison it will be helpful first to construct a somewhat novel diagrammatic illustration[1] of the standard public good solution — for a simple world of two individuals A and B. In Figure 5.1, x_A on the horizontal axis represents A's production of the public good while x_B on the vertical axis represents B's contribution. A's indifference curves U^o_A, U'_A, U''_A, ... on these axes are drawn solid, while B's U^o_B, U'_B, U''_B, ... are shown as dashed. The shapes of the U_A curves can be explained as follows. First of all, other things equal, an increase in x_B always benefits A, hence any move north in the diagram gets A onto a higher indifference curve. Moving east, on the other hand, means that for given x_B individual A is producing a larger amount of the public good. He will derive some marginal utility benefit from doing so, but will also incur a marginal cost. It is reasonable to suppose that as he increases x_A from zero at the vertical axis, utility at first rises but ultimately begins to fall. These conditions dictate the shapes of the U_A curves in the diagram. A corresponding argument explains the shapes of the U_B curves.

Evidently, for any given x_B, the optimum x_A will be found where the associated U_A curve is *horizontal*. Hence, under Nash–Cournot assumptions, a reaction curve R_A can be passed through all these points of horizontality; the curve R_A shows A's chosen output of the public good, given B's output. The negative slope of R_A reflects the fact that B's production of the public good substitutes for A's own production in A's utility function. Hence diminishing marginal utility for A's own production of the public good sets in earlier, the larger is x_B.

It may be helpful to introduce some symbolism at this point. Individual $i = A,B$ is maximizing $U_i(X,y_i)$, where $X \equiv x_A + x_B$, and y_i represents his consumption availability of an ordinary private good. His choice between x_i and y_i is constrained by some production function $Q_i(x_i,y_i) = 0$. Then the private optimality solution can be written in two alternative self-explanatory notations as:

$$\frac{dy_i}{dX}\bigg|_{U_i} = \frac{dy_i}{dx_i}\bigg|_{Q_i} \tag{1a}$$

or

$$MRS_i(X) = MC_i(x_i) \tag{1b}$$

Given our standard assumptions about the shapes of the marginal rate of substitution (MRS) and marginal cost (MC) functions, a rise in x_B tends to lower $MRS_A(X)$ without affecting $MC_A(x_A)$ — assuming, as we usually do, that the individuals' production functions are not interdependent. A's indifference-curve slope on x_A,x_B axes in Figure 5.1 can be written.[2]

$$\frac{dx_B}{dx_A}\bigg|_{U_A} \equiv -\frac{\partial U_A/\partial x_A}{\partial U_{A/\partial x_B}} \equiv -\frac{MRS_A(X) - MC_A(x_A)}{MRS_A(X)} \tag{2}$$

Since upon moving north in the diagram $MRS_A(X)$ tends to decrease

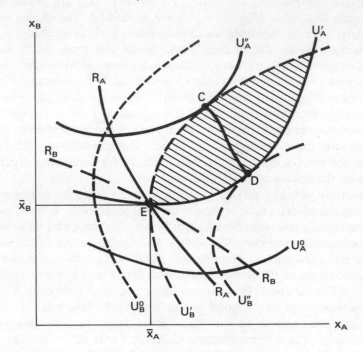

Figure 5.1 *Efficient and equilibrium solutions, Summation
composition function*

and $MC_A(x_A)$ remain unchanged, the indifference-curve slope becomes
less negative or more positive. Thus, the indifference-curve minima
shift to the left, explaining the negative slope of the R_A curve as
asserted above.

For the other individual, we have:

$$\left.\frac{dx_B}{dx_A}\right|_{U_B} \equiv -\frac{\partial U_B/\partial x_A}{\partial U_B/\partial x_B} \equiv -\frac{MRS_B(X)}{MRS_B(X) - MC_B(x_B)} \qquad (3)$$

A corresponding argument explains the negative slope of individual
B's Reaction Curve R_B.

Evidently, the Nash–Cournot solution is at point $E = (\bar{x}_A, \bar{x}_B)$ in
Figure 5.1, the intersection of the two Reaction Curves. (The equilibrium is stable if, as shown here, the R_A curve is absolutely steeper
than the R_B curve.) Equally evidently, this equilibrium is not efficient.
In fact, the shaded portion of the diagram pictures the familiar region
of mutual advantage. The curve CD is the portion of the contract curve
(set of mutual indifference-curve tangencies) included within the region

of mutual advantage, and the efficient solution must lie on this curve. The mutual-tangency condition can be written:

$$\frac{MRS_A(X) - MC_A(x_A)}{MRS_A(X)} = \frac{MRS_B(X)}{MRS_B(X) - MC_B(x_B)} \tag{4}$$

Imposing the additional necessary condition for efficiency that $MC_A = MC_B$, this reduces to the familiar:

$$MC_A(x_A) = MC_B(x_B) = \sum_i MRS_i(X) \tag{5}$$

That is, for efficiency in the production of a public good, each producer should set the marginal cost of his output equal to the *sum* of the individuals' separate marginal rates of substitution. This condition will be met only by a subset of the points, or perhaps only by a unique point within the range CD of the contract curve in Figure 5.1.

With this standard solution for the Summation rule of social composition as background, now consider the Weakest-link function of the Anarchia fable.

Figure 5.2 is constructed on the same principles as Figure 5.1. However, the 45° line where $x_A = x_B$ now plays an important role. In drawing individual A's indifference curves (solid), we clearly need only consider the region where $x_A \leq x_B$: A would never choose to produce more output than B does, since he would incur additional costs without generating any benefits for anyone under the social composition function $X = \min(x_A, x_B)$. And similarly, B's indifference curves (dashed) are shown only in the region where $x_B \leq x_A$.

Consider A's indifference curves U_A^0, U_A^I, U_A^{II}, ... Equation (2) continues to define their slopes. But within the interesting region North-west of the 45° line, along any vertical line the slopes now will be the same — since $MC_A(x_A)$ depends only on x_A, while $MRS_A(X)$ remains unchanged when $X = \min(x_A, x_B)$. For low levels of utility, A's indifference curves will have negative slope where they contact the 45° line, but eventually a point F will be reached where the contact occurs at a horizontal indifference-curve slope. Between points F and K in the diagram, contact occurs along a positive-sloped portion of indifference curve. And, finally, above K, indifference curves will not touch the 45° line at all. Correspondingly for individual B: below point G the indifference curves have negative slope where they contact the 45° line; above point G, they have positive slope; while above point L they do not touch the 45° line at all.

As for the Reaction Curves, it will be evident that R_A must lie along the 45° line until point F is reached, after which it becomes vertical. A similar analysis for individual B indicates that R_B must also at first overlie the 45° line. But eventually, at the point G where a vertical-sloped indifference curve contacts the 45° line, the R_B curve becomes horizontal.

Under the strict logic of the Nash–Cournot equilibrium concept, the outcome may equally well fall anywhere along the entire range where R_A and R_B both overlie the 45° line, that is, anywhere in the range *OF*. (Note that F corresponds to the preferred X on the part of the individual *least desirous* of the public good, relative to its private marginal cost to him.) I want to argue, however, that in the spirit of 'rational expectations' we would expect to find the final equilibrium at point F, the upper limit of this range, where $X = x^*$. While all the potential equilibria along *OF* are possible, there is a gain to all parties the nearer the outcome is to point F. Apart from the possibility of learning via repeated play of the game, it is not difficult to imagine a dynamic that would lead directly to this solution. Specifically, if the players moved *in sequence*, the first player (A, let us say) would 'rationally' pick output $x_A = x^*$ in the confident belief that player B would then follow his lead. If B were the first player, knowing A's situation he would also choose point F.[3] So long as the choices are visible,[4] the economic logic leading to the solution at F seems compelling.[5] It should be noted, also, that this outcome is *not* vulnerable to the Prisoners' Dilemma paradox. In the Prisoners' Dilemma, once having achieved a mutually profitable outcome it pays each party to 'defect'. Here defection is not an issue — the cooperative outcome at F is perfectly stable, if only it can be achieved in the first place.

The (modified) Nash–Cournot equilibrium, then, can be said to be where all parties produce output $X = x^*$ such that:

$$MC_i(x_i^*) = MRS_i(x_i^*) \quad \text{for some } i \in I$$

and   (6)

$$MC_j(x_j^*) \leqq MRS_j(x_j^*) \quad \text{for all } j \neq i.$$

Note: Individual i is the one who *first* hits the equality in the upper equation.

As for the *efficient* solutions, inspection of Figure 5.2 will make it clear that these all lie along the 45° line in the range between points K and L — which corresponds to the portion of the contract curve within the region of mutual advantage. Along the 45° line below K, both parties move onto higher indifference curves the closer they get to K. Similarly, above point L there is a mutual gain as the parties move down toward L. Along the segment KL, however, neither can gain without some loss being imposed upon the other party. Within

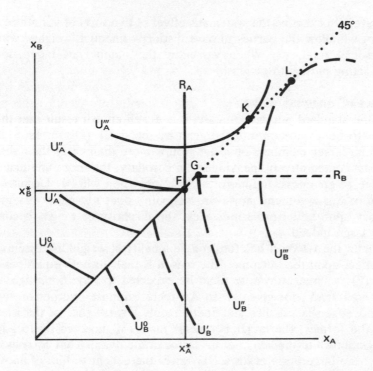

Figure 5.2   Efficient and equilibrium solutions, Weakest-link composition function

KL, a subset or possibly a unique point will also meet the production condition:

$$\sum_i MC_i(x_i) = \sum_i MRS_i(x_i) \qquad (7)$$

THE EXTENT OF VOLUNTARY PROVISION — DISCUSSION

Is there reason to believe that, under the Weakest-link composition function, voluntary provision of the public good will more nearly approximate the efficient amount?

The first point to note from Figures 5.1 and 5.2 is that, for both the Summation and Weakest-link functions, under-provision is to be anticipated. Nor is it immediately obvious that the extent of under-provision should be systematically greater in either case — so long as we stick to the two-party interaction pictured on the diagram. I want, however, to examine the systematic effect of two sorts of variation: (1) When we allow the parties to have distinctly unequal 'weights' within the social total. (2) When we allow the number of independent interacting parties to increase.

Effect of unequal weight

For the standard Summation case, it is a well-known result that there tends to be 'exploitation of the great by the small' (Olson, 1965: 29). That is, larger members of social groups more than carry their share, at least comparatively speaking. As a corollary, the more unequal the degree of greatness, the more the total provision will be. Despite the force of this argument, however, inequality does not have very great impact upon under-provision unless the disparity of weight becomes very large indeed.

Under the Weakest-link function, inequality of weight has essentially no effect upon the outcome. The reason is that, in both equations (6) and (7), a large individual i can be expected to have *both* high MC_i and high MRS_i, for given x_i. In Anarchia, suppose one person has a large wedge-shaped slice and another only a small slice of the island. For the former, the larger perimeter makes it more costly to add a marginal inch to the height of his sector of the dyke — but correspondingly, the larger area of his sector raises the benefit to him of another inch added to dykes all around.

Effect of larger numbers

In the standard Summation situation, it is well known that at the Nash–Cournot equilibrium: (1) total production X of the public good rises as the population size I grows, but (2) the absolute and relative under-provision also increase with I (see Chamberlin, 1974, 1976). (These results follow if neither the public good nor the private good is inferior.) Intuitively, think of a typical individual A in Figure 5.1 where B represents 'everyone else'. When others provide more of the public good, individual A now being in effect wealthier will want to consume more X, as well as more of the private good. Then his Reaction Curve R_A will have negative slope (x_A falls as x_B rises) but its absolute slope will be greater than unity ($x_A + x_B$ rises as x_B rises.) As X rises with population size I, eventually the typical individual A finds himself almost saturated with the public good X, and hence relatively unwilling to sacrifice consumption of the private good to generate even more X. We can say that A's weight in the social total relative to 'everyone else' diminishes; being small, he will 'exploit the great' by cutting x_A back almost one-for-one as x_B rises (the slope of his reaction curve approaches − 1). But in the efficiency condition of equation (5), the rising ΣMRS on the right-hand side as I increases dictates that each individual i should *increase* his output x_i — whereas, we have just seen, our typical individual A will want to decrease his output. So the degree of under-provision will rise sharply as numbers increase.

The result for the Weakest-link social composition function is quite different. The degree of under-provision may increase, but, if so, only weakly as I increases. Equation (7) says that the *efficient* social output X will tend to be unchanged as I increases, since the summations on both left-hand side and right-hand side of the equation rise more or less equally. Equation (6) indicates that the *actual* output will surely be unchanged, except when one of the new entrants is less desirous of the public good (relative to his private marginal cost) than the least desirous old member of the population. If the populations, old and new, were quite uniform there would be no change at all, but with heterogeneous populations there would remain some tendency for increased underprovision as I rises. Intuitively, think of each individual as supplying a link in a linear chain, whose strength is the public good enjoyed by all. If all individuals had identical marginal cost MC and marginal rate of substitution MRS, adding another link would not affect either the equilibrium strength or the efficient strength of the chain. However, as a second approximation, a new entrant relatively undesirous of strength would tend to reduce the equilibrium amount provided relative to the efficient amount.

BEST-SHOT COMPOSITION FUNCTION

I shall discuss the third social composition function, the Best-shot formula, only briefly. Recall that here the social total X of the public good represents the *largest* of the individual contributions x_i.

In the two-party case, if we suppose as a first approximation that the individuals are identical, each would surely want to escape the burden — leaving the other to bear the cost. But if the parties diverge sufficiently in desire for the public good (relative to its private cost), the one most desirous will very likely end up being the provider. It is difficult to set up a plausible dynamic leading to a definite equilibrium under visible conditions, however.

The efficient solution has two parts: choosing the low-cost supplier, and determining the quantity he produces. We can say:

For some individual k such that $TC_k(x_k) \leqq TC_j(x_k)$ for all $j \neq k$:

$$MC_k(x_k) = \sum_i MRS_i(x_k)$$

and   (8)

$$x_j \qquad = 0, \text{ for } j \neq k.$$

The output should be produced by the individual whose total cost TC_k is lowest, and the amount provided should be such that his marginal cost MC_k *equals the sum of all the marginal rates of substitution MRS_i.* (There may be more than one productive arrangement meeting these conditions.) But it is immediately clear that the actual provision will not get anywhere near this. Even if the most efficient producer were to become the single generator of the public good for the entire community, he would clearly produce only to the point where marginal cost equalled his *individual* marginal rate of substitution:

$$MC_k(x_k) = MRS_k(x_k)$$ (9)

As numbers increase, the amount provided might rise slightly whenever a new entrant turns out to be the new low-cost provider. Nevertheless, it is clear that as I grows the Best-shot function implies drastically and increasingly unsatisfactory outcomes.

SUMMARY AND REMARKS

In the provision of public goods, our standard textbook assumption — that the amount X socially available is simply the *sum* of the private amounts x_i individually produced — is only one of a number of possible important social composition functions. Two other social composition functions were selected for comparative investigation: under the Weakest-link rule the socially available quantity corresponds to the *minimum* of the individual x_i, while under the Best-shot function the social availability X corresponds to the *maximum* of the x_i. It was shown that each of the three functions applies to important types of social phenomena. Furthermore, other public-good situations correspond to mixtures of composition functions or to more complicated functions than were discussed here. Consequently, exclusive concentration upon the Summation formula has led to a seriously distorted view of the private provision of public goods.

Each of the three social composition functions leads to a distinct pattern of provision of X, and in particular of underprovision of the public good as population size I increases. Without pretending to any degree of rigour, overall results are roughly summarized in Figure 5.3. The bold curves indicate the general trend of the efficient social total

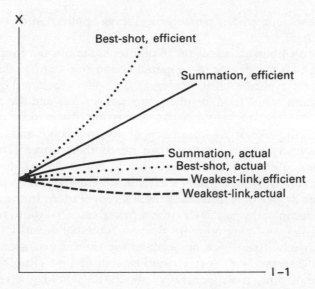

Figure 5.3   Trend of efficient and actual solutions as population grows

of *X* as population size *I* grows, while the faint curves indicate the equilibrium provision. The solid pair of curves indicate the working of the Summation function, the dashed pair stand for the Weakest-link function, and the dotted pair the Best-shot function. At *I* = 1, the public good is of course merely a private good; all curves coincide along the *X*-axis where *I* − 1 = 0.

When the social composition function for public goods represents the standard textbook Summation situation (solid curves), efficient provision rises rapidly with *I* but actual provision only very slowly, hence absolute and relative underprovision of the public good tend to increase strongly with numbers. When the social composition function follows the Weakest-link formula (dashed curves) — i.e. when the socially available amount *X* is the *minimum* of the amounts privately produced — the efficient amount tends to remain unchanged as *I* grows while the actual equilibrium provision may fall slowly as *I* increases. Under-provision is mild, particularly when the population is homogeneous. (In fabled Anarchia, under-provision was alleged to amount to just 1.83 per cent, a figure selected for dramatic rather than veridical illustration.) Finally, when the social composition function follows the Best-shot rule (dotted curves) — i.e. when the socially available amount *X* is the *maximum* of the quantities privately produced — efficient provision rises very sharply with *I*, while actual provision may rise, but very slowly. Clearly, underprovision is the most severe in this case.

I shall conclude with a possibly significant application of the ideas proposed here.[7]

Observers of human behaviour in disaster situations have repeatedly been struck by the degree of cooperation and self-sacrifice that these tragic events typically elicit. Refugees are often sheltered gratis in private homes, while food, blankets, medical services and the like flow copiously into the stricken area. An interesting observation: after the Alaskan earthquake of 1964, suppliers of essential goods and transport services actually reduced rather than raised their prices (Dacy and Kunreuther, 1969).[8] Furthermore, this is not merely a matter of assistance coming from outside: the victims themselves often display a remarkable degree of restraint and mutual cooperation. In the Alaskan case, for example, the purchasers of low-priced essential goods refrained from hoarding and took no more than an equitable quantity. Reports of a similar tenor have been made about the Halifax explosion of 1917 (Prince, 1920), the New York power blackout of 1965 (Rosenthal and Gelb, 1965), and, more generally, about the bombing disasters of World War II (Iklé, 1958). The sociologist C. E. Fritz (1961) has contended that shared communal disaster is a unifying experience without equal.

More specifically, the strong feeling of community identification, and the consequent unselfish cooperative efforts in repair and relief activity, are characteristic of the immediate postimpact period. The motivation for mutual assistance appears to erode after some days or weeks, and jealousies over relief distribution and the like typically lead to widespread recrimination as a more normal society is restored. And similarly for the 'counter-disaster syndrome', the tendency of outsiders to rush assistance to the disaster zone. Some time later a reaction tends to set in, frequently leading to bad relations between victim and support populations.

Before seeing the evidence, it would have been plausible to conjecture that the weakening of normal control mechanisms in the immediate disaster period would allow antisocial elements to violate laws and customs, and that even normally law-abiding individuals would attach much higher priority than before to the selfish necessities of personal survival as against serving community interests. Certainly, popular novelistic treatments typically paint a lurid picture of disaster aftermaths. And indeed there is some divergence of opinion and evidence on this score. The sociologist Sorokin (1942) maintained that disaster releases a variety of extreme behaviours both good and bad. And incidents of looting in the Chicago blizzard of February 1967 counterbalance the good fellowship observed during the 1965 New York blackout. Or to cite military experience: front-line troops who have heroically withstood an enemy may, as at Waterloo, suddenly dissolve into a frantic, pushing mob. It is this juxtaposition or alternation of good and bad behaviour that needs explaining.

Dacy and Kunreuther (1969) argued that disaster increases 'community feeling'. De Alessi (1975) pointed out that we need not call upon a shift of the utility function: the evidence is consistent simply with a movement on a given utility map. In particular, potential donors with a positive 'taste' for charity now find new groups of impoverished targets for benevolence.

Without necessarily disagreeing with these explanations, so far as they go, I want to emphasize the public good aspect of the problem. The alliance we call society, normally not in danger of collapse, is threatened in time of disaster. In these circumstances alliance-supportive activities, cooperativeness and self-sacrifice, become an important public good. But, I also want to argue, a public good in large part describable in terms of the Weakest-link social composition function.

In our Anarchia example, the public need for flood protection was met by a technological solution — construction of dykes. Here we are speaking of behavioural solutions. While the underlying principles remain the same, the greater volatility of behaviour allows variation over time in response to the perceived magnitude of the threat. In normal periods when the threat is small, the dykes already in place are sufficient and there is no need for exceptional behaviour. In effect, the 'permanent' component of individuals' adjustment to the long-term probability distribution of threats provides more than enough protection. But as the specific threat grows and appears to be overwhelming the existing permanent defences, the Weakest-link formula elicits a 'transitory' additional adjustment: members of the community turn out to plug the leaks, to add sandbags on top, to dig out alternative water channels, etc.

While not intrinsic to the logic of the Weakest-link rule, behavioural response to disaster may be intensified by a critical mass aspect of the social alliance. Instead of the loss rising more or less in proportion to the magnitude of the non-countered threat, an all-or-nothing situation may be involved. In terms of the dyke metaphor: if the dyke is not breached, little or no loss will be suffered, but once breached even by a little bit the whole structure may give way. In terms of human cooperative behaviour, a critical-mass situation (see Schelling, 1978) implies two stable equilibria: survival of the alliance intact, or its complete collapse.

Thus, consistent with the evidence, the goodness of behaviour to be expected in disaster will vary in response to the magnitude of the threat. In normal times people behave in a conventionally cooperative way because individually they find it profitable to do so: while there is some slippage around the edges, on the whole the social control mechanisms deter evildoing. As the threat grows, eventually the balance may hang by a hair — so that any single person can reason that his own behaviour might be the social alliance's weakest link. It is in these circumstances that the Weakest-link rule elicits extraordinary heroism and self-sacrifice even from normally selfish people. But once the balance seems to be swinging the other way, so that even heroism can no longer rescue the situation — or, at least, once many people believe that *others* might so perceive matters — social collapse is likely to be swift.

NOTES

1. Similar diagrammatics are employed, for a somewhat different purpose, in my 'Natural Economy Versus Political Economy' (1978).
2. More explicitly:

$$\left.\frac{dx_B}{dx_A}\right|_{U_A} \equiv -\frac{\dfrac{\partial U}{\partial X}\dfrac{dX}{dx_A}+\dfrac{\partial U}{\partial y_A}\dfrac{dy_A}{dx_A}}{\dfrac{\partial U}{\partial X}\dfrac{dX}{dx_B}}$$

$$\equiv -\left(1+\frac{dy_A}{dx_A}\frac{\partial U/\partial y_A}{\partial U/\partial X}\right)$$

$$\equiv -(1-MC_A/MRS_A)$$

$$\equiv -\frac{MRS_A-MC_A}{MRS_A}$$

3. Lacking this knowledge, B might tentatively choose point G, but then would dismantle or liquidate his 'excessive' output after A's choice of point F.
4. If the choices are not visible (e.g. if no citizen of Anarchia could observe the height of other citizens' dykes), the problem becomes more complex. Presumably, some kind of probabilistic mixed strategy will become privately optimal. (A logically parallel example, though for a much simpler binary strategy rather than continuous strategy interaction, is the 'Battle of the Sexes' game analysed by Luce and Raiffa, 1957: 90–4). Such a situation will probably lead to a greater shortfall of output in comparison with the efficient solution. Of course, under the Summation Rule as well, invisibility may lead to a greater shortfall of output.
5. A somewhat related issue is discussed in Luce and Raiffa (1957: 106–7). In a game with multiple Nash equilibria, those equilibria with pay-offs inferior for both players to the pay-offs of some other strategy pair are termed 'jointly inadmissible'. In our situation the equilibria along the 45° line short of point F are all dominated by point F, and so are jointly inadmissible. On the other hand, as is evident from Figure 5.2, point F itself is jointly inadmissible in view of the possibility of outcomes even higher up on the

45° line. Thus, like the Prisoners' Dilemma, the game pictured here does not have what Luce and Raiffa call *a solution in the strict sense.* But the equilibrium at *F*, like the 'uncooperative' solution for the Prisoners' Dilemma, seems entirely stable.

6. As under the Weakest-link rule, we would expect invisible interactions to lead to a choice of a mixed strategy by each party.
7. These ideas derive in part from my 'Disaster and Recovery: A Historical Survey' (1963), 'Disaster Behavior: Altruism or Alliance?' (1975 [1967]), and from the discussions in De Alessi (1975) and Douty (1972).
8. To underline the anomalous element for conventional theory, truck rates to Alaska were lowered only for those commodities that could *not* be conveniently shipped by boat — the competitive mode of transport!

REFERENCES

Chamberlin, J. (1974) 'Provision of collective goods as a function of group size', *American Political Science Review* 68 (June).
—— (1976), 'A diagrammatic exposition of the logic of collection action', *Public Choice* 26 (Summer).
Dacy, D. C. and Kunreuther, H. R. (1969) *The Economics of Natural Disasters: Implications for Federal Policy*, New York
De Alessi, L. (1975) 'Toward an analysis of postdisaster cooperation', *American Economic Review* 65 (March).
Douty, C. M. (1972) 'Disaster and charity: Some aspects of cooperative economic behavior', *American Economic Review* 62 (September).
Fritz, C. E. (1961) 'Disaster', in R. K. Merton and R. A. Nisbet (eds.), *Contemporary Social Problems.* New York: Harcourt, Brace, and World.
Hirshleifer, J. (1978) 'Natural economy versus political economy', *Journal of Social and Biological Structures* 1 (October).
Hirshleifer, J. (1963) *Disaster and recovery: A historical survey*, Santa Monica: The Rand Corporation. Memorandum RM-3079-PR. April.
Hirshleifer, J. (1975 [1967]) 'Disaster behavior: Altruism or alliance?', UCLA Economics Department Discussion Paper No. 59 (May 1975 [March 1967]).
Iklé, F. C. (1958). *The Social Impact of Bomb Destruction*, Norman: University of Oklahoma Press.
Luce, R. D. and Raiffa, H. (1957) *Games and Decisions*, New York: Wiley.
Olson, M. (1965) *The Logic of Collective Action*, Cambridge, Mass.: Harvard University Press.
Prince, S. H. (1920) *Catastrophe and Social Change*, New York: Columbia University Press.
Rosenthal, A. M. and Gelb, A. (1965) *The Night the Lights Went Out*, New York: Signet.
Schelling, T. C. (1978) *Micromotives and Macrobehavior*, New York: Norton.
Sorokin, P. A. (1942) *Man and Society in Calamity*, New York: Dutton.

FROM WEAKEST-LINK TO BEST-SHOT: CORRECTION

My recent paper in *Public Choice*, on alternative social composition functions governing the voluntary provision of public goods (Hirshleifer, 1983), contained a regrettable error in one of the diagrams.

Figure 5.2 was intended to picture the extreme case of a 'Weakest-link' social composition function, corresponding to:

$$X = \min_{(i)} x_i \tag{1}$$

Here X is the socially available amount of the public good in a community of I individuals, while x_i represents the contribution of individual i ($i = 1, \ldots, I$). In this weakest-link situation, for two individuals A and B, the respective preference maps take on drastically different shapes northwest of the 45° line (where $x_A < x_B$) and southeast of it (where $x_A > x_B$). In particular, A will never contemplate operating outside the northwest region, while B will always choose to be in the southeast region.

I should have noticed that A's indifference curves must be strictly *vertical* in his relevant region, while B's must be strictly *horizontal* in his relevant region. (A degree of curvature does exist, in each case, but only in the non-relevant region.) The diagram here, showing only the indifference curves in the relevant regions, is a corrected version of Figure 5.2 in the original paper. In the corrected diagram there is a best vertical indifference curve for individual A, $\hat{U}_A$, associated with the maximum x_A that A would ever be willing to contribute — regardless of how much greater B's production may be. Consequently, A's Reaction Curve R_A runs from the origin to point F along the 45° line, and thenceforth along the vertical $\hat{U}_A$. For B similarly, his Reaction Curve R_B runs from the origin to point G on the 45° line, and thenceforth along his best indifference curve — the horizontal $\hat{U}_B$.

Consistent with the argument of the original paper, the *equilibrium* will be at the upper limit of the range where the Reaction Curves overlie one another along the 45° line — point F. The range between points F and G is like a 'contract curve' in that one party can gain only at the expense of the other. When marginal costs are equalized between the two parties, some single point like H in this range will be the efficient solution (assuming the MC functions are rising).

The erroneous diagram in the original paper would have been closer to correct for *intermediate* cases between Summation and Weakest link, for example:

$$X = w_1 x_1 + w_2 x_2 + \ldots + w_I x_I \tag{2}$$

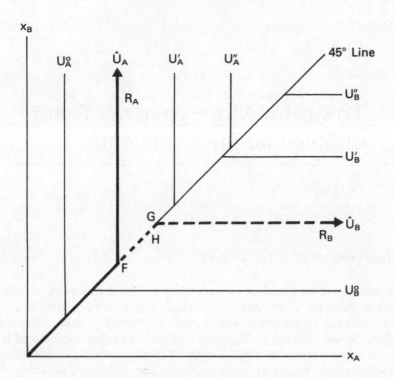

Figure 5.4 Efficient and equilibrium solutions, Weakest-link composition function (corrected)

Here the w_i are weights attached to the individuals' respective contributions, when these are ranked from the smallest to the largest. In the standard Summation case, all the weights would be unity. In the Weakest-link case, the weights are $w_1 = 1$, $w_2 = \ldots = w_I = 0$. I have discussed this intermediate range of cases, constituting the class of 'descending-weight' social composition functions, in a later paper (Hirshleifer, 1984).

Bibliography

Hirshleifer, J. (1983), 'From weakest-link to best-shot: The voluntary provision of public goods', *Public Choice* 41: 371–86.
—— (1984), 'The voluntary provision of public goods: Descending-weight social composition functions', UCLA Economics Dept. Working Paper No. 326 (May).

6 Toward a More General Theory of Regulation: Comment*

*   *   *

Background of this Chapter

A conference was held in January 1976 on The Economics of Politics and Regulation, in honour of George J. Stigler on his 65th birthday. The opening presentation was a paper by Sam Peltzman, 'Toward a More General Theory of Regulation'. The brief paper reproduced here was a comment on Peltzman's study. The note introduces two themes which are, I hope, of some novelty and importance. First, that democratic government typically acts in a redistribution-buffering role, leaning against the wind to moderate the redistributive consequences of changing events and circumstances (apart from those initiated by government itself). And second, that social interactions constitute a hierarchy along the dimension of constraints or rules of the game. The most constrained game is market exchange with established property rights. The intermediate level is constitutional politics, which permits invasions of property rights subject to established 'rules for changing the rules'. Finally, the least-constrained, the truly hardball game, is the raw politics of power and conflict.

*   *   *

In the broadest sense Sam Peltzman's paper[1] aims at developing — to quote his own words as applied to Stigler — *a theory of the optimum size of effective political coalitions*. The novelty and excitement of the results obtained are all the more impressive as Peltzman's analysis

---

* Originally published in the *Journal of Law & Economics* 19: 241–4 (1976). Reproduced by permission of The University of Chicago Press.

seems entirely independent of the literature in the public choice tradition that has grown from the pioneering work by Downs and by Buchanan and Tullock.[2] The penetrating power of the analysis displayed here is, however, in part due to limiting the field of attention to the specific area of regulation, a limitation that makes possible a fruitful interaction of economic and political conceptualizations.

In Peltzman's model the contending interest groups are supposed to be seeking, simply, *wealth redistributions through the regulatory process*. In effect, each group bids for the right to tax the remainder of the community. The regulator, taken as equivalent to an elected politician, arbitrates among the interest groups in seeking to maximize his majority — that is, his probability of election or re-election. All the results obtained derive from these simple assumptions. It is remarkable how far they carry us.

The interest groups, of course, really do have more complex aims. But I do not quarrel with postulating, as a strategic simplification, the one-dimensional materialistic goal of wealth-maximization. There are two things wrong with taking the regulators' goal as majority maximization, however. First, and most obviously, *the regulators themselves constitute an interest group*. They should, therefore, also be aiming at wealth-maximization. Indeed, the pathbreaking work of Downs really started from the question: Are Chicago aldermen guided by goals any different from or higher than the goals of Chicago factory workers or Chicago economics professors? A question answered in the negative, of course. If wealth is the ultimate goal, majority maximization can only be an instrumental and partial aim. The politician should be willing to accept some risk of defeat in exchange for a sufficient direct or indirect monetary payment. If majority maximization is not the only goal, we get the important implication that there are diminishing returns to size of majority from the politician's point of view — which is quite apart from the dilution effect of coalition size that Peltzman recognizes from the interest group's point of view.[3]

Even more fundamental, Peltzman's identification of the regulator with the elected politician is too radical a simplification. This assumption precludes analysis of the substantially different roles played by the various classes of actors in the political drama. To mention only one instance, Eckert[4] has shown that there are significant differences in the behaviour of regulators in local governments — depending upon whether they hold positions as civil servants in administrative bureaus or as commissioners in independent agencies. (Note that *neither* of these categories is elective, nor can they be regarded as more than distantly sensitive to electoral results.) A civil servant has permanent tenure and generally stands to gain by expansion of the size and rate of activity of his agency.[5] This implies a motivation on his part to increase the scope and level of detail of regulatory activity. An independent commissioner, on the other hand, is appointed for a limited term of years and normally has other business interests apart from his governmental position. He is consequently not nearly so motivated to multiply the administrative burden of regulatory activity requiring his supervision, or aggrandize agency size. More generally different types of constitutionally empowered agents on the political scene — bureaucrats, judges, legislators, and elected executives — each bring distinct motivations, authorities and constraints into the process of political exchange that leads to the final regulatory outcome.

In this connection I would like to suggest a possibly significant variation or extension of Peltzman's model. He allows for competition among different majority-seeking candidates for the regulatory power and also for competition among interest groups as they bid for the favour of the regulator. But he does not allow for possible *competition among different regulatory agencies*. This can be an important feature of a number of political situations. One case of particular interest has free entry into the regulation business, combined with freedom on the part of the targets of regulation to 'vote with their feet' for the regulatory jurisdiction of their choice. So an appropriate constitutional arrangement can lead to a kind of long-run zero-profit equilibrium in the regulation industry, in which 'do-nothing regulation' is the final outcome! (Some good news, at last.) The most notorious example is the deplorable competition in laxity that has led to the improbable selection of the state of Delaware as the legal domicile of most major American corporations.[6]

Consider now the key substantive result obtained by Peltzman — which I will call the principle of 'share the gain and share the pain'. His *regulatory equilibrium* is one where a balance is struck among the marginal costs and benefits of the different interest groups affected and which includes (through the impact of these costs and benefits upon electoral competition) the interest of the regulators as well. After achievement of such an equilibrium, what happens if an exogenous change in market determinants (for example, in technology, wealth, demand, and so on) occurs? It is then generally in the political interest of the regulators, given certain diminishing returns conditions, to 'correct' the new market solution that would ensue. The correction tends to be such as to assure that some benefits go to all interest groups involved, if there is a social gain to be distributed. For example, in some circumstances a technological advance might lead to a new market solution lowering cost but not lowering price so that all the benefit would otherwise go to the producers and none to the consumers. In these circumstances the regulators would impose a price reduction, assuring that some portion of the social gain goes to consumers as well. (And some of the gain goes to the regulators also, of course.) Similarly, the regulators tend to assure that burdens are spread among all parties, if a social loss has been incurred. And where some would gain and others lose from the unconstrained market process, the regulators 'lean against the wind' so as to moderate the final outcome.

This redistribution-buffering activity might at first seem inconsistent with the fact that the regulators are in the business of initiating or facilitating wealth redistributions themselves. However, there is no contradiction. Once having found the optimal redistribution from their point of view and established a regulatory equilibrium, the regulator-politicians naturally will resist and try to counter any further changes brought about by forces not under their control.

So much for disturbances of an established regulatory equilibrium. It was not entirely clear to me whether Peltzman finds an analogous regulatory policy — one of moderating distributive effects of market solutions — always politically optimal for the *initial* regulatory equilibrium. He does explain the prevalence of cross-subsidization in terms of a 'share the gain and share the pain' argument. A customer of a regulated industry who can only be served at high cost (for example, a water-user in a remote location) is generally favoured by regulation in being required to pay less than the full additional costs of service — the burden being borne in part by the low-cost customers. Far more important an example than cross-subsidization, of course, is the equalizing or Robin Hood effect of the overall tax expenditure process.

The distribution-corrective tendency of government suggests a result that oddly echoes Becker's work on the family.[7] Becker argues that a family head, who acts to redistribute the benefits stemming from activities of the various family members, tends to make the latter all behave 'altruistically' — that is, each member will be motivated to act in the overall family interest. Tying this in with Peltzman's analysis provides us with a nice argument for paternalistic regulation! By rounding off some of the rough edges of social interaction, regulation induces 'altruistic' behaviour on the part of the regulated. Perhaps this explains why members of regulated industries always seem to be such awfully nice folk.

This brings me now to my final and most important point. Like the political analyses of other economists (Downs, Buchanan and Tullock, Niskanen, and so on), Peltzman's is a theory of *constitutional politics*. In constitutional politics there exist what the economist would interpret as property rights: initial endowments of resources and powers that can only be modified by specified permissible modes of behaviour —

excluding, most importantly, violence. The economist approaching the study of politics naturally tends to assume constitutionality; in the market interactions that dominate his thinking, endowments are given and rules of behaviour are strictly spelled out. Peltzman goes beyond the conventional limits of economics to show how politics in the form of regulation changes the rules of the contest in the market arena. We can think of a hierarchy of games. On the strictest, most constrained, level is 'constitutional economics' — market interactions. The 'constitutional politics' game is at a higher level, as it can be played to change the rules or conditions of market rivalry, for example, by redistributing wealth. But constitutional politics is itself limited by accepted man-made constraints in the form of initial distributions of legitimate power. The highest and biggest game of all is *non-constitutional politics* (or, better perhaps, *meta-constitutional* politics). This biggest game of social interaction is subject only to the laws of nature. There are no property rights, and the ultimate arbiter is the physical force of individuals or of the coalitions they can form. (Alexander the Great, asked on his deathbed who should inherit his empire, answered: 'He who can hold it.') There are, for better or worse, reasons to believe that the artificial constitutional rules under which we have been living are rapidly eroding, suggesting that a somewhat different set of analytical tools needs to be developed for purposes of social science.

NOTES

1. Sam Peltzman, 'Toward a More General Theory of Regulation', 19 *J. Law & Econ.* 211 (1976).
2. Anthony Downs, *An Economic Theory of Democracy* (1957); James M. Buchanan and Gordon Tullock, *The Calculus of Consent* (1962). A work that is closely related to Peltzman's topic is Mancur Olson, Jr, *The Logic of Collective Action* (Harvard Economic Studies, vol. 124, 1965).
3. See William A. Riker, *The Theory of Political Coalitions* (1962).
4. See Ross D. Eckert, 'On the Incentives of Regulators: The Case of Taxicabs', 14 *Public Choice* 83 (1973).
5. As emphasized by William A. Niskanen, Jr, *Bureaucracy and Representative Government* (1971), and earlier by C. Northcote Parkinson, *Parkinson's Law and Other Studies in Administration* (1957).
6. Another nice example, suggested by Milton Friedman, is the ability of banks to choose between state and national regulation — and, if the former, between membership and non-membership in the Federal Reserve and the Federal Deposit Insurance Corporation.
7. Gary S. Becker, 'A Theory of Social Interactions', 82 *J. Pol. Econ.* 1063 (1974).

7 Natural Economy Versus Political Economy*

*   *   *

Background of this Chapter

The distinction between competition subject to property rights or other socially enforced rules of the game ('political economy') versus the harder forms of competition subject only to the laws of Nature ('natural economy') is developed further in this paper. While humans may perhaps be credited for inventing political economy, the persistence of crime, war and politics teaches us that actual human affairs still remain largely subject to the underlying pressures of natural economy. Nevertheless, positive cooperation can evolve even under natural-economy conditions — cooperation with some partners being, however, only a means of more effective competition against other parties.

*   *   *

ABSTRACT

In political economy, competitive striving is limited by a system of law and property; in natural economy, no such limitations exist. In the one case competition characteristically takes the form of *vying* for exchange partners; in the other, of *taking*. The actual world of human affairs is only an imperfect political economy, since natural-economy forms of competition are evident in such activities as externalities, crime and redistributive politics.

Nevertheless, conflict tends to be limited and positive cooperation can emerge even under natural-economy conditions. Biologists have dis-

* Originally published in *Journal of Social and Biological Structures* 1: 319–37 (1978). Reproduced by permission of Academic Press, Inc. (London) Ltd. An earlier version of this paper was presented as the Gilbert Memorial Lecture, University of Rochester, New York, 30 March 1978.

tinguished three forms of cooperation: (1) helping others where merely incidental to self-help, (2) helping kin, and (3) reciprocal exchanges. These interact in various ways. The viability of a helping pattern depends importantly upon the intensity of competition and upon the reaction of the aided organism to the help provided. The techniques for achieving cooperation in the absence of contractual enforcement in the biological realm have analogs in the human sphere, including: dealing with relatives, merger of interests via the division of labour, repeated business association and commitment to a reward–punishment mode of behaviour.

ECONOMICS AND SOCIOBIOLOGY

Charles Darwin thought like an economist. One of his favourite phrases was 'the economy of nature', and in his analysis of the workings of biological mechanisms he regularly used economic concepts like scarcity, cost, competition, specialization and the division of labour (Ghiselin, 1974).

The revival of Darwinian evolutionary selection theory as applied to problems of social behaviour, which has come to be known as *sociobiology* (Wilson, 1975), also has a distinctly economic aspect. Looking over the whole realm of life, sociobiology is attempting to find the general laws determining the multifarious forms of association among organisms. For example: Why do we sometimes observe sex and families, sometimes sex without families, sometimes neither sex nor families? Why do some animals flock, others remain solitary? Within groups, why do we sometimes observe hierarchical dominance patterns, sometimes not? Why do organisms in some species partition territories, others not? What determines the selflessness of the social insects, and why is this pattern so rare in Nature? When do we see resources allocated peacefully, when by means of violence? These questions are both posed and answered in recognizably economic terms. Sociobiologists ask what are the net advantages of the observed association patterns to the organisms displaying them, and what are the mechanisms whereby these patterns persist in social equilibrium states. It is perhaps this assertion of *economic-behavioural continuity* between man and other life-forms (termed 'genetic capitalism' by one detractor) that explains the hostility of some ideologues to sociobiology — just as Darwin's assertion of *physical continuity* between man and other species was found offensive by many Victorians.

Since there is such a striking similarity between the *basic problems* attacked by economics and by social biology, we can expect to find parallels in the corresponding *logical structures of thought*. The common root problem is scarcity. But why are resources necessarily scarce? Ultimately, scarcity is the consequence of the multiplication of populations — a keystone of Darwin's theory, arrived at by his study of the economist Malthus. More broadly, we can say that scarcity of resources is inevitable because of the expansive tendency of ways of life that have proved successful at extracting those resources.

As for logical structures, economics and biology both involve an intertwining of two levels of analysis. On the *individual or organism level* the acting units or entities choose (or at any rate somehow hit upon) strategies or techniques that promote their own success in the struggle (competition) for advantage. These techniques will, importantly, involve greater or lesser degrees of friendly or hostile interaction with other individuals or organisms, but the economic man or the sociobiological organism does not gratuitously act to help, or for that matter to hurt, others. He or it will do one or the other, will help or hurt, only in response to what is, ultimately, self-advantage (Ghiselin, 1974; Dawkins, 1976). It is at this point that sociobiology becomes disturbing to the Rousseau–Marx school[1] of philosophers who want to believe that *unselfishness* is normal in Nature or at any rate in the natural man. And in consequence that selfishness in man as he actually behaves in the world is an anomaly due to bad institutions, rather than to anything intrinsic in his essential make-up. (That so often these dedicated believers in the fundamental goodness of man are found viciously abusing anyone with opposed opinions is perhaps revealing of the underlying truth of the matter, but this point need not be pursued here.) Returning to the parallelism of biology and economics as systems of thought, on the *social level* of analysis the outcome is an equilibrium (or, at least, a time-path of movement toward equilibrium) in which, on the margin, every surviving life-form and every strategy adopted by life-forms is just barely viable given the choices of all the others. For, if it is more than barely viable, on the margin, that life-form or strategy will multiply and expand until the law of diminishing returns eliminates the advantage.

There are, on the other hand, certain real or seeming differences between economics and biology in modes of thought and logical structures, three of which can be mentioned here:

1. The first is the question of *rationality*. The human being can rationally choose or 'optimize' his course of action (or so we like to think) whereas, below the human level and except possibly for a few of the higher animals in limited degree, biologists who speak of 'choice' and 'strategy' are only using metaphors. What happens in the biological realm is that, given a sufficiently long run, *natural*

selection under Malthusian competition allows survival only of the most successful among the possible strategies. So the result ends up almost *as if* baboons or rats or crabgrass plants were consciously optimizing. Even in the economic literature, curiously, there is a school of thought (Alchian, 1950; Enke,1951; Winter, 1964; Nelson and Winter, 1974) that minimizes the role of subjective 'rational' *choice* of, as opposed to environmental *selection* of, successful strategies. And coming at things from the opposite direction, a number of economists (Kagel *et al.*, 1975; Fredlund, 1976) have conducted experiments or otherwise observed that animals faced with economic choices are really not so dumb! For the purposes of this paper, rational forethoughtedness is best thought of as simply *one of the possible mechanisms or strategies of striving for advantage* — like long necks for giraffes or fleet-footedness for deer. Certain organisms face environments where 'hard-wired' or instinctive responses suffice for viability; others live in circumstances such that reserving a degree of freedom for purposive choice has won out in the game of life.

2. The second divergence is epitomized by the difference between the biological term 'fitness' and the economic concept of 'tastes'. For the biologist, natural selection has inevitably shaped life into organisms driven as if they were maximizing something quite objective and unambiguous: reproductive survival, or *fitness*. Social scientists generally, and economists among them, find unappealing the idea that our deep-seated desires and our superficial whims reduce down to serving biological fitness, to multiplying the number of our descendants. Rejecting the reductionism of the biological explanation of human aims or goals, the modern economist has jumped to the opposite extreme. He takes our goals for living, to which he attaches the demeaning term 'tastes', as purely subjective and arbitrary, something totally inexplicable (or at any rate belonging in someone else's explanatory jurisdiction). Economists today would do well to go back to the master, Adam Smith, who did not regard the fundamental drives of men as arbitrary and inexplicable, who clearly understood that *human desires are ultimately adaptive responses* shaped by man's biological nature and situation on earth (Coase, 1976, p. 539).[2]

3. The central theme here will be another main difference between the analytical approaches of economics and of biology toward social behaviour, a difference summarized in the distinction between 'natural economy' and 'political economy' — both being sub-categories of *universal economy* (Ghiselin, 1978).

In traditional political philosophy, or legendary political history, the step from natural economy to political economy was taken only by man — in the form of the social contract of Rousseau or Hobbes. The thesis of comparative sociobiology is that there is no such sharp discontinuity in social organization, just as there is no sharp discontinuity in physical form, between man and other branches of life. Within a social group, *law* emerges when what might be called 'moralistic aggression' (Trivers, 1971) by third-party intervenors serves to control internal conflict. We see this already wherever parents regulate offspring rivalry — behaviour widespread in the animal kingdom. *Government* may be said to exist when, in groupings larger than a single family, control tasks are performed by specialists in that function. In the biological realm, some species have dominant individuals or cliques that approach primitive government within packs or troops. The immunities from invasions thus created prefigure the human institution of *property* (Fredlund, 1976).[3]

These political economy institutions provide two classes of advantages. On the first level, law and government deter or limit the internal fighting and consequent losses of strength that would be disfunctional for the group as a whole. Individuals need not divert effort to continual patrolling and monitoring. This is a kind of minimal or negative cooperation. On the second level, positive cooperation in the form of *exchange* of resource entitlements becomes a possibility — and, ultimately, the more sophisticated dealings in deferred reciprocations that constitute the essence of *contract*.

Yet the institutions of political economy can never be so perfect as to entirely displace, even in human societies, the underlying realities of natural economy. Every living organism remains to some degree in a Hobbesian 'state of nature'. In particular, the intercourse among the nations of mankind lies outside the scope of effective law. Even under law and government, the rational self-interested individual will strike a balance between lawful and unlawful means of acquiring resources — between production and exchange on the one hand and theft, fraud and extortion on the other. For that matter a perfectly law-abiding individual (if there is any such) could not have such confidence in third-party enforcement as to entirely forgo personal vigilance and self-defence. And setting aside *violation* of law, the structure of the law itself will necessarily have greater or lesser imperfections. It is not always practicable to define rights to property in such a way as to ban socially wasteful activities designed to capture benefits while imposing costs on others (what the economist calls 'externalities'), or, much more important, to foreclose efforts aimed at influencing government or revising the law *so as to redefine rights in one's favour*. This latter activity is of course the stuff of redistributive politics. In short, while the intellectual division of labour whereby biologists concentrated on natural economy and economists on an idealized political economy is an entirely understandable one, in the actual world the separations are by no means clean-cut. Mankind still lives, to an important degree, outside the sway of the cooperation-supporting institutions of political economy. Yet, as we shall see, forms of cooperative association can emerge even under natural economy!

COMPETITION IN RELATION TO COOPERATION AND CONFLICT

Competition is the all-pervasive law of natural economy interactions. The source of competition is the limited resource-base of the globe in the face of the universal Malthusian tendency to multiply. By natural selection the biosphere has come to be filled by life forms successful at multiplying and pressing upon one another for command over resources. This teeming of life is therefore both cause and consequence of biological competition.

Figure 7.1 portrays what competition looks like from the biological point of view. For two interacting biological entities F and G — whether species or genes or characters or strategies — the essential is that the equilibrium viable number of each decreases with the actual number of the other. That is, the curve $\hat{N}_F$ (showing the level of N_F where its time-rate of change becomes zero) is a decreasing function of N_G. Similarly, $\hat{N}_G$ is a decreasing function of N_F. As the directional change arrows indicate, Figure 7.1 shows a *competitive* coexistence equilibrium at the intersection of the $\hat{N}_F$ and $\hat{N}_G$ curves. (By changing the values of the parameters determining $\hat{N}_F$ and $\hat{N}_G$ we could also display *corner* equilibria, where F drives G to extinction or vice versa.) Figure 7.2 is the corresponding picture of a *cooperative* interaction between F and G, where the equilibrium viable number of each entity is an *increasing* function of actual numbers of other. (Again, the diagram shows a stable coexistence equilibrium, other cases being also possible.) And finally, in Figure 7.3, a mixed or asymmetrical 'predator–prey' situation in which (so to speak) G is helpful to F — since $\hat{N}_F$ is an increasing function of G — but F is hurtful to G. (Here the arrows indicate a cyclic pattern, which may be either damped or explosive.) These biological equilibria correspond to what the economist calls Nash–Cournot solutions, in which each party takes the actions of the other as given, thus ruling out *purposive* pursuit of mutual gain.

One puzzle immediately comes to mind here. From the biological

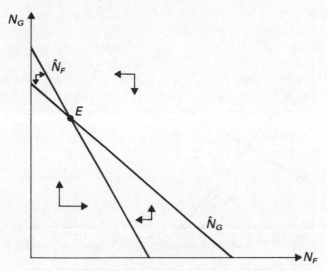

Figure 7.1 Stable competitive equilibrium (coexistence)

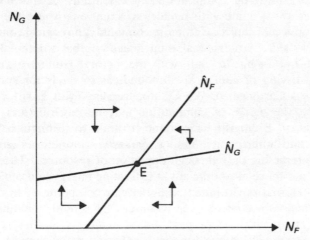

Figure 7.2 Stable cooperative equilibrium (coexistence)

picture in Figure 7.1 it appears that competition is necessarily anti-social: any benefit for F comes at the expense of G. And yet economic tradition, starting with the 'invisible hand' of Adam Smith, has always viewed competition as ultimately a force for harmonizing interests. How can this divergence be resolved?

First of all, competition for the economist ordinarily refers to a *three-sided* interaction: vying *against* a rival or rivals, but *for* the opportunity

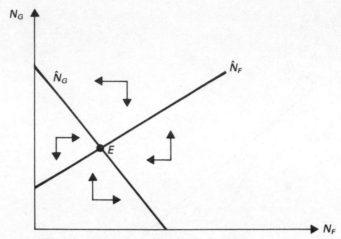

Figure 7.3   Stable asymmetrical equilibrium (coexistence)

to engage in mutually advantageous exchange with a third party. Some instances of biological competition are essentially of this nature, as when males vie to mate with females in situations where the females retain the option of choice. But, more commonly, biological competition is direct *two-sided* striving (as when males combat for females, who are left no option but to mate with the victor). Human examples of two-sided striving of course also abound, as in duels for survival — Rome versus Carthage, or Ike Clanton versus Wyatt Earp.

Secondly, the *modes* of competition may be more or less wasteful and anti-social. Biologists have found it useful to distinguish between 'scramble' and 'interference' modes. *Scramble* competitors ignore one another, interacting only through depletion of resources. The winning organisms are those most efficient at extracting energy and other inputs from the external environment. *Interference* competitors, in contrast, gain and maintain control over resources by directly fighting off or hampering their rivals, a process that is evidently inefficient for the social aggregate. Of course, under (idealized) institutions of political economy 'interference' competition is not permitted. A businessman is allowed to compete in various ways, but not by blowing up his rival's shop. This does not quite get to the heart of the matter, however. Even 'scrambling' competition may be socially wasteful, and even if the resources scrambled for are to be used for exchange with third parties. Though less obviously so than in the case of interference competition, scrambling also is socially inefficient in that *effort is being invested to preclusively appropriate resources that would have been socially available even without that effort* — or to redistribute them or

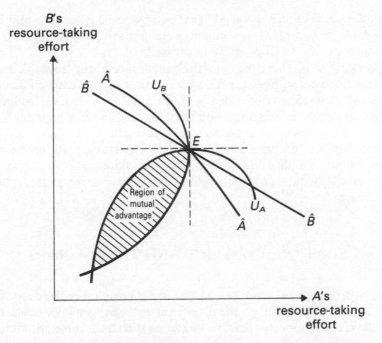

Figure 7.4   Nash equilibrium for preclusive competition

to prevent such redistribution. This is the source of the difficulty in the classic 'overfishing externality' model (Gordon, 1954), a situation which corresponds exactly to biological scramble competition.

Figure 7.4 displays the nature of the social loss from preclusive competition (as in scrambling or fishing) between two maximizing entities A and B. The $\hat{A}$ and $\hat{B}$ curves correspond to the $\hat{N}_F$ and $\hat{N}_G$ curves of Figure 7.1. Figure 7.4 provides a 'utility' interpretation of the derivation of these curves. Since B's preclusive efforts are always a bad for A, the indifference curves for A represent higher levels of satisfaction moving south. And, similarly, B's indifference curves are higher moving west. A's own effort is a good to himself, up to a point (he receives a positive net marginal product), but eventually becomes a bad (negative net marginal product). And, similarly, for B. These properties explain the general shapes of the indifference curves. Since A controls his own effort only, for any level of B's effort A's optimum is found where his indifference curve U_A becomes horizontal (zero net marginal product.) Similarly B finds his optimum where his indifference curve U_B becomes vertical. These conditions determine the $\hat{A}$ and $\hat{B}$ curves, whose intersection is the coexistence equilibrium E (as in Figure 7.1). The region of mutual advantage shows that a social gain over this equilibrium could be achieved. That is, organisms A and B could both be made better off if agreement were possible, or if rights to the resources could be appropriately preassigned.

We have seen, therefore, that the beneficence of the 'Invisible Hand' is associated not with competition *per se*, but with a severely constrained type of competition that ideally characterizes the market economy: vying to engage in exchange with third parties, by offering them better terms, and under circumstances where resources all have assigned ownership so that no effort is wasted in striving to preclusively appropriate or redistribute them. These conditions of course require a system of law and property rights, as can only arise under political economy.

COOPERATION, CONFLICT AND THEIR LIMITS

If competition is the basic law of life, and if competition leads to social advantage only under an ideal political economy with its institutions of law and property that facilitate cooperation through mutually advantageous exchanges, how is it that cooperation is often observed in the biological sphere *in the absence of law and property*? Consider the 'mutualism' of the flowers and the bees, a relation that seems very much like exchange in that it involves reciprocal conferring of benefits. Or another example: small cleaner fish that provide grooming services to larger fish while feeding on their external parasites. This is even closer to exchange since the cleaner fish do not groom at random, but have a regular clientele of customers (larger fish who can be trusted not to eat their barbers!). Furthermore, even one-way transfers — gifts, *unilateral* conferring of benefits — take place on both the human and non-human levels. And where conflict occurs, as of course it does, how and why is it that the battle is often *limited* rather than all-out, as it might have been (Lorenz, 1966)?

Biologists have examined the problem of social cooperation (Trivers, 1971; West Eberhard, 1975; Wilson, 1975) under the rubric of 'altruism' in which they have been followed by a number of economists (Becker, 1976; Kurz, 1977). Terminologically, this is most unfortunate. The word 'altruism' has psychological connotations that are often irrelevant or misleading. More important, it leads almost inevitably to semantic confusions. For example: 'If the well-being of organism B is desired by (enters into the utility function of) organism A, isn't A's seeming altruism toward B just pursuit of A's own goals, and so not really altruism?' A total pseudo-issue, of course. Here's another one: 'If an altruism choice of strategy is to be *viable* in competition with non-altruism, altruism must contribute to self-survival more than non-altruism does, and therefore it can't really be altruism.' All such muddles could be avoided if we drop the term 'altruism' and ask instead: What are the determinants of the entirely objective phenomenon that can be called *helping*? Patterns of helping can usefully be analysed under three main headings proposed by biologists: (1) helping that is merely *incidental* to selfish behaviour, (2) helping associated with *kinship*, and (3) helping that is involved in *reciprocal* interactions.

Incidental helping poses no problems. It is the kind of unwitting or unwilling assistance that animals give to parasites — in the case of mankind, the 'foreign aid' programmes we provide for rats, houseflies and common cold germs. (How absurd to call this *altruism*!) But incidental helping overlaps also with reciprocal helping, in cases like the flowers and bees where species have become *co-adapted* to help one another incidentally to helping themselves.

Kinship helping raises more interesting economic issues. The biologists' basic helping rule (Hamilton, 1964) is shown in inequality (1): evolutionary selection impels a Donor organism D to aid a Recipient organism R if

$$c_D/b_R < r_{DR}, \tag{1}$$

that is, if the cost–benefit ratio, c_D/b_R of the action is less than the *degree of relatedness* r_{DR} between the pair. Biological cost and benefit are measured in terms of reproductive survival or *fitness W*; cost c_D is a decrement to Donor's own-fitness W_D and benefit b_R is an increment to Recipient's own-fitness W_R. The biological logic is that the gene controlling helping behaviour in Donor D values its own survival (using the language of conscious optimization metaphorically, though the actual process is the result of blind natural selection) equally with survival of any identical copy itself, and r_{DR} measures the chance of organism R having an identical copy. Specifically, a gene for kinship helping instructs a man (other things equal) to give his life if he can thereby save two siblings, four half-sibs, eight cousins, etc.

Looking at this as the economist would, optimal action always involves an interaction of *preferences* and *opportunities*. The relatedness factor is the operative preference element. In effect, Donor organism D is maximizing an 'inclusive fitness' concept W_D^*, of which his own-fitness W_D is only one component. Specifically,

$$W_D^* = W_D + r_{DR}W_R. \tag{2}$$

Inclusive fitness is then a weighting of the W's by degree of relatedness to Donor (he is, of course, always 100 per cent related to himself).

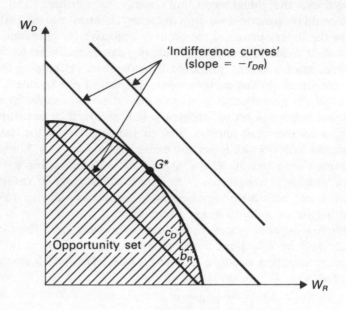

Figure 7.5   Maximization of 'inclusive fitness'

Diagrammatically (Figure 7.5), inclusive fitness W_D^* as the biological utility function leads to linear 'indifference curves' with slope $-r_{DR}$ on W_D, W_R axes. The shaded opportunity set represents the attainable region for Donor D. At the optimum point G^*, the cost–benefit ratio c_D/b_R (the absolute slope $-dW_D/dW_R$ along the boundary of the opportunity set) just equals the absolute indifference-curve slope r_{DR}.

In the diagram, relatedness r is shown as a constant feature of the interaction between two organisms, as of course it always is, but the cost—benefit ratio c/b is a diminishing-returns function of the amount of helping. The c/b ratio can also be a function of a number of other determinants, and in particular may vary over the life-cycle as between organisms of given relatedness. One example relevant for humans: because offspring generally need help more urgently, and parents are in a position to give it, from cost–benefit considerations we would expect to see parents aiding children more than children aid parents — even though relatedness r is the same both ways. Some biologists (e.g. Dawkins, 1976) have argued that kinship helping can scarcely be important beyond the immediate family, since *r* falls off very rapidly toward zero as kinship distance increases. But as West Eberhard (1975) points out, one individual might sometimes be able to influence fitness of a great many others — so that increase in numbers affected may offset decrease in average *r*. In human endeavours this provides a biological explanation for the gruelling hours and selfless devotion often observed of leaders in war, politics or even business.

A couple of interesting complications concerning kinship helping can be pursued here — the first having to do with *competition* and the second with the question of Recipient's *reaction* to Donor's help.

First, with regard to competition. Under kinship helping it certainly seems that the Recipient *R* is getting the better of the deal. But our fundamental premise is that all forms of life and all strategies are in competition. Then why should not a gene *NH* for *not helping* one's kin out-compete the help-kin gene *H*? The organism bearing the *H* gene will sometimes be a Donor, sometimes a Recipient of aid — but the carrier of the *NH* gene will be exclusively a Recipient. Since we are ruling out the reciprocation element, non-helpers cannot be punished for being bad boys. The *NH* gene is thus a 'freerider', and other things equal it always pays to be a freerider rather than pay the fare. Indeed, the economist Tullock (1978) claims that this argument refutes Hamilton's helping rule. Where the critic went wrong was in failing to appreciate that helping only one's kind means that helping acts will be *preferentially directed to fellow carriers of the helping gene*. It is true that the *H* gene tends to lose sway within the *family* but it nevertheless (if the condition is met) gains in prevalence within the *population*.

This can be shown explicitly, for a simplified special case (a 'sexual haploid' organism) by asking under what conditions W_H will exceed W_{NH} — the 'fitness' or viability of the helping gene *H* will exceed that of the non-helping gene *NH*?[4] Here *c* and *b* are cost and benefit as before, *N* is the population number and *p* the proportion bearing the helping gene. The key variable is the discrimination factor, *m*, which represents the *proportion of helping acts received by fellow helpers*. Then, $W_H > W_{NH}$ requires

$$-c + \frac{bmNp}{Np} > \frac{b(1-m)Np}{N(1-p)}.$$ (3)

On the left-hand side, the first term $-c$ represents the cost of the helping act to Helper (in fitness units, and normalized so that there is one helping act per time-period). The numerator of the second term, $bmNp$, represents the aggregate benefit of helping acts per time-period that are directed at fellow helpers — while the denominator Np is the number of helpers in the population. The ratio of the two then shows the average per-helper benefit of helping acts, in fitness units per time-period. The right-hand side, analogously, shows the average per non-helper benefit of having helpers in the population. Inequality (3) reduces to:

$$\frac{c}{b} < \frac{m-p}{1-p}. \tag{4}$$

Thus we see that for helping to be competitively viable, a necessary (though not sufficient) condition is $m > p$ — fellow helpers must receive helping acts *in bigger proportion than their proportion in the population*.

Let us suppose we are talking about helping one's siblings, for whom relatedness r_{DR} equals $\frac{1}{2}$. Supposing that the helping gene H arose as a new mutation in one's parent, p being at first effectively zero in the population at large, then the probability that one's sibling also bears the H gene is one-half. And as p goes to unity, m must also approach unity. Indeed, it is algebraically clear that for sibling helping, in general:

$$m = (1 + p)/2. \tag{5}$$

Making this substitution in (4) we directly verify the helping rule (1) for siblings:

$$c/b < \tfrac{1}{2} = r_{DR}. \tag{6}$$

Note that this viability analysis leads to *corner solutions*, $p = 1$ or $p = 0$, according as the inequality condition is or is not satisfied. What might lead to *interior solutions* for p? This could come about if, for a particular type of helping act, c/b were an increasing function of p — i.e. if there are diminishing returns to helping as the proportion of Helpers rises. The interpretation would be that competition is becoming increasingly severe, perhaps because with larger p and thus more helping acts the population N tends to grow until it presses increasingly upon its external resources.[5]

The cost–benefit ratio c/b is therefore importantly a function of *intensity of competition*. Several further aspects of competition are brought out if we look at what might be called the *generalized helping/ hurting rule*:

$$\sum_{\substack{\text{losers} \\ (i)}} r_{iD}\, c_i < \sum_{\substack{\text{gainers} \\ (j)}} r_{jD}\, b_j. \tag{7}$$

Here the Donor's acts help some, and hurt others. His 'as–if' optimization of inclusive fitness sums the costs versus benefits for all affected parties, weighted by relatedness. Of course, he counts himself, with a relatedness of unity, in either the loser or the gainer group, whichever is appropriate.

Again, competition enters in the form of some constraint connecting the costs and benefits. The most extreme such constraint, which may be called *absolute competition*, is defined by the condition:

$$\Sigma c_i = \Sigma b_j. \tag{8}$$

That is, benefits conferred on some organisms must be exactly balanced by costs imposed on others, equal in aggregate. In *two-party* absolute competition ('It's either him or me!') the c/b ratio must be unity, hence kinship helping could not be viable — except for identical twins, for whom $r = 1$. If absolute competition governs, the generalized helping rule can be written in the following special form, where $\bar{r}$ is the average relatedness of members of the population to Donor:[6]

$$\sum_{\substack{\text{losers} \\ (i)}} c_i(r_{iD} - \bar{r}) < \sum_{\substack{\text{gainers} \\ (j)}} b_j(r_{jD} - \bar{r}). \tag{9}$$

Under absolute competition it is not the simple relatedness, but relatedness greater or less than the average in the population that serves as the factor for weighting cost or benefit.

As a further special case, suppose now that for all losers of fitness, the c_i equal a common value c — and for all gainers of fitness, the b_j equal a common value b. Then, if $\bar{r}_{iD}$ is the average relatedness of losers to Donor and $\bar{r}_{jD}$ is the average relatedness of gainers to Donor, the generalized helping rule under absolute competition reduces to:[7]

$$\bar{r}_{iD} < \bar{r}_{jD}. \tag{10}$$

That is, help any group more closely related to you at the expense of groups less closely related. Crudely speaking, *under absolute competition anyone is your enemy who is less closely related to you than the average in the population*!

Absolute competition is not universal, of course. But even apart from that, there is an important consideration which mitigates the rather terrifying xenophobic implications of the above rule. To wit, that (as Darwin emphasized) *organisms more closely related tend to be in closer competition*. If we consider birds in a nest, in terms of relatedness a single nestling would 'choose' to take food from inhabitants of other nests rather than deprive his own sibling. But of course he is only in a position to compete for food with his own siblings, the inhabitants of his own nest. This phenomenon operates to *increase enmity within* and to *reduce enmity between* families, groups and species. The bottom line is that since the motive to help (the relatedness factor r) and the competitive gain from hurting both tend to be increasing

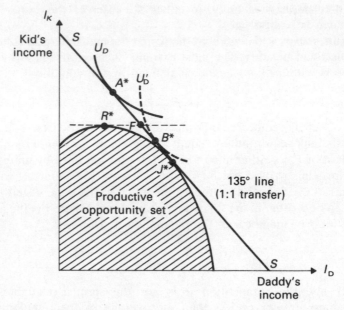

Figure 7.6   Daddy versus Kid: hard-core versus pragmatic cooperation

functions of closeness of kinship, the final outcome is delicately balanced and depends upon the specific details of the situation. Sociobiological considerations may lead sometimes to xenophobic wars, but under other circumstances to often equally bloody civil wars. Or, looking at matters more optimistically, to mutual help sometimes among close relatives, sometimes between distantly related organisms. In each case it is the balance of the preferences and opportunities, of relatedness and cost–benefit considerations, that governs.

We can now turn to the second complication — Recipient's *reaction* to Donor's helping (or hurting). From the economic point of view, Donor's aid or injury will affect Recipient's 'fitness wealth' one way or the other and thereby change the balance of preferences versus opportunities for the latter. Specifically, depending upon the directionality of these wealth effects, Recipients may *react* by helping or hurting Donor (or third parties) in a way that Donor should take into account.

One instructive instance studied by economists is the 'Rotten Kid theorem' (Becker, 1976). Here we postulate an utterly selfish 'Rotten Kid' K, who simply wants to attain a position with highest I_K in Figure 7.6 (on axes representing Daddy's income I_D versus Kid's income I_K). Daddy, on the other hand, has a degree of love and concern for Kid as shown by his normal looking indifference curve, U_D, on these axes.

But the two are not in absolute competition, and indeed can mutually benefit from cooperation. Suppose that Kid is in a position to make the first move, and Daddy the last. Then if Kid were shortsightedly selfish, he would choose an optimum at R^*. But, knowing that Daddy is unselfish and will react positively to aid, Kid should choose the joint-income optimum J^*. The reason is that Daddy will then make $1 : 1$ transfers of income to Kid, by moving along the 135° line SS to an optimum at A^*. Note that Daddy is a truly unselfish or 'hard-core' cooperator (Wilson, 1977), Kid a merely pragmatic one, but they both benefit.[8]

We have here an opportunity set rewarding cooperation (in a context excluding *contractual* reciprocation). In these circumstances one way of achieving cooperation is for either or both parties to evolve 'love' for the other — more specifically, to become motivated to share any increments of income with the other. Evidently, the mechanism can work, as shown in the diagram. Indeed, it is easy to see that if Daddy were *less* loving (if his indifference curve were to shift to the somewhat more selfish pattern U'_D), he would only react to Kid's aid by more limited income transfers along SS to an optimum at B^* — but this would be insufficient to motivate Kid to cooperate in the first place. So Daddy is better-off not only 'altruistically' in utility terms for being unselfish, but (and this is essential for the viability of such 'Golden Rule' behaviour) he is better-off even in terms of *real measurable income*![9] Where the economist would say that Daddy had a 'taste' for helping his offspring, for the biologist this attachment or affection can only have evolved as a *means* of achieving higher fitness.

We have already crossed over into a discussion of the third category of aid — *reciprocal* helping, a pattern which can come about even in the absence of relatedness. But relatedness, since it provides a degree of initial payoff in inclusive-fitness units for helping, seems to make it easier to evolve what looks like an extra 'irrational' degree of love. Note also that Nature seems to allow for scarcity of love power — the greater is Daddy's degree of affection, the less need Kid's be to achieve mutual gain through cooperation.

Let us focus more closely now on the *reactive* aspect of helping. Consider first interactions among non-kin, where $r_{DR} = 0$. Then the helping rule (1) reduces simply to $c_D < 0$; in the absence of kinship, there must be a negative cost (positive selfish benefit) to the Donor of any help he gives Recipients. We can think of this cost c_D as decomposed into a *primary* cost term c^0_D and a *reactive* cost term c'_D:

$$c_D \equiv c^0_D + c'_D \tag{11}$$

'Incidental' helping is associated with a negative $c^0{}_D$ (the helping act has a primary selfish benefit to Donor): 'reciprocal' helping is associated with a negative $c'{}_D$ (Recipient's reaction to help aids Donor D).

Reciprocation of help brings us close to the *exchange* interactions of the economist. The basic rule of reciprocal interactions is, 'Help your helper!' In biological terms, 'Increase an unrelated organism's fitness, assuming there is direct cost to yourself, only if he will react by increasing your fitness (and do so by a large enough amount)!' But there are two main paths of reciprocation. First, it may be that Recipient R is an individual who would *unconditionally* help you in return. His reactive 'wealth effect', in terms of helping you, is positive and quantitatively large enough to make your negative reactive cost term $c'{}_D$ overbalance your positive direct cost $c^0{}_D$. If the beneficiary is your kin, there will in general be some favourable reaction on his part to your aid — but, as we saw in the Rotten Kid example above, possibly not quantitatively enough to motivate your sacrifice. In that case, your potential beneficiary can guarantee to reactively help you *more* than he otherwise would by evolving a degree of uncontrollable or 'irrational' love for you (like Daddy above) and this may serve the purpose of warranting your aid to him. Among unrelated organisms, perhaps the bond *between dog and man* (under natural economy, since you cannot write a contract with your dog) exemplifies how love or its functional equivalent gratitude motivates helping. Essentially the same phenomenon clearly occurs in a negative sense as well. Animals and even humans do sometimes react with uncontrollable or 'irrational' rage to punish those who hurt them. So we have deterring of hurting as well as inducement of helping in the natural economy through reactive responses whose delivery is guaranteed by emotion.

The second type of Recipient who will reactively help you, unconditionally, is someone who is (on the margin) an incidental helper to you. Again, the reaction must be quantitatively great enough if it is to warrant your sacrifice. This process is presumably what leads to co-adaptation for mutual aid between unrelated organisms like the flowers and bees.

However, *cheating* is a pervasive phenomenon that tends to limit all these cooperative arrangements. Cheating in Nature takes many forms. A Recipient may pretend to a higher degree of relatedness r (as when a cuckoo lays her egg in another bird's nest). Or Recipient can fake a higher potential benefit from aid, as when a nestling screams for food as hard as it can, whether or not truly hungry. Or it can pretend to be a reactive helper, as when a mimic cleaner fish upon being allowed to approach a 'client' just takes a bite and escapes! Or an even more extreme case of pseudo-reactive helpers: there are carnivorous plants who prey on their would-be pollinators. Of course, analogous phenomena are not unknown in human affairs.

It may be that, for any or all of the reasons suggested above, *unconditional* positive reactions are inadequate to induce the initial helping act even though there does still exist a *potential* mutual gain from reciprocated help. That is, *exchange* would be mutually beneficial but, having received his end of the bargain, the initial Recipient party lacks sufficient motivation to make the required reciprocal sacrifice. We have here a classical Prisoners' Dilemma situation, which can be solved by shifting from natural economy to political economy — that is, to a system of *third party enforcement of contract*. (Of course, cheating remains a problem under political economy, indeed it is given a number of new dimensions.)

We have now located the context in which political economy can become an element in the picture of social cooperation. But the main emphasis here has been upon seeing the picture as a whole: since political economy institutions are always and necessarily imperfect, social cooperation rests to a degree upon foundations that must remain viable even under natural economy. There have to be human makeshifts and substitutes for enforcement of contract, and these can be better understood if we examine the working of the same mechanisms in the non-human sphere.

Some of these makeshift arrangements can be briefly discussed here, with comments on their relevance for the human economy.

Cooperation among relatives
Relatedness provides warrant in fitness terms for some helping acts even without reciprocation (as we saw under the heading of kinship helping). But somewhat more subtly, it also promotes *mutual* helping by tending to increase the probability and magnitude of unenforced reciprocation. In human affairs, we know that business enterprises very often are undertaken by family units: examples include the Rothschilds, the Medicis, the new publishing house charmingly named Thomas Horton and Daughters and even the Mafia! And of course an enormous fraction of all economic activity takes place within the bosom of the family.

Repeat business
Suppose that two parties have the opportunity to engage not in an isolated business transaction, but in a *sequence* of repeated interchanges each of which would be mutually beneficial. Evidently, then, the motivation for either party to cheat at any point in the series is attenuated by the prospective loss of future benefit. In the case of

cleaner fish, the bigger client fish does not usually eat his barber. The little fellow has provided good service in the past, has proved himself not one of those mimic cleaners who bite and run, and so can be relied on in the future. In human affairs the prospect of repeated association is obviously an extremely potent force motivating good behaviour in all types of social interchanges. As one example of specific relevance to business association in the narrower sense, the sociologist Macaulay (1963) has shown that appeal by commercial firms to judicial enforcement of contract is relatively rare, largely because of the effectiveness of this alternative mechanism for enforcing cooperation — fear of loss of future business.

Merger of interests

To the extent that members of a group share a common fate or outcome, helping one another becomes self-help. Merger can be regarded as an extreme form of repeated business relationship, in which each participant has made himself irreversibly vulnerable to severe loss should the association break down. There are two main types of merger, which may be called *complementation* versus *supplementation* relationships (Hirshleifer, 1977a, p. 38). *Complementation* involves division of labour through acceptance of specialized roles. An obvious example is the division of labour between males and females in bearing and caring for offspring. In the human realm, this is also a kind of familial cooperation, but one which must not be confused with cooperation among relatives — since male and female parents are not ordinarily closely related. They are more in the nature of business partners, with 50 per cent shares in the business of producing offspring. *Supplementation* as a pattern of merger, on the other hand, is particularly valuable where the advantage of grouping stems not from specialization of role but rather essentially from *size* of the cooperating unit: i.e. where returns to scale exist. *Cartels* are associations of this nature, but cartels are ordinarily rather vulnerable to disruption through cheating. Much more important in animal and human affairs are the returns to scale associated with military power ('God is on the side of the bigger battalions' — Voltaire). There is reason to believe that the need to fight and to fight off other human groups has very strongly influenced the social instincts of mankind (Alexander, 1975).

Conditional commitment

The Prisoners' Dilemma arises in all sorts of interchanges, from business transactions to criminal partnerships to military deterrence of conflict. The essence of the problem is that the recipient of aid or injury — however desirous *ex ante* of receiving aid or avoiding injury — may not find it rational *ex post* to reciprocate in kind. Having received the loan, the borrower is not directly motivated to repay. If an aggressor were to destroy most of our population in a surprise nuclear attack, little or nothing might be gained after the fact by having our surviving forces engage in a punitive retaliatory strike against enemy population. But guaranteeing in advance to return (even though irrational *ex post*) good for good or evil for evil affects the other party's *ex ante* calculations — and thus tends to promote cooperation and limit conflict (Schelling, 1960). Uncontrollable emotions of loving gratitude or vengeful rage achieve this object in natural economy. Of course, sophisticated human contrivances may provide other mechanisms of uncontrollable reaction. A neat modern example is the 'Doomsday machine', which (if all goes well!) deters aggression by guaranteeing to blow up the whole world should an aggressor initiate a nuclear attack.

We have seen how what might be called the Silver Rule — to return good for good and evil for evil — can be socially effective in deterring aggression and rewarding cooperation. What about the Golden Rule — to return good for good and good for evil? One's first impression is that the Golden Rule could never be viable. After all, in the competitive picture there will always be followers of what could be called the 'Brass Rule' — be well-behaved if absolutely necessary but otherwise grab the marbles. Brass types can be kept in line when Silvers are around to mete out reward and punishment, but the Golds would seem to be natural prey. Yet the rotten-kid example above showed that a Brass–Gold combo might indeed be viable for both parties! So even unconditional love seems to have a place in natural economy.[10]

CONCLUDING REMARKS

The central thesis of sociobiology, the continuity of forms and patterns of social organization over all the realms of life, has surely been adequately established — as far back as Darwin, at least. What is a less familiar and accepted idea is that these patterns of social organization *respond to universal economic laws*. They are the product of scarcity of resources, of the limited availabilities of materials and energy in the face of the unlimited expansive tendency of life. Depending upon the specifics of the situation, different types and intensities of association will win in this all-pervasive competition. It is the great law of diminishing returns, in its multifarious forms, which assures that no single tendency will win everywhere, so various forms of life will maintain sway over different resource bases or niches. Thus in certain circumstances the economics favour sexual reproduction, in others asexual; sometimes parental care, sometimes parental indifference; sometimes we will see packs and herds, sometimes solitary individuals; partitioning of resources sometimes by territory, sometimes by dominance, sometimes by inter-individual or inter-species specialization by area or food type or size or hunting times or seasons and so on in infinite variety.

That economics can contribute to biology is evident, and indeed we are seeing more and more explicit use of economic models in biological studies of optimal foraging, of investment in offspring, of selfish versus unselfish behaviour, etc. But to look at the other side of the picture, can biology contribute to economics? The contributions that biology might make fall into two categories: the *analogical* and the *substantive*. Where the two sciences have studied formally similar problems, but results achieved by one remain unknown to the other, analogical borrowing is clearly possible. One example: biologists have a more elaborately structured theory, and one that is far more empirically validated, of the phenomena described under the heading of specialization and the division of labour (see Ghiselin, 1974, Ch. 8). But what is more important, substantively sociobiology claims (Wilson, 1977) that it will provide an ultimate foundation for the sciences of man — in the same sense that chemistry is ultimately founded upon atomic physics.

Economists, like other social scientists, have tended to resist the application of biological categories to human beings. Frank Knight (1922), one of the few great modern economists who attempted to say something about the intrinsic nature of man, his wants and goals in relation to his economic behaviour, nevertheless declared: 'On every count this biological interpretation of human conduct falls down; no hunger and sex theory of human motive will stand examination.' To make the statement is to appreciate its absurdity. Hunger and sex, though not *all*-important, are scarcely *un*important motivators of human beings. And we have seen that much subtler phenomena — love and rage, family feeling and group loyalty — can all emerge as motivators under the pressures of natural selection.

The potential substantive contributions of sociobiological thinking to economics relate most obviously to the nature of man. *Contra* Frank Knight, man's nature is importantly channelled by his biological heritage. His wants and goals are not 'mere' arbitrary tastes, nor are they entirely his to choose. Not only the obvious drives of hunger and sex, but subtler aspects of his wants like the desire for novelty or the urge to nurture his children, or the impulse of gratitude for benefits received, may be deeply ingrained in his evolutionary past. The economist's working hypothesis should be not that preferences are arbitrary, but that beneath the ephemeral surface phenomena men's wants have certain permanent analysable characteristics, which came about because they are adaptive — or at least *were* adaptive in the evolutionary past — to his form of life. Of course, man as a rational or rationalizing animal can, to a degree, oppose these inbuilt drives — sometimes to his advantage, sometimes not — but never without difficulty.

Perhaps the grossest flaw in the economist's traditional view of the human being is illustrated by the attention we devote to his *man–thing* activities as opposed to *man–man* activities. Our textbooks talk of tastes for cheese or shoes or automobiles, rarely of desires for children or mates or subordinates or fraternal associates. Other social scientists, though without having been able to provide a better analytical model, have justly scorned this view of man as rational unaffiliated thing-consumer, interacting with others only through market exchange. There is however a thrust within modern economics to overcome this limitation and use our analytical tools to study the human interactions involved in phenomena like mate choice and crime and charity and politics. Sociobiology provides a foundation for this widened view of economics.

Interaction via market exchange under the rules of the game here called *political economy* is only a part, often a small part, of the economic picture. Not only plants and animals, but human beings as well, interact economically to a very large degree under *natural economy* rather than political economy, without benefit of law or property or contract. Economists have been studying only a chapter of the book of economic life. By following in the direction pointed out by sociobiology, we will be able for the first time to take cognizance of the book as a whole.

NOTES

1. Marx himself was an enthusiastic Darwinist. He saw in Darwin's exposition of the competitive struggle for existence a biological 'basis in natural science for the class struggle in history' (Himmelfarb, 1959, Ch. 19).
2. There is one important difference, however. Smith tended to regard the innate qualities of man as serving *the good of the species*. In contrast, the modern biological view emphasizes that characters are selected if they promote the fitness *of their bearers*, even though possibly disfunctional for the species as a whole (Williams, 1966; Ghiselin, 1974).
3. Property as a social institution must be distinguished from mere *de facto* control over resources: e.g. where animals succeed in excluding competitors from territory only by dint of continual patrolling and combat. Whether a

given pattern falls into the one category or the other could be tested by observing what happens to an animal who falls ill or otherwise suffers weakened ability to defend his dominion. Does he nevertheless retain control?

4. The development here is an adaptation of that given in Charnov (1977).

5. On this, see also Frech (1978).

6. Since under absolute competition $\Sigma_{(i)} c_i = \Sigma_{(j)} b_j$, this condition can be combined with condition (7) in the form:

$$\sum_{(i)} r_{iD} c_i - \bar{r} \sum_{(i)} c_i < \sum_{(j)} r_{jD} b_j - \bar{r} \sum_{(j)} b_j.$$

This leads immediately to inequality (9) in the text.

7. If b and c are constants, the helping rule (7) can be written:

$$c \sum_{(i)} r_{iD} < b \sum_{(j)} r_{jD}$$

or

$$cNp\bar{r}_{iD} < bN(1 - p)\,\bar{r}_{jD}.$$

But the absolute competition condition (8) can also be written:

$$cNp = bN(1 - p).$$

The form of inequality (10) then follows by cancellation in the preceding.

8. Provided that, as asserted, it is Daddy who 'has the last word'. Since Kid as merely pragmatic helper acts cooperatively only in the hope of inducing reactive aid from Daddy as hard-core helper, actual cooperation can only ensue where the latter has the final free choice of action (Hirshleifer, 1977*b*).

9. However, while Daddy can gain from being unselfish, he need not be *so* unselfish as to end up at point A^* in the diagram; any solution along SS northwest of point F would suffice to induce Kid to cooperate. Presumably, natural selection would tend to produce only the degrees of unselfishness represented by a tangency position at F (Wintrobe, 1978).

10. The Silver Rule, on the other hand, is clearly more effective in promoting social cooperation over a wider range of situations. The rotten-kid type of cooperation, Figure 6 shows, can come about only if rather restrictive conditions hold. But the Golden Rule does have one practical advantage over the Silver Rule. An organism can follow the Silver Rule only if it has both reward and punishment in its repertory. The Golden Rule requires no such ability to discriminate.

BIBLIOGRAPHY

Alchian, A. A. (1950) 'Uncertainty, evolution and economic theory', *J. Polit. Econ.* **58**, 211.

Alexander, R. D. (1975) 'The search for a general theory of behavior', *Behav. Sci.* **20**, 77.

Becker, G. S. (1976) 'Altruism, egoism and genetic fitness: economics and sociobiology', *J. Econ. Lit.* **14**, 817.

Charnov, E. L. (1977) 'An elementary treatment of the genetical theory of kin-selection', *J. Theor. Biol.* **66**, 541.
Coase, R. H. (1976) 'Adam Smith's view of man', *J. Law Econ.* **19**, 529.
Dawkins, R. (1976) *The Selfish Gene*, New York: Oxford University Press.
Enke, S. (1951) 'On maximizing profits: a distinction between Chamberlin and Robinson', *Am. Econ. Rev.* **41**, 566.
Frech, H. E. III. (1978) 'Altruism, malice and public goods: does altruism pay?' *J. Social Biol. Struct.* **1**, 181.
Fredlund, M. C. (1976) 'Wolves, chimps and Demsetz', *Econ. Inquiry* **14**, 279.
Ghiselin, M. T. (1978) 'The economy of the body', *Am. Econ. Rev.* **68**, 23.
Gordon, H. S. (1954) 'The economic theory of a common-property resource: the fishery', *J. Polit. Econ.* **62**, 124.
Hamilton, W. D. (1964) 'The genetical evolution of social behavior, I', *J. Theor. Biol.* **7**, 6.
Himmelfarb, G. (1959) *Darwin and the Darwinian Revolution*. Garden City, New York: Doubleday.
Hirshleifer, J. (1977*a*) 'Economics from a biological viewpoint', *J. Law Econ.* **20**, 1.
—— (1977*b*) Shakespeare *vs.* Becker on Altruism: the importance of having the last word. *J. Econ. Lit.* **15**, 500.
Kagel, J. H., Battalio, R. C., Rachlin, H., Green, L., Basmann, R. L. and Klemm, W. R. (1975). Experimental studies of consumer demand behavior using laboratory animals. *Econ. Inquiry* **13**, 22.
Knight, F. (1922) 'Ethics and the economic interpretation', *Q. J. Econ.* **36**. 454.
Kurz, M. (1977) 'Altruistic equilibrium' in *Economic Progress, Private Values and Policy* (B. Balassa, ed.). New York: Elsevier-North Holland Pub. Co.
Lorenz, K. (1966) *On Aggression*. New York: Harcourt, Brace & World. (Original German publication, 1963.)
Macaulay, S. (1963) Non-contractual relations in business', *Am. Sociol. Rev.***28**, 55.
Nelson, R. R. and Winter, S. G. (1974) 'Neoclassical versus evolutionary theories of economic growth: critique and perspectives', *Econ. J.* **84**, 886.
Schelling, T. C. (1960) *The Strategy of Conflict*, Cambridge, Mass.: Harvard University Press.
Trivers, R. L. (1971) 'The evolution of reciprocal altruism', *Q. Rev. Biol.* **46**, 35.
Tullock, G. 'Altruism, malice and public goods', *J. Social Biol. Struct.* **1**, 3–9.
West Eberhard, M. J. (1975) 'The evolution of social behavior by kin selection', *Q. Rev. Biol.* **50**, 1.
Williams, G. C. (1966) *Adaptation and Natural Selection*. Princeton, N.J.: Princeton University Press.
Wilson, E. O. (1975) *Sociobiology*. Cambridge, Mass.: The Belknap Press.
Wilson, E. O. (1977) 'Biology and the social sciences', *Daedalus: Journal of the American Academy of Arts and Sciences*, Fall 1977, 127. (Issued as vol. 106, no. 4 of the *Proceedings of the American Academy of Arts and Sciences*.)
Winter, S. G. (1964) 'Economic "natural selection" and the theory of the firm', *Yale Econ. Essays* **4**, 225.
Wintrobe, R. (1978) 'It pays to do good, but not to do more good than it pays: A note on the survival of altruism', University of Western Ontario, mimeo.

8 Privacy: Its Origin, Function, and Future*

*   *   *

Background of this Chapter

This paper was originally presented at a conference held in November 1979 on The Law and Economics of Privacy. The organizers of the conference were thinking of privacy as a rather narrow legal issue — the proper extent of a protected enclave of *secrecy* about one's own affairs. I took the liberty of addressing a much broader topic: the sources, social functions and prospects of a *private sphere* of behaviour ('private rights') within organized society.

Individual competition always threatens to be destructive of social cohesion. To constrain or channel this competition, I suggest here that all social spheres have evolved one or another kind of 'social ethic'. Three main types of social ethics are visible in Nature: Iron Rule (dominance), Golden Rule (sharing) and Silver Rule (private rights). I contend that all three of these have played, and will always play, important roles in human affairs.

*   *   *

The first man who, having enclosed a piece of ground, bethought himself of saying 'This is mine,' and found people simple enough to believe him, was the real founder of civil society.

Rousseau, Discourse on the Origin of Inequality

Explorers must accept the bad with the good. In the new-found lands gold may lie on the ground for the taking, but pioneers are likely to encounter rattlers and desperadoes. Recently a new territory has been discovered by economists, the intellectual continent we call 'privacy'.

---

* Originally published in the *Journal of Legal Studies* 9: 649–64 (December 1980). Reproduced by permission of The University of Chicago Press.

194

The pioneers are our peerless leaders Posner and Stigler whose golden findings have already dazzled the world. It is high time for rattlers and desperadoes — that's the rest of us — to put in an appearance. Of course, I ought to add parenthetically, 'new' is relative to one's point of view. Our pioneering economists, like explorers in other places and other times, found aborigines already inhabiting the territory — in this case intellectual primitives, Supreme Court justices and such. Quite properly, our explorers have brushed the natives aside, and I shall follow in that honourable tradition.

WHAT IS PRIVACY?

So much for flowery introduction. The first issue I shall address is whether our pioneers have correctly mapped the major features of the privacy continent. Have they possibly mistaken a peninsula for the mainland, foothills for a grand sierra, or perhaps even misread their compass so as to reverse north and south? Well, not quite so bad as the last, but I shall be contending that the mainland of privacy is not the idea of *secrecy* as our pioneers appear to believe: secrecy is only an outlying peninsula. The central domain of what we mean by privacy is, rather, a concept that might be described as *autonomy within society*. Privacy thus signifies something much broader than secrecy; it suggests, as I shall be maintaining in detail below, a particular kind of social structure together with its supporting social ethic.

In his 1978 article Posner deals *only* with aspects of privacy as secrecy, as ability to control dissemination and use of information about (or possessed by) oneself.[1] Stigler's recent paper has much the same narrow orientation.[2] This limited angle of view perhaps explains why our pioneers' attitude toward privacy is — occasional qualifications aside — on the whole hostile. Their tone suggests that we have more privacy than ever before — probably more than is actually good for us or, at any rate, good for economic efficiency — and, furthermore, that any person displaying a special desire for privacy is probably just out to hoodwink the rest of us.

In his later paper Posner does however glimpse the central massif of the privacy continent.[3] He there considers a category of privacy he calls *seclusion*. The desire for seclusion is regarded by Posner as a more or less inexplicable taste — and one that is not, probably, very widely shared. Seclusion approaches but does not yet arrive at what I take to be the heart meaning of privacy; seclusion denotes *withdrawal from* society, whereas I am speaking of privacy as a *way of organizing society*. Still, seclusion does suggest one of the major aspects of the situation, the human desire for autonomy — for independence from control by others. Among the group of us assembled here today, due respect for this desire should not be difficult to find. Autonomy of the individual is the bedrock value of that classical liberalism still popular hereabouts.

The etymology of the word 'privacy' is suggestive. The basic Latin form is the adjective *privus*, the original archaic meaning being 'single'. Standard later use signified that which is particular, peculiar, or one's own — the implied context being not the solitary human being but rather the individual facing the potential claims of other persons. Clearly, this root idea is what the word 'private' still means when we speak of *private property*. Secrecy, which is an information preserve maintained about oneself, is but one aspect of (or is perhaps an instrumentality of) privacy in this more fundamental sense. Being rung up on the telephone only to hear a recorded message hawking some product would be regarded as an invasion of our privacy, even though no secret information about ourselves is thereby elicited.

The desire for privacy in the sense of private property is most intense in so far as it concerns control of one's own person and one's own time. The felt urgency gradually diminishes in moving outward to embrace family, home and possessions. But even in the case of material objects, I would argue, our desire to have and to hold them transcends the merely physical benefits derivable therefrom. Possessions are not just things. They are guarantors or at least symbols of our autonomy from others, of our status as self-sustaining individuals.

So far I have addressed the privacy of an individual as against other members of society. A special case of enormous importance concerns individual autonomy as against those other members of society who constitute the government. This is the privacy meant in the line we draw distinguishing the *private sphere* from the public sphere. In this connection, failure to perceive the centrality of the autonomy conception of privacy leads Posner to decry the Supreme Court's recent constitutional doctrine of sexual privacy, as applied for example in striking down anti-abortion statutes.[4] I would be among the last to defend the usual thought-processes of the present occupants of the Supreme Court bench. But their judgment setting sexual matters outside the reach of government control, whether or not soundly based in law or morals, is surely a declaration of a *privacy right* in the most essential meaning of that term.

Autonomy as against the *state* is more than the leading special case of the general problem of privacy. Privacy can be attained, to some *de facto* degree, simply by individual patrolling and self-defence. Nor is this an unimportant phenomenon even today; a person who remains passive in the face of invasions of his rights is unlikely to retain them.

But for defending privacy we rely, for the most part, upon the support of *law*, a system of impersonal third-party definition and enforcement of private property rights. Laws can be enacted by a general town meeting and enforced by a general hue and cry as need arises. But society long ago arrived at (or had imposed upon it) the alternative system of *specialized coercion* that is government. A dangerous solution, evidently. How to defend autonomous private rights against the organized professional guardians of those rights is the key problem of liberal political philosophy. But I am not going to solve that problem today. Instead, my purpose is to look both into the sources and the social consequences of what our pioneers regard as the somewhat peculiar taste for privacy.

ON THE EVOLUTION OF TASTES

Economics has not done a good job on tastes. The use of this trivializing word, suggestive of the choice of French dressing versus Thousand Island, is itself an evasion. If we spoke of human drives or aims, of ingrained ethics, or of value systems or goals for living, we should be inclined to treat the subject with more respect. One hardly need emphasize that *what* we want is often of greater significance for personal and social life than how precisely we manage to balance marginal cost against marginal benefit in achieving our desires. Even if preferences were arbitrary brute facts, independent of economic forces, simply mapping them should have aroused more interest than it has. But what we call tastes are *not* completely arbitrary. On the most elementary level, it is not difficult to understand why ice water is more desired in July than in December. In what has been called 'the new theory of consumption',[5] economists have begun to interpret preferences for observable market goods as derived from and dependent upon more fundamental desires. But lacking an analytical explanation of these latter, our theories have only pushed the underlying arbitrariness back a notch.

Starting with Alchian,[6] a number of economists have analysed how the market environment selects for commercial survival only those firms choosing the 'best' decisions — even though those decisions were very likely made via a process of at best limited rationality.[7] Thus, the blind forces of environmental selection lead to a *simulation* of conscious rationality. The solutions we see in the world about us tend to be well-adapted *because* they have survived, however arrived at.

Curiously, and undoubtedly because of the tunnel vision that enables us not to see tastes as an economic problem, economists have never attempted to apply the idea of evolutionary selection to the essential makeup of the human fabric itself. Even in the new theory of consumption, the provenance of our underlying deeper desires remains an unanalysed mystery. But the biologists, in a long tradition starting with Darwin's *Descent of Man* and recently flowering as a topic under the heading of sociobiology, have been better economists than we. They have shown that not only our physical but our psychic constitution — what we desire, what 'tastes sweet' to us[8] — is what has been found by natural selection to work as a genetically implanted motivator. I hasten to interpolate a word of warning, however: our implanted structures and orientations represent successful evolutionary solutions *in the past*, and there is no implication that they will continue to succeed in the future. Nor is there any implication that these solutions are 'right' by any standard other than success — for example, by the standard of ethics.

We do not usually dignify the implanted tropisms of primitive organisms, to seek or avoid light or heat or water, by calling them desires. They are 'hard-wired' controls on behaviour. Higher organisms have genetic controls that tend to be increasingly 'soft-wired' as we approach the human level. Such controls permit the organism to choose, to some degree, among the implanted ends — for example, by deferring gratification. More important for our purposes, the controls are subject to social influence. Man is, pre-eminently, the *indoctrinable* — the teachable — animal.[9] Western man does not munch grass, like the cows, because his genetic constitution forbids it; he does not drink animal blood, like the Masai, because his cultural constitution forbids it.

Culture is evidently important, exceptionally so on the human level, but it does not abolish biology. For one thing, the genetic foundation sets a limit upon the cultural superstructure: human beings cannot even be taught to digest grass. For another, the human capacity for culture — the fact that our innate instructions *are* soft-wired — is itself a biological adaptation. Finally and most important of all, cultural and genetic factors are simultaneously under the sway of natural selection. Within economics this idea has played a notable role in the thinking of the Austrian school, which emphasizes that human social structures typically emerge without rational planning on anyone's part.[10] Nor need they be any the worse for that lack; there is not only a wisdom of Nature but a wisdom of culture. Of particular relevance for us is the *law* as one of the social structures that follows an evolutionary course,[11] possibly doing better the less the purportedly rational element in its unfolding development. Again, however, a word of caution. Nature is not always wise,[12] and cultures (including our own) are also likely to have evolved seriously dysfunctional characteristics. Natural selection selects for survivability pure and simple, and a trait *may* survive that is bad for the ecology or for the species or even for its individual bearer.

Having made these general points about tastes, it is time to become more specific about privacy. Has the genetic origin of mankind or, alternatively, have successful cultures like our own implanted within us as individuals a 'taste for privacy'? In this context, the word *ethic* is a more accurate term than 'taste'. We are dealing with a two-sided situation, a balancing of autonomy and sociality. The privacy ethic, whether internalized as Adam Smith's Impartial Spectator or some analogous metaphor, would urge the individual to insist on his own claims to inviolability of person and property *while being prepared to concede corresponding rights to others*. The question is whether we are, as individuals, driven internally (at least to some degree) by this ethic.

Consider economic man. This intellectual creation, acting dispassionately yet ruthlessly in pursuit of self-interest, is free of implanted social controls. If he concedes rights to others, it is only as a means of self-gratification: honesty *may* be the best policy. But actual man as we know him does sometimes sacrifice his interests for others in a way not purely instrumental to his own goals. The biological explanation is interesting. There *is* ultimate relentless selfishness in Nature, but on a level deeper than the individual — on the level of the gene.[13] Organisms are just survival machines designed to carry packets of genes over from generation to generation. Most obviously when it concerns one's offspring, therefore, a selfish gene might instruct the *individual* to be unselfish. Generalizing from this, the biologists have shown that shared genetic endowments among kin lead to natural selection in favour of the trait of helping one's relatives.[14] And even beyond the kinship tie, *group selection* may lead to the genetic implanting of an ethic of loyalty to neighbours and allies,[15] as will be discussed below. And finally, building upon this genetic base, natural selection operating on cultures undoubtedly has promoted ethics of self-sacrifice for larger groups identified by language or ethnicity or ideology.

THREE STRUCTURES OF SOCIALITY AND THEIR SUPPORTING ETHICS

There are some animal species whose members are social isolates, whose biologically driven coming together is limited to the sexual act. Jean-Jacques Rousseau put natural man in this category:

... wandering up and down the forests, without industry, without speech, without home, an equal stranger to war and to all ties, neither standing in need of his fellow-creatures nor having any desire to hurt them, and perhaps even not distinguishing them one from another; let us conclude that, being self-sufficient and subject to so few passions, he could have no feelings or knowledge but such as befitted his situation.[16]

This passage sounds rather like economic man. Egoistic economic man might, in view of the material advantages of cooperation (in production, in trade, or in defence), associate with others — but only on a *quid pro quo* basis as expressed in the famous *social contract*. This is not quite the line of Rousseau's thinking, which is rather more complex (not to say confused); Rousseau also postulated a certain natural goodness and sense of compassion in primitive man. The early Sophists were more consistent in their view that our basic nature is entirely selfish, that the social contract is only of instrumental significance for mankind.[17]

Theories of a social contract among truly economic men have difficulty with the problem of enforcement. In the absence of a social ethic, individuals carry out their shares of the social bargain only as they can be forced to do so. But enforcement services are a public good in many respects: punishing a malefactor tends to benefit the community, whether or not the agent who punishes gains thereby. Hence we would expect enforcement services to be undersupplied by economic men. There is no doubt that, from the most primitive to the most advanced stages of society, a higher degree of cooperative interaction (including 'moralistic aggression'[18] against malefactors) takes place than can be explained simply as a pragmatic option for totally egoistic man.

But the mere fact of natural association does not tell us enough. The often-bruited idea of a generalized 'social instinct' omits essential distinctions. There are many different kinds of natural societies. While still leaving matters seriously oversimplified, since none of these is probably ever observed as a pure form, as a first approximation it seems possible to classify the main structures of sociality in animals and men on the basis of their reliance on the principles of: (1) communal sharing, (2) private rights, or (3) dominance. It may be easiest to remember these in terms of their underlying ethics. If sharing is the Golden Rule, mutual recognition of private rights is the Silver Rule, while the struggle for dominance is the Iron Rule of social interaction.[19] These structures and ethics have evolved, each only in particular ecological contexts, because individuals so organized turned out to have a survival advantage (through group selection) over those expressing different behavioural traits.

Dominance in social groups, the Iron Rule, does not require any very roundabout explanation. In the evolutionary competition for survival and reproduction, no particular subtlety is involved when selfish genes instruct their bearers to attempt to subordinate other organisms in a continuing pattern of association. The only problem is why the dominated individuals, having lost the struggle for the alpha position, submit rather than secede. And, in fact, defeated contenders or other dissatisfied group members sometimes do secede. But there are advantages to group affiliation even in a subordinate position; as Hobbes contended, isolation may be worse. There are lone baboons, but they do not survive the leopard long. Furthermore, in an uncertain world there always remain possibilities of promotion; today's subordinate may become tomorrow's alpha.

Is there an ingrained ethic associated with the Iron Rule of dominance? Yes, and this can be seen in various ways. In the combat for top position, animals typically fight by limited conventional means, often not using their most lethal weapons.[20] The defeated animal thus does not fight to the death, and his submission is accepted. More generally a degree of *noblesse oblige* constrains the leader — for example, he might have to protect weaker group members against predators. And followers must do more than prudently know their place. If the group is to survive severe competition, they must act with a measure of loyal enthusiasm.[21] That the dominance pattern is indeed two-sided is also revealed by the fact that the alpha animal does not always monopolize the male reproductive role.

What of the Golden Rule of sharing? That this might be viable (to some degree) in a world of selfish genes is only superficially paradoxical. As an obvious example, all mammals are tied to a way of life requiring maternal unselfishness toward infants. More generally, kin selection leads to many types of mutual helping among nuclear or extended families in Nature. The extent to which unselfish sharing among *unrelated* individuals may be favoured by group selection is a much debated matter among biologists, but is clearly operative to some degree.[22] In any case, most natural groupings do involve an important kinship element as well.

The underlying ethic of sharing is not all hearts and flowers. The kin selection process may have implanted the supportive emotion of love, as in the instance of maternal care, so that no external pressure is required.[23] Beyond this case, there may be two sides to the story. At least on the human level the less attractive emotions of *envy* and *fear of envy* (the latter perhaps internalized as conscience or guilt) may serve as enforcers of the noble Golden Rule.[24] And, as is well known, Adam Smith emphasized *self-esteem* as a major motivator of unselfish action.[25] So sharing behaviour is supported by a complex mixture of internal drives. Nevertheless, imposed societal sanctions may always be required to help repress egoistic self-interest.

The really interesting problems for our purposes concern the Silver Rule. Can Nature actually evolve a social system of private rights with its supporting ethic? It has in fact done so in the social structure known as *territoriality*. Members of many animal species, humans among them, carry about them a bubble of personal space, invasion of which is resisted. How human cultural differences modify the detailed expression of this kind of 'taste for privacy' is entertainingly described by Hall.[26] Many animals also defend geographically fixed territories, defined on the level of the family or of larger bands or troops.

But *de facto* possession of space is not enough. The supporting ethic is still needed, namely, a complementary *reluctance to intrude*. In Nature, this does occur. Among many, possibly all territorial species (man excluded, perhaps) it has been found that proprietors defending their territories are almost always able to fight off incursions. Such intrusions as do take place tend to be exploratory rather than determinedly invasive.[27] Internalized respect for property is what permits autonomy to persist within society.

More than one mechanism for the evolution of this social pattern can be imagined. It has been contended that Nature has somehow gotten the individuals to so behave for the good of the species,[28] an explanation which fails to cope with the free-rider problem. That is, even if propensity to intrude is bad for the species on average, it may be good for the genes carried by the intruder. A more plausible argument starts from the observation that, other things equal, a territory is *worth more* to its proprietor than to the intruder. The proprietor will have a more accurate knowlege of its resources, and indeed may have to a degree adapted them to his own personal requirements (or himself to them). It therefore pays the proprietor to fight harder and longer. This being the case, evolution might have hard-wired defensive belligerence into proprietors together with the complementary traits of reluctance to intrude and willingness to retreat on the part of potential challengers — the two together comprising what I have called the privacy ethic. And Maynard Smith has shown that such a 'bourgeois' strategy can be viable in evolutionary terms even if proprietorship is founded upon no more than a convention like 'first come, first served'.[29]

As indicated above, social structures and their supporting ethics tend to evolve where they are adaptive in particular ecological contexts. The unselfish sharing represented by maternal care is adaptive where high 'quality' of offspring[30] pays off more than large numbers. Selfless sharing in mated pairs is typically observed where severe environments make close teamwork essential to survival.[31] Territoriality, by eliminating duplication of effort in exploiting the resource field, is a kind of minimal teamwork; it tends to emerge where resources are fixed in place and more or less uniformly distributed.[32] Territories may be held at individual, family or group levels, depending mainly upon returns to scale. Under severe ecological pressure, individual territoriality has been observed to break down in favour of a group dominance structure.

To summarize, all three main social principles — dominance, sharing and private rights — have evolved in Nature, each as an adaptation to a particular type of social niche. Each principle also tends to be associated with an ingrained supporting ethic, since a mere 'social contract' entered into by purely egoistic individuals is unlikely to survive the free-rider problem. Typically, strands of all three may be woven together in the behavioural pattern of each species. And of course the merely egoistic element probably never totally disappears. Indeed, sometimes what seems superficially to represent an organized social unit may be only a 'selfish herd' lacking any real cooperative element.[33]

ON THE NATURAL HISTORY OF PRIVATE RIGHTS

Hayek has argued that the transition from the small human band to settled communities and civilized life resulted from man's learning to obey the abstract rules of an emergent market order.[34] The alternative to this cultural constraint, Hayek supposed, was for man to remain under the guidance of 'innate instincts to pursue common perceived goals' (our Golden Rule). The way of face-to-face communal sharing, probably adaptive to the primitive hunter-gatherer economy in which man may have lived for 50,000 generations, allegedly had to be bypassed if progress was to be made.

There are curious parallels and divergences between Hayek's ideas and those of the Marxist anthropologist Sahlins.[35] For Sahlins also, human social development required overcoming innate instincts. But in his view the innate instincts are those of 'animality' — selfishness, indiscriminate sexuality, dominance and brute competition. Sahlins agrees with Hayek once again, as to the sharing ethic of the primitive human band.[36] But for Sahlins the shift to the Silver Rule ethic — associated with the transition from a hunting to an agricultural way of life — represented moral degeneration rather than progress.[37]

As indicated earlier, the degree to which alternative social ethics may have been *genetically* implanted rather than *culturally* renewed in each human generation will not be emphasized here. Both genetic and cultural inheritances are subject to natural selection; both track environmental change. However, genetic adaptation has much more inertia. It is therefore reasonable to believe that the untold aeons of man's primate heritage laid down a foundation of behavioural as well as structural traits that still remain with us; that the 50,000 generations of hunter-gatherer life have also left their mark; that man has partially yet probably only incompletely adapted genetically to the life of regular labour that began with agriculture; and, finally, that modern urban patterns in some ways clash considerably with our deeper ingrained attitudes.[38]

Turning to the historical question, primeval communism and sharing, as an Eden-like stage of early human societal evolution[39] is a myth.[40] Essentially all known primitive communities have been found to possess relatively elaborate structures of property rights. Though these private rights are defined in ways that vary from society to society, invasions of them are always strongly resented. Golden Rule motivations were probably present in early man, as they may still be today. But only as one element, probably the smallest element, in the human mixed brew of motivations: sheer egoism competing with overlapping (partially conflicting, partially reinforcing) elements of dominance, privacy and sharing ethics.

I shall be following Hayek and Sahlins in going back to the origins of these social ethics. But in contrast with their views, to me it seems clear that the first and deepest layer of human sociality was the Iron Rule of dominance.[41] It is generally agreed that man evolved from a primate line that left the forest to live in the African savannah. In this highly dangerous environment, primates lacking biological weaponry could initially survive only by banding in groups. Sharing is essentially unknown in the primate heritage, and territoriality was not a viable principle in the savannah ecology. In consequence, dominance had to be the governing rule holding the band together. (The baboons, a currently successful savannah-dwelling species, are at this stage today.) That all human history testifies to the importance of the struggle for power and status is too obvious to require underlining. I shall add only two points: (1) the instinctive drive for leadership could only succeed in tandem with the complementary quality of willing *followership*,[42] and (2) dominance need not be the result of strictly individual force but may involve also the ability to form effective coalitions.

The crucial step toward moderation of the Iron Rule was, it seems, the shift to a largely carnivorous diet. Hunting of big game probably placed a greater premium upon a more egalitarian form of cooperation, requiring distributed individual enterprise and cleverness. The consequence was a reduction in the steepness of the dominance gradient. Something approaching monogamous sexual pairing — private rights in mating — may have been the result of the sexual division of labour associated with hunting.[43] At some point the development of tools and weapons opened up another dimension of the division of labour, between hunter and specialized craftsman. It seems likely that the first systematic pattern of exchange of material goods was between tools and weapons on the one side and meat on the other.[44] The possibility of such exchange required prior mutual recognition of private rights. Already at the primate level, the beginnings of private sexual rights as well as material property rights (in meat) have been observed. *Exchange* of material goods seems uniquely human, however.[45]

Parallel with the evolution of the privacy ethic, we need not exclude a tendency to broaden the Golden Rule of sharing beyond immediate kin. Successful 'begging', a normal behaviour pattern between offspring and parent, is found to some extent between unrelated adults among the higher primates, once again in connection with meat.[46] In primitive human societies, anthropologists have emphasized, *patterns of redistribution* are nearly universal as limitations upon property rights. However, it would be misleading to place excessive emphasis upon the Golden Rule aspects of redistributive sharing; among primitive peoples, reciprocation of 'gifts' is almost always expected.[47] Under conditions of resource variability, sharing may also serve a mutual insurance function.[48] And, finally, in some cases where resources are held in common rather than privately partitioned, productive efficiency may provide a satisfactory explanation.[49]

The uniquely human development of language led to an open-ended increase in the complexity and subtlety of behaviour patterns. One point of great interest concerns interband relations. When primate bands split up, for demographic or other reasons, they shortly become strangers. But human bands could retain recognition of kinship ties, could form clan and tribe alliances. The widening field of interaction opened up further possibilities of specialization and exchange, both on the group and on the individual level.

The ecological shift to pastoralism and to agriculture was not, if this argument is correct, the origin of private rights. But pastoralism requires private ownership of flocks, and agriculture private ownership of crops. The two systems tend to develop rather different human types. Pastoralism is typically associated with extended family or clan units, relatively strong dominance, and polygyny (as in the patriarchical period pictured in Genesis). Agriculture tends to be associated with the monogamous peasant homestead, unmatchable in efficiency terms by any form of group farming. On the other hand, the military helplessness of a dispersed farming population tends to lead to their subjection or enslavement by dominant overlords or invaders.

In fact, the role of war in selection of human types and social

structures has been enormous. From the most primitive times, it seems
impossible to doubt that man as superpredator also preyed on his own
kind,[50] particularly in times of resource stress. Warfare as an economy
activity is characterized by an overwhelming economy of scale leading
to larger group size: 'God is on the side of the bigger battalions.'
Against this, however, has to be balanced diminishing returns to scale
in exploiting game or crops or other localized resources. Warfare has
undoubtedly had complex and multi-directional effects upon the human
makeup itself. On the one hand, it selects for selfless loyalty and
dedication — Golden Rule properties within the group. It also selects
for the strong charismatic leadership typical of dominance structures.
Yet the more individualistic virtues associated with private rights may
also play an important role in war, for a variety of reasons: private
men are more likely to have developed habits of ingenuity and
enterprise, they may fight more strongly for what they regard as their
own, and the commercial societies organized on the principle of private
rights will have become richer and more innovative. Thus, while Adam
Smith along with other philosophers[51] deplored the loss of heroic
qualities due to the spread of affluence and commerce, the outcome
of the contest between Athens and Sparta is not in general predictable.
(It was 'a nation of shopkeepers' that defeated Napoleon.) And, finally,
reinforcing the fact that each separate individual represents a mixture
of motivations, the large scale of modern societies makes it possible to
combine many *different human types* into a mutually supportive alliance.

SOME CONCLUDING POINTS

I shall finish by setting down, not in any very systematic order, some
points that may reinforce the key ideas and perhaps provide hints as
to where they might lead.

1. To distinguish, as is common, between 'selfish' and 'unselfish'
behaviour, between pursuit of private goals and public goals, is a very
serious oversimplification. Man does have egoistic, purely selfish drives.
But his social instincts are more complex, involving (at least) the three
principles of *dominance, sharing* and *private rights*. Each of these is
not a simple one-sided urge, but a two-sided ethic.

2. These ethics have evolved and have become ingrained in the
human makeup in association with various forms of social organization
over the history of mankind. Each ethic and associated social structure
has been adaptive to certain of the ecological contexts and constraints
in which humanity has lived.

3. The 'taste for privacy' is a misleading term. It *may* represent

nothing more than a selfish claim, of which we may appropriately be suspicious. But insistence on one's own rights is also part of a two-sided ethic involving willingness to concede corresponding rights to others, and even willingness to participate as a disinterested third-party enforcer against violators.

4. Like the privacy ethic, each of the other two-sided ethics has a selfish aspect. This is obvious for the dominance drive, but even sharing involves the supportive emotions of envy and fear of envy.

5. Economic study of market interactions may yield satisfactory results while postulating purely egoistic men, acting within an unexplained social environment of regulatory law. But as the power of economic analysis comes to be employed outside the traditional market context, for example in the area of public choice, the egoistic model of man (as in social contract theories) will not suffice.[52]

6. The privacy ethic is an enormously powerful device for creating wealth, but beyond a certain point affluence creates great social dangers in permitting or perhaps even promoting a relaxation of social discipline together with the spread of disruptive ideologies.[53] Pursuit of affluence may be self-defeating, not only on the individual level as moralists have always contended, but in terms of social survival as well. This ought to raise doubts in our minds about too-ready use of 'efficiency' (which is essentially maximization of aggregate wealth) as the criterion of social policy.[54]

7. The conflict between the privacy ethic and its competitors (alternative social ethics on the one hand and sheer egoism on the other) takes place partly within social groups, partly between them. Man has ingrained within him elements favouring each of these social tendencies, soft-wired so as to leave a range of ideological choice. So the future of the privacy ethic rests in part upon its ability to capture the hearts and minds of men. At least equally important is the competition between groups, primarily military competition. While it is conventional to deplore merely 'commercial' ethics, societies organized on this principle have given a good account of themselves historically — not only militarily, but in terms of the values we consider civilized. I shall not attempt here to forecast the future prospects of privacy as a social structure balancing individual autonomy with communal responsibility except to say: They don't look very good!

208   *Cooperation and Conflict*

NOTES

1. Richard A. Posner, 'The Right of Privacy', 12 *Georgia L. Rev.* 393 (1978).
2. George J. Stigler, 'An Introduction to Privacy in Economics and Politics', 9 *J. Legal Stud.* 623 (1980).
3. Richard A. Posner, 'Privacy, Secrecy, and Reputation', 28 *Buffalo L. Rev.* 1 (1979).
4. Ibid.
5. Kelvin J. Lancaster, 'A New Approach to Consumer Theory', 74 *J. Pol. Econ.* 132 (1966).
6. Armen A. Alchian, 'Uncertainty, Evolution, and Economic Theory', 58 *J. Pol. Econ.* 211 (1950).
7. Herbert A. Simon, 'A Behavioural Model of Rational Choice', 69 *Q.J. Econ.* 99 (1955).
8. David P. Barash, *The Whisperings Within* (1979).
9. Edward O. Wilson, *Sociobiology: The New Synthesis* 562 (1975).
10. Friedrich A. Hayek, *The Three Sources of Human Values* (1978).
11. Paul H. Rubin, 'Why Is the Common Law Efficient?', 6 *J. Legal Stud.* 51 (1977).
12. Michael T. Ghiselin, 'The Economy of the Body', 68 *Am. Econ. Rev.* 233 (1978).
13. Richard Dawkins, *The Selfish Gene* (1976). I should not imply that there is unanimity on this point among biologists; various strands of opinion have their supporters. For example, some detect a deep cooperative or sympathetic urge in the life principle. See Lewis Thomas, *The Lives of a Cell: Notes of a Biology Watcher* (1974). Others question the saliency of the acting-gene metaphor, as genes do not act alone nor are they entirely distinct particles.
14. W. D. Hamilton, 'The Genetical Evolution of Social Behavior', 7 *J. Theoretical Biology* 1 (1964).
15. 'When two tribes of primeval man, living in the same country, came into competition, the tribe including the greater number of courageous, sympathetic, and faithful members would succeed better and would conquer the other.' Charles Darwin, *The Descent of Man*, in *The Origin of Species and the Descent of Man* 498 (Modern Library edn., n.d.).
16. Jean-Jacques Rousseau, *A Discourse on the Origin of Inequality,* in *The Social Contract and Discourses* 230 (Everyman's Library 1950).
17. Roger D. Masters, 'Of Marmots and Men: Animal Behavior and Human Altruism', in *Altruism, Sympathy, and Helping: Psychological and Sociological Principles* 59 (Lauren Wispé ed., 1978).
18. Robert L. Trivers, 'The Evolution of Reciprocal Altruism', 46 *Q. Rev. Biology* 35 (1971).
19. In another context I distinguished behaviours in accordance with the golden, the silver and the brass rules. The last of these represented 'economic man', free of implanted constraints. I shall not need the brass metaphor here. See Jack Hirshleifer, 'Natural Economy versus Political Economy', 1 *J. Soc. & Biological Structures* 319 (1978).
20. Konrad Lorenz, *On Aggression*, Marjorie Kerr Wilson trans. (1966).
21. An instructive instance of a two-sided dominance ethic, implanted not by natural but by artificial selection over many generations, is the relation

between the dog and his human master. This example shows that a 'society' may cut across the species barrier.

22. W. D. Hamilton, 'Innate Social Aptitudes of Man', in *Biosocial Anthropology* (R. Fox ed. 1975).
23. Gary S. Becker, 'Altruism, Egoism, and Genetic Fitness: Economics and Sociobiology', 14 *J. Econ. Lit.* 817 (1976).
24. See Helmut Schoeck, *Envy: A Theory of Social Behavior* (1970) and F. H. Willhoite, Jr, 'Rank and Reciprocity: Speculations on Human Emotions and Political Life', in *Human Sociobiology and Politics* (Elliot White ed. 1980).
25. R. H. Coase, 'Adam Smith's View of Man', 19 *J. Law & Econ.* 529 (1976).
26. Edward T. Hall, *The Hidden Dimension* (1966).
27. See Robert Ardrey, *The Territorial Imperative* (1966). A wolf pack will even respect a human being's territorial claims, if asserted in proper wolf language. (If you're interested, correct wolf etiquette requires urinary marking of the boundary of your claim. See Farley Mowat, *Never Cry Wolf* (1963).)
28. V. C. Wynne-Edwards, *Animal Dispersion in Relation to Social Behavior* (1962) and Ardrey, *op. cit.*
29. John Maynard Smith, 'The Evolution of Behavior', *Sci. Am.*, September 1978, 176.
30. Gary S. Becker, 'A Theory of Social Interactions', 82 *J. Pol. Econ.* 1063 (1974).
31. Wilson, *op. cit.*, ch. 15.
32. Ibid., Ch. 12.
33. W. D. Hamilton, 'Geometry for the Selfish Herd', 31 *J. Theoretical Biology* 295 (1971).
34. Hayek, *op. cit.*
35. Marshall D. Sahlins, 'The Origin of Society', *Sci. Am.*, September 1960, 76 and *Stone Age Economics* (1972).
36. A contradiction leaps to the eye here. Suppression of 'indiscriminate sexuality' sounds rather like a move from group-sharing to private rights, which Sahlins ought (in the interests of consistency) to deplore rather than approve.
37. Sahlins, *Stone Age Economics*. A fascinating strand to this argument, which unfortunately cannot be pursued here, is the claim that even in material terms — leisure, health, protein consumption, etc. — the tiller of the soil was far worse-off than had been the cooperative hunters of the earlier era. See also Marvin Harris, *Cannibals and Kings: The Origins of Culture* (1977).
38. See Desmond Morris, *The Naked Ape* (1967): *A Zoologist's Study of the Human Animal* and *The Human Zoo* (1969). Wilson, *op. cit.*, p. 569, is somewhat unusual in the degree of lability he assigns to genetic traits; he would be inclined therefore to minimize their possible current maladaptedness.
39. Frederick Engels, *The Origin of the Family, Private Property, and the State* (1902).
40. See Ernest Beaglehole, 'Property', in 12 *Int'l Encyclopaedia of the Soc. Sci.* 359 (1968).
41. Lionel Tiger and Robin Fox, *The Imperial Animal* (1971); Fred H. Willhoite, Jr, 'Primates and Political Authority: A Biobehavioral Perspective', 70 *Am. Pol. Sci. Rev.* 1110 (1976).

42. Willhoite, *op. cit.*
43. Morris, *op. cit.*
44. The exchange of interpersonal cooperative *services* (sex, grooming, mutual aid) long anteceded this, of course.
45. On sexual rights among baboons, see Willhoite, *op. cit.* An economic analysis of rights in meat, maintained even against dominant animals among chimpanzees, appears in Melvin C. Fredlund, 'Wolves, Chimps, and Demsetz', 14 *Econ. Inquiry* 279 (1976). For 'the propensity to truck, barter, and exchange' as an exclusively human trait, see Adam Smith, *The Wealth of Nations*, Book 1, ch. 2, p. 13 (Modern library edn. 1937).
46. Wilson, *op. cit.*, ch. 26.
47. The 'norm of reciprocity' seems to be universal in the human species. And, so far as we can tell, it is uniquely human (see Adam Smith, *op. cit.*). The need to form and to manage reciprocal ties is likely to have played a critical role in the evolution of man's individual intelligence as well as his social repertory. See Willhoite, *op. cit.*
48. Richard A. Posner, 'A Theory of Primitive Society, with Special Reference to Law', 23 *J. Law & Econ.* 1 (1980).
49. Harold Demsetz, 'Toward a Theory of Property Rights', 57 *Am. Econ. Rev.* 347 (Papers & Proceedings, May 1967). Even though what appears to be sharing *may* often represent disguised egoistic or private right motivations, economists ought not be too hasty in excluding the possibility that Golden Rule sharing is actually taking place.
50. Richard D. Alexander, 'The Search for a General Theory of Behavior', 20 *Behavioral Sci.* 77 (1975); Harris, *op. cit.*
51. Edward C. Banfield, *The Contradictions of Commercial Society: Adam Smith as a Political Sociologist* (Mont Pelerin Society Lecture, 1976).
52. Note Stigler's inability to satisfactorily explain privacy (secrecy) legislation without bringing in an element he calls 'social altruism'. Stigler, *op. cit.* See also H. Margolis, *Selfishness, Altruism, and Rationality* (1979) (unpublished paper at Center for Int'l Studies, Mass. Inst. of Technology).
53. J. A. Schumpeter, *Capitalism, Socialism, and Democracy* (1942).
54. At this point my analysis diverges from that of Harold Demsetz, 'Ethics and Efficiency in Property Rights Systems', in *Time, Uncertainty, and Disequilibrium* (Mario J. Rizzo ed. 1979), with which it otherwise has many points of agreement. I shall note here one other significant divergence. Demsetz, concerned to counter certain naive ethical views held by ideological defenders of private property as a 'natural' right of man, strongly emphasizes the socially conventional (not to say arbitrary) aspects of how rights are actually defined. In contrast, it seems to follow from my approach that there is, indeed, some 'natural' element in property rights, that there are intrinsic limits constraining what is merely contingent and artificial. I cannot develop this idea further here, however.

9 Evolutionary Models in Economics and Law: Cooperation versus Conflict Strategies*

* * *

Background of this Chapter

The original version of this paper was the main presentation at a seminar on Evolutionary Theory in Law and Economics, held in May 1980. In line with one of the central themes of this volume, the paper traces the interplay of cooperative and conflictual motivations in the evolution of legal systems and of economic forms. The analysis questions certain excessively harmonistic views as to the supposed triumphant progress of the law or of the economy in the direction of efficiency.

Cooperation and conflict are not simple opposites but rather are typically intertwined, though in a number of distinctly different patterns. Using game-theory models like Prisoners' Dilemma and Chicken, the paper categorizes ways in which cooperation may fail, and explores the very different consequences of such failures in differing environmental circumstances.

Note: The evolutionary game-theory modelling in this paper has some striking parallels with the well-known work of Robert Axelrod, unknown to me at the time, which has since appeared in his volume, *The Evolution of Cooperation* (New York: Basic Books, 1984).

* * *

Attempting to address the combined topics of economics, law and evolution in a single paper is hubris indeed. All the more so, as I shall be adopting very broad interpretations of what we might mean by both economics and law. Economics, as understood here, is *not* limited to

---

* Originally published in *Research in Law and Economics* 4: 1–60 (1982). Reproduced by permission of JAI Press, Inc.

selfish, rational 'economic man' interacting with his fellows only through impersonal market relationships. For my purposes, all human motivations and interactions constitute the subject matter of economics, so long as they respond to the pervasive fact of resource scarcity. As for law, I shall take that term as covering essentially all modes of *coercive social control* of behaviour, thus including much of what might conventionally be considered under the headings of politics or sociology. However, the evolutionary standpoint sets some bound upon the field of discussion. Also, I shall be considering only one aspect of interpersonal interactions — though that is perhaps the most important of all — to wit, the determinants of *cooperation versus conflict* in human affairs.

ECONO-LEGAL THINKING AND THE MISSING TREND TOWARD HARMONY

In recent years there has been growing intellectual interchange between legal and economic scholars. The dominant influence, it seems fair to say, has been economics, in the sense that economic propositions have been borrowed or applied to provide new or more fundamental explanations of certain legal phenomena.[1] The influential economic ideas in question, together with their seeming legal implications, can be stated rather baldly (shorn of needed qualifications and possible adornments) as follows:

1. *Smith's Theorem* ((60), Book 1, ch. 2). Voluntary exchange is mutually advantageous for participants. Implication: The law ought, presumptively at least, to promote trade — negatively, by removing artificial legal barriers, positively, by facilitating and enforcing private exchange agreements.

2. *Coase's Theorem* (11). All available mutually advantageous exchanges will be voluntarily undertaken by the parties involved. Even where individuals impose what are said to be 'external' injuries upon others, as when an upstream user of water degrades the quality of the flow to a downstream user, a resolution of the conflict will tend to take place through the exchange process. This conclusion does not depend upon the initial assignment of property rights, provided the entitlements are well defined. If the upstream user has the legal right to degrade quality, the downstream party can offer him compensation for not doing so. If on the other hand the downstream user has a legal right to unimpaired quality, the upstream party can purchase the other's tolerance of damage. Either way, the upstream use will continue to

take place if and only if it can pay its way in comparison with the downstream damage. Given such an assignment of property rights, and if there are no transaction costs, the final outcome will be *efficient* (in a sense to be made more precise below). Implication: In addition to removing artificial barriers to transactions, the law ought to assign well-defined property rights to all resources of economic value. And if transaction costs (barriers to exchange) are absent, the law need not otherwise concern itself with regulating external damage.

3. *Posner's Theorem* (49).[2] Where unavoidable transaction costs (that is, barriers other than those due to the law itself) preclude achievement of a fully efficient result by private negotiation, some particular initial assignments of property rights may constitute or lead to more nearly efficient outcomes than others. Implication: Recognizing the presence of unavoidable transaction costs, the law ought to choose the most efficient of the possible assignments of property rights.

I have in each case stated the seeming legal implication in *normative* terms, the operative phrase being: 'The law ought to . . .'. An alternative *positive* interpretation would be indicated by the assertion: 'The law will in fact tend to . . .'. In its normative version, this entire line of econo-legal thinking might be summarized: 'Market transactions among individuals operate in the direction of economic efficiency, and the law *ought* to aid and where necessary supplement this trend.' The positive version would be: 'Market interactions tend toward economic efficiency, and the law *will in fact tend to* assist and supplement this tendency.'

On either interpretation, a generally Panglossian aura surrounds the entire discussion. In the positive version, it would seem, we scholars need only chronicle the unfolding harmonious progress of law and economy toward the best (most efficient) of all possible worlds. The normative version of the argument, while it suggests some doubt as to the matter (why else concern ourselves with what *ought* to be done?), has the offsetting advantage of providing a more muscular role for savants like us. Whatever blemishes may mar its present complexion, the law can be improved, and we are the ones who know how to do so! Indeed, it seems reasonable to suppose, as scholarly understanding advances and as education of the public broadens and deepens over time, the various mistaken ideas that have in the past interfered with sound econo-legal thinking should have decreasing sway.

I have injected a note of sarcasm, for we know that there must be something seriously wrong with this picture. On the most fundamental matter, the rule of law has always fallen short of universal coverage of mankind. The potential mutual gains from cooperation have not abolished war, crime or politics. Turning to less cataclysmic though

still momentous issues, the advanced systems of law that are the proud
possessions of western nations have in fact been changing for at least
a century in directions that are on the whole pernicious from the
viewpoint of economic efficiency. Rather than increasingly supportive
of property and exchange, the trend has clearly been in the direction
of harassment, increasing uncertainty, and even confiscation. Parallel
developments taking place in other aspects of life — rising crime rates,
increasingly grave race-class conflicts, growing political polarization —
suggest that these pernicious legal trends are due not simply to errors
in the design of laws, but rather to deeper social realities. The forces
promoting harmonious reciprocal exchanges among individuals and
leading toward legal structures supporting and facilitating such exchanges are evidently weaker than recent econo-legal thinking might have
led us to suppose. The central thrust of this paper will be an attempt
to see how far this unfortunate fact is explained by evolutionary theory.

Evolutionary ideas are relevant to our question of the scope of
harmonious interaction among men in two main ways. First, regarding
the nature of man. What capacities for cooperation or for conflict lie
innate within members of the human species, either as universal
tendencies of life or as the particular results of the evolution of
mankind? In short, are we humans essentially fighters or lovers?
Second, regarding social institutions. Whatever the intrinsic pattern of
individual human drives may be, the overall outcome is also a function
of the social constraints regulating personal interactions. Adam Smith's
((60), Book IV, ch. 2) principle of the 'invisible hand' has shown us
how even selfish individuals may be led by appropriate social institutions
to cooperate to their mutual advantage. Conversely, even selfless
generosity may sometimes be subverted for lack of supportive social
arrangements. The first element, our innate make-up, constitutes a
background which has been largely constant over the evolutionarily
brief span represented by the historical experience of mankind.
Furthermore, it is also largely uniform over the human species. The
second element, the institutional or cultural foreground, is in contrast
highly volatile over historical time and amazingly varied among different
human societies. Both elements are essential for understanding the
prospects for and limits upon cooperative versus conflictual interactions
among men.

EFFICIENCY

It is time to address the problem of 'efficiency', to ask whether this
concept is robust enough to bear the weight placed upon it in recent
econo-legal thinking.

The root idea is *Pareto-preference*. A social configuration Λ is said to be Pareto-preferred to another social configuration Ω if no affected member of the society prefers Ω to Λ, and at least one member actually prefers Λ. (As we shall see, the proper interpretation to be placed upon 'affected' raises difficulties, but let us set this problem aside for the moment.) Any *voluntary* transaction, if the participants can be assumed to be rational, leads to a Pareto-preferred outcome. In particular, since an act of voluntary exchange is mutually beneficial (the Smith Theorem), its outcome is Pareto-preferred to the pre-exchange situation—provided no other members of the society are adversely 'affected' thereby. Furthermore, rational decision-makers will eventually execute *all* mutually advantageous transactions available to them. The final outcome, when there are no further opportunities for mutual gain, is called *Pareto-efficient*. Note that only a small subset of the outcomes that are Pareto-preferred to some initial situation are Pareto-efficient (that is, leave no room for further improvement in the way of mutual gain). Conversely, there will generally be Pareto-*efficient* configurations that are not Pareto-*preferred* to some particular initial situation. That is, there may be outcomes which could not be improved upon (in terms of mutual gain) once arrived at, but which are not achievable by mutually advantageous transactions from a given specified starting point. Nevertheless, the Coase Theorem asserts, any starting point will eventually lead to *some* Pareto-efficient outcome—if existence of property rights and absence of transaction costs permit unrestricted exchange.

Practically all important social issues, however, involve comparisons among situations that cannot be ranked by Pareto-preference considerations. That is, almost always, social changes make some parties better off but others worse off. This even holds for 'voluntary' exchange, since in general third parties will be affected. Suppose that women were previously barred from some line of employment, and now the barrier has been removed. The females who enter that line of employment gain from the increased scope of exchange, as do their employers. But the previously protected (male) employees will be adversely affected, yet do not have any legal entitlement to retain their old terms of employment. It is a standard proposition of economics that such pecuniary externalities balance out in aggregate value terms. The loss to the male workers (of receiving a lower wage) is exactly counterbalanced by the gain to their employers (in not having to pay a higher wage). Nevertheless, absent compensation it remains true that some parties are now worse off; removal of an artificial barrier to trade is thus *not* in general a strictly Pareto-preferred (SPP) change.

To get around this difficulty, the concept of 'potentially Pareto-preferred' (PPP) social changes has been proposed.³ Suppose everyone's well-being could simply be scaled in terms of the amount of pie he consumes. Then any way of increasing the overall size of society's aggregate pie meets the PPP criterion. For a larger pie can *potentially* be redivided so that everybody gains (or, at least, so that some gain while nobody loses). Put more generally, the PPP criterion is satisfied by any change such that the gainers could (*even if they do not*) compensate the losers. Any such change is, in the modern econo-legal literature, called a movement in the direction of 'efficiency'. A final position in which no such PPP changes remain to be made is called simply 'efficient'.

In terms of changes from an arbitrary initial position, not every potentially Pareto-preferred change (movement in the direction of efficiency) will generally be strictly Pareto-preferred. In particular, the PPP criterion would (subject to some qualifications to be mentioned below) give a favourable response to our example of removing barriers to employment of women, where the strict Pareto criterion does not. Since the losses to the male employees are exactly counterbalanced by the gains to their employers, with a further net gain flowing to the new female workers and their employers, clearly the losers from the change could be compensated. The PPP criterion, if we accept it, thus justifies exchange even where pecuniary externalities are imposed on other parties (as almost always they will be).

Our discussion has suggested that there are a number of ethical or ideological problems associated with efficiency criteria, and it is time to mention three of these explicitly.

1. Voluntarism

The key issue in approving only strictly Pareto-preferred (SPP) changes versus approving all potentially Pareto-preferred (PPP) changes is voluntarism. The PPP criterion overrides dissent. There is an irony in the history of thought here: proponents of the market process usually contend that it is a way of achieving economic efficiency without compulsion or dictation, yet we have seen that market transactions will be unambiguous movements in the direction of efficiency only if we depart from a strictly voluntaristic interpretaion of what 'efficiency' means. Indeed, excessive emphasis upon the saliency of the efficiency criterion, in the nonvoluntaristic PPP sense, would seem to open the gates even to rather brutal social processes that might conceivably still operate in accordance with a PPP rule.

2. Enshrining the status quo

Matters may appear in a somewhat different light, however, once we appreciate that voluntary changes are necessarily relative to some starting point. Why should the starting point, the initial distribution of wealth and talents, be given such a privileged position in our social thinking? This objection holds with greatest force against the strict Pareto criterion. The PPP criterion is somewhat less bound to the status quo, as it allows some non-unanimistic departures therefrom. Nevertheless, even what is potentially Pareto-preferred may still depend upon the initial position.

One example which has received some attention is the so-called reversal paradox (Scitovsky (59)). Consider an initial social configuration Λ, with its vector of produced goods and associated income distribution. It may be that a change to some other configuration Ω with a different vector of produced goods and income distribution is PPP-indicated, in that compensating payments *could* make everybody better off in comparison with Λ. That is, Ω makes possible some other configuration Ω' which *would* be strictly Pareto-preferred to Λ. But it might also be the case that Λ meets the PPP criterion relative to Ω! That is, there might be a Λ' that is strictly Pareto-preferred to Ω. (It is the change in income distribution, shifting the market weights assigned to individuals' preferences, that makes this possible.) Probably a much more significant phenomenon is the paradox put in inverted form: starting at Λ a change to Ω may be ruled out as a PPP-inferior movement, yet starting at Ω the move to Λ may also be PPP-inferior! A non-trivial example: an enslaved person might not be able to afford to buy his freedom from his master, yet were he free to begin with he might not be willing to sell himself into slavery at any price the master would pay. Which configuration is then the more efficient?

3. Meddlesome preferences

Suppose that some individuals have preferences that are not 'self-regarding'. For example, lowering the barriers to female employment in coal mines might be found disturbing by some third parties even though the latter are unaffected in material terms. Ought such preferences to be taken into account, under either the strict Pareto (SPP) or potential Pareto (PPP) criterion? Assuming that individuals are actually willing to pay (to sacrifice their own resources or potential consumption) in order to further such 'meddlesome' goals, I see no basis for excluding them from consideration. However, when non-self-regarding tastes are taken into account, it no longer follows that voluntary exchange necessarily leads to efficiency even in the PPP sense.

What is the upshot of this discussion? If you now find yourself less than fully confident as to the normative validity of efficiency (either in the SPP sense or the PPP sense) as a criterion for social policy, you are in agreement with me. And notice that I have nowhere diverged from the premises of utilitarian individualism—the idea that the proper social goal can be expressed entirely in terms of the achievement of individual desires, rather than (for example) the pursuit of abstract ideals like justice or service to God—though in fact I do have reservations about strict utilitarianism. Nor have I attempted to bring in paternalistic arguments—to the effect that some individuals (or all individuals at some times) do not really know their true desires or are not able to choose what is best for them—and I would not entirely reject paternalism either. For all these reasons efficiency criteria fall short of being fully attractive. This is less threatening a thought for those of us who are doubtful in any case about the prospects of purposive social reconstruction in the pursuit of efficiency (or indeed in pursuit of any social goal); a doubt which is, for reasons that will become clear at the end of the next section, more or less consistent with an evolutionary approach to societal phenomena. But, as a matter of *positive* analysis, the difficulties that have been revealed may partially explain the seeming recalcitrance of the politically influential public to the efficiency argument of modern econo-legal thinkers.

Finally, one under-emphasized aspect of the efficiency criterion is crucial for our purposes: efficiency is always relative to the boundaries of the society or group envisaged. An act of voluntary reciprocal exchange is beneficial for the 'society' comprised by the two participants; it is when we consider third parties that questions begin to arise. If competing merchants were to form a cartel the move would be efficient from their point of view, though not so when consumers are taken into account. Or consider theft. If we set aside long-term effects upon the incentive to produce, theft as such would be purely redistributive. It is only the resources consumed in defences erected against theft, and the consequent increased costs of thieving, that reduce the aggregate size of society's pie. Would it then be PPP-efficient to ban defences against theft? Presumably, the answer would be yes (apart from the aforesaid long-run problems) if the thieves are considered members of the society, but no, if as *outlaws* they have placed themselves outside the social unit. (I myself prefer the latter answer!) In a broader context, outcomes efficient for our nation as a whole may be adverse to the well-being of other nations; even gains for the whole human species may be achieved at the expense of other species. My point is that no one, probably, favours efficiency in a totally universalistic sense. We all draw the line somewhere, at the boundary of 'us' versus 'them'.

Efficiency thus is ultimately a concept relating to group advantage over other competing groups.

ELEMENTS OF EVOLUTIONARY MODELS

The word 'evolution' primarily suggests to us the biological succession of living types, but the underlying concept is of course much broader. Stars evolve: initially a localized concentration of gases in space, a star goes through several stages as it burns its nuclear fuel, ending up eventually as a white dwarf or black hole. According to current cosmological theories the universe as a whole is evolving, under the sway of the second law of thermodynamics, to an eventual steady state of maximum entropy — a uniform distribution of energy throughout space. On the human level we know also that languages evolve, though following what course I am not prepared to suggest. Thus it is by no means illegitimate to argue that patterns of economic interaction and legal structures may evolve. Yet, I want to say, not everything that changes can usefully be said to *evolve*. Evolution represents a particular type or pattern of change.

1. Evolution versus randomness
Evolution is not random variation (totally inexplicable change). The outcomes of successive spins of a roulette wheel vary, but do not evolve. Yet random change on a micro or component level may be an element of evolutionary change at the level of a larger entity or collection. In biology genetic mutations occur randomly, yet they contribute to the evolutionary development of species.

2. Evolution versus cyclicity
Regular cyclical change, which plays a role in certain theories of social processes, is best not regarded as evolution. Cyclicity is a kind of generalized stationarity. Put another way, evolutionary changes have an *irreversible* element, so that things are never quite the same afterward (Lotka (38), ch. 2).

3. Evolution versus revolution
In evolutionary models, transitions on the macro level result from the accumulation of small changes in micro-elements over time. Species evolve through the gradual working of forces contributing to variations in the characters of individual organisms, and to differential multiplication thereof. Stars evolve via a multitude of infinitesimal changes operating over the aeons on their atomic or subatomic constituent particles.

Where custom is the dominant element, law tends to follow an evolutionary course: the law emerges from a host of small transactions. But a Moses or a Solon hands down the law from above, all at once as a *revolutionary* change. Similarly, in earlier times the economic system changed mainly through the gradual discovery and slow diffusion of new techniques and new social relationships. In modern times, of course, revolutionary economic transformations are occurring with increasing frequency, often (though not necessarily) imposed from above.

Whether a change is revolutionary or evolutionary is sometimes a matter of relevant timespan or scope of unit. Fusion of a pair of hydrogen atoms within a star is a revolutionary change for the specific atoms involved, but only a tiny component of the evolutionary process for the star. In primitive times, within a small human band the invention of the bow, or the promulgation of a successful new law, may have been revolutionary. But among the larger group of related bands comprising what we now perceive as a single culture, the change may have progressed only at an evolutionary pace, perhaps being repeatedly reinvented or slowly diffusing before becoming characteristic of that culture.

4. Evolution versus design
When we speak of evolutionary changes in human affairs, we generally have in mind 'unintended' ones. Once again, we must distinguish different levels of analysis. Purposive planning by individuals, or by small groups, might be consistent with unintended evolutionary change on a macro level. The inventor of the bow had an intention, but it was only to help himself or his band; the spread of a new technique of hunting, not to mention the more remote social consequences following upon that spread, was surely beyond his purpose. Or, modern statute writers may intend some purposive redesign of the social order — but, since 'legislation is based on folk notions of causality' (Moore (44), p. 7), the result may be very different from that planned.

One of the inferences I draw from this discussion is that the applicability of evolutionary models ought not to be oversold; evolution is not the sole important pattern of social change. In particular, with the increasing connectivity of the human world-system — due mainly to advances in communication and to the development of technology with worldwide impact (most notably, military technology) — 'revolutionary' and 'designed' changes are playing larger and larger roles. Nevertheless, models of evolutionary change have not lost all relevance. First, many areas of life continue to be subject to evolutionary principles. Language, custom, the sphere of private economic activity and the common law can still be said to evolve. Second, the *present-day* starting point, even for revolutionary or designed change, is in large part the product of *past* genetic and cultural evolution. The social evolution of the human species places constraints upon the nature and pace of planned future change.

Evolutionary models share certain properties. First of all, they concern populations. Even where we seem to be speaking of single entities, if the course of change is evolutionary it can be described in terms of changing populations of micro-units. Thus, the evolutionary course of a disease within a single human body is a function of the relations among populations of bacteria, antibodies, cells, and so on. Or the evolution of a single nation's economy is the result of changing relations among populations of individuals, trading units, and the like.

Evolutionary models represent a combination of constancy ('inheritance') and variation. There must be an unchanging as well as a changing element, and even the changing element itself must be heritable if a system can be said to evolve. In biological evolution, the emphasis is upon differential survival and reproduction of organismic types or characters from one generation to the next. Here the constancy is due to Mendelian inheritance of permanent patterns of coded genetic instructions (genes). Variation stems from a number of forces, including internal mutations of these instructions (genetic copying errors), recombination of genes in sexual reproduction, and the external pressure of natural selection. Socioeconomic evolution mainly concerns the differential growth and survival of patterns of social organization. The main 'inheritance' element is the deadweight of social inertia, supported by intentionally taught tradition. As for variation, there are analogues to mutations ('copying errors' as we learn traditions). Also, natural selection is still effective. Finally, *imitation* and *rational thought* constitute additional non-genetic sources of socioeconomic variation.

Biologists have been much interested in the question of the 'direction' of evolution. The main principle recognized is *adaptation*. That is, organisms and their lines of descent over the generations tend to fit themselves into niches of viability offered by their environments. They do so mainly under the pressure of selective competition from other organisms and species, all of which have an irrepressible Malthusian tendency[4] to multiply so as to fill any unsaturated places in the environment.

A number of philosophers have perceived a directional trend toward 'complexity' in biological, cultural and even cosmological evolution. I believe this is mistaken. If complexity is adaptive, the trend of development will be in that direction, but often the direction of adaptation may be toward simplicity. We see movement towards complexity when, for example, a few 'founders' enter and proliferate within a new environment that contains many different yet unfilled niches. We see movement towards simplicity, on the other hand, whenever homogenization of the environment reduces the number of distinct niches available.

The adaptation principle suggests that the external environmental determinants must ultimately govern in the evolutionary process.[5] But biological evolution is opportunistic, and must work with the internal materials at hand. The available internal materials — the genetically coded instructions — will have been shaped by a variety of past irreversible transformations. These transformations were perhaps responsive in their own day to then-current environmental requirements, but persisting today they remain more or less recalcitrant constraints upon adaptive change. Despite this, there are extraordinary examples of parallel evolution in Nature, for example, where traits usually associated with fishes have been independently evolved by quite different biological taxa moving into aquatic environments, among them the mammals (seals, whales), birds (penguins), and lizards (sea-going iguanas). There are also failures of parallel evolution, however. Nothing like the kangaroo has evolved outside Australia, despite large geographical regions where kangaroo-like qualities would seem to be highly adaptive.

The second qualification of the adaptation principle is of greater interest for our purposes. What is adaptive for the individual organism (and its descendants) may or may not be adaptive for the species. Fleetness of foot helps the gazelle escape the lion, but the gain to being exceptionally fleet may largely be that some other gazelle is eaten instead. If the gazelles were making a cooperative group adaptation, presumably somewhat less fleetness than what has actually evolved would be optimal. A different type of imperfect species adaptation is illustrated by the peacock. The enormous tail pleases the female's fancy and so its bearer sires more offspring, yet a heavy price is paid. As a group adaptation, it seems that the peacocks ought to have found a mode of sexual competition involving less energy loss and vulnerability to predators. In economic terms we would say that these forms of biological competition impose *adverse externalities* upon other members of (what we perceive as) a larger potentially cooperating group — in this case, the species.

Group adaptation remains imperfect in such cases because the biological payoff in reproductive competition depends mainly upon *relative* achievement. An organism can get ahead in evolutionary terms either by pulling itself up or by pushing its competitors down:

'It is crucial to understanding the behaviour of organisms, including ourselves, that in evolutionary terms success in reproduction is always *relative*; hence, the striving of organisms is in relation to one another and not toward some otherwise quantifiable goal or optimum.' (Alexander (1), p. 17)

The evolutionary emphasis upon *relative* reproductive competition has important implications for the question of efficiency discussed above. If it were strictly true that only relative status counted, the efficiency concept would be meaningless. If one party's advance automatically means that other parties lose, there is no scope for *mutual* gain, actual or potential (see Becker (6), pp. 1089–90; Hirshleifer (30), pp. 329–30). In the case of the peacock, other males' reproductive survival is not even a neutral but probably on balance a harmful consideration; the descendants of other cocks will use up resources and multiply to the disadvantage of its own descendants.[6]

It was argued at the end of the previous section that efficiency must be interpreted as relative to the boundaries of the group. We can now see that for group efficiency to be economically meaningful as a criterion, the group must be one within which individuals do *not* compete mainly in terms of relative achievement. In nature, *species are mainly fields of relative reproductive competition*. This is why, so often, adaptations tend to be selected that are harmful to the species as a whole.

Nevertheless, truly cooperating groups within species[7] are also often evolved by Nature. Among the more evident examples are families, packs, and insect communities, extending on the human level to tribes and nations. What is happening here, in so far as evolutionary reproductive competition is controlling, is that some individuals have allied to achieve a mutual gain *relative* to other members of their species.

That intra-group cooperation and mutual gain typically take place within a larger context of intergroup competition and conflict is essential to keep in mind in speaking of efficiency. Failure to appreciate this fact is an important weakness of modern econo-legal thinking, which the evolutionary approach has exposed. Even within an actual or potential alliance there remain, however, mixed motives — individual advantage is generally not wholly consistent with group advantage. The theoretical approach to the viability of cooperation strategies in such mixed incentives situations is the topic of the next two sections.

PATTERNS OF CONFLICT AND COOPERATION: EVOLUTIONARY EQUILIBRIUM

Cooperation and conflict are not simple opposites. The two are complexly intertwined, but in ways that fall into a limited set of mixed incentive patterns. I shall illustrate some of these patterns here in terms of game theory matrices.[8] (I shall be considering only the especially simple class of two-person binary-strategy interactions at this point.)

The most famous of these patterns is the game known as Prisoners' Dilemma. It will be helpful to start with a simpler pattern, a game I shall call Tender Trap (Matrix 1).[9] Tender Trap illustrates the binding force of convention (of an agreed rule) even where all players realize that the wrong convention has been chosen. We tacitly agree upon many conventions to order our daily lives: for example, rules of the road, rules of language, rules of courtesy. Their function is to coordinate activities, so that any person can reasonably anticipate what others will do.

In Matrix 1 the parties can agree on either convention #1 or convention #2; the first is superior to the second in that each party gains 5 units of income instead of 2, but either is superior to following opposite strategies (such that each party receives 0). For example: everyone might agree that it would be better if Americans spoke Esperanto rather than English, but in any case all Americans are better-off speaking the same language. I begin with this pattern because *here there is no conflict of interests* whatsoever; the problem is purely one of coordination. (The game of Tender Trap can be generalized to allow a degree of conflict of interest, however, by having the off-diagonal elements display different returns to the two players: see below.)

The standard solution concept which mathematicians employ for such 'non-zero-sum' games is the *Nash equilibrium* (NE) (Nash (45)). A strategy pair is an NE if, taking the strategy of the other party as given, neither player can improve his position by revising his own strategy. In Matrix 1 the two agreed 'conventions' (the two cells on the main diagonal) are both Nash equilibria. If the players had chosen the first convention (row 1 and column 1), either would lose by shifting, but the same holds if they had initially chosen the inferior second convention (row 2 and column 2).

A subtly different solution, which wc will call the *evolutionary equilibrium* (EE), has been proposed by the biologist John Maynard Smith.[10] The idea is that the two parties are members of a homogeneous population meeting randomly in pairwise interactions. One strategy may be 'defeated' by another, and therefore eventually be driven out in the evolutionary sense, if it yields on average a lower return than the other. The average returns received will be a function of the proportions of the population choosing each of the strategies, so that we are dealing with possible equilibria of a dynamic process.

In Matrix 1 it may be verified that if the proportion p of the population choosing strategy #1 were initially greater than 2/7, the

		Matrix 1 Tender Trap				Matrix 2a Chicken	
						C_1 (Coward)	C_2 (Hero)
		C_1	C_2				
	R_1	5,5	0,0	(Coward)	R_1	0,0	−10,20
	R_2	0,0	2,2	(Hero)	R_2	20,−10	−100,−100

		Matrix 2b Hawk–Dove				Matrix 3 Prisoners' Dilemma	
		C_1 (Dove)	C_2 (Hawk)			C_1 (Omertà)	C_2 (Fink)
(Dove)	R_1	2,2	0,10	(Omertà)	R_1	−1,−1	−20,0
(Hawk)	R_2	10,0	−5,−5	(Fink)	R_2	0,−20	−10,−10

	Matrix 4 Generalized Symmetrical Game				Matrix 5 Battle of the Sexes	
	C_1	C_2			C_1	C_2
R_1	1,1	y,x		R_1	2,1	0,0
R_2	x,y	0,0		R_2	0,0	1,2

average return from choosing #1 would exceed the return from #2. In this circumstance strategy #1 will tend to drive out #2. Then the 'efficient' solution, in the potentially Pareto-preferred (PPP) sense of maximizing the 'pie' of aggregate income[11] — the upper-left corner outcome (5,5) — will be attained as an evolutionary equilibrium EE. Furthermore, the efficient solution here is also strictly Pareto-preferred in comparison with any other starting point (it is *unanimously* preferred over any alternative outcome cell of Matrix 1). If, on the other hand, the initial proportion were less than 2/7, the attained EE would be at the lower-right corner.[12] So the two NEs are also both EEs. The dividing line p = 2/7 is a kind of threshold or critical mass for reaching the mutually preferred solution. Something like a shift from a generally less preferred to a more preferred EE actually occurred among Jews of Palestine, who managed to put together a critical mass for shifting from Yiddish (mainly) to Hebrew as a common language. But it is unlikely that a population could shift from driving on the left to driving on the right, or from the Imperial to the metric system of units, without support by the force of law.

Moving now to mixed incentive interactions, Matrix 2a illustrates the famous game of Chicken. The two players drive towards one another at full speed, the one who turns aside (Coward) becoming an object of contempt. If it turns out that each plays Hero, the result is death (−100 for each). Or, both might be Cowards (0 return for each). The really desirable situation, of course, is for the other to be a Coward (−10) and you a Hero (+20).

The Nash equilibrium (NE) is double here again, but occurs at the two *off*-diagonal outcomes. That is, from an initial position at either off-diagonal cell, it does not pay either party to change his strategy. The numbers in Matrix 2a are such that the off-diagonal outcomes are also jointly efficient (maximum sum of returns), though in this case neither NE is strictly Pareto-preferred in comparison with *all* the other possibilities. However, the essential features of Chicken would persist even if the sum of incomes in the off-diagonal cells were *not* maximal. For example, if the (+20, −10) cells were changed to (+5, −10) the off-diagonal outcomes would remain the Nash equilibria (NEs). But, whether or not the off-diagonal outcomes are efficient, these solutions are not available as evolutionary equilibria (EEs) in a homogeneous population. The reason is that they require *complementary* pairing of strategy choices, which is not possible in random encounters within a homogeneous population.

Let us now find the evolutionary equilibrium for Chicken. We can do so by calculating the average returns to each of the strategies as a function of the population fraction p choosing strategy #1 (Coward). In Matrix 2a the evolutionary equilibrium occurs at p = 9/11. The population being homogeneous, the interpretation is that each player chooses the Coward strategy 9/11 of the time and the Hero strategy 2/11 of the time. (This is known as a 'mixed' as opposed to a 'pure' strategy choice.) The average return will then be −20/11 to each player.[13] Even if the off-diagonal outcomes cannot be attained, there evidently remains a potential cooperative gain from both being Cowards (each receiving 0 rather than a negative amount). But this cooperative outcome is not an evolutionary equilibrium; if Cowards became too numerous, they would lose out on average to those making choices closer to the EE mixed strategy.

My picturesque description may perhaps suggest that the game of Chicken is a somewhat pathological class of social interaction. Such an inference would be quite false. The pattern of Chicken, in the more interesting version characterized by positive efficiency gains if the off-diagonal outcomes can be achieved, fits the *very* common situation of two parties in a position of potential conflict over a prize. Using a different ornithological metaphor, Maynard Smith calls what is essentially the same game 'Hawk–Dove'. In Matrix 2b a Hawk player encountering a Dove player wins a prize of 10, Dove receiving nothing. But Hawk–Hawk encounters involve a big loss (–5) to each. Dove–Dove encounters yield a modest gain (2) to each; the two do not suffer injury, but some potential gain (e.g. nutrition) is lost from lack of aggressivity. The EE here has the proportion p = 5/13 playing the Dove strategy. (Rather than assuming that every individual follows a mixed strategy, we can equally well interpret the EE as a population balance of individuals each of whom separately has a fixed Hawk or Dove nature.)

There are, of course, many examples in Nature of organisms faced with Hawk–Dove choices (whether to fight or retreat). Nor is it at all hard to imagine human analogues in the realms of warfare, politics, business, or anywhere that jockeying for position is important.[14] The essential feature is that each player must balance 'cowardly' loss of the prize against the even greater loss should potential conflict become actual.

In Tender Trap, putting together a *critical mass* provided a way of escaping the inferior of the two solutions. In Chicken or Hawk–Dove (I shall more usually employ the latter metaphor from now on), the trap takes the form of the EE mixed strategy with some positive probability of inefficient mutual losses due to Hawk–Hawk interactions. Critical mass does not provide any route out of Hawk–Dove. Instead, the obvious mode of escape is to somehow arrange that at each meeting one party will take the role of Hawk and the other the role of Dove. Any means of doing this would be PPP-efficient, but for the method to be viable each organism would have to be able to play each role about half the time. In effect, a convention is needed to assure that when two parties meet their behaviour will be *non-parallel*, in contrast with the parallelism convention needed under Tender Trap.

If the two parties can be regarded as arriving randomly (as in search or exploration situations) at the location of the prize, 'first come first served' would provide such a convention. Each organism would be first about half the time. Remarkably, this precursor of ownership or property rights has evolved in Nature in a number of ecological circumstances.[15] Mathematically, the convention, 'last come first served' would do as well, but I know of no examples of this in Nature (and few in human affairs).[16]

First come first served as the basis for conventional avoidance of conflict is an example of what Maynard Smith (43) calls an *uncorrelated asymmetry*. Another example might be sex (for example, males defer to females). At least as important are *correlated asymmetries*[17] — for example, differences in their valuations of the prize. Perhaps the most obvious such convention would be 'weaker defers to stronger'. In Nature it is very commonly observed that after only a test of strength (taking the form of *limited combat*, in which the parties do not use their most lethal weapons or tactics) the weaker party does give way (Lorenz (37); Maynard Smith (43)).

Now for the Prisoners' Dilemma (Matrix 3). The tale is probably familiar. Two prisoners, held incommunicado, can be convicted only of a misdemeanour and suffer mild punishment (-1) if they both refuse to confess; they can be convicted of a felony and will suffer heavier punishment (-10) if they both confess. But if one confesses and the other does not, the authorities will release the first (0 penalty) and throw the book at the second (-20). Here mutual choice of the omertà strategy #1 provides a large efficiency gain. Yet, it is in each party's selfish interest to choose the fink strategy #2 — regardless of what the other does! (That is, strategy #2 'dominates' #1.) The fink–fink outcome is the sole Nash equilibrium (NE) and the sole evolutionary equilibrium (EE). It might be regarded as a tough trap, in contrast with the tender trap of Matrix 1.

The Prisoners' Dilemma model has a wide range of applicability. The typical economic 'externality' or 'commons' problem falls into this pattern. If all nations were to cut back whaling activities, there would be a collective benefit (efficiency gain) to be shared from preservation of this valuable resource. Yet, it pays each alone to engage in whaling without regard to long-run considerations. Note that this is not a merely 'defensive' policy made necessary by others' greed; even if other nations practised restraint, each separate nation is motivated to engage in unrestrained whaling. (Indeed, it may often be the case — though not for the particular numbers shown in our Matrix 3 — that restraint on the part of others *increases* the gains of the selfish or fink strategy.) On the other hand, Prisoners' Dilemma need not be socially dysfunctional in the larger sense; the cooperation it subverts may be a conspiracy against the public.[18] This is presumably the case for the two prisoners of the initial example. And similarly for cartel agreements to restrict production.

Before turning to the large question of possible escapes from the Prisoners' Dilemma trap, it will be very useful to note that all three classes of mixed motive games considered to this point can be put in the general format of Matrix 4. A generalized Tender Trap would have $x < 1$, $y < 0$. (In this generalized form, Tender Trap will not be a pure game of coordination; there is *some* conflict of interest whenever $x \neq y$.) Hawk–Dove has $x > 1$, $y > 0$ (with $x + y > 2$ in the more interesting case for which the off-diagonal cells are efficient outcomes). And Prisoners' Dilemma has $x > 1$, $y < 0$. I do not mean to suggest that all two-person symmetrical games with mixed conflict/cooperation incentives can be put in this format; Matrix 5, known as 'Battle of the

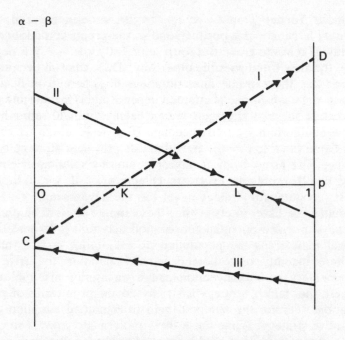

Figure 9.1   Three classes of cooperation failures

Sexes' (see Luce and Raiffa (39), ch. 5) represents a mixed incentive game characterized by a somewhat different kind of symmetry. But I shall consider only the generalized Matrix 4 pattern here, in order to explore a little more rigorously the nature and determinants of evolutionary equilibrium.

The evolutionary equilibrium (EE) strategy is one that, broadly speaking, will drive others out of existence by 'defeating' them in binary encounters. If the population can be regarded as of infinite size, the average return α to the first strategy in Matrix 4, where p is the population fraction adopting that strategy is:[19]

$$\alpha = (p)1 + (1 - p)y. \tag{1}$$

Similarly, the average return β to the second strategy is:

$$\beta = (p)x + (1 - p)0. \tag{2}$$

The first strategy will on average defeat the second, and therefore drive it out, whenever $\alpha - \beta$ exceeds zero, where:

$$\alpha - \beta \equiv p(1 - x) + (1 - p)y. \tag{3}$$

There are three qualitatively different types of situations, as illustrated by the three lines in Figure 9.1: The dashed line I corresponds to the generalized Tender Trap ($x < 1$, $y < 0$). As can be seen, for p sufficiently large $\alpha - \beta$ is positive, and so the proportion adopting the first strategy tends to grow. But for p sufficiently low, $\alpha - \beta$ is negative and the dynamic trend goes the other way. Thus, the two evolutionary equilibria are the extreme final situations C (where $p = 0$) and D (where $p = 1$); which one is attained depends upon the starting point. (At point K the two strategies are in balance, but K represents an unstable equilibrium.) The dashed line II corresponds to Chicken or Hawk–Dove ($x > 1$, $y > 0$). Here the *less* prevalent strategy has the advantage, the result being a mixed or interior solution at point L. Finally, line III represents Prisoners' Dilemma ($x > 1$, $y < 0$) for which the first (cooperative) strategy never has the advantage.[20]

I would have liked to claim that these simple curves represent *the* three ways in which potential cooperation may fail: (1) where lack of a critical mass traps the population at an inferior corner solution; (2) where inability of a homogeneous population to arrive at a complementary pairing convention leads to an inferior mixed solution,[21] (3) where the 'selfish' strategy is strictly dominant in terms of private calculations, despite the potential gain from mutual adoption of the cooperative strategy. While these three patterns do cover a surprising amount of territory,[22] it would be absurd to claim full generality. The underlying model remains excessively restrictive, in *at least* the following respects:

1. Not all symmetric patterns of mixed cooperation–conflict incentives have been covered (see, for example, Matrix 5).
2. The symmetry restriction (equivalent to assuming a homogeneous population) is severely limiting. More generally, at any moment of time a population would be characterized by a probability distribution along many relevant dimensions. For example, as already mentioned in connection with the Hawk–Dove game, some individuals may be better fighters than others, or may need the food more, etc.
3. Equally severe, perhaps, is the limitation to *dyadic* interactions. This is particularly relevant for us here, since the law is (at least in part) a way of converting dyadic into *triadic* social interactions. (There are the two contending agents, plus a third 'uncommitted' party to decide between them.)
4. We have considered only binary strategy situations (2×2 game matrices).
5. Finally, we have implicitly been ruling out any structuring of the interactions among individuals that might make possible binding agreements to cooperate, as by exchange. The difficulty is that

contractual agreement does in general require some kind of outside (third party) enforcement, for example, law. What I am trying to do here, in effect, is to get a better focus upon the need for law by exploring the obstacles that cooperation encounters without it.

It follows that there are more complex forms of mixed-incentive cooperation/conflict interactions than we have yet gone into. Indeed, the number of qualitatively different mixed-incentive cases increases at a frightening rate when we depart from the simplifying assumptions of this section, which is undoubtedly why the problem of cooperation versus conflict remains so baffling. In the next section I shall mainly pursue one particular line of enquiry, into the possible modes of escape from the Prisoners' Dilemma — the 'tough trap' for potential cooperators. These escape routes typically involve relaxing one or the other of the restrictive conditions mentioned above. Yet, as we shall see, a plausible escape route often leads toward other, more intricate traps that subvert cooperation in subtler ways.

ESCAPES, MAINLY FROM THE PRISONERS' DILEMMA

The Prisoners' Dilemma has been by far the most studied pattern of cooperation failure — failure to achieve a potential mutual benefit in the strict Pareto sense, or possibly even an aggregate 'efficiency' gain in the potentially Pareto-preferred (PPP) sense. Also, as we have seen, the Prisoners' Dilemma does represent the toughest trap, mainly because the noncooperator strategy is actually *dominant* (preferred whatever the choice of the other participant).

However, it will be of interest to show more rigorously how the ownership (first come first served) convention mentioned in the preceding section can actually provide an escape route from cooperation failures of the Chicken or Hawk–Dove type. Following Maynard Smith (43) we can suppose that the Hawk–Dove game (Matrix 2b) is expanded by the addition of a third 'Bourgeois' strategy (Matrix 6). The Bourgeois rule is: when you are the first-comer in possession of the resource, play like a Hawk; when the late-comer, play like a Dove. That is, when an owner, fight to defend your property; when an interloper, defer to others' ownership.

The elements of the R_3, C_1 interaction (Bourgeois encountering Dove) in the lower-left cell of Matrix 6 are derived as follows. On average, half the time Bourgeois will be in an ownership situation against Dove, thus reaping the 10 units of income that Hawk would

Matrix 6
Hawk-Dove-Bourgeois

		C_1 (Dove)	C_2 (Hawk)	C_3 (Bourgeois)
(Dove)	R_1	2,2	0,10	1,6
(Hawk)	R_2	10,0	−5,−5	+2 1/2,−2 1/2
(Bourgeois)	R_3	6,1	−2 1/2,+2 1/2	5,5

Matrix 7
Prisoners' Dilemma
(Cost-Benefit Format, b > c)

		C_1 (Helper)	C_2 (Nonhelper)
(Helper)	R_1	−c+b,−c+b	−c,b
(Nonhelper)	R_2	b,−c	0,0

Matrix 8
Prisoners' Dilemma with Retaliators

		C_1 (Helper)	C_2 (Nonhelper)	C_3 (Retaliator)
(Helper)	R_1	−c+b,−c+b	−c,b	−c+b,−c+b
(Nonhelper)	R_2	b,−c	0,0	0,0
(Retaliator)	R_3	−c+b,−c+b	0,0	−c+b,−c+b

obtain against Dove; the other half of the time, Bourgeois as non-owner would receive only the 2 units of income that Dove would obtain against Dove. Averaging the two, the return to Bourgeois against Dove is 6. By analogous reasoning, the second element of the lower-left cell (the return to Dove against Bourgeois) is 1. The elements in the other new cells can be derived in the same way.

How about efficiency? Note that the maximum aggregate income of 10 units is attained at the old off-diagonal outcomes (R_1,C_2 and R_2,C_1) as well as at the Bourgeois–Bourgeois (R_3,C_3) outcome. All three solutions are therefore equally efficient in the PPP sense. Furthermore, each is a Nash equilibrium (NE).

But it still has to be shown which, if any, is an *evolutionary* equilibrium EE. The first step is to calculate the expected returns α, β, and γ to the three strategies Hawk, Dove and Bourgeois, respectively — as functions of the corresponding population proportions p,q,r (where, of course, r = 1 − p − q). Then we have to find the ranges of values for p,q,r in which each strategy defeats the others, and the implied dynamic directions of change in those proportions. The algebra is rather tedious, but the result can be shown in Figure 2 (which is a

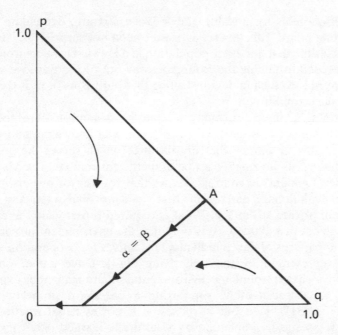

Figure 9.2 Convergence to 'Bourgeois' EE (Hawk–Dove–Bourgeois Game)

kind of generalization of Figure 1). As the arrows indicate, there is a dynamic convergence toward the origin — that is, toward $p = q = 0$, which implies $r = 1$. In other words, only the Bourgeois strategy survives in the evolutionary equilibrium. (In Figure 2, at point A the gains from the three strategies are in balance, but this is a dynamically *unstable* equilibrium like point K in Figure 1.)

There is a fly in the ointment, however. Ability to play a Bourgeois strategy would seem to require a more complex mentality, or at least biochemistry: the Bourgeois strategist must be able to distinguish between owner and interloper situations, and must be able to execute the appropriate behavioural manoeuvres of both Hawk and Dove. It seems reasonable to suppose that these capacities impose a certain burden; if so, the elements of the R_3, C_3 cell might become (for example) 4,4 rather than 5,5. This would mean, first, that a population of Bourgeois players is definitely a less efficient solution than complementary pairings of Hawk and Dove. In Figure 10.2, it also suggests that point A would become a stable rather than unstable equilibrium. Thus, making due allowance for the costs of a more elaborate behavioural repertory, the overall result might be an analogue of Tender Trap — the population might tend toward either an evolutionary equilibrium at pure-Bourgeois, or a stable Hawk–Dove mixture, depending upon the starting point. This theoretical result need not surprise us. Since it seems plausible that not every population in a Hawk–Dove environment has succeeded in finding the Bourgeois way out of the trap, we would have proved too much in demonstrating that pure-Bourgeois is the *only* evolutionary equilibrium.

Nevertheless, there are many fascinating examples of respect for ownership in nature. Robert Ardrey (3), in a well-known popular work, attributed this to a somewhat mystic force which serves the good of the species by minimizing the scope of inefficient combat. The Maynard Smith development, in contrast, shows that respect for ownership is a possible evolutionary emergence that need not call upon any force other than private advantage. What is required (apart from the critical mass problem just alluded to) is only that the environment provide the particular patterns of mixed individual incentives for cooperation versus conflict represented by the underlying Hawk–Dove game. On the human level, a corresponding environmental situation might be expected to lead to a 'social ethic' supporting a system of property rights (Hirshleifer (31)). (For our purposes, it is not essential whether this ethic is a genetically implanted or a culturally learned pattern.)

We can now turn to the tougher cooperation trap represented by the Prisoners' Dilemma (PD). In this section it will be convenient to set up the PD matrix in a cost–benefit format (Matrix 7). Each act of 'helping' costs the donor organism c, and benefits the recipient organism by the amount b, where $b > c$. Mutual helping is evidently efficient, but the parties are trapped at the Non-helping (0,0) equilibrium. Critical mass provides no escape route here; even if 99 per cent of the other organisms one is likely to encounter are behaving as Helpers, it still pays to play Non-helper.[23] Nor is there a possible gain from any kind of ownership convention — Non-helping remains dominant no matter what the other player does.

There is, of course, the valid escape route through reciprocation or contractual exchange: each party promises to act cooperatively, *provided* the other does. Smith's Theorem is potentially at work in Prisoners' Dilemma as it is in *all* mixed cooperation–conflict situations.

In what follows, a number of escape routes *not* requiring third party intervention or support will be discussed in turn. There is a certain sense in the sequence of topics, though no attempt will be made at a taxonomy of escape modes apart from a major division between symmetrical and asymmetrical strategy games.

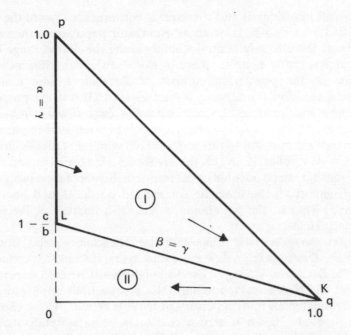

Figure 9.3   Neutral EE range (Prisoners' Dilemma with Retaliator Strategy)

Symmetric Strategies

1. The Silver Rule

Determined uncontingent Helpers are following the *Golden Rule* of social interaction; selfish Non-helpers, the *Brass Rule*. How about the *Silver Rule* — responding to help with help, to non-help with non-help? Matrix 8 represents an expansion of Matrix 7 by addition of such a 'Retaliator' strategy. This game has two symmetrical Nash equilibria — Non-helper–Non-helper and Retaliator–Retaliator. The latter, if it can be attained, would be just as efficient as the ideal Helper–Helper outcome. Both these NEs are 'weak', in that there is in each case a second equally attractive strategy available for either player. Consequently, in an evolutionary model we might expect some random drift away from each of the NEs. The dynamic calculations to obtain the evolutionary equilibria (EEs) are rather troublesome but the results are pictured in Figure 3. Here α, β, γ represent the expected returns to Helper, Non-helper and Retaliator, respectively. In Zone I (above the line where $\beta = \gamma$), there is strong convergence toward point K (q = 1, or an all-Non-helper population). But point K, while a stable equilibrium with respect to Zone I, is unstable with respect to Zone

II. So drift into Zone II and consequent convergence toward the origin
O ($r = 1 - p - q = 1$, or an all-Retaliator population) then occur.
However, there is only neutral stability along the dotted range of the
vertical axis (up to point L where $p = 1 - c/b$). If a sufficiently large
fraction of the population consists of Retaliators, any individual
organism can do as well being a pure Helper. (But if the proportion
of Helpers ever exceeded $1 - c/b$, we are in Zone II where it becomes
profitable for Non-helpers to enter.) At point L itself all three strategies
yield equal returns, and so this endpoint of the dotted range is unstable.
Subject to a fuller study of the dynamics, it seems reasonable to
conclude that after a possible initial transient the population proportions
would, almost all the time, lie somewhere on the dotted interval in
Figure 3. That is, the population would be a mixture of Retaliators
and pure Helpers.

So far, so good, but this otherwise attractive escape from the
Prisoners' Dilemma has a flaw analogous to that discussed in connection
with the Bourgeois strategy. The Retaliator must be able to recognize
Helpers and Non-helpers, and must also possess both helping and non-
helping capabilities in its repertory of feasible actions. These capacities
again probably impose a certain cost upon being a Retaliator rather
than pure Helper. Then, in an all-Retaliator population ($r = 1$), it
would be *strictly* more profitable (rather than only equally profitable)
to be a pure Helper instead. Thus the all-Retaliator population is not
an equilibrium, and in fact the final outcome will be an all-Non-helper
population. We are back in the Prisoners' Dilemma. Note that the
'cost of complexity' difficulty subverts the Bourgeois strategy in a
Hawk–Dove environment situation only to the extent of requiring a
critical mass before Bourgeois can become an EE, whereas it entirely
destroys any hope of a Retaliator EE in a Prisoners' Dilemma
environment.

Another type of Silver Rule strategy has received somewhat more
discussion in the literature: actual or potential retaliatory behaviour in
repeated plays of the Prisoners' Dilemma game. The idea here is that
to escape the trap, parties tend to pair up in a long-term pattern of
business association. Given the mutual gain from continuance of the
association. Non-helper behaviour may be checked by the retaliatory
response of the other party breaking off a mutually advantageous
relationship.[24]

But again a paradox is encountered. No matter how many times the
PD game is repeated, on the *very last* play it remains dominant strategy
to act as a Non-helper. Knowing that his partner-opponent will
rationally behave in this way, each player will then have no incentive
to act cooperatively on the *next-to-last* play. Following this logic the

entire game unravels, and Non-helper remains the dominant strategy throughout.[25]

2. *Nepotism and Other Discrimination Techniques* Under the heading of 'altruism', biologists have devoted a great deal of attention to cooperation among living forms, as seeming exceptions to the rule of reproductive competition in Nature. The psychological or ethical term 'altruism' is, however, an unfortunate terminological choice for what is better described in operational terms simply as *helping*. The clearest instances of helping behaviour are associated with kinship (nepotism). That parents care for offspring, that blood is thicker than water, is commonly though by no means universally observed in Nature or in human affairs. To some extent at least, relatedness seems to provide a way out of the Prisoners' Dilemma. My purpose here is to explore how this mechanism works, and more generally to understand how analogous mechanisms can apply to other forms of mutual aid.

We can think of a population in which a 'gene for helping' H is in competition with a 'gene for non-helping' N. It might be thought that Non-helpers will always be free riders upon helpers, so that the H gene could never be viable.[26] But, as we shall see, helping can be viable despite free-riding if the ecological circumstances provide for a sufficient degree of *discrimination* in which aid is preferentially directed toward fellow Helpers. Kinship is one mechanism that provides the basis for such discrimination.[27]

The basic kin-selection model is due to Hamilton (25), but a more tractable version has been put forward by Charnov (9).[28] Quite generally, before bringing in nepotism, we can ask under what conditions W_H will exceed W_N — the 'fitness' or viability of the helping gene H will exceed that of the non-helping gene N. Let b and c be the benefit conferred and cost incurred of each helping act, let p be the proportion of the population bearing the helping gene, and finally let m be the discrimination factor — *the fraction of helping acts received by fellow Helpers*. Then, the viability condition $W_H > W_N$ can be expressed as:

$$-c + bm > b(1 - m)\frac{p}{1 - p}. \tag{4}$$

On the left-hand side, the first term $-$ c is the cost incurred by the Helper (measured in fitness units, and normalized so that there is one helping act per time period). The second term, bm, represents the average per-Helper benefit of helping acts (per time period) that are directed at *fellow Helpers*. The right-hand side, analogously, shows the average *per-Non-helper* (free rider) benefit of helping acts per time period. Inequality (4) reduces to:

$$\frac{c}{b} < \frac{m - p}{1 - p}. \tag{5}$$

Thus we see that for helping to be competitively superior to non-helping, a *necessary* (though not sufficient) condition is m > p — helping acts must be disproportionately directed to fellow Helpers.

All that has been said so far is perfectly general; kinship has not entered specifically at all. Still deferring the specifics of kinship, we can use Matrix 9 to gain a better understanding of the role played by the discrimination factor m. Matrix 9 is in the standard form of Matrix 7 except for the introduction of new 'recognition coefficients' v_H and $\bar{v}_N$. The first of these, v_H, is the conditional probability that an encountered Helper will be recognized as such by a fellow Helper and therefore will be 'correctly' granted aid (in the form of the benefit b). The conditional probability that an encountered Non-helper will be helped (because of being *incorrectly* recognized as a fellow Helper) is denoted $\bar{v}_N$. These two coefficients are in principle independent; for example, an organism might never fail to recognize a fellow Helper yet often treat Non-helpers as Helpers. The discrimination factor m will generally be functionally related to v_H and $\bar{v}_H$, as well as to p. More specifically, m/(1 − m) — the ratio of correctly to incorrectly directed helping acts — can be expressed as:

$$\frac{m}{1 - m} = \frac{p\,v_H}{(1 - p)\bar{v}_N}. \tag{6}$$

Or,

$$m = \frac{pv_H}{pv_H + (1 - p)\bar{v}_N}. \tag{7}$$

Example: If $v_H = .8, \bar{v}_N = .4$, and p = .25, then m = .4. Evidently, m will rise as v_H increases, and fall as $\bar{v}_N$ increases.

We now want to compare the expected returns α and β to the Helper and Non-helper strategies, respectively:[29]

$$\alpha = pv_H(b - c) - (1 - p)\bar{v}_N c \tag{8}$$
$$= pv_H b - c[pv_H + (1 - p)\bar{v}_N]$$
$$\beta = p\bar{v}_N b. \tag{9}$$

The condition for α to exceed β is then:

$$p > \frac{\bar{v}_N c}{(b - c)(v_H - \bar{v}_H)}. \tag{10}$$

We see that the ratio on the right-hand side is a kind of critical mass. Should p ever exceed it, Helping will grow until the population consists

Matrix 9
Prisoners' Dilemma
with Recognition

		C_1 (Helper)	C_2 (Nonhelper)
(Helper)	R_1	$v_H(b-c), v_H(b-c)$	$\bar{v}_N(-c), \bar{v}_N b$
(Nonhelper)	R_2	$\bar{v}_N b, \bar{v}_N(-c)$	0,0

Matrix 10
Prisoners' Dilemma
with Asymmetrical Commitment

		C_1 (Helper)	C_2 (Nonhelper)
(Helper)	R_1	$-c+b, -c+b$	$-c, b$
(Nonhelper)	R_2	$b, -c$	0,0
(Committer)	R_3	$-c+b, -c+b$	0,0

exclusively of Helpers. The critical mass will be more difficult of attainment the higher are c and $\bar{v}_N$ and the lower are b and v_H.

The incorporation of constant recognition factors thus converts the Prisoners' Dilemma into a Tender Trap situation, as discussed above, for which the stability considerations are as pictured by the line labelled I in Figure 1. But, unfortunately, if the population is initially in a Non-helping mode, putting together the critical mass needed to escape the trap will not be easy.

Example: Using our previous numbers $v_H = .8; \bar{v}_N = .4$, and supposing that b = 10 and c = 5, the critical value for p is 1! Thus, if the population were already all Helpers, they might remain so — but any smaller initial proportion of Helpers would spiral downward to the pure Non-helper situation p = 0. And this despite a favourable 2 : 1 benefit–cost ratio b/c, and a similarly favourable recognition ratio $v_H \bar{v}_H$.

While constant recognition coefficients v_H and $\bar{v}_N$ lead to a Tender Trap type of situation as in line I in Figure 9.1, a constant discrimination factor m would lead to a Hawk–Dove class of solution with a stable interior equilibrium as in line II of Figure 9.1[30] That is, in equilibrium a certain proportion p^* of the population would be Helpers and the remainder Non-helpers. A stable m implies varying v_H and $\bar{v}_N$. In particular, for m to be actually or nearly constant, it must be that as p rises either v_H falls or $\bar{v}_N$ rises (or both). This might characterize a 'mimicry' situation, in which Non-helpers try to cheat by disguising their identities. Then, it seems reasonable to believe, as the proportion of true Helpers rises it is easier for the few cheaters to successfully disguise themselves.

Now we can turn to *kinship* as a means of escape from the Prisoners' Dilemma trap. We may note from Eq. (7) that, for any *constant* recognition coefficients (however favourable), the discrimination factor m approaches zero as p goes to zero. This is what makes it hard for a critical mass of Helpers to evolve. But, for kinship helping, there is a considerably better lower bound on m. Suppose we are talking of siblings, for whom genetic relatedness is $r = 1/2$. (The probability of two siblings having received the same gene at any given haploid locus — that is, of both having inherited the mother's gene or both the father's gene — equals 50 per cent.) What happens when p approaches zero? We can imagine that the helping gene arose as a single new mutation in one parent. Then, if a given offspring of that parent is a Helper, there is a 50 per cent chance that its sibling is a fellow Helper. Thus, at the limit, $m = r = 1/2$. And in fact, for sibling helping the relation between m and p is:

$$m = \frac{1 + p}{2}.$$
(11)

Even when p approaches zero, the proportion of helping acts directed at fellow Helpers never goes below 50 per cent, and m rises toward unity as p increases.[31]

It follows immediately that the population will evolve toward cooperation ($p = 1$) of the Help-your-sibling variety if and only if:

$$c/b < 1/2.$$
(12)

Or, more generally for any degree of relatedness r, if and only if:

$$c/b < r.$$
(13)

Thus, helping relatives will be more viable in evolutionary terms than non-helping whenever the cost–benefit ratio of the helping act is less than the degree of relatedness. For efficiency in the PPP sense, however, the rule 'should' be to help whenever $c/b < 1$. Thus, *even within the kinship group* the kin-selection process provides only a partial escape from the Prisoners' Dilemma.

3. Group Selection   A topic much debated among biologists is the degree to which evolution of cooperative behaviour may be due to *group selection*. Under kin selection, the favourable discrimination factor m needed to make helping viable is achieved because helping one's relatives is likely to mean helping fellow carriers of one's own helping gene H. In the genetic sense, a relative *is* partially one's self. Under group selection, the discrimination needed for viability of H is supposed to be achieved simply by propinquity, combined with improved survival of groups containing helpers.

In anthropological terms, it seems reasonable to infer that the shift from small kinship-based bands to large nations has been associated with a corresponding shift from kin selection to group selection as the major winnowing process in human evolution. Kin selection still, it is evident, retains importance today for eliciting helping actions within the family. But we are much more interested in the viability of cooperative behaviours among *unrelated* individuals in the group structures of modern life.

Kin selection and group selection are often hard to distinguish in practice. Neighbours are more likely than random members of a population to share common ancestry. To illustrate the power and limitations of group selection, we will analyse a simple model containing no element of kinship.

Suppose an entire population swarms together at mating time, but otherwise divides itself quite randomly into propinquity subgroups. Then, by sheer chance, certain subgroups will be characterized by higher-than-average fractions of help-your-neighbour H genes — even though members of a given subgroup are not otherwise any more closely related than average. The mechanism of group selection postulates that the viability of subgroups will be strongly correlated with the proportions of helpers they contain. Differential subgroup survival will then tend to raise the overall fraction of H genes in the population. The problem, however, is that *within* each subgroup containing Helpers, it pays Non-helpers to free ride upon them. It has been shown that it is nevertheless mathematically possible for the proportion p of Helpers in the population to increase; the intergroup gain from helping may overcome the intragroup loss. But the dominant opinion among biologists is that the conditions for this to occur are so special that, *factually* speaking, group selection essentially never operates[32] in Nature — at least, below the level of *Homo sapiens*.

Analysis in terms of the discrimination factor m sheds some additional light upon the difficulty with group selection. If in fact a population broke up merely randomly into binomially distributed samples of unrelated carriers of H and N genes, then propinquity alone would dictate that m — the overall proportion of helping acts directed at fellow Helpers — would just equal p! Condition (5) could not be met, and helping would not be viable. To make it viable, some other conditions would have to be modified. For example, it might be that the per-act benefit b is not a constant but increases with the number of Helpers per group, thanks to some kind of increasing returns. Alternatively, it might be that grouping causes the recognition coefficients v_H and v_{-N} to take on more favourable values.

Whatever the mechanism may be, it can only work through differential survival of Helper and Non-helper genes as a function of the number of cooperative individuals falling into any given subgroup. To take the simplest case, suppose that after the initial mating swarm the population divides into subgroups of exactly two members each. With random segregation, if the proportion of H genes in the population is p then the proportion of groups containing two Helpers will be p^2, the proportion containing just one Helper will be $2pq$ (where $q = 1 - p$), and the proportion containing zero Helpers will be q^2.

Let s_{2H} be the per-capita survival probability of Helper individuals in groups of two Hs, let s_{ON} be the per-capita survival probability of Non-helper individuals in groups of two Ns, and let s_{1H} and s_{1N} be the respective survival chances of each type of individual in mixed groups. We would expect the survival probabilities to rank as follows: $s_{1N}, s_{2H} > s_{1H}, s_{ON}$. That is, the more profitable situations are (1) to be a free rider upon a Helper partner (s_{1H}), or (2) to be one of the two Helpers in an all-H group (s_{2H}). The less profitable situations are (3) to be a Helper with a Non-helper partner (s_{1H}), or else to be one of two Non-helpers (s_{ON}). (The proper rankings within the upper and the lower pairs will be left open for the moment.)

After the differential selection of H and N genes[33] represented by these survival probabilities takes place, in the next mating swarm the new Helper/Non-helper ratio $(p/q)'$ in the overall population will be:

$$(p/q)' = \frac{p^2 s_{2H} + pq s_{1H}}{q^2 s_{ON} + pq s_{1N}}. \tag{14}$$

At equilibrium, $(p/q)'$ would have to equal p/q, so:

$$1 = \frac{p s_{2H} + q s_{1H}}{q s_{ON} + p s_{1N}}.$$

Or,

$$\frac{p}{q} = \frac{s_{1H} - s_{ON}}{s_{1N} - s_{2H}}. \tag{15}$$

It may be verified that this is a stable interior solution if both numerator and denominator on the right-hand side of Eq. (15) are positive. The H gene will remain present in the population at large if $s_{1H} > s_{ON}$, and the N gene if $s_{1N} > s_{2H}$. When these conditions are met, *within* each subgroup we have a Hawk–Dove type of game (as described above). If we had instead a true within-subgroup Prisoners' Dilemma, so that it *always* paid to be a Non-helper whatever the other party played, the survival probabilities would show $s_{1N} < s_{ON}$ as well as $s_{2H} < s_{1N}$ — the H gene would not be viable at all in the population.

Put another way, for the H gene to survive in this model despite the advantage of being a free rider when one's partner is a Helper (that is, where the denominator in Eq. (15) is positive), it must be that when one's partner is a Non-helper it is *selfishly* advantageous to be a Helper (that is, the numerator must be positive). This seems rather implausible; we would probably expect the numerator in Eq. (15) to be negative. But there is another route to viability of helping — the denominator might be negative. If *only* the denominator were negative, q would go to zero and all the population would be Helpers in equilibrium. In what is probably the most interesting case, where *both* numerator and denominator are negative, the interior equality will be unstable — the population will go to all-H or all-N depending upon the initial situation. Then, a critical mass would be necessary for viability of helping behaviour. (Compare the Tender Trap game above.)[34]

If we think in terms of selection operating among (and within) human groups, the increasing-returns factor mentioned earlier tends to make s_{2H} very big, thus contributing to a negative denominator in Eq. (15). One arena where increasing returns to within-group cooperation are particularly effective is warfare,[35] and warfare among humans has been a potent selective force (Alexander (1), ch. 4). Suppose it is the case that $s_{2H} > s_{1N}$. That means your survival chances, if your partner is a Hero, are better fighting alongside him than running away. If in addition $s_{1H} > s_{ON}$ (even if your partner runs away, it is still better to fight on), the numerator in Eq. (15) is positive and the Non-helper gene will be driven out. This does seem implausible. But even if the latter condition fails, there will still be a critical mass for p beyond which only helping behaviour is viable so long as s_{2H} exceeds s_{1N}. And the critical mass is the more easily achieved the greater is this difference.

The other force tending to raise the discrimination factor m is improved recognition within groups, which allows carriers of the H gene to modify their behaviour so as to reward fellow-Hs and punish Ns. This seems a likely result of human intelligence. In particular, suppose it really does not make sense to fight on if one's partner runs away ($s_{1N} < s_{ON}$). Then, a smart Hero will act accordingly — that is, will run away himself. If his recognition coefficient for Non-helper partners were perfect ($\bar{v}_N = 0$), his recognition-adjusted survival probability would then be $s_{1'H} = s_{ON}$ rather than $s_{1H} < s_{ON}$. Even short of this, any improved $s_{1'H}$ relative to s_{ON} would reduce the negative balance in the numerator of Eq. (15) and thus tend to make Helping more viable.

Nonsymmetric strategies

We have already seen how a kind of asymmetry may lead to *complementary* strategic choices in the Hawk–Dove game — converting the solution from an interior mixture of Hawks and Doves to fully efficient Hawk–Dove pairing. We are here considering possible asymmetries in the Prisoners' Dilemma context. There are, of course, many possible dimensions along which some degree of asymmetry may obtain: the pay-offs might diverge from the fully symmetrical form of Matrix 7, or there might be differential knowledge of these elements, or differential communication capacities, or the players might vary in their ability to recognize fellow Helpers, and so on. In this section, however, I will mainly consider an asymmetry in ability to employ threat or promise strategies.

A more general statement is in order first. We have so far been considering only interactions within homogeneous populations, encounters where the player choosing Row comes from the same population as the player choosing Column. In all such cases Non-helpers are free riders on Helpers. A bird that endangers itself by calling out to others when a predator appears would be subject to free-riding on the part of those who never call warnings. In Matrix 7, this feature is represented by the advantage of Non-helpers over Helpers in the off-diagonal cells. But when the interacting players come from *different* populations, free-riding disappears. A bee following a Non-helper strategy of refusing to pick up pollen from a flower does not gain thereby; the flower loses, but so does the bee. Evidently, there is no Prisoners' Dilemma trap here at all; if a mutual benefit exists, the Helper strategy is dominant for both players. It is quite generally easier, therefore, to convert potential into actual cooperation when the players come from *different* populations, or are otherwise in less direct competition with one another. One advantage of sexual over asexual reproduction, perhaps, is that sex divides the population into largely non-competing halves. Males compete with males, and females with females, but the male–female interaction is complementary.[36]

Turning back to the Prisoners' Dilemma, I shall consider a particular form of non-symmetrical strategy — *commitment to a threat or a promise*. Commitment is very much like the Retaliator strategy represented in the symmetric Matrix 8: the player cooperates with Helpers but not with Non-helpers. But here we allow only *one* of the players to adopt such a strategy, as shown in Matrix 10.

The type of commitment strategy dealt with here represents adoption of a fixed *conditional-reaction function*. Its essence is restricting in advance one's freedom to select a response to the other party's choice.[37] It is, first, an engagement to do something one would otherwise not do in order to influence the behaviour of the other party. Second, the difference between commitment to a threat versus a promise is not fundamental. Threat, strictly speaking, would involve Committer in a self-damaging 'punishment' response to Non-helper behaviour; promise, in a self-damaging 'reward' response for Helper behaviour.[38] Third, threats or promises involve *communication* as well as commitment. If the other party does not know of the commitment, or does not believe it, his behaviour will not be affected. But only one-way communication is required, and indeed threats and promises may typically be more effective if only one-way communication is possible.

Incorporation of a Commitment strategy into the options of one player allows achievement of the efficient outcome. In Matrix 10, upon Row's commitment to R_3, and communication of that commitment, Column player will choose the Helper strategy C_1, so long as $b > c$ — that is, whenever mutual helping satisfies the criterion of efficiency.

To achieve this result in pairwise interactions, the players would have to combine into subordinate–superordinate teams. For larger groupings, this form of teaming generalizes to a hierarchical ranking system in which each player makes a commitment-plus-communication move in relation to those below him.[39] One further implication may be of interest for our purposes. It was suggested above that law could be thought of as an institutionalized 'impartial' third party whose function is to enforce agreements between members of potentially cooperating dyads. This left open the question of who is to play that role, and what would be his incentive. The present discussion illustrates another institutional model of law: hierarchy. Here the suggestion is that one possible basis of law is the threat (or promise) on the part of superordinate parties to mete out punishment should subordinates engage in non-cooperative behaviour (or to grant rewards for cooperative behaviour). As an interesting point, it is not logically necessary that the superordinate player actually ends up any better off than do the subordinates! And, in fact, in our otherwise symmetrical Matrix 10 the two players do equally well. (In such a situation there might be unanimous agreement on the *principle* of hierarchy, even if the actual ranks were to be randomly chosen.) However, as a practical matter it seems likely that only an initial asymmetry of power will lead to this form of solution to the Prisoners' Dilemma, and consequently that the superordinate player will set up the terms of the association (the elements of the pay-off matrix) so as to reap the superior outcome (see below).

The Committer in Matrix 10 is promising to reward the other player by not playing his Non-helper strategy R_2 if the latter plays the cooperative strategy C_1. But the other player knows that if he should

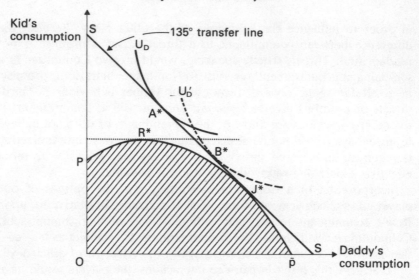

Figure 9.4   Rotten Kid and Big Daddy

play C_1, the Committer would be better off reneging (choosing R_2 anyway). How can threats (or promises) be made credible? As a means of providing the needed guarantee, Nature has evolved 'uncontrollable' emotions — of loving gratitude or vengeful rage as the case may be. Put another way, it sometimes pays off to be irrational, to lose the capacity for optimizing choice. Even on the human level, emotions limit the possible scope of rational behaviour — not always to our disadvantage.[40]

One interesting example of these ideas is the 'Rotten Kid' model.[41] A selfish individual (the Rotten Kid) can be induced to engage in cooperative behaviour by an appropriate promise of reward. One way of guaranteeing such reward is for the other member of the dyad (Big Daddy) to evolve a sufficient degree of benevolence for Rotten Kid. The strategic situation must be asymmetrical, in that Big Daddy must be able to *commit* himself to rewarding cooperation by distributing enough of the gain back to Rotten Kid. (And of course he must be able to communicate the fact of that commitment.) The emotion of love provides the needed guarantee. The crucial point is that *Big Daddy himself also ends up better off.* And better off not merely in terms of emotional satisfactions, but in terms of the actual material gains needed to make the commitment-to-benevolence strategy a viable one.

In Figure 9.4, on axes representing Daddy's income I_D versus Kid's income I_K, Rotten Kid simply wants to attain a position highest up in the I_K direction. (In effect, Kid's indifference curves are horizontal.)

Daddy's degree of love and concern for Kid is illustrated by his normal-looking indifference curve U_D. We now must suppose that Kid makes the first move, and Daddy the second: Kid proposes, but Daddy disposes.[42] If Kid were short-sighted as well as selfish, he would choose point R*. But, knowing Daddy's emotion-based commitment, Kid in his long-run self-interest should choose position J* — which is jointly optimum (efficient) in the sense of achieving the highest sum $I_K + I_D$. From J*, Daddy makes a love-induced transfer along the 135° line SS to his indifference-curve tangency optimum A*. Kid's 'pragmatic' cooperation has been repaid, since A* is higher up (involves larger I_K) than R*. But, what is more remarkable, Daddy's 'hard-core' cooperation[43] has also paid off in material terms: I_D too is higher at J* than at R*. And in fact, if Big Daddy were somewhat less loving, as represented by his alternative indifference curve U'_D, he would only react to Kid's cooperative move by more limited income transfers to point B*, which would be insufficient to motivate Kid to cooperate in the first place.

Benevolence or love on the one hand, rage or jealousy on the other, are the sorts of preferences or 'tastes' that the economist is likely to regard as arbitrary brute facts. The evolutionary approach, in contrast, suggests that at least some aspects of preferences are not accidental, but have evolved as ways of restraining freedom of choice where such restraint can conduce to advantageous cooperation. More broadly speaking, it suggests (as will be brought out later) that social ethics, such as ingrained respect for property rights or obedience to constituted leaders, may also have evolved to aid group efficiency by allowing the Prisoners' Dilemma to be overcome.

A number of econo-legal scholars have suggested that 'altruism' is a partial substitute for law in eliciting cooperative behaviour.[44] The thrust of our theoretical development in the above Sections has been to the effect that the situation is far, far more complex than that. The likelihood that cooperative behaviour will be viable depends on the details of the ecological situation (summarized, in our simple models, by the game matrices). Furthermore, helping can emerge among organisms evidently incapable of altruism in any ethical or psychological sense of the word. On the other hand, among more advanced animals, including man, emotions like benevolence and love can indeed serve to promote helping interactions — but it may well be that emotions like hate and rage are at least equally important (to induce, for example, 'irrational' efforts to punish non-cooperators).

Summarizing at this point: in this and the previous section we have explored a number of alternative routes along which cooperation might evolve. In a binary–strategy world of random dyadic encounters between members of a homogeneous population, the possible pay-off patterns (environmental situations) fall into a limited set of classes. In Tender Trap all the motivation is to cooperate, yet the population might (depending upon the initial situation and the required critical mass) not end up in the *best* cooperative solution. In Hawk–Dove there are mixed motives. The cooperative strategy (Dove) can be the more advantageous, up to a point, but not to the extent of driving out Hawk. (That is, each strategy is the more profitable once sufficiently rare in the population.) Thus, the result tends to be a mixed population (or a homogeneous population playing a mixture of strategies). What was rather significant is that some structuring of the possible encounters in Hawk–Dove may allow fully complementary efficient pairing. In particular, the evolutionary equilibrium achievable under the rule 'first come first served' is a possible precursor of territoriality and property rights. This solution is associated with a Bourgeois strategy: playing Hawk against intruders, but Dove against possessors.

But if the environmental circumstances correspond to the game of Prisoners' Dilemma, where the cooperative strategy is always dominated by the non-cooperative evolution of mutual-aid interactions will be much more difficult. A Retaliator strategy would be the analogue to Bourgeois in the Hawk–Dove game. Like Bourgeois, Retaliator represents self-enforcement of cooperation: Retaliator reacts favourably to good behaviour, while punishing bad behaviour committed against himself. But Retaliator seems not to be viable under Prisoners' Dilemma. Various other routes to cooperation do promise a degree of success. Nepotism (aiding only one's kin) facilitates cooperative interactions, but not so far as to achieve full efficiency even within the kinship group. Much the same can be said for other 'discrimination' techniques, as in group selection, which focus aid upon individuals more likely to be fellow helpers. Ability to interact repeatedly with the same partner may also provide a partial escape. More interesting for our purposes here is the asymmetrical or hierarchical route out of the Prisoners' Dilemma. A player in a superordinate role can make a pattern of cooperation effective by becoming *committed* to a threat of punishment for bad behaviour (or, what is essentially equivalent, a promise of reward for good behaviour).

COMPETITION AND EFFICIENCY

For ecobiologists in the Malthus–Darwin tradition, competition — in the ruthless sense of the struggle for existence — is the fundamental principle of Nature's economy. The source of competition is the limited resource base of the globe in the face of the universal tendency of populations to multiply. By natural selection the biosphere has come to teem with life-forms successful at pressing upon one another to obtain the nutrients needed to sustain life.

Biologists have found it useful to distinguish three main classes of competitive strategies: *scramble, interference,* and *predation*.[45] Scramble competitors interact only through depletion of resources. The winning organisms are those most effective at extracting energy and other needed inputs from the external environment. *Interference* competitors, in contrast, gain and maintain control over resources by attacking (or otherwise reducing the efficiency of) other contenders, mainly, though not exclusively, their conspecifics. (Members of the same species, having a higher overlap zone of resource needs, are typically closer rivals than members of different species.) *Predation,* finally is mainly interspecific[46] — the competitor organisms have been made part of the resource field.[47]

Competition in Nature, in all these forms, tends to be both antisocial and wasteful of resources. And yet the economist views market competition as a harmonizing force, one that leads to productive efficiency. What are the special features of market competition making this possible? First, under idealized institutions of political economy only the more innocuous form of scramble competition is permitted in the market. When one businessman finds a customer for his output or a supplier for needed input, he does indeed deplete the resource field for other businessmen. But he is not permitted to blow up his rival's shop (interference), or to stock his own store by raiding the other's inventory (predation). Second, again under idealized conditions, the adverse externalities that the businessman imposes on his competitors are only pecuniary, as discussed above. A less successful business competitor may have to lower his product price quotation to customers, or raise his hire price offer to input suppliers, but in efficiency terms the effects of such price adjustments cancel out. Another way of looking at this is to note that market competition for the economist is not a two-sided but a three-sided interaction. The market competitor vies not just *against* a rival, but *for* the opportunity to engage in mutually advantageous exchanges with other parties. The gain to third parties in this 'vying competition' counterbalances any loss suffered by competitors. In simple two-sided 'taking competition', in contrast, there is no such offsetting gain. The really useful distinction (so far as efficiency is concerned) is therefore not along the scramble/interference/predation dimension but rather is the dichotomy of competitive *vying* versus *taking*.

While the more downright *taking* form of competition is far more

common in Nature, important instances of vying competition have
evolved as well. In sexual competition there are two main modes of
resolving rivalry for females: [48] (1) male combat and (2) female choice.[49]
The latter comes close to what the economist would regard as mutually
advantageous exchange. Where female choice obtains, males defer to
the female's 'property right' in her own reproductive capacity, which
she will dispose of at her option to the most desired partner.

On the human level, *taking* in its extreme interference version is
clearly the mode of competition in duels for survival such as Rome
versus Carthage, or Ike Clanton versus Wyatt Earp. Such competition
obviously tends to adopt inefficient or even violent methods. Turning
back to male combat as an example of taking competition in Nature,
the wasteful results include not only the direct damage which one
or both combatants may suffer, but the consequent misdirected
evolutionary trends, such as sexual dimorphism (the development of
excessive male size, or weapons like horns and claws, that serve only
for fighting other males). The consequences of human interference
competition are entirely parallel, whether we speak in terms of genetic
or cultural evolution.[50] But even the scramble form of taking competition
is inefficient in the absence of property rights. An organism chancing
upon a food source will consume it until the marginal benefit to itself
falls to zero, even though stopping earlier might be more efficient for
the species or other larger group, that is, might provide greater
nourishment for the next searcher.

What has come to be known as *rent-seeking* is a less violent scramble
form of competition in human affairs.[51] Where an asset exists that has
not been reduced to recognized property, an inefficient struggle for the
resource (or for the fruits thereof) tends to take place. This struggle
takes two main forms. If the asset can be sequestered (for example, if
it can become legally protected property), its value will thereafter be
maintained even though valuable goods or services may have been
initially wasted in the two-sided competition for it. An example would
be a political struggle for a television channel or an airline route.
Where the asset cannot be or is not sequestered at all, as in the case
of common property resources like hunting grounds or underground
aquifers, unlimited taking competition tends to sharply reduce the net
social yield.

To achieve an ideal state of efficiency, property rights in all resources
would have to be preassigned and perfectly respected. Remove these
conditions and there will be 'excessive' efforts to acquire assets (if they
can be sequestered) or to seize their fruits (if they cannot be
sequestered). Such efforts include unlawful activities like theft (but
recall that defending against theft is also inefficient).[52] Resource-taking

may also occur because there is no relevant law, as when nations contend for power or territory. Or, finally, taking competition may take place even under law (which may or may not be regarded as an 'imperfection' of the legal order). One example is the search for undiscovered resources like petroleum, fish or ideas (whether patentable or not). Such search is, evidently, not totally wasteful. The increments to the community's stock of resources are socially useful, but it remains true that the degree of effort devoted to searching tends to be excessive.[53] The costly contests that take the form of redistributive politics, on the other hand, are unqualifiedly inefficient.[54]

We are not surprised that male combat for females, or struggle for territory, or pecking-order dominance (and their human analogues) represent wasteful forms of competition. Much more puzzling is why highly inefficient competition has evolved in Nature even in cases where the equivalent of pre-assigned and respected 'property rights' does exist, specifically, in male competition for mates *even where female choice governs*. The peacocks with their burdensome tails are an obvious instance. Another case is that of the bower bird males, who toil at constructing attractive (rather than merely utilitarian) domiciles for prospective mates. Two explanations have been offered. First, that the evolution of attractive sexual characters is a self-sustaining pattern, rather on the order of a chain letter or a speculative bubble (see Fisher (18), p. 152; Dawkins (15), p. 170). It pays a peahen in the current generation to choose the cock with the largest tail, because her male offspring will then also tend to have big tails, thus attracting the next generation's peahens, who will prefer big-tailed cocks so that *their* sons will have big tails, and so on indefinitely. Alternatively, it has been suggested (Zahavi (75)), that we have here what the economist would call a 'signalling equilibrium' (see Spence (61); Riley (51)). The big tail is a kind of advertisement. It does not *contribute* to the male cock's quality as a mate, but it *signals* quality, since only a very strong bird can successfully carry a big tail.[55] Note that this explanation also has a rather fragile or unstable 'self-sustaining' element; it pays for hens of this generation to respond to this signal only to the extent that future hens will read the signal the same way.

EVOLUTION AND LAW

Man's laws are subject to the deeper rules of Nature. The first of these rules is that all living forms are in reproductive (Malthusian) competition with one another. However, and here we come to what might be called the second rule of Nature: it is often more effective for separate organisms to come together and engage in cooperative association. But such alliances are merely secondary and contingent, in at least two respects: (1) in-group cooperation is only a means for more effectively and ruthlessly competing against outsiders; and (2) there is never perfect parallelism of interest among the members of a group, hence cooperation must generally be supported by sanctions to punish 'antisocial' behaviour. Indeed, one of the greatest obstacles to cooperation is the fact that those individuals having the best opportunities to engage in mutual aid — because they are nearest in terms of propinquity or similarity or relatedness — are commonly the most closely competitive in their needs for resources.

Forms of Association, and Precursors of Law

Forms of association vary widely in degree of cooperativeness. What seems to be a social unit may be only a 'selfish herd' (Hamilton (26)): the term refers to animals who seek protection against predators by moving toward the centre of the crowd, thus placing others at risk on the periphery. Here the element of cooperation is entirely lacking. Then there are cases of merely parallel mutual interests, as when birds return annually to a mating area where they can expect to find other birds. In patterns of association like territoriality or dominance hierarchies there is at least a negative cooperative element, a tendency to avoid strife. And, finally, there are true communities, most notably families, characterized by more or less intense positive helping.

The theoretical analysis above suggested two possible situations serving as precursors of *law*, interpreted as a system of retaliation that deters non-cooperative behaviour: (1) Bourgeois strategies under Hawk–Dove and (2) hierarchy under Prisoners' Dilemma. In the relatively benign environment corresponding to the conditions of the Hawk–Dove game, the regulation of behaviour is egalitarian and decentralized. In the severer environment corresponding to Prisoners' Dilemma, it is hierarchical and centralized. In each case a 'social ethic' is also involved, in the sense that one or more of the parties is required to engage in behaviour that is not in its private interest in terms of the immediate situation. In Matrix 6, playing Bourgeois (R_3) means forgoing the more profitable Hawk strategy (R_2) upon encountering a Dove (C_1), as well as the more profitable Dove strategy (R_1) upon encountering a Hawk (C_2). And in Matrix 10 the superordinate Committer strategist (R_3) foregoes the more profitable Nonhelper choice (R_2) against Helper (C_1), that is, he rewards cooperative behaviour.

The Bourgeois solution under Hawk–Dove can be generalized to a population of any size, in which everyone possesses some property or territory which he is prepared to defend. The Committer solution under Prisoners' Dilemma also extends to a group of any size, each member being ranked relative to all others. Nevertheless, the limitation of the analysis to binary-strategy dyadic encounters in a homogeneous population remains very restrictive, and I do not mean to imply that there are not other archetypes or primitive forms of law that arise out of more complex interactions. And in particular I believe that another source of law arises out of the balance of power or coalition considerations that emerge when more than two parties interact.

More specifically, this other source corresponds to what biologists have called *moralistic aggression* (Trivers (66)): intervention of 'uninvolved' third parties on the side of the victim of hostile or uncooperative behaviour (on this see also Hamilton (27); Aubert (4)). I am not prepared to provide a formal analysis, but I conjecture that moralistic aggression will be a viable strategy, at least as part of a mixed solution, in multiparty Prisoners' Dilemma interactions. If moralistic aggression is operative, coalitional power in an egalitarian social structure serves essentially the same role as the dominant power of a superordinate player in a hierarchical structure. Like the other sources of law, moralistic aggression also involves a social ethic; the intervenor forgoes the short-run advantage of shirking the third-party enforcer role.

Finally, we should keep in mind that forces promoting cooperation may amplify and support one another. Kin selection and group selection are perhaps weak forces regarded separately, but they tend to be mutually reinforcing since members of propinquity groupings are almost always more closely related than average in the population. Parent–child nepotism may also support a cooperative superordinate–subordinate commitment interaction (Big Daddy in our example above). And similarly, parents might be more inclined than mere outsiders to play the 'moralistic aggressor' role so as to enforce mutual helping among their offspring.

On the Historical Evolution of Law

A number of legal historians and philosophers have viewed the law as following an evolutionary course of change. Before commenting on these interpretations, it is elementary though perhaps still useful to notice that the evolution of law must be considered in conjunction with the evolution of societal forms. Very primitive men lived in small bands based primarily upon a hunting economy. Later on pastoralism and agriculture emerged, followed ultimately by industry. To bring out a slightly less familiar point, at least one other economic way of life has been important probably in all historical periods: predation upon other human groups. In response to accumulated technological advances and other forces (climatic change, population growth, pressure of non-human and human predators), the typical *scale* of human association has gradually increased over time, culminating eventually in the large modern nation-state based upon diversified economic activity and the division of labour.

The characteristic laws of an era when most of the world's population lived in sparsely distributed hunting bands must have diverged from the types of law in force now, when most people live in urban environments within huge national states. There is a question of cause versus effect here. I am suggesting that the law responds to larger social changes governing forms of economy and state. But, to some extent at least, legal systems tend to bring about these larger changes. For example, Marxist communism as a system of law has not proved to be very conducive to economic advance, but its effectiveness in organizing and using military strength against internal and external enemies has led to its enormous extension over the face of the globe.

Returning to the traditional legal historians,[56] they have — not surprisingly, in the light of the foregoing — tended to agree that the dominant evolutionary trend is from laws suitable for an intimate face-to-face community to a legal system capable of governing impersonal public life among strangers (from *Gemeinschaft* to *Gesellschaft*).[57] More specifically, Sir Henry Maine contended that the directions of historical change were from family responsibility to individual obligation, and from legal relations based on family status to those based upon contract. Max Weber emphasized progress toward abstract rationality, decisions being made in accord with logic and principle rather than personality, magic, or emotion. A somewhat similar position was taken by Roscoe Pound, who tended to emphasize moral as well as procedural improvements in this unfolding development. Somewhat more specifically, primitive law was said to be characterized by strict liability, self-help and collective responsibility; modern law by liability only for moral fault, recourse via impartial public law rather than self-help, and individual rather than collective responsibility for behaviour.[58]

There is considerable disagreement among scholars on both the broad sweep and the finer details of these trends. For instance, important elements of strict liability remain in modern American law, and their scope may even by expanding (as in workmen's compensation). But, far more importantly, the drastic events suffered by humanity in the twentieth century cast a dubious light upon the generally optimistic tone of this entire line of thinking, and especially upon the implied trend toward ethical as well as procedural progress in systems of law governing the majority of men.

Thrasymachus in Plato's *Republic* says that 'Justice is the interest of the stronger.' If we interpret this as a positive statement (rather than as a principle of normative ethics), it is difficult not to concede a degree of validity to the Sophist's contention.[59] A revisionist interpretation of past legal trends might seek to explain why the more powerful groups have been led to favour collective responsibility in some areas and times, individual responsibility in others, and so forth. Or perhaps more correctly, why the *balances* of power among groups of varying strength brought about such developments.

Social Ethics and Systems of Law

While I shall not be able to tie things all together in a neat package, I shall begin to connect the theoretical development with actual legal trends.

First, consider the hierarchical Committer solution to the Prisoners' Dilemma. This has a rather close correspondence to the power structures sometimes observed among animals and men. I have called it elsewhere (Hirshleifer (31)) the 'Iron Rule' of social order.[60] One odd feature of the previous analysis was that the superordinate or dominant individual did not end up any better-off than the subordinate. And curiously enough, something like this does occasionally occur among animals, where it is found that the dominant male in the band does not always father the most offspring. Nevertheless, we would be quite surprised if this were normally the case. Equality of *result* despite inequality of *role* is, I want to suggest, a special case due mainly to the assumption of a homogeneous population in the theoretical analysis. When there are strong asymmetries of power in the population, even before the form of association is fixed, it is more than likely that the stronger will be able to set up a hierarchical system in which he reaps most of the mutual gain, as Thrasymachus suggested. (On the other hand, since individuals striving for dominance may not achieve it, and may suffer damage in the process, the *average* payoff of a 'seek power' strategy may be no greater than that of an 'accept inferiority' strategy.)

There is a social ethic associated even with the Iron Rule of dominance. In our simple Matrix 10, we saw that good behaviour by the subordinate must be rewarded, even though it is against the Committer's immediate interest to do so. In more general contexts (where injury strategies are allowed in the contest for the top position), it has been observed also that animals typically fight by conventional means, often not using their most lethal weapons (Lorenz (37); Tinbergen (65)). The defeated animal does not fight to the death, and his submission is accepted.

Let us now consider the more egalitarian precursors of law mentioned earlier. If the environment corresponds to the conditions of the

Hawk–Dove game, we saw that a Bourgeois strategy (under our assumed conditions) was an evolutionary equilibrium. The strategy of fighting to defend your own property but deferring to the corresponding rights of others was superior to always seeking short-run gain (Hawk) or always deferring (Dove). The territoriality observed in Nature is such a social structure. Members of many animal species, humans among them, have either a fixed or a mobile bubble of personal space, invasion of which will be resisted. The supporting social ethic here involves both willingness to defend and reluctance to intrude, each action being against the immediate interest of the territory holder. This is indeed what occurs. 'Irrational' fury on the part of property owners and corresponding fearfulness or timidity on the part of intruders lead to the defeat of most incursions (see especially Ardrey (3)).

However, while the Bourgeois ethic undoubtedly plays a role even on the human level, it does not conduce to more affirmative forms of group cooperation. Egalitarian *coalitions*, we suggested above, enforce good behaviour through the social ethic of moralistic aggression. Again, emotions like indignation (see Trivers (66); Willhoite (70)) may have evolved to overcome the short-run disadvantage of becoming involved in third-party punishment of offenders. Moralistic aggression is open-ended in its scope of application; it can be used to support a variety of different social norms. Among the many possibilities observed among mankind are sharing, reciprocation and heroism. Human beings seem able to learn alternative ideologies, but once learned the support for any particular ideology stems probably at least in part from an innate pattern of behaviour.

The social behaviour of human beings is subject to many other influences, some mentioned in the preceding analytical discussions. In particular, *kinship* as a source of cooperative or even self-sacrificial behaviour has always been of great historical importance; as a biologically determined universal, it is unlikely ever to lose its sway. Early human societies were very largely made up of close kin (though exogamy provided a counterbalancing force setting some bound upon xenophobia).[61] Associations broader than family groupings tend to be supported by ideologies *simulating* family relationships: the dominant individual in a hierarchical society becomes 'the father of his country'; in an egalitarian society, participants become 'brothers'. Culture, it seems, permits humans to learn to fool themselves, in ways that are often, though by no means always, socially productive.

Does the Law Evolve toward Efficiency?

It follows from Coase's Theorem that, *given* any initial assignment of property rights, there will be a trend toward efficient use of resources.

All possibilities for mutually advantageous exchanges will gradually be discovered and consummated, except as prevented by the barrier of transaction costs.

However, it is not in general true that trade makes *all* affected parties better off; the result of exchange is only potentially rather than strictly Pareto-preferred to the pre-exchange situation. Still, the net balance of such losses must be less than the gain to the contracting parties. (Otherwise, the Coasian argument goes, these third parties would enter the transaction and induce a change in its terms.)

Recent thinking has suggested that the process by which the law itself changes, so as to *redistribute* established property rights, is not essentially different from the Coasian process of *exchange* of rights that is conditional upon an initial structure of property entitlements. This is clear enough when a change in the law is unanimously approved, either because it benefits everyone directly or because appropriate compensations are paid. A possible instance is the privatization of hunting rights for fur-bearing animals that took place among certain Indian tribes in North America. This change came about after the arrival of European traders opened up a larger market for furs, thus increasing the social gains achievable by shifting away from the previous inefficient regime of common property rights.[62]

The more difficult case, which is (with only rare exceptions) the one of practical concern, is when the law changes in ways that clearly help some individuals while injuring others. Traditional 'welfare economics' implicitly viewed this process as a benign one in which a paternalistic government apparatus balances considerations of equity against efficiency in the light of changing external circumstances. A degree of optimism seemed warranted, since ongoing improvement in analytical understanding could be expected to aid performance in this regard, with the added nice feature of suggesting that lots of economists should be hired at all levels of government.

The 'new political economy'[63] literature, in contrast, is much more pessimistic. It regards all the actors on the political scene — voters, legislators, bureaucrats, and even judges — as making choices so as to maximize personal utility subject to the constraints imposed by laws and institutions (and the behaviour of other actors). While it might theoretically be possible to redesign the constraints of duties and rights so as to lead to more efficient outcomes, there seems to be no particular reason to suppose that any such improvements are likely to come about.

One of the most exciting new ideas in recent years has been the proposition that the law does after all tend to evolve in the direction of efficiency. (This is the positive, rather than normative, version of

Posner's Theorem as described above.) It supposedly does so evolve not because of the wise benevolence of lawmakers, but as an inevitable result of the conflictual process of litigation.[64] The basic idea is quite simple. Suppose we are dealing with a situation where mutually advantageous *exchanges* of entitlements are partially or wholly unfeasible, so that the initial assignment of property rights may make a real efficiency difference. An inefficient assignment leaves more scope for improvement; that is, the net balance of gains and losses will be greater in shifting from an inefficient to an efficient set of rights than for the reverse change.[65] It follows that, other things equal, those individuals and groups whose interests will be served by legal changes in the direction of efficiency will be motivated to bring more pressure and strength to bear than will their opponents in the contest for judicial determination of rights.[66]

Different models have been proposed for the actual mechanism of this process. In the original version of Rubin the emphasis is upon relitigation. If precedents are not absolutely binding, attempts will be made repeatedly to overturn an inefficient one. Even if judges never become any more enlightened, intellectually speaking, as long as there is a random element in their decisions the efficient outcome will eventually be hit upon so as to become the new precedent.[67] In an alternative version, those standing to benefit from the efficient precedent will be induced to make the greater investment (for example, hire more able lawyers) so as to influence the outcome of the action (Goodman (22)).

Finally, what is very important, the thrust of this efficiency through strength argument is by no means limited to the arena of common law litigation. With minimal modifications the same logic can be applied also to the forces determining statute law and constitutional interpretation.[68] For that matter, since the process is essentially one of 'trial by combat', why not apply it also to civil wars and international conflicts? Dr Pangloss, it seems, may have been right after all!

To refute the idea that strife and contention lead to efficiency in any all-encompassing sense we need only look about us. Still, it is important to appreciate how and to what degree the argument goes wrong, at least in its application to the evolution of law. I see three major flaws, which I shall try to explain in order of increasing importance.

First, while I would support the contention that judicial or political results are ultimately determined by *strength* (by pressures brought to bear upon decision-makers), the link is weak between result-relevant strength and the underlying costs and benefits imposed upon individuals. Rubin mentions that there is a 'public good' situation here; others who may gain from overturning the precedent are free-riding upon the actual litigant. Put more generally, each side has the problem of *mobilizing* its strength. Among the forces favouring the ability of one side or the other to mobilize so as to bring potential strength to bear are such familiar considerations as compactness (small numbers, geographical concentration), perceived unity of interest, cheapness of communications, and perhaps a group-centred social ethic. In this model, it is interesting to note, litigation emerged in the first place because of negotiation breakdowns[69] between the interests on each side. And yet, negotiations *within* each side aiming at mobilizing forces so as to present a common front are quite essential for winning the contest. The overall conclusion, then, is that there are at least two sets of forces at work in this conflictual process: on the one hand the balance of efficiency considerations, but on the other hand comparative effectiveness at mobilization.

Second, and in part a related consideration, once the outcome is seen to depend in part upon ability to mobilize we would expect to observe a kind of arms race between the contenders. Each would be motivated to trade off some of the potential efficiency gain in order to increase the chance of defeating the other. In the animal world, we have seen, male combat for females leads to the diversion of resources to the development of otherwise unproductive weapons of contest. The same effect is highly visible in the sphere of international conflict. Thus, any trend towards efficiency gains from improved precedents (or, more generally, from reallocation of resources in accordance with the outcome of contests) must be weighed against losses due to the pressure to 'meet the competition' by adding to combative capacity. Increased armaments, furthermore, may raise the costs of the process of coming to a decision (determining who wins and who loses). In warfare among nations, the costs of producing armaments are generally minor in comparison with the direct damage should war actually come about.

Third, and most important, is the question of *whose* efficiency? That is, what are the boundaries of the relevant group? Even if economic benefits and costs translate directly into combat strength, even if no resources are wasted in arms races or direct damage, the loss to the defeated can be said to be outweighed by the gains to the victors only if the transaction changing the structure of rights is internal to the group, which thereby gains collective power for the purpose of competing against others. An example might be military conscription of a particular age cohort. If an external enemy presented a sufficiently urgent threat, many of us might think that such a drastic revision of rights was nevertheless warranted in the interests of national survival. But suppose it were a question of one nation enslaving another. Even if the enslavers were willing and able to 'bid higher' than their victims in a military contest, we would be disinclined to regard the transaction as improving efficiency in any meaningful way.[70] (Conceivably, this process of 'efficient enslavement' might aid the entire human species in its competition for survival against other species, but such competition is not sufficiently urgent at this time to be a major consideration.)

CONCLUSIONS

I shall not attempt any general summary of the paper but instead will present a number of the more interesting or noteworthy implications of the evolutionary approach as it applies to conflict versus cooperation strategies in human affairs.

1   The central tradition of economic reasoning emphasizes the harmony of interests among men. Under the guidance of the 'invisible hand', even entirely self-interested individuals are led to cooperate so as to achieve the mutual gains of trade. Economists have paid much less attention to conflict and aggression, to attempts to reap one-sided gains at the expense of others, although this aspect of behaviour is also entirely amenable to economic analysis.

2.   Recent economic approaches to the study of political interactions reflect a similar harmonistic tilt in viewing the political problem as one of 'collective choice' rather than as fundamentally a contest for power and domination. And, analogously in the legal sphere, recent economic approaches have viewed the main function of law as that of facilitating (and possibly supplementing) the process of market exchange in its triumphant progress toward economic 'efficiency'. The alternative view which has some claim to our attention is that law is a system of coercion imposed on the weaker by the stronger party, or at least that it represents a balance of pressures among parties each contending to achieve or resist such domination.

3.   The evolutionary approach suggests that this darker picture is the true one. As a generalization holding over the entire realm of living forms, *reproductive competition* is the first imperative of Nature. Furthermore, in the last analysis no holds are barred — all means of struggle will be employed in this competition, so long as one contender or another finds it advantageous to do so.

4.   Nevertheless, it is true that in a multitude of ways and on all levels of life organisms have found it profitable to come together in patterns of cooperative association. But such cooperation is always secondary and contingent, in at least two respects: (1) in-group cooperation is

only a means for more effectively and ruthlessly competing against outsiders, and (2) even within the group there will not be perfect parallelism of interests, hence cooperation must generally be supported by sanctions.

5.   From this point of view, the ultimate test of any group's constitutive law is whether it makes the group a more effective collective competitor. A very major concern of law must always be to prevent internal subversion of the collective effort by members pursuing their private interests.

6.   *Efficiency*, on this interpretation, is meaningful only as a measure of group strength or advantage relative to competing groups in the struggle for life and resources. Forming a cartel may be an efficient course of action for a group of firms, even if the net balance is adverse when the interests of consumers are also counted in. Outcomes efficient for our nation may be inimical to the well-being of other peoples; gains for the entire human species may be achieved at the expense of other forms of life. A totally universalistic measure of efficiency is pointless; we must draw the line somewhere, at the boundary of 'us' versus 'them'.

7.   Whether in fact cooperative or helping behaviour will be elicited from individuals with mixed motivations depends ultimately upon the ecological situation (the pay-offs from hostile versus friendly interactions). This paper provided a systematic analysis for the simplest case: random dyadic encounters in a homogeneous population, individuals having only a binary choice between a more and a less cooperative strategy. Three qualitatively different sets of environmental circumstances (pay-off matrices) each led to a characteristic result: (a) In the Tender Trap class of interaction, the gain from choosing either strategy *increases* with the proportion of the population adopting it. The more cooperative (more mutually advantageous) strategy will then be unanimously adopted if the proportion following it comes to exceed a critical mass in the population; otherwise, the result goes the other way. (b) In the Chicken or Hawk–Dove class of interaction, the gain from either strategy *decreases* with the proportion adopting it. The characteristic result is then a mixed equilibrium, with the more and the less cooperative option each being pursued a given fraction of the time (or by a given percentage of the population). In both Tender Trap and Hawk–Dove, typically the potential efficiency gain from cooperation is only partially realized. (c) In the Prisoners' Dilemma class of interaction the selfish strategy *always* dominates, and cooperation will not be viable at all despite the potential mutual gain.

8.   In extending the analysis beyond this very simple case, innumerable analytical variations become possible. Among the cases of greatest

interest for our purposes are the following: (i) Generalization of the Hawk–Dove game to allow a Bourgeois strategy — defence of one's own established control over resources, while deferring to the corresponding priority of others — can lead to an equilibrium characterized by a high degree of cooperation. This suggests how a sense of *property*, one of the possible preconditions supporting a system of law, might have evolved. (ii) With regard to the Prisoners' Dilemma, biologists have been much concerned with evolutionary solutions that turn upon ability to direct helping acts preferentially toward fellow cooperators. Aiding only one's relatives (kin selection) or only members of one's own propinquity group (group selection) may, under certain conditions, provide partial ways out of the trap — that is, some but typically not all of the efficiency gains can be thus achieved. This analysis again is suggestive of major features of human cooperative association, to wit, that observed helping largely takes place within kinship or other closely knit groups. (iii) If an asymmetrical environmental situation permits one player to commit himself to a threat–promise strategy relative to the other, full cooperation can in principle be induced even in the Prisoners' Dilemma context. Curiously, it does not necessarily follow that the individual in the superordinate hierarchical role reaps more gain than the other from the interaction. Nevertheless, in practice the circumstances making an asymmetrical strategy choice possible are likely to coincide with an inequality of power and thus of realized gain. This analytical model can therefore be regarded as patterning the Sophist view of law as the imposed will of the stronger. (iv) In a more egalitarian environmental context, coalitional power of the majority can serve a function analogous to that of the dominant individual in an unequal situation. Cooperative behaviour is enforced by moralistic aggression on the part of third parties against malefactors. This interaction mode therefore provides the elementary pattern for a democratic structure of law.

9.   To the extent that these systems of eliciting cooperation or punishing subversion require organisms to act in ways opposed to their immediate interests (for example, when a superordinate player has to carry out a threat or deliver on a promise), a social ethic in the form of ingrained emotional drives may provide the overriding motivation. Rage on the part of the victim and/or indignation on the part of third parties, for example, each irrational in terms of the direct interest of the party affected, may serve to raise the costs of cheating or other group-subversive activities. Or, equally 'irrational' love and gratitude may lead to enough unenforced reciprocation to make mutual helping viable. Different social ethics are required according to whether the structure is hierarchical or egalitarian. Among more advanced animals, and

humans in particular, typically each individual will have a mixture of ingrained hard-core cooperativeness (appropriate for the social context in which he is placed) as well as merely prudential cooperativeness based upon immediate considerations of cost and benefit.

10. Turning specifically to economics, the following are among the suggestive implications:

(a) The image of economic man has been much denounced, but the evolutionary approach suggests that self-interest is ultimately the prime motivator of human as of all life. This theme is, however, subject to several qualifications, among them that one's kin are in the genetic sense partly one's own self. Also, as just indicated, even economic man's behaviour is constrained by inbuilt emotions and tastes. While these no doubt contain accidental elements, they are not completely arbitrary. What tastes sweet to us is mainly what serves our own interest, and our 'irrational' or 'unselfish' drives have largely met the evolutionary test of enabling us the better to compete via group membership.

(b) 'Economic imperialism' — the use of economic analytical models to study all forms of social relations rather than only the market interactions of 'rational' decision-makers — is similarly entirely consonant with the evolutionary approach. All aspects of life are ultimately governed by scarcity of resources. But our use of the powerful tools of economic analysis must not lead us to unconsciously carry over harmonistic preconceptions, valid for the domain of mutually advantageous market exchanges, to the sphere of struggles for power and dominance. It is with that sphere that politics and law are mainly concerned.

(c) I find this thought somewhat disconcerting, but the evolutionary approach also suggests that, after all, the mercantilists were really not so wrong! Failing to appreciate the significance of the *mutual* advantage of exchange, they viewed trade essentially as an instrument in the international struggle for power. Mutual advantage is very nice, but trade still must be looked at with suspicion if it strengthens a potential enemy in war. This point is not without topical interest, for example when we consider the sale of industrial technology to the Soviet Union.

11. And now, turning to law:

(a) In the great debate between natural law and social contract philosophies — that is, between those who view association under law as fundamental and intrinsic in man as against those who regard it as merely a contingent and pragmatic option — the evolutionary approach suggests an intermediate position. Human social behaviour is enormously variable. That man is a social animal, often capable of great heroism and self-sacrifice, is true for some and perhaps true in part of all men. It is also true of other men, or perhaps the same men at other times, that they will help others only to the extent that they thereby serve themselves. And indeed the latter is the deeper truth, since ingrained social ethics are themselves viable only if ultimately of selfish advantage.

(b) The analysis here suggests that law, in the sense of coercive social control of group-subversive behaviour, has two elementary forms, each of which corresponds to an associated social structure. The first form is hierarchical, control being achieved by the superordinate player's commitment to a threat–promise strategy. The second is egalitarian, with control effected by third-party moralistic aggression. Of course, these elements are interwoven in highly complex ways in any actual society. The circumstances making one or other form more effective in the competition among groups remain to be explored.

(c) As to the historical evolution of law itself, such alleged trends as the movement from status to contract or the shift from strict liability to moral fault do not seem valid except over limited segments of human history. The only really clear unidirectional trends are the fairly obvious developments associated with the greatly increased scale of human societies over historical time. The law necessarily became more impersonal, systematic, predictable and professonalized as bands and tribes gradually gave way to huge industrial nations.

(d) The adversarial processes of law themselves engender a certain tendency toward efficient solutions, since supporters of the more productive legal rule can bid higher in the struggle to establish precedents. But too much ought not be claimed. For one thing, the struggle itself is likely to lead to a wasteful arms race as each side attempts to mobilize its strength. Even more fundamental is the question of *whose* efficiency is being achieved: is it really meaningful to balance off the loss of some parties against the gains to others? Are these redistributions only internal to that group whose competitive viability is of valid concern for the contending parties?

12. What might be called the Smith–Coase message tells us that, under a system of perfectly effective law, there will be a continuing tendency to seek out and achieve all mutually advantageous exchanges. How generalizable is this message to transactions in a world of imperfect law, or subject to no law at all? The harmonistic or Panglossian argument, which economists are perhaps predisposed to favour, is that wherever mutual advantage is present we can expect continual progress toward its achievement. Refuting that contention has been the main concern of this paper. At every point in time, each decision-making agent will be weighing the relative attractiveness of cooperation and conflict strategies — of seeking *mutual* advantage on the one hand, or

on the other hand *unilateral* advantage even at the expense of others. And indeed, the latter is the more fundamental evolutionary force; ultimately, cooperative association is only a means for more effectively competing *against* others in the struggle for reproductive survival.

NOTES

1. Professionals in both fields, most notably the double-threat economist-legist Posner [see especially (49)], have contributed to these developments.
2. See also Calabresi (8).
3. Also known as the 'Kaldor criterion' (Kaldor (33)).
4. As is well known, reading Malthus's *Essay on Population* played a key role in the shaping of Darwin's thought.
5. As emphasized, for example, by Alexander (1), ch. 4.
6. This is somewhat of an oversimplification. For one thing, descendants of other cocks would provide less-inbred mates for one's own descendants.
7. There are also many fascinating examples of across-species cooperation, but these are only means whereby individual members of both species compete more effectively against their own conspecifics.
8. My analysis is in the spirit of Schelling (56, 57) and Luce and Raiffa (39), ch. 5.
9. In these matrices one player chooses a row strategy, the other a column. The first number in each cell is the income return to row-player, the second the return to column-player.
10. Maynard Smith (42); the biologists call this solution an 'evolutionarily stable strategy' or ESS. For economic interpretations of the ESS concept, see Hirshleifer and Riley (32), Cornell and Roll (13), Schotter (58).
11. Since there is only a single 'income' commodity, no reversal paradox can arise.
12. If the proportion were exactly $p = 2/7$ the two strategies would yield equal returns, so that neither would tend to drive out the other. But this is an unstable situation; any small accidental shift of p in one direction or the other would be self-reinforcing.
13. Since the zero point is arbitrary, the negativity of average achieved returns need cause no concern.
14. Cornell and Roll (13) suggest a number of examples in economic affairs, including seniority ladders and stock market analysis.
15. Maynard Smith (42) cites several instances: for example, male hamadryas baboons recognize conventional prior 'ownership' of females by other males. For a more general discussion of the emergence of property rights among animals, see Fredlund (20).
16. A possible explanation is that 'last come first served' conflicts with the adaptive incentive to search diligently for resources. A large fraction of the time, diligent searchers can expect to find and consume the prize before any competitors even put in an appearance. (For a different explanation see Cornell and Roll (13).)
17. For an economic discussion of uncorrelated versus correlated asymmetries, see Cornell and Roll (13).

18. Recall the argument in the section above about the relativity of the efficiency criterion with regard to the boundaries of the group.
19. The analysis that follows derives in part from Hirshleifer and Riley (32).
20. An important complication arises, however, where the populations are taken as of finite rather than of infinite size (Riley (52)). Once only a single member of the population is following a given strategy, it can no longer encounter any other playing the same strategy. For small populations (by no means uncommon in Nature, or in human affairs) this effect can be significant. In Figure 9.1, the cross-over cases I and II are affected. What can happen, essentially, is that the cross-over point can come so close to either end of the p scale that one strategy *is* driven out even though the infinite-population model calls for a mixed solution (line II) or for a possible Tender Trap EE at that strategy (line I).
21. Recall that the interesting case is where x + y > 2. In such a situation the mixed solution is more 'efficient' (in the PPP sense) than either of the diagonal outcomes, but still falls short of what could be achieved by complementary pairing.
22. For example, a large fraction of the problems analysed in Schelling's fascinating *Micromotives and Macrobehavior* (57) can be fitted under these headings.
23. Schelling (57), ch. 7, is perhaps misleading on this score. He shows that with a sufficient proportion p of Helpers in the population there may be an absolute expected gain to playing Helper — that is, for large p it may be that p $(-c+b)$ + $(1-p)$ c = $-c$ + pb>0. Nevertheless, the absolute gain from playing Nonhelper is even greater (it is in fact pb), and so the Helper strategy remains nonviable in the evolutionary sense.
24. The saliency of this threat in actual modern business practice has been discussed by Macaulay (40).
25. This paradox can be overcome if there is no 'last play'; for example, if the game is to be played an infinite number of times. Or, more realistically, if at each play there is a certain constant probability of the game continuing further. See Luce and Raiffa (39), p. 102, and Telser (62).
26. See Tullock (68), and the countering arguments of Frech (19), Hirshleifer (30), and Samuelson (55).
27. In the previous discussion, the presence of Retaliators provided in effect a degree of discrimination in the population as a whole.
28. I have used Charnov's simplest 'sexual haploid' model.
29. To reconcile these expected returns in Eqs. (8) and (9) with condition (4), note that in (4) one helping act was supposed to occur per time period. To renormalize α and β in this way, divide both α and β by the bracketed expression at the right of Eq. (8). From Eq. (7), this expression equals pv_H/m. The results are the 'fitnesses' compared in inequality (4):

$$\alpha \frac{m}{pv_H} = W_H = -c + bm$$

$$\beta \frac{m}{pv_H} = W_N = b\frac{p\bar{v}_N}{bv_H + (1-p)\bar{v}_N} = b\frac{p(1-m)}{1-p}$$

30. If m is constant, the left-hand side in Eq. (4) is a constant. But the right-

hand side will be an increasing function of p. So W_H α − β W_H is a *decreasing* function of p, from which α − β must behave similarly — leading to a picture like that of line II in Figure 1. (But in this case α − β will be a negatively sloped curve rather than a line.)

31. In terms of the underlying recognition coefficients, if $m = \dfrac{1+p}{2}$ then it follows from Eq. (6) that $\dfrac{1+p}{p} = \dfrac{v_H}{v_N}$. So the ratio v_H/v_N falls as p rises, but never goes below 2.

32. See Williams (71), Maynard Smith (41). The major instance of group selection commonly cited is the tendency toward reduced virulence of disease germs (Barash (5), ch. 4). But even this is not a pure group-selection case, as there is a kin-selection element involved (Alexander and Borgia (2)).

33. The standard biological literature on this subject (see, for example, E. O. Wilson (73), ch. 5; Barash (5), ch.4) places undue emphasis upon differential *group extinction* as the critical factor in group selection. This is somewhat misleading. Differential rates of group extinction play an important role, but are by no means a sufficient statistic for determining the proportions of H and N genes in the next generation; it is also necessary to take account of differential H and N survival *within* groups, both those going extinct and those not doing so. In the biological literature, the model here is generally consistent with that of D. S. Wilson (72), and (I believe) with the views of Hamilton (27).

34. More complicated models, involving groups larger than two, or partial in-group mating rather than simple swarming, will of course have more complex stability conditions. But the simple model here lays bare the key issues.

35. 'God is on the side of the bigger battalions.' — Voltaire.

36. This is not entirely true, of course. For one thing, at the genetic level, a 'gene for having male offspring' can be regarded as being in competition with a 'gene for having female offspring'. But given that the population is sexually divided, intrasex competition is much more intense than intersex competition.

37. For a fuller discussion, see Schelling (56), chs. 2, 5.

38. In these terms, R_3 in Matrix 10 represents a promise rather than a threat. (Row promises not to play his more advantageous R_2 *if* Column plays C_1.)

39. This situation is analysed in detail in Thompson and Faith (63, 64).

40. The difficulty of guaranteeing to behave in a way that is ex post irrational is exemplified by the 'Mutual Assured Destruction' (MAD) problem in nuclear deterrent strategy. The underlying theory is that a potential attacker will be deterred if the target nation can retain enough strength to impose sufficient retaliatory damage. Yet, having suffered the attack, the victim's 'rational' incentive to retaliate is not very strong. One's own losses are no longer remediable, and it seems pointless to engage in mass murder of the other population. A semi-whimsical solution for the problem is the 'Doomsday Machine', which would make retaliation automatic rather than subject to human control or recall.

41. Becker (7). Becker's discussion is in the context of the family, so there is some danger of confounding this route to cooperation with mutual aid due

to relatedness (kin selection). The mechanisms are entirely separate, and relatedness plays no role in the present analysis.

42. The necessity for this 'hierarchical' asymmetry is emphasized in Hirshleifer (29).

43. For further discussion of pragmatic versus hard-core cooperation, see E. O. Wilson(74).

44. See, for example, Kurz (35), Landes and Posner (36).

45. This classification represents only one of the dimensions along which distinctions might be made. One might distinguish also strategies of competing by high survival versus high fertility, by adventurous versus risk-avoiding behaviour, by specializing versus generalizing in use of resources, by adaptation to mountain or desert or polar conditions, etc. Another strategic dimension which is very crucial for our purposes is competition via isolated versus group struggle.

46. Cannibalism occurs widely in Nature, but is still far less common than eating other species. Conceivably, this is the result of group selection.

47. The predator–prey interaction has a cooperative aspect, though a one-sided one. A rational predator would be concerned to promote the survival of its prey species, but generally speaking the prey would do better without the predator.

48. Males are essentially always in severer competition for females than females for males. The female's more costly investment in facilities for reproduction is the scarce resource sought after by males. (On the other hand, females may compete for higher quality males, especially where monogamy governs.)

49. In Darwin's words, males strive 'to conquer other males in battle' or, alternatively, 'to charm the females'.

50. Culturally, humans learn that a degree of willingness to fight for resources does pay off in this world. Whether this message has become *genetically* implanted in the human species may be left an open question for the moment. As to sexual competition, male superiority in size and strength suggests that the principle of male combat may have governed even in human evolution. (On sexual competition as a cause of possible masculine intellectual as well as physical superiority, see *The Descent of Man*, ch. 19.)

51. See Krueger (34), Tullock (67), Posner (48). The term 'rent-seeking' is another unfortunate terminological choice. All economic agents are seeking 'rents' — that is, returns to resources under their control. The loss of efficiency is not due to *rent-seeking*, but to effort expended in *resource-taking*.

52. At least in the short run, and if the thief is regarded as a member of the group within which efficiency is calculated.

53. For the fishery case, see Gordon (23). On the possibility of 'excessive' searching for ideas, see Cheung (10) and Hirshleifer (28).

54. Again, only if both gainers and losers are considered part of the group within which efficiency is calculated. From the point of view of the gainers alone, the losers may merely constitute a resource field — like a prey species.

55. For an analogous theory of advertising, see Nelson (46, 47).

56. For citations and discussion, see Friedman (21); Moore (44).

57. Ferdinand Tonnies, cited in Friedman (21), p. 282.

58. For a general discussion, see Moore (44), especially ch. 3.
59. That law is whatever serves the interest of the Soviet state is (I believe) openly professed as the main principle of Soviet justice.
60. For an analysis of dominance patterns among humans and other primate species, see Willhoite (69).
61. The origin of exogamy is subject to some question. Close inbreeding leads to expression of more genetic defects, but on the other hand a more closely related group will tend to be more cooperative and thus more effective. It has been suggested that exogamy is of 'political' advantage in enabling groups to form alliances with others.
62. See Demsetz (16). For a somewhat analogous treatment of the enclosure movement in England, see Dahlman (14).
63. I shall cite only the major seminal work of Downs (17).
64. Rubin (54), and see also Gould (24), Priest (50).
65. Note that the 'reversal paradox' problem is being ignored.
66. Perhaps this is the prophetic meaning of the otherwise mysterious riddle of Samson: 'Out of the eater came forth meat, and out of the strong came forth sweetness' (Judges xiv : 14).
67. Rubin (54). Similarly motivated attempts to overturn even efficient precedents will also probably take place. In consequence, we would expect to observe both the more and less efficient precedents, each governing with a certain fractional probability or a corresponding fraction of the time — see Cooter and Kornhauser (12). However, the more efficient rule will tend to prevail more frequently, increasingly so the larger the efficiency improvement it represents.
68. As already suggested by Rubin (54) and Priest (50).
69. As emphasized by Cooter and Kornhauser (12).
70. A somewhat similar argument is put forward by Rothbard (53), though I am sure he would reject my suggestion that military conscription might (even hypothetically) be said to be efficient.

BIBLIOGRAPHY

1. Alexander, Richard D. (1979) *Darwinism and Human Affairs*, Seattle, University of Washington Press.
2. ——, and Borgia, G. (1978) 'Group Selection, Altruism, and the Levels of Organization of Life', *Annual Review of Ecology and Systematics*, Vol. 9: 449–75.
3. Ardrey, Robert (1966) *The Territorial Imperative*, New York, Atheneum.
4. Aubert, Vilhelm (1963) 'Researches in the Sociology of Law', *American Behavioral Scientist*, Vol. 7: 16–21.
5. Barash, David P. (1977) *Sociobiology and Behavior*, New York, Elsevier.
6. Becker Gary (November/December 1971) 'A Theory of Social Interactions', *Journal of Political Economy*, Vol. 82 (6): 1063–93.
7. ——, (September 1976) 'Altruism, Egoism, and Genetic Fitness: Economics and Sociobiology', *Journal of Economic Literature*, Vol. 14: 817–28.
8. Calabresi, Guido (1961) 'Some Thoughts on Risk Distribution and the Law of Torts', *Yale Law Journal*. Vol. 70: 499.
9. Charnov, Eric L. (1977) 'An Elementary Treatment of the Genetical Theory

of Kin-selection', *Journal of Theoretical Biology*, Vol. 66: 541–51.
10. Cheung, Steven N. S. (1979) 'The Right to Invent and the Right to an Invention', University of Washington, Institute of Economic Research Report No. 79–13.
11. Coarse, Ronald H. (October 1960) 'The Problem of Social Cost', *Journal of Law and Economics*, Vol. 3: 1–45.
12. Cooter, Robert and Kornhauser, Lewis (1980) 'Can Litigation Improve the Law without the Help of Judges?', *Journal of Legal Studies*, Vol. 9: 139–63.
13. Cornell, Bradford and Roll, Richard (Spring 1981) 'Strategies for Pairwise Competitions in Markets and Organizations', *Bell Journal of Economics*, Vol. 12: 201–13.
14. Dahlman, Carl J. H. (1976) 'The Economics of Scattered Strips, Open Fields, and Enclosures', Ph.D. thesis, University of California, Los Angeles.
15. Dawkins, Richard (1976) *The Selfish Gene*, New York, Oxford University Press.
16. Demsetz, Harold (May 1967) 'Toward a Theory of Property Rights', *American Economic Review*, Vol. 57 (2): 347–60.
17. Downs, Anthony (1957) *An Economic Theory of Democracy*, New York, Harper.
18. Fisher, Ronald A. (1958) *The Genetical Theory of Natural Selection*, New York, Dover Publications (original publication 1929).
19. Frech, H. E. III. (1978) 'Altruism, Malice and Public Goods: Does Altruism Pay?' *Journal of Social and Biological Structures*, Vol. 1: 181–6.
20. Fredlund, Melvin C. (June 1976) 'Wolves, Chimps and Demsetz', *Economic Inquiry*, Vol. 14: 279–91.
21. Friedman, Lawrence (1975) *The Legal System*, New York, Russell Sage Foundation.
22. Goodman, John C. (1978) 'An Economic Theory of the Evolution of the Common Law', *Journal of Legal Studies*, Vol. 7: 393–406.
23. Gordon, H. S. (April 1954) 'The Economic Theory of a Common Property Resource: The Fishery', *Journal of Political Economy*, Vol. 62: 124–42.
24. Gould, John P. (1973) 'The Economics of Legal Conflicts', *Journal of Legal Studies*, Vol. 2: 279–301.
25. Hamilton, W. D. (1964) 'The Genetical Evolution of Social Behavior, I', *Journal of Theoretical Biology*, Vol. 7: 1–17.
26. ——. (1971) 'Geometry for the Selfish Herd', *Journal of Theoretical Biology*, Vol. 31: 295–313.
27. ——. (1975) 'Innate Social Aptitudes of Man: An Approach from Evolutionary Genetics', in R. Fox (ed.), *Biosocial Anthropology*, New York, Wiley.
28. Hirshleifer, J. (September 1971) 'The Private and Social Value of Information and the Reward to Inventive Activity', *American Economic Review*, Vol. 61: 561–75.
29. ——. (June 1977) 'Shakespeare vs. Becker on Altruism: The Importance of Having the Last Word', *Journal of Economic Literature*, Vol. 15: 500–2.
30. ——. (October 1978) 'Natural Economy versus Political Economy', *Journal of Social and Biological Structures*, Vol. 1: 319–38.
31. ——. (1980) 'Privacy Its Origin, Function, and Future', *Journal of Legal*

Studies, Vol. 9: 649–65.

32. —— and Riley, J. (August 1978) 'Elements of the Theory of Auctions and Contests', UCLA Department of Economics, Working Paper No. 118B.

33. Kaldor, Nicholas (1939) 'Welfare Propositions in Economics and Interpersonal Comparisons of Utility', *Economic Journal*, Vol. 49: 549–52.

34. Krueger, Anne O. (June 1974) 'The Political Economy of the Rent-seeking Society', *American Economic Review*, Vol. 64: 291–304.

35. Kurz, Mordecai (1977) 'Altruistic Equilibrium', in Bela Balassa and Richard Nelson (eds), *Economic Progress, Private Values, and Policy*, Amsterdam, North-Holland Publishing.

36. Landes, William M. and Posner, Richard A. (May 1978) 'Altruism in Law and Economics', *American Economic Review*, Vol. 68: 417–22.

37. Lorenz, Konrad (1966) *On Aggression*, New York, Harcourt, Brace, & World (original German publication 1963).

38. Lotka, Alfred J. (1956) *Elements of Mathematical Biology*, New York, Dover Publications.

39. Luce, R. Duncan and Raiffa, Howard (1957) *Games and Decisions*, New York, John Wiley.

40. Macaulay, Stewart (February 1963) 'Non-contractual Relations in Business', *American Sociological Review*, Vol. 28: 55–67.

41. Maynard Smith, John (14 March 1964) 'Group Selection and Kin Selection', *Nature*, Vol. 201: 1145–47.

42. —— (January–February 1976) 'Evolution and the Theory of Games', *American Scientist*, Vol. 64: 41–5.

43. —— (September 1978) 'The Evolution of Behavior', *Scientific American*, Vol. 239: 176–92.

44. Moore, Sally Falk (1978) *Law as Process: An Anthropological Approach*, London, Routledge & Kegan Paul.

45. Nash, J. F. (1951) 'Non-cooperative Games', *Annals of Mathematics*, Vol. 54: 286–95.

46. Nelson, Phillip (March–April 1970) 'Information and Consumer Behavior', *Journal of Political Economy*, Vol. 78 (2): 311–30.

47. —— (July–August 1974) 'Advertising as Information', *Journal of Political Economy*, Vol. 82 (4): 729–55.

48. Posner, Richard A. (August 1975) 'The Social Costs of Monopoly and Regulation', *Journal of Political Economy*, Vol. 83 (4): 807–29.

49. —— (1977) *Economic Analysis of Law*, 2nd edn, Boston, Little, Brown.

50. Priest, George L. (1977) 'The Common Law Process and the Selection of Efficient Rules', *Journal of Legal Studies*, Vol. 6: 65–83.

51. Riley, John G. (April 1975) 'Competitive Signalling', *Journal of Economic Theory*, Vol. 10: 174–87.

52. —— (1979) 'Evolutionary Equilibrium Strategies', *Journal of Theoretical Biology*, Vol. 76: 109–25.

53. Rothbard, Murray N. (1979) 'Comment: The Myth of Efficiency', in Mario J. Rizzo, (ed.), *Time, Uncertainty and Disequilibrium*, Lexington, Mass., D. C. Heath.

54. Rubin, Paul H. (1977) 'Why Is the Common Law Efficient?' *Journal of Legal Studies*, Vol. 6: 51–63.

55. Samuelson, Paul A. (1980) 'Complete Genetic Models for Altruism, Kin Selection, and Like-gene Selection', mimeo.

56. Schelling, Thomas C. (1960) *The Strategy of Conflict*, London, Oxford

University Press.
57. ——. (1978) *Micromotives and Macrobehavior*, New York, W. W. Norton.
58. Schotter, Andrew (February 1979) 'Evolutionarily Stable Market Equilibria', New York University, Department of Economics.
59. Scitovsky, Tibor (1941) 'A Note on Welfare Propositions in Economics', *Review of Economic Studies*, Vol. 9: 77–89.
60. Smith, Adam (1937) *The Wealth of Nations*, New York, Random House (original publication 1776).
61. Spence, A. Michael (1974) *Market Signalling: Informational Transfer in Hiring and Related Processes*, Cambridge, Mass., Harvard University Press.
62. Telser, L. G. (January 1980) 'A Theory of Self-enforcing Agreements', *Journal of Business*, Vol. 53: 27–45.
63. Thompson, Earl A. and Faith, Roger L. (1980) 'Social Interaction under Truly Perfect Information', *Journal of Mathematical Sociology*, Vol. 7: 181–97.
64. ——. (June 1981) 'A Pure Theory of Strategic Behavior and Social Institutions', *American Economic Review*, Vol. 71: 366–80.
65. Tinbergen, N. (21 June 1968) 'On War and Peace in Animals and Men', *Science*, Vol. 160: 1411–18.
66. Trivers, Robert L. (March 1971) 'The Evolution of Reciprocal Altruism', *Quarterly Review of Biology*, Vol. 46: 35–58.
67. Tullock, Gordon (June 1967) 'The Welfare Costs of Tariffs, Monopolies, and Theft', *Western Economic Journal*, Vol. 5: 224–33.
68. ——. (January 1978) 'Altruism, Malice, and Public Goods', *Journal of Social and Biological Structures*, Vol. 1: 3–10.
69. Wilhoite, Fred H., Jr. (December 1976) 'Primates and Political Authority: A Bio-behavioral Perspective', *American Political Science Review*, Vol. 70: 1110–26.
70. ——. (1979) 'Rank and Reciprocity: Speculations in Human Emotions and Political Life', mimeo.
71. Williams, George C. (1966) *Adaptation and Natural Selection*, Princeton, N.J., Princeton University Press.
72. Wilson, David S. (January 1975) 'A Theory of Group Selection', *Proceedings of the National Academy of Sciences*, Vol. 72: 143–6.
73. Wilson, Edward O. (1975) *Sociobiology*, Cambridge, Mass., Belknap Press.
74. ——. (Fall 1977) 'Biology and the Social Sciences', *Daedalus*, Vol. 106 (4): 127–40.
75. Zahavi, A. (1975) 'Mate Selection — A Selection for a Handicap', *Journal of Theoretical Biology*, Vol. 53: 205–15.

10   The Economic Approach to Conflict*

Background of this Chapter

This paper was originally one of the contributions at a colloquium in June 1984 that was organized under a rather unpoetic heading: 'The Economic Approach Applied Outside the Traditional Areas of Economics'. The published volume emerging from the conference, I am glad to say, carries the more forceful title *Economic Imperialism*.

In line with the theme of several of the preceding papers, the emphasis here is upon conflict as a strategy or way of doing business. Where such a strategy is advantageous, we must expect some people to adopt it, so that even persons with very cooperative predispositions must be prepared to encounter other parties playing a tougher game. The three main topics addressed are: (i) *The causes of conflict* — what are the respective roles of divergent material interests, of ingrained or learned malevolence or hatred, and of misperceptions? (ii) *The conduct of conflict* — what are efficient strategies in situations with differing patterns of partially congruent, partially opposed interests (e.g. Prisoners' Dilemma and Battle of the Sexes) and what is the nature of the equilibrium achieved? (iii) *The consequences of conflict* — how does the tendency towards interior solutions in some cases, towards corner solutions in other cases, help explain real-world phenomena like the size and shape of nations?

In racing for a prize you can better your chances by running faster yourself, or by making your opponents run slower. More generally

---

* Originally published in Gerard Radnitzky and Peter Bernholz (eds), *Economic Imperialism: The Economic Method Applied Outside the Field of Economics* (New York: Paragon House, 1986). Reproduced by permission of Paragon House.

there are two main classes of strategies in life's contests: improving your own performance, or hindering your competitors'. When one or more competitors adopt hindrance strategies, the result is *conflict*. The term conflict does not necessarily imply actual violence — for example, we speak of industrial conflicts (strikes) and legal conflicts (lawsuits). But my discussion will mainly be directed to the use of violence.

A rational decision-maker, the economist presumes, will engage in conflict whenever doing so represents the most advantageous way of competing in a world where prizes are scarce. My primary concern will be to show that economic analysis — i.e. models of rational choice on the decision-making level, and of equilibrium on the level of social interaction — can do much for the study of conflict. But it is also true, and this is my secondary theme, that the study of conflict can do much for economics. Attending to the darker aspects of how humans might and do compete is absolutely essential even for a proper understanding of the relatively benign nature of market competition.

Returning to my primary theme, I want to show how the economic approach to conflict sheds light upon questions such as:

What circumstances lead the parties to engage in conflict, i.e. to 'agree to disagree'?

In conflict interactions, when do we observe an interior or balanced solution, and when a tendency toward corner outcomes — total victory for the one side, unrelieved defeat for the other?

Is conflict always or largely a mistake on the part of one side or the other, so that better information can be relied upon to promote peaceful settlement?

In this brief presentation I cannot actually answer all these questions, or even resolve any of them very adequately. I want only to show how the economic approach may permit us to effectively address them. The sequence of topics that I will follow is indicated in Table 10.1.

ELEMENTARY STATICS OF CONFLICT AND SETTLEMENT[1]

Let me plunge right in with some extremely simple pictures designed to illustrate the interacting decision problems of two individuals as a function of their (1) opportunities, (2) preferences, and (3) perceptions.

Figure 10.1 illustrates alternative 'settlement opportunity sets' QQ, drawn on axes representing consumption incomes c_B and c_R for Blue and Red, respectively. (Note: These are the *non-conflictual* opportunities — what the parties might achieve in the absence of

Table 10.1 Sequence of Topics

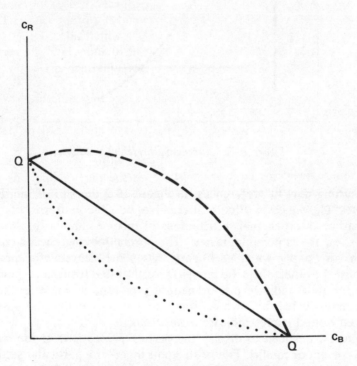

Figure 10.1 Alternative opportunity sets

fighting.) Three possible shapes for QQ are illustrated: positive complementarity (dashed curve), neutral complementarity, i.e. the constant-sum case (solid 135° line), and negative complementarity (dotted curve).

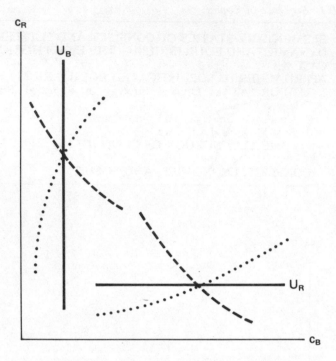

Figure 10.2   Alternative preference patterns

Turning now to preferences, in Figure 10.2 the trio of indifference curves U_B suggests Blue's alternative possible patterns of 'tastes' regarding interpersonal distributions of income. Similarly, the curves U_R show Red's possible 'tastes'. The normal-looking dashed curves in each case apply when each party has some degree of *benevolence* toward the other; the solid curves (a vertical line for Blue, a horizontal line for Red) indicate merely neutral preferences, where each of the two simply values his own consumption income; finally, the positively-sloped dotted curves indicate *malevolence*.

Finally, we need to display the parties' *perceptions* of the outcome in the event of conflict. Figure 10.3 puts together a particular settlement opportunity set QQ (complementary in this case), indifference curves for the two parties (both pictured as displaying a degree of benevolence), and two 'conflict perception points' designated P_B and P_R, respectively. Then the shaded area is the 'potential settlement region' (PSR), the set of possible income combinations representing improvements over what each perceives as attainable by conflict.

Under the plausible hypothesis that the larger the PSR the greater

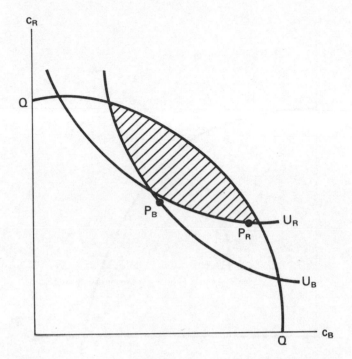

Figure 10.3   Mutual benevolence with pessimistic perceptions

the likelihood of peaceful settlement, it will be evident that this likelihood is increased by: (1) greater complementarity of the settlement opportunity set QQ, (2) greater benevolence on the part of both parties, and (3) less 'optimistic' perceptions of the likely outcome of conflict.

Several other possible combinations are shown in the diagrams. Figure 10.4 illustrates how, in a situation with complementary opportunities and agreed conflict perceptions (i.e. P_B and P_R coincide), malevolent preferences compress the size of the PSR. Figure 10.5 illustrates how anti-complementary opportunities (concave curvature of QQ) also tend to constrict the shaded PSR region, in a situation of neutral preferences together with agreed perceptions. As for the effect of differential perceptions, Figure 10.6 illustrates how in the situation of the previous diagram, a shift of P_B to a new position P'_B (P_R remaining unchanged) has enlarged the PSR by the dotted area — Blue has become more *pessimistic* about the outcome of conflict. On the other hand, as illustrated in Figure 10.7, when each party is optimistic about the

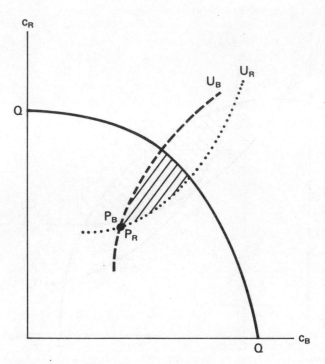

Figure 10.4   Mutual malevolence with agreed perceptions

outcome it may well be that the PSR entirely disappears, suggesting that conflict has become inevitable.

The effect of complementarity on the international level has recently been documented by Polachek (1980). His data indicate that those country-pairs with the most to gain from trade tend to engage in the least conflict.[2] And of course there are many other instances on the human and animal levels. For example, some small cleaner fish operate actually inside the jaws of their bigger fish clients; the latter forgo a quick and easy meal in return for the benefits of trade in the form of grooming services.

As for interpersonal preferences, individuals and nations with close ties of culture and kinship that lead to mutually benevolent preferences very likely do less frequently engage in conflict — but again, only in an 'other things equal' sense. In particular, since brothers are often close competitors for resources, fratricidal conflict is not uncommon despite the closeness of kinship ties.[3]

As an instance displaying the role of changing perceptions and beliefs, some authors (e.g. Blainey (1973) on war, Ashenfelter and

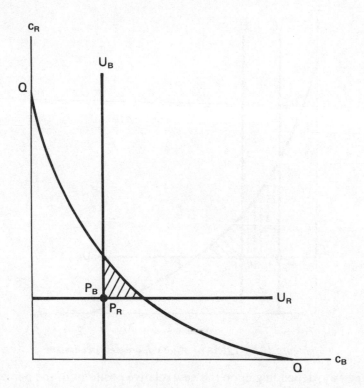

Figure 10.5 Anti-complementary opportunities with agreed perceptions and neutral preferences

Johnson (1969) on strikes and lockouts) make the important point that conflict is in large part *an educational process*. Struggle tends to occur when one or both parties is overoptimistic (see Figure 10.7). The school of actual combat teaches the parties to readjust their conflict perception points to more realistic levels. Eventually, a potential settlement region PSR emerges (or an existing region grows larger) so that conflict tends to end by mutual consent.

Two qualifications must be kept in mind, however. First, as Wittman (1979) emphasizes, while the results of continuing struggle may lead the losing party to more realistic (pessimistic) perceptions, the winning party is likely to revise his perceptions upward. The loser becomes more willing to settle but the winner tends to increase his demands — so that the conflict may well continue.[4] Second, the damage due to struggle may impoverish both parties and impair the settlement opportunities as well. The effect on prospects for settlement could go

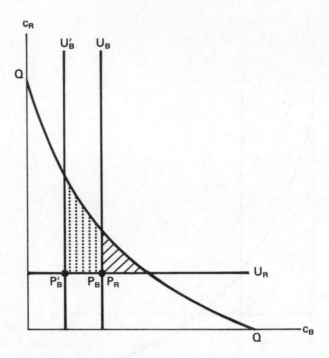

Figure 10.6   Effect of Blue's Increased pessimism

either way, depending upon the new relative positions of the perception points P_B and P_R and the revised QQ curve.

There is more to be said about elementary statics, for example, introducing *asymmetries* in the parties' preference functions (one may be benevolent, the other malevolent), or in the shape of the settlement opportunity set (Blue's non-conflictual activities may confer benefits on Red, while Red's impose costs on Blue). But I must set this topic aside in order to move on. How small a slice of our topic has been even touched on so far is suggested by Table 10.2, which indicates *some* of the directions in which the analysis needs to be extended.

In what follows, I shall only be able to address the first of these topics in any detail. Among other things, I shall be asking, granted that a mutually advantageous settlement opportunity exists, under what circumstances can conflict actually be avoided?

DYNAMICS AND EQUILIBRIUM (THE UNSOPHISTICATED CASE)[5]

Under the heading of elementary statics I indicated how preferences, opportunities and perceptions combine to influence individual decisions.

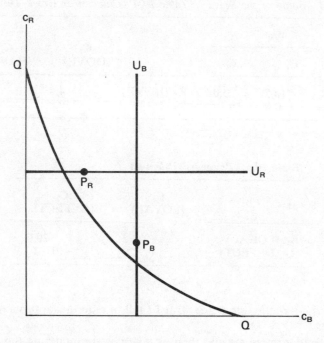

Figure 10.7   Mutual optimism eliminates potential settlement region

Table 10.2   Directions for fuller analysis

1. From statics to dynamics and equilibrium
2. From individuals to organizations
3. From 2-party to n-party interactions
4. From atemporal to intertemporal analysis
5. Allowing for risk and uncertainty
6. Conflict at varying levels — 'escalation'

But I did not progress very far towards showing how an *equilibrium* emerges when the parties' decisions interact. The nature of the equilibrium turns out to depend critically upon the detailed dynamics of the interaction — or, I shall sometimes say, upon the 'protocol' that specifies how and in what sequence the parties make their choices. These specifications are most clearly expressed in the language of game theory. This language is adopted at a cost, since game theory drastically compresses the separate categories of preferences, opportunities, and perceptions into a single numerical tabulation representing the net

Table 10.3		*Battle of the Sexes*
		She	
		C_1	C_2
He	R_1	*10,5	0,0
	R_2	0,0	*5,10

Table 10.4 *Chicken or Hawk–Dove*

	C_1 (DOVE)	C_2 (HAWK)
R_1 (DOVE)	4,4	*0,10
R_2 (HAWK)	*10,0	−24,−24

Table 10.5 *Prisoners' Dilemma*

	C_1 (LOYAL)	C_2 (DEFECT)
R_1 (LOCAL)	−2,−2	−20,0
R_2 (DEFECT)	0,−20	*−10,−10

payoffs to alternative strategies. But I shall pursue this approach for the moment.

The familiar game matrix, then, is taken as summarizing the players' decision environment. I shall begin with a comparative discussion of three famous elementary 2 × 2 games — Battle of the Sexes (BOS), Chicken, known also in the biological literature as Hawk–Dove (HD), and Prisoners' Dilemma (PD) (Tables 10.3, 10.4 and 10.5). These are non-zero-sum interactions; each represents a somewhat different combination of complementary versus anti-complementary elements. While the abstract game representation fails to distinguish between *conflict* as such versus other types of cooperation failures (for example, those associated with 'externalities'), I shall assume here that whenever efficiency is not achieved, the explanation is the adoption of a conflict strategy by one or both parties.

The most common solution concept for the non-zero-sum game is the 'Nash non-cooperative equilibrium' (NE) — sometimes called the 'equilibrium point'. The key idea is that there is no equilibrium so long as either player can gain an advantage by shifting his strategy. (The pure strategy NEs are marked with asterisks in Table 10.3, 10.4 and 10.5, the first two cases having also a mixed strategy NE not shown in the tables.) The NE equilibrium concept might or might not be objectionable, depending upon the assumptions as to the players' capacities or the dynamics of the interaction. I want to make these assumptions quite explicit.

To divide the difficulties I first consider equilibrium in 'unsophistica-ted' play. The players may perhaps lack the ability to reason *strateg-ically* — i.e. to conceptualize that 'if I do this, then he will do that, in which case I would respond by ...' More interestingly for the economist, unsophisticated play might be appropriate even for intelligent parties in certain environmental situations, especially those associated with large numbers of players (as in the standard pure competition model). Specifically, think of a 'war of all against all', in which members of a large population encounter one another randomly in one-time pairwise interactions. This leads to a concept I shall call *evolutionary equilibrium* (EE). If the average return to each strategy depends upon the population proportions adopting one or the other, a dynamic process is set up leading eventually to an equilibrium distribution of strategies in the population. This evolutionary equilibrium could be either pure (one strategy eventually drives out all the others) or else mixed. It can be shown that the evolutionary equilibria are a subset of the Nash equilibria; to wit, the EEs are the 'dynamically stable' NEs.

The dynamic process and the EEs for our three cases are pictured in Figure 10.8, in terms of the population proportion p characterized by the strategy in the first row and column of each table. Starting with Battle of the Sexes (BOS), as the directions of the arrows suggest there are two EEs — at the limiting proportions, p = 0 and p = 1. The mixed solution at p = 0.5 is an NE, but not being dynamically stable it is not an EE. The simplest interpretation is as follows. Assume that in each encounter the He and She roles are randomly assigned. In the initial population there are a fixed number of players having permanently chosen strategy #1, the remainder playing strategy #2. However, the population fractions will evolve in accordance with the relative success of the two strategies. It follows that if more than half the population are already committed to the first strategy, that strategy will be more successful and will multiply further, and similarly in the opposite case.[6] A possible application would be the struggle for language dominance in an initially bilingual population, there being a strong tendency towards a corner solution despite the *comparative* disadvantage suffered by native speakers of the losing language.

In contrast with the very mild 'battle' involved in Battle of the Sexes, the game of Chicken or Hawk–Dove (I shall usually employ the latter designation) can entail serious conflict. When one HAWK encounters another, a lot of feathers may fly. For the payoff numbers in Table 10.4, the diagram indicates a single EE at p = 0.8, a mixed solution. That is, the equilibrium strategy is to play DOVE 80 per cent of the time and HAWK the other 20 per cent. (Or else, there will be a mixed population, 80 per cent Doves and 20 per cent Hawks.)[7] The HD game

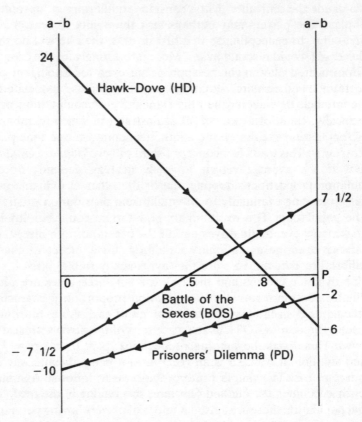

Figure 10.8   Evolutionary equilibria for 3 famous games

is sometimes thought to describe industrial or international conflict, the idea being that sometimes you have to play tough, for example, go out on strike, or else the other party will know you are a DOVE and take advantage of you. This interpretation, involving strategy in repeated games, does not really belong under our 'unsophisticated play' heading, although the analogy is suggestive. A more precise interpretation is as follows. If there are only a few tough people around, it pays to be aggressive — only rarely will you get into costly fights. But when most of the population are aggressive, the smart play is to be quiet and stay out of trouble.

As for the Prisoners' Dilemma, Figure 10.8 indicates that there is a unique EE, in which everyone adopts the DEFECT strategy.[8] The international arms race is often described as a Prisoners' Dilemma, though once again this is only an analogy; the arms race corresponds to a repeated-play rather than a one-time-only game. A more accurate interpretation would be the famous 'commons' problem, where it pays to impose costs upon one's neighbours whether or not they refrain from doing the same to you.

In the EE (and NE) solution to the Prisoners' Dilemma, the players are trapped in their third-best (i.e. next to worst) outcome, even though it seems that they should be able to achieve their jointly second-best outcome (which is on the settlement opportunity frontier) by mutually LOYAL play. What prevents their doing so is assumed *non-enforceability of agreements*. Similarly in Hawk–Dove, there is a potential mutual gain on average (in comparison with the mixed strategy equilibrium) if the parties were to agree: 'In each encounter one of us will be randomly designated to play HAWK, the other to play DOVE.' To escape some real-world conflictual encounters it *is* sometimes possible to make binding agreements, but not always. Lawsuits can be settled without going to trial, via an agreement that the court may (perhaps) be relied on to enforce. But, except perhaps for small nations both subject to a common suzerain, no such outside enforcement is available in international conflict. More generally, enforceability of agreements is a matter of degree, depending in part upon the motives of the 'enforcer' — which means that a three-party game is being played. Sometimes, however, agreements are said to be *self-enforcing*. This can only be the case, under HD or PD environments, when some kind of expanded game is being played. Such considerations lead to the topic of 'sophisticated' equilibrium, the subject of the next section.

APPROACHES TO SOPHISTICATED EQUILIBRIUM[9]

While the very unsophisticated models so far discussed are by no means devoid of applicability, to make further progress we have to consider more complex types of conflictual encounters. I can only address here topics associated with three types of complications:

1. When there are repeated plays of the game, so that the parties can modify their choices in the light of opponents' earlier moves.
2. When one or both parties can *commit* to a strategy.
3. As a generalization of the preceding, when there are different 'protocols', for example when one party or the other has the first move, or when one or the other outcome is the *status quo ante*.

Tit-for-Tat as Optimal Strategy in Repeated Prisoners' Dilemma Games

The topic here considered is: In the repeated-play Prisoners' Dilemma, can the 'trap' outcome be escaped by having one or both parties adopt the strategy of rewarding the other for LOYAL play and punishing him for playing DEFECT?

It is a well-known result in the theory of repeated games ('supergames' in the unfortunate current jargon) that the PD trap cannot be escaped for any finite numbers of plays. For, DEFECT surely will always be optimal on the last round. But then LOYAL on the next to last round cannot be rewarded and thus will not rationally be chosen, and so on back to the very first round. The prospects are somewhat better for an infinite number of plays, or where there is merely some positive probability of play always continuing for another round. Each of these cases involves heavier mathematics than I want to go into here, however.

Axelrod (1984) (see also Axelrod and Hamilton (1981)) summarizes a number of his researches concerning the repeated-play Prisoners' Dilemma. By now quite famous are the two computer round-robin tournaments among candidate strategies submitted by various experts. In the first tournament each of fifteen different strategies was paired against every other (and against itself) in 200-round interactions. In the second tournament there were 62 entries; this time, instead of each pairwise interaction lasting a fixed number of rounds, a probability of continuation was chosen which worked out to make the average contest length 151 rounds.

The two tournaments were both 'won' by the simple conditional-cooperation strategy known as TIT-FOR-TAT. Against any opponent the TIT-FOR-TAT player initially chooses LOYAL, but thenceforth simply mirrors his opponent's choice in the previous round. Thus, an opponent who plays DEFECT at any point is punished, but in a proportionate eye-for-an-eye way that leaves open the possibility of mutual reversion toward more cooperative play. The success of TIT-FOR-TAT was due primarily to its 'robustness'. Even though TIT-FOR-TAT never outscored any single opponent strategy in a one-on-one encounter in these tournaments, it piled up points by doing quite well against almost every opponent (and very well indeed when paired against itself).

The claim has been made, on the basis of these tournament results, that mutually profitable adoption of TIT-FOR-TAT is *the* explanation for the evolution of cooperation.[10] Put another way, the contention is that, if social cooperation evolves at all, it will be because populations initially pursuing a variety of strategies for coping with the repeated-play Prisoners' Dilemma have ended up in an evolutionary equilibrium in which everyone plays TIT-FOR-TAT. This claim must however be treated with some reserve, and certain cautions will be indicated here:

1. First of all, Prisoners' Dilemma is only one of a vast number of mixed-incentive payoff environments in which cooperation might or might not emerge. Battle of the Sexes and Hawk–Dove as discussed above are two other such environments. Notice also that each of these three patterns is a two-person game characterized by two strategy options for each player. More generally, of course, there are games with any number of players, and any number of strategies for each player. In fact, there is a multiple infinity of pay-off environments that pose cooperation problems, and which do not take the special form of a repeated-play Prisoners' Dilemma.

2. A *round-robin* tournament is also a very special type of contest. In many circumstances, particularly if we are thinking of evolutionary selection, the competition among strategies might be better characterized by an *elimination* tournament. TIT-FOR-TAT would do very badly in elimination tournaments, since (as has been noted) it rarely if ever can defeat any other strategy in a one-to-one encounter.

3. Finally, there is a flaw in the logical development which will be clarified by an example. Consider the strategy triad consisting of LOYAL, TIT-FOR-TAT and DEFECT — which may respectively be termed Golden Rule, Silver Rule and Brass Rule. Should the population ever evolve to 100 per cent TIT-FOR-TAT, followers of the Golden Rule (LOYAL) can successfully invade, as LOYAL and TIT-FOR-TAT players would then be indistinguishable. This suggests that there will be an indeterminate equilibrium involving only these two strategies, but such a conclusion is unwarranted. Because, once LOYAL becomes sufficiently numerous, DEFECT becomes profitable again! The upshot is a mixed or cyclic equilibrium.

The 'proof' that TIT-FOR-TAT would be the evolutionary equilibrium (Axelrod (1984), Appendix B) rests upon an assumption that, in order to enter, the invader strategy must actually *do better than* the incumbent. This is an unwarranted requirement; *doing equally well* suffices to permit entry, and in any case precludes extinction if there are any representatives already present in the population. Furthermore, even if definite superiority were required for entry, it can be shown that the EE still would not be a 100 per cent TIT-FOR-TAT population — if allowance were made for the fact that TIT-FOR-TAT is a demanding strategy. Specifically, TIT-FOR-TAT requires ability to discriminate between experienced behaviours, to remember which individuals among those encountered have displayed each type of behaviour in the past, and to recognize those individuals when encountered again. Since they do not require these capacities, both LOYAL and DEFECT are less burdensome to adopt and live by. Once a proper accounting is made for the *cost* of the extra abilities that TIT-FOR-TAT requires, the economics of the situation will preclude the population evolving toward 100 per cent TIT-FOR-TAT.[11]

Contingent Strategies and Commitment

TIT-FOR-TAT was an example of a *contingent strategy* in a repeated-game context. It is also possible to have contingent strategies even with single-play games, which leads to what is called the theory of 'meta-games' (another unfortunate choice of terminology).

Commitment represents the ability to foreclose one's own future freedom of choice, to guarantee to your opponent that you will not diverge from a specified chosen strategy. (Since one can only achieve any useful effect from commitment by communicating that fact to the other party, I will always be assuming that such communication occurs.) Particularly interesting results ensue from *commitment to contingent strategies*, which correspond to what we call in ordinary language 'threats' and 'promises'. But commitment to a simple strategy is also entirely possible.

Consider Battle of the Sexes (Table 10.3). If He can commit to strategy #1, the only rational response for She is also to play, #1, allowing the committer the higher return. Correspondingly, She would like to commit to strategy #2, forcing He to go along. In either case, the one with power to commit reaps the greater benefit from the interaction (10 versus 5).

Commitment to a contingent strategy makes sense, as has been emphasized by Thompson and Faith (1981), only in a situation of *sequential play* — where the parties move in some definite order over time. Such a protocol opens up a route of escape from the trap outcome of the Prisoners' Dilemma. It is important here to distinguish between 'strategy' and 'move'. By assumption, the only actual *moves* are those available to the players in the original matrix — LOYAL or DEFECT. A *strategy* is a plan for playing the moves in a context of a particular sequential protocol, the governing rules of the game. The 'Expanded Prisoners' Dilemma' of Table 10.6 illustrates such a situation.

In Table 10.6 we suppose that Row has the power to commit to a contingent strategy, Column being limited as before to his simple LOYAL versus DEFECT options. The interesting contingent strategy for Row is CONCUR: threaten DEFECT if Column's move is DEFECT but promise LOYAL if Column plays LOYAL. (But for completeness the rather illogical DIVERGE strategy is also shown.) Row's optimal

Table 10.6 Expanded Prisoners' Dilemma

	C_1 (LOYAL)	C_2 (DEFECT)
R_1 (LOYAL)	−2,−2	−20,0
R_2 (DEFECT)	0,−20	−10,−10
R_3 (CONCUR)	−2,−2	−10,−10
R_4 (DIVERGE)	0,−20	−20,10

Table 10.7 Deterrence without commitment

	C_1 (REFRAIN)	C_2 (ATTACK)
R_1 (FOLD)	3,2	1,3
R_2 (RETALIAT.	3,2	2,1

Table 10.8 Deterrence requiring commitment

	C_1 (REFRAIN)	C_2 (ATTACK)
R_1 (FOLD)	3,2	2,3
R_2 (RETALIATE)	3,2	1,1

play is to *commit* to CONCUR, in which case Column will surely play LOYAL — the result being (-2, -2). Thus, the Prisoners' Dilemma has been escaped; the parties achieve their second-best outcomes, as compared with the third-best (i.e. next-to-worst) results that constitute the trap solution. It is also interesting to note here that having the power to commit has not led to any comparative advantage for Row over Column.

The significance of commitment for the problem of *deterrence* is illustrated by Tables 10.7 and Table 10.8. Table 10.7 is another version of the Expanded Prisoners' Dilemma just discussed. In the deterrence context, for the party with the first move (the Column player), DEFECT in Table 10.6 becomes ATTACK in Tables 10.7 and 10.8, while LOYAL in Table 10.6 corresponds to REFRAIN in Tables 10.7 and 10.8. For the responding (Row) player, two strategies have been deleted. DIVERGE has been omitted because of its evident irrationality. Also, ATTACK (= DEFECT) has been dropped, since if Row can consider attacking regardless of what Column does we do not have a deterrence situation. Thus, the implication is, Row is incapable of attacking *except* in response. Responding to attack is, of course, the RETALIATE strategy. Failing to do so is the FOLD strategy, corresponding to LOYAL in the original Prisoners' Dilemma. (The actual numerical values given in the table represent the *ranking* of the outcomes in the underlying Prisoners' Dilemma matrix, 1 being lowest and 3 highest.)

It is evident that deterrence succeeds *even without commitment* in Table 10.7. If attacked, Row prefers to RETALIATE, and this suffices to deter attack. But Row in Table 10.8 is more pacifically inclined, and if attacked, really would prefer FOLD to RETALIATE. Unfortunately, that guarantees he will be attacked! Here is where the power to commit provides an escape. If Row can guarantee in advance that RETALIATE will occur, despite his aversion to that course of action, deterrence succeeds. If he can reliably threaten to do what he does not want to do, he won't have to do it!

An interesting question is: What are the mechanisms of commitment in cases like this? Here we can go back to our fundamental categories of *opportunities, preferences* and *perceptions*. If Row is pacifically inclined, as pictured in Table 10.8, he can try to shift the situation towards Table 10.7. If possible, he might alter his preferences in the direction of bellicosity. Alternatively, he could try to manipulate elements of the opportunity set. For example, he might make a wager with outsiders, staking a considerable sum that he will *not* choose FOLD. Or, he could make the current encounter into a visible precedent and test case, it being clear that his choosing FOLD here and now will invite future costly confrontations. Or, Row might work on Column's perceptions by putting out misleading indicators of bellicosity.

The emotion of *anger*, which might otherwise seem to be only a 'primitive' hindrance to human rationality, appears here in a new light. Anger provides the needed commitment to RETALIATE. My psychological 'loss of control', that leads me to punish aggression even where it is not to my short-run material advantage to do so, may be just what is needed to deter invasions.[12] And by a reverse argument, the same may hold for *love*. 'Unselfish' willingness to share gains, even when not required to do so, can be not only psychologically but materially rewarding when cooperation on the part of others is elicited thereby.[13] Thus, both anger and love can serve as 'enforcers' of implicit contracts between two parties.

First Move Versus Last Move

With outcomes specified by a given game matrix, quite different results may ensue depending upon whether the players choose simultaneously

Table 10.9 'Dominated'-strategy equilibrium

| | | First-mover | |
		C_1	C_2
Second-mover	R_1	*4,2	2,1
	R_2	1,4	+3,3

Table 10.10 Battle of the Sexes

| | | She | |
		C_1	C_2
He	R_1	3,2	1,1
	R_2	1,1	2,3

Table 10.11 Hawk–Dove (or Chicken)

	C_1 (DOVE)	C_2 (HAWK)
R_1 (DOVE)	3,3	2,4
R_2 (HAWK)	4,2	1,1

Table 10.12 Last-move advantage

	C_1	C_2
R_1	1,4	3,2
R_2	4,1	2,3

or sequentially — and if the latter, depending upon which moves first and which moves last. The latter topic has some suggestive implications for the choice between offence and defence in war, or pre-emptive moves in diplomacy. Without getting into these applications here, it will be of interest to look at some of the advantages and disadvantages of priority.

Consider a sequential-move single-round game. In such a game it may pay a player to follow a so-called 'dominated' strategy of the corresponding simultaneous-move game. (Since the Nash equilibrium NE cannot involve playing a dominated strategy, it follows that the NE will not be an appropriate solution concept here.)[14] In Table 10.9 Column is supposed to be the first-mover. His strategy #2 is payoff-dominated by strategy #1. Nevertheless, he does better at the sequential-play equilibrium R_2, C_2 (marked with a +) than at the Nash equilibrium R_1, C_1, (marked with an asterisk) that would be reached had he played his dominant strategy.

A more central question for our purposes is, who has the advantage, first-mover or second-mover? In Battle of the Sexes (BOS), as has already been noted, first-mover can force achievement of the common-strategy outcome that favours him or her (see Table 10.10). And in

Chicken or Hawk–Dove (HD) also, by playing HAWK the first-mover can force his opponent into DOVE with an inferior outcome (Table 10.11). Can last-mover ever have the advantage? Yes, as illustrated in Table 10.12. Here, if Column has the last move he can force R_2, C_2, with outcome (2,3) — whereas Row having the last move leads to R_1, C_2 with returns (3,2). Thus, the last-mover here has the advantage.

Interpreting these results, notice that both BOS and HD are characterized by strong parallelism of interest between the players. In contrast, Table 10.11 is a constant-sum case (if we interpret the tabulated numbers as cardinal magnitudes). The players' interests being strictly opposed, the first-mover knows that his opponent's final move will be entirely adverse to his interests. Hence, the non-terminator is induced to settle for a 'safe' but relatively unsatisfactory intermediate pay-off; that is to say, he must accept the bad to avoid the worst. But when the parties' interests are not strictly opposed, first-mover can commonly adopt a strategy such that he will benefit more by second-mover's optimal response than second-mover can gain himself.

A nice illustration of the relative advantages of first-move versus last-move arises in oligopoly theory. In the homogeneous-product duopoly case, with *quantity* as the decision variable, the first-mover has the advantage — the so-called 'Stackelberg solution'. Being able to predict and therefore allow for his competitor's subsequent constrained optimization, the first-mover can produce a level of output such as to pre-empt most of the joint duopoly gain. If however *price* is the decision variable (as might be the case if the duopolists' products were not identical), the last-mover clearly has the advantage. For, regardless of the price selected by his opponent, the last-mover can undercut it so as to engross most of the joint sales. Thus, once again the first-mover tends to have the advantage where there is strong parallelism of interest — the case where quantity is the decision variable, the parties having a strong joint interest in keeping the common price high. But the last-mover has the advantage where interests are more strictly opposed, as when he can largely deprive the other of sales by undercutting on price.

ON THE TECHNOLOGY OF CONFLICT[15]

Conflict is a kind of 'industry' — a way in which economic agents compete for resources. Just as the economist without being a manager or an engineer can apply certain broad principles to the processes of industrial production, so, without claiming to replace the military commander he can say something about the possibilities for 'producing' desired results through violent conflict.

Under this heading I shall only address one topic here: *increasing versus decreasing returns in the sphere of conflict.*

As an historical generalization, *battles* generally proceed to a definitive outcome — victory for the one side, defeat for the other. *Wars*, while sometimes terminating in complete overthrow of one side or the other, are somewhat more likely to end inconclusively or with a compromise settlement. I argue that this is related to the scope of increasing versus decreasing returns to the application of violence. A related phenomenon is the fact that the world is divided into a system of nation-states: while each government has a near-monopoly of power within a limited region, the struggles that continue to take place along the frontiers reveal that there is typically a periphery along which forces are about equally balanced.

Thus, there seem to be two general principles at work. (1) Within a given geographical region, as the scale of military effort grows there tend to be *increasing returns* — and hence a 'natural monopoly' of military power within each sufficiently limited base area. (2) But in attempting to extend military sway over larger regions, *diminishing returns* are encountered to the projection of power away from the base — hence, we do not see a single universal world-state.

What is it that underlies the scope of the increasing returns principle? Simply that the stronger contender can steadily inflict a more than proportionate loss upon his opponent, thus becoming (relatively) stronger still. In a situation where only pairwise relative strength counts, this process tends to proceed to the limit of total annihilation (unless flight or surrender intervenes).

Simple yet important special cases of this process are modelled in Lanchester's equations. In linear warfare, for example, the military units (soldiers, ships) arranged in line distribute their fire equally over the enemy's line. Symbolizing the Blue force size as B and the Red force size as R, the relevant process equations are:

$$dB/dt = -k_R R$$
$$dR/dt = -k_B B$$

where k_B and k_R are the respective attack efficiencies (reflecting factors like vulnerability versus accuracy of fire). The condition for equality is:

$$k_B B^2 = k_R R^2$$

Thus, military strength in linear warfare varies proportionately with force effectiveness but as the square of force size. Even where this exact rule does not apply,[16] it still is quite generally the case that in the combat process the strong become stronger and the weak weaker, ending in total victory for the one side and defeat for the other.

The logic of this is so compelling[17] that we may well wonder why it sometimes fails to hold. Among the possible complicating factors are:

1. Force effectiveness may not be uniform in time or in scale. The initially more powerful army may tire more rapidly. Or, the initially losing commander may turn out to have a comparative advantage in handling the smaller forces that remain once both sides have suffered attrition.
2. Actual battle is of course typically too complex to be modelled in a simple linear way. For one thing, the field of combat may be inhomogeneous: the losing side may have an 'area of refuge' within which it retains sufficient strength to avoid annihilation.
3. In the confusion of war, sometimes the winning general does not know he has won. Hence, he may withdraw the forces capable of achieving total victory.
4. While battles are almost always two-sided interactions, wars normally are at least potentially multi-sided. Rather than suffer further losses in order to annihilate a defeated army, the winning commander may choose to conserve the forces needed to meet other opponents.[18]
5. But by far the most important of the disturbing factors is the fickle finger of Fate. Recognizing the multitude of unpredictable chance events in warfare that sometimes favour one side, sometimes the other, the prudent commander may be happy to settle for 'good enough' rather than push matters to the extreme.

Allowing for these moderating factors, Figure 10.9 illustrates the applicability of the increasing returns principle. There will be some critical ratio of forces, indicated by the dashed vertical line, where the probabilities of victory are equal. In the neighbourhood of this critical ratio, small changes in the balance of forces tend to bring about disproportionately large effects upon the chances of victory.

My second broad generalization, that *decreasing returns* apply to the geographical extension of military power, is pictured in Figure 10.10.[19] Writing the military strengths at the parties' respective home bases as M_B and M_R, for a balance of power over distance to exist the following must hold:

$$M_B - s_B d_B = M_R - s_R d_R$$

Here s_B and s_R are the loss-of-strength gradients in geographically projecting power. And d_B and d_R are the respective distances from

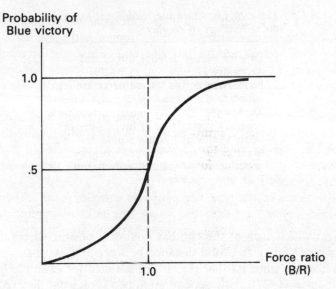

Figure 10.9   Increasing returns to force size

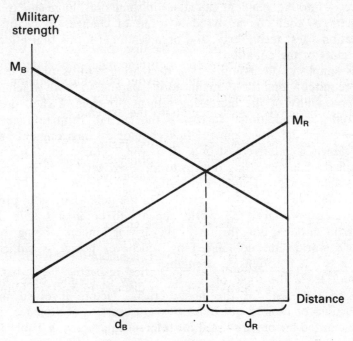

Figure 10.10   Decreasing returns to extension of power

Cooperation and Conflict

Table 10.13 *Illustrative additional topics in
the technology of conflict*

1. Offence versus defence forces and
   weaponry
2. First-strike versus second-strike move;
   counterforce versus countervalue targets
3. Trade–offs: Mobility versus fortification,
   accuracy versus rate of fire, forces in
   being versus mobilization potential, etc.
4. Maintaining organizational integrity
   under stress — military and civilian
5. Risk and its control

base over which each of the two has dominant power, where $d_B + d_R$ = D, with D being the total distance between the two bases.

This analysis suggests that the size of nations, for example (on this, see Friedman (1977)), will depend upon two somewhat distinguishable abilities: (1) to organize power at the base, and (2) to project power over distance. Major historical trends in the partition of the earth's surface — into independent city-states in some eras, huge superpowers in others — could be analysed in terms of changes in factors like population sizes, technology, and organizational forms that affect the parameters of the equation.

This simplistic discussion of the decreasing returns principle once again requires a long list of qualifications, parallel to those which hedge the applicability of the increasing returns principle. I shall mention here only one additional factor — the crucial distinction between offensive and defensive power. In technological environments where the defence is relatively strong, decreasing returns to distance are intensified while increasing returns to force size tend to be moderated. So a stable system of smaller sovereign states tends to emerge. But where offensive technology overbalances the defensive, as in present-day strategic warfare, the world appears to be in a fragile if not downright unstable equilibrium — the driving tendency being toward a single world-state dominated by whichever power is sufficiently ruthless to use its offensive strength.

I must leave the topic of the technology of conflict here, having discussed only one of the many crucial factors involved in the 'production' of desired outcomes through exercise of violence. Some of the omitted factors are listed for reference purposes in Table 10.13.

CONFLICT, ECONOMICS, AND SOCIETY

So far I have been able only to drop hints about what I described as my secondary theme — to wit, that the study of conflict is important for economics. I can only expand a little bit on those hints here.

We have seen that the technology of conflict helps explain the size and shape of nations. Apart from the overwhelming importance of that fact, the underlying principle has even broader applicability. Many types of competitions among individuals and organizations have conflictual aspects, and violence always remains as a coercive threat in the background. While the law may attempt to prevent thieves from stealing, business firms from sabotaging competitors' premises, lawyers from filing groundless lawsuits, or trade unions from intimidating non-members, control of such behaviours will never be perfectly effective. And in consequence, even entirely law-abiding individuals and organizations must, at the very least, plan on devoting some resources to extra-legal (not necessarily illegal) ways of protecting themselves. It will be evident that these invasive and counter-invasive efforts surely absorb a very substantial fraction of society's resources.

A related set of implications concern the internal structures of organizations. Thompson and Faith (1981), for example, make the extreme assertion (to put it mildly) that democracy is always an illusion, that every state is ultimately a military dictatorship (p. 376).[20] But inspection of the world reveals an enormous range of social structures adopted by animals and humans — ranging from extremes of hierarchical dominance to highly egalitarian systems. A more profitable line of inquiry is to ask what the factors are that affect the steepness of the social dominance gradient. Where there is a single concentrated key resource, as in the irrigation systems of ancient empires, we might expect the struggle for its control to lead to a highly hierarchical social structure.[21] In addition, concentrated populations can be dominated without excessive diminishing returns to the geographical projection of military power. On the other hand, more broadly distributed resources and populations, as in the pioneer days of America's settlement, conduce toward egalitarian social systems. It is also well known that *external* conflict promotes the adoption of internal command economies and dictatorship. The explanation of this fact is, I believe, connected with the increasing returns aspect of war and the consequent urgency of controlling free-riding, but unfortunately space does not permit development of this theme here.

My main message can be simply summarized. The institutions of property and law, and the peaceful process of exchange, are highly beneficent aspects of human life. But the economist's inquiries should not be limited to such 'nice' behaviours and interactions. Struggle, imposing costs on others, and downright violence are crucial phenomena of the world as we know it. Nor is the opposition between the 'nice' and the 'not nice' by any means total. Law and property, and thus the possibility for peaceful exchange, can only persist where individuals are ultimately willing to use violence in their defence.

ACKNOWLEDGEMENTS

The author would like to express his grateful thanks to the Earhart Foundation and to the GSM Research Center for Political Economy for support of this research. The author also had the benefit of helpful comments from Robert Axelrod, Craig McCann, Gordon Tullock and Donald Wittman.

NOTES

1. The discussion in this section builds upon Boulding (1962, Ch. 1); Friedman (1980); and Wittman (1979).
2. Of course, any such unicausal explanation must not be taken too far, lest we fall into the error of Angell (1910), who argued just before World War I that the growing web of international commerce had made war impossible.
3. This type of consideration leads to the very interesting question of just what are the factors that tend to generate benevolent versus malevolent interpersonal attitudes. The possible sources of human 'altruism' have been much discussed by biologists and to some extent by economists (see, for example, Hirshleifer (1977, pp. 17–26)) but for our purposes here, it is more instructive to look at the other side of the picture — malevolence or hatred. While it is quite possible to have 'cold-blooded' fighting without hatred, there seems to be a feedback between the two in the human psyche. It appears that the ability to hate one's enemy has been selected in the evolution of the human species, a factor that leads to 'hot-blooded', less rationally controllable warfare.
4. Sparta, after its defeat by the Athenians at Cyzicus (410 BC), offered peace on moderate terms, and did so once again after Arginusae (406). But the over-confident democratic party controlling Athens rejected both offers. The war continued until the irremediable naval disaster at Aegospotami culminated in the total capitulation of Athens (404).
5. The discussion here develops certain ideas in Hirshleifer and Riley (1978), and Hirshleifer (1982, pp. 13–20).
6. Let the average returns to following the first and second strategies be a and b respectively. In Battle of the Sexes a following of the first strategy will be in the 'He' situation one-half of the time and a 'She' situation the other half. Thus:

$$a = .5 (10p) + .5 (5p) = 7.5p$$

Similarly, for a follower of the second strategy:

$$b = .5 [10(1 - p)] + .5[5(1 - p)] = 7.5 (1 - p)$$

Since $a - b$ is positive for $p > .5$, whenever more than half the population is initially pursuing the first strategy, that strategy will be the more successful and the population will evolve toward an EE at $p = 1.0$. In the opposite case similarly, if p is initially less than .5 the population will evolve toward $p = 0$.

7. In Hawk–Dove, the pay-off to DOVE will be: $a = 4p + 0 (1 - p)$. And for Hawk the pay-off will be: $b = 10p - 24 (1 - p)$. The two strategies have equal pay-offs when $p = 0.8$. In contrast with Battle of the Sexes, in Hawk–Dove this interior p is an evolutionary equilibrium EE. Whenever the DOVE proportion exceeds 0.8, $a - b$ is negative; HAWK being now more profitable, the DOVE population proportion p will retreat back toward 0.8 — and similarly in the opposite case.
8. In Prisoners' Dilemma the respective returns are:
$$a = -2p - 20 (1 - p)$$
$$b = 0 p - 10 (1 - p)$$
Here $a - b$ is negative for any value of p between zero and unity. Thus the population will evolve toward $p = 0$, so that the only EE is an all-DEFECT population.
9. This section builds especially upon Schelling (1960); Axelrod (1984); Thompson and Faith (1981); and Hirshleifer (1982) and (1983).
10. The common title of the Axelrod volume and the Axelrod–Hamilton paper, 'The Evolution of Cooperation', does indeed suggest such a sweeping claim. However, at various points, appropriate qualifying disclaimers do appear in the cited works.
11. For further details on these points see Hirshleifer (1982, pp. 20–35).
12. On this, see Simmel (1955 (1923)). More generally, an outraged sense of justice which leads to 'moralistic aggression' (Trivers, 1971) by third parties may be an important force in maintaining the possibility of social cooperation. Again, it is essential that justice be pursued even where *not* in accordance with cost-benefit analysis. ('Let justice be done though the heavens fall.').
13. The 'Rotten Kid' paradigm (Becker, 1976) is a famous instance under this heading. Benevolent willingness of a parent to share the mutual gains can induce a merely selfish Kid to act in the overall family interest — with material benefit to all concerned.
14. It is true that if the choice situation were written in expanded-matrix form, allowing second-mover to employ contingent strategies, the correct solution would always be *one* of the Nash equilibria. But since these equilibria rapidly become excessively numerous with larger ranges of strategy choice, the NE remains not very useful as a solution concept. (On this, see also Brams and Wittman (1981).)
15. This section makes use of discussions by Tullock (1974, Ch. 9); Boulding (1962, Ch. 12–13); and especially Lanchester (1956 (1916)).
16. Lanchester shows, for example, that where forces *occupy areas*, rather than *extend in lines*, relative strengths vary linearly with force sizes rather as the square of force sizes.
17. Exactly the same logic underlies what is known as 'Gause's exclusion principle' in evolutionary theory: when two species compete to occupy any

single niche, the more effective competitor must drive the other to extinction. This principle is subject to much the same qualifications as those which limit the scope of increasing returns in conflict interactions (see text below).

18. Harold II of England, having totally defeated the invading Norwegians at Stamford Bridge on 15 September 1066, was left with insufficient strength to avoid disaster at Hastings on 14 October.
19. Such a diagram appears in Boulding (1962, p. 230).
20. This conclusion only very doubtfully follows from their analysis, which is, in any case, of a highly special sequential-play game protocol. The games being played in the network of associations that comprise a society are many times more complex than they allow for.
21. This point is the key theme of Wittfogel (1957).

BIBLIOGRAPHY

Angell, Norman (1910) *The Great Illusion*.
Ashenfelter, Orley A. and George E. Johnson (1969) 'Bargaining Theory, Trade Unions, and Industrial Strike Activity', *American Economic Review*, vol. 59 (March).
Axelrod, Robert (1984) *The Evolution of Cooperation*. New York: Basic Books, Inc.
—— and Hamilton, William D. (1981) 'The Evolution of Cooperation', *Science*, vol. 211 (27 March).
Becker, Gary S. (1976) 'Altruism, Egoism, and Genetic Fitness: Economics and Sociobiology', *J. of Economic Literature*, vol. 14 (September).
Blainey, Geoffrey (1973) *The Causes of War*. New York: The Free Press.
Boulding, Kenneth E. (1962) *Conflict and Defense*. New York: Harper & Bros.
Brams, Steven J. and Donald Wittman (1981) 'Nonmyopic Equilibria in 2 × 2 Games', *Conflict Management & Peace Science*, vol. 6 (Fall).
Friedman, David (1980) 'Many, Few, One: Social Harmony and the Shrunken Choice Set', *American Economic Review*, vol. 70 (March).
—— (1977) 'The Size and Shape of Nations', *J. of Political Economy*, vol. 85 (February).
Hirshleifer, J. (1977) 'Economics From a Biological Viewpoint', *J. of Law & Economics*, vol. 20 (April).
—— (1982) 'Evolutionary Models in Economics and Law: Cooperation Versus Conflict Strategies', *Research in Law and Economics*, vol. 4.
—— (1983) 'Equilibrium Concepts in Game Theory', UCLA Dept. of Economics Working Paper No. 291 (May).
—— and J. Riley (1978) 'Elements of the Theory of Auctions and Contests', UCLA Economics Dept. Working Paper No. 118B (revised, August).
Lanchester, Frederick William (1916) *Aircraft in Warfare*, extract reprinted as 'Mathematics in Warfare', in James R. Newman (ed.), *The World of Mathematics*, vol. 4. New York: Simon & Schuster, 1956, pp. 2138–57.
Polachek, Solomon W. (1980) 'Conflict and Trade', *J. of Conflict Resolution*, vol. 24.
Schelling, Thomas C. (1960) *The Strategy of Conflict*. London: Oxford University Press.

Simmel, Georg (1955) 'Conflict', trans. Kurt H. Wolff, in *Conflict and the Web of Group-Affiliations*. New York: The Free Press. (Original German publication, 1923).

Thompson, Earl A. and Roger L. Faith (1981) 'A Pure Theory of Strategic Behavior and Social Institutions', *American Economic Review*, vol. 71 (June).

Trivers, Robert L. (1971) 'The Evolution of Reciprocal Altruism', *Quarterly Review of Biology*, vol. 46 (March).

Tullock, Gordon (1974) *The Social Dilemma: The Economics of War and Revolution*. Center for the Study of Public Choice, Virginia Polytechnic Institute and State University.

Wittfogel, Karl A. (1957) *Oriental Despotism: A Comparative Study of Total Power*. New Haven: Yale University Press.

Wittman, Donald (1979) 'How a War Ends: A Rational Model Approach', *J. of Conflict Resolution*, vol. 23 (December).

Name Index

Subject Index

A and B country, 23, 25, 79
Adaptation, 221–3
Agriculture, 205
  during Black Death, 103, 108
  in Confederacy, 24, 25, 34, 35, 36
  in Japan, 40, 44, 45, 56
  in Russia, 18–19
Alaskan earthquake, 1964, 134,
  135–7, 139, 158
Alliance, society as, 138–40, 159
Altruism, 11, 134–40, 146, 158–9,
  167, 178–9, 237, 247
  see also Cooperation, Helping
American Confederacy, 1861–5,
  23–34
  agricultural production, 24, 25,
    34, 35, 36
  city-countryside trade, 31–2
  class antagonism, 33
  cotton, 25, 27–8
  economic collapse, 24–5, 26–7, 73
  government budget and finance,
    27–31
  impressment, 29, 31–2, 75
  industrial production, 25–6
  inflation and money supply, 28–9,
    31
  move into cities, 25, 76
  postwar recovery, 33–4
  price control, 31
  self-sufficiency of, 25
American Occupation of Japan,
  43–55
  trade policy, 27–8
Anomalies, 134
Atomic bomb *see* Bombing, Nuclear
  war
Autonomy of individual, 195–6

Barter, 28–9, 40, 55, 69, 74, 75
Battle of the Sexes *see under* Game-
  theory models and strategies
Behaviour *see* Altruism,
  Psychological patterns
Belgium, 78
Benevolence *see* Altruism
Best-shot model *see* Public goods
Biology *see* Evolutionary model,
  Sociobiology
Black Death, 95–111
  aftermath, 101–10
  causes of, 98
  'economic depression of the
    Renaissance', 103, 108–9, 111
    and feudal system, 109–10
  mortality rates, 98–101, 110
  occurrences of, 98
Black Market, 75
  in Germany, 60, 68, 72
  in Japan, 40, 55, 56
  in Russia, 17, 18
Bolshevik revolution, 15–23, 77
Bombing, 57, 73, 76
  risk, 121, 123
  see also Hamburg, Hiroshima,
    Nagasaki, Nuclear War
Budget Bureau, USA, 119–20, 127–8

Cartels, 188, 218, 261
  see also Decartelization
Charity *see* Altruism
Cheating, 186–7
Chicago blizzard, 137, 158
Chicken *see under* Game-theory
  models and strategies
China, 76

Subject Index

306

Cities, fluctuations in population,
25, 76, 106
see also Depopulation
Civil war
in Russia, 15, 23
in USA, 23–34
Climate, 106–7
Coalitions, political, 164–8
Coase's Theorem, 212–13, 215,
256–7, 264
Collapse, economic see Economic
collapse
Commitment strategies, 288–90
Communism, 53, 65, 74, 254
see also War communism
Community feeling, 135–7, 158
Compensation for war damage see
War damage insurance
Compensation trade, 68–9
Competition, 169, 174–8, 207
absolute, 183–5
and efficiency, 248–51
and kinship, 181
modes of, 176
in natural economy, 174–5
preclusive, 177
as related to cooperation and
conflict, 174–8
strategies, 174–8, 249–50, 261
Confederate States of America see
American Confederacy
Conflict, 259, 273–98
as competitive strategy, 273–4, 283
and cooperation, 174–8, 223–48
definition of 273–4
dynamics and equilibrium, 280–5
economic approach, 274
as educational process, 279
equilibrium, 285–92
increasing vs decreasing returns,
293–6
Lanchester equations, 293
and opportunities, 274, 281, 290
and perceptions, 274, 276, 277,
281, 290
and preferences, 274, 276–8, 281,
290
and society, 297–8
Stackelberg solution, 292
statics, 274–80
technology of, 292–6
Constitutional politics, 167–8
Consumer-resource ratio, 11
Consumption, new theory of, 197

Cooperation, 174–89, 252, 261–5
and altruism, 178–9
and conflict, 174–8, 223–48
failures of, 230
and kinship, 179–87
as mode of competition, 181
Counter-disaster syndrome, 10, 158
Cuba, 76
Currency
conversion in postwar Japan, 54
printing of, 17, 19–20, 22, 29, 31,
41, 74
reform, 31, 67, 70–2, 77

Decartelization, 65–6
see also Cartels
Demographic statistics, 21
Denazification, 65
Depopulation of cities, 21, 55, 76,
78–9, 105
Deterrence, 289–90
Disaster
behaviour, 6, 134–40
common themes, 73–80
consumer-resource ratio, 11
counter-disaster syndrome
definition of, 6, 73
elasticity of resources, 11
generalized, 7, 74, 78
localized, 7, 9–14, 74
organizational/technological
difficulties, 8, 14
population survival and recovery,
76, 78–9
rebound phenomenon, 8–9, 12, 79
relief, 11, 138
socialism, 15, 21
syndrome, 9, 74
zones of effect, 9
see also Recovery, specific
disasters (e.g. Alaskan
earthquake, Hamburg)
Dominance, 200–1, 255

Economic collapse
of Confederacy, 24–5, 26–7
definition of, 6, 73
of Germany, 57–8
of Japan, 37
Economic man, 199–200, 263
Economics
and law, 211–65
and sociobiology, 170–4, 190–1
subject matter of, 212